EMMETT TILL IN LITERARY MEMORY
AND IMAGINATION

Southern Literary Studies

FRED HOBSON, SERIES EDITOR

EMMETT TILL

IN LITERARY MEMORY
AND IMAGINATION

Edited by

HARRIET POLLACK *and*

CHRISTOPHER METRESS

LOUISIANA STATE UNIVERSITY PRESS

BATON ROUGE

PUBLISHED BY LOUISIANA STATE UNIVERSITY PRESS
Copyright © 2008 by Louisiana State University Press
All rights reserved
Manufactured in the United States of America
An LSU Press Paperback Original
FIRST PRINTING

DESIGNER: Amanda McDonald Scallan
TYPEFACE: Whitman
PRINTER AND BINDER: Thomson-Shore, Inc.

Library of Congress Cataloging-in-Publication Data

Emmett Till in literary memory and imagination / edited by Harriet Pollack and Christopher Metress.
   p. cm. — (Southern literary studies)
   Includes bibliographical references (p.   ) and index.
   ISBN 978-0-8071-3281-4 (pbk. : alk. paper) 1. American literature—20th century—History and criticism. 2. American literature—21st century—History and criticism. 3. Till, Emmett, 1941–1955. 4. Race in literature. 5. United States—Race relations—History—20th century. 6. Politics and literature—United States—History—20th century. 7. African Americans—Crimes against—Mississippi. 8. Lynching in literature. 9. African Americans in literature. 10. Civil rights movements in literature. I. Pollack, Harriet. II. Metress, Christopher.
   PS228.R32E46 2007
   810.9'358—dc22

                                                                     2007021770

"Afterimages," from The Collected Poems of Audre Lorde by Audre Lorde. Copyright © 1997 by The Audre Lorde Estate. Used by permission of W. W. Norton and Company, Inc.
   "Mississippi," from The Collected Poems of Langston Hughes by Langston Hughes, edited by Arnold Rampersad with David Roessel, associate editor, copyright © 1994 by The Estate of Langston Hughes, printed here as originally published in a slightly adapted form in the Chicago Defender under the title "Mississippi—1955" (October 1955).

The paper in this book meets the guidelines for permanence and durability of the Committee on Production Guidelines for Book Longevity of the Council on Library Resources. ∞

CONTENTS

Acknowledgments
vii

The Emmett Till Case and Narrative[s]
An Introduction and Overview
HARRIET POLLACK *and* CHRISTOPHER METRESS
1

On That Third Day He Rose
Sacramental Memory and the Lynching of Emmett Till
CHRISTOPHER METRESS
16

The Murder of Emmett Till in the Melodramatic Imagination
William Bradford Huie and Vin Packer in the 1950s
SHARON MONTEITH
31

Flesh That Needs to Be Loved
Langston Hughes Writing the Body of Emmett Till
MYISHA PRIEST
53

James Baldwin's Unifying Polemic
Racial Segregation, Moral Integration, and the Polarizing Figure of Emmett Till
BRIAN NORMAN
75

Maids Mild and Dark Villains, Sweet Magnolias and Seeping Blood
Gwendolyn Brooks's Poetic Response to the Lynching of Emmett Till
VIVIAN M. MAY
98

It Could Have Been My Son
Maternal Empathy in Gwendolyn Brooks's and Audre Lorde's Till Poems
LAURA DAWKINS
112

Silence and the Frustration of Broken Promises
Anne Moody's Struggle with the Lynching of Emmett Till and the Civil Rights Movement
KATHALEEN AMENDE
128

This Corpse So Small Left Unavenged
Nicolás Guillén and Aimé Césaire on Emmett Till's Lynching
SYLVIE KANDÉ
143

Childhood Trauma and Its Reverberations in Bebe Moore
Campbell's *Your Blues Ain't Like Mine*
SUZANNE W. JONES
161

Grotesque Laughter, Unburied Bodies, and History
Shape-Shifting in Lewis Nordan's Wolf Whistle
HARRIET POLLACK
178

(Dis)embodying the Delta Blues
Wolf Whistle *and* Your Blues Ain't Like Mine
DONNIE MCMAHAND
202

Literary Representations of the Lynching of Emmett Till
An Annotated Bibliography
CHRISTOPHER METRESS
223

Contributors
251

Index
255

ACKNOWLEDGMENTS

A collection of this kind is not possible without the hard work, long support, and good will of many people. Our first thanks go to Rebecca Mark and Alferdteen Harrison, organizers of the 2004 international conference "Unsettling Memories: Culture and Trauma in the Deep South." This landmark gathering, sponsored by Jackson State University, Tougaloo College, and Tulane University, brought together more than a hundred activists and scholars for an energizing conversation about the Deep South's troubled past, and this current collection is an outgrowth of one panel from that conference: a session devoted to literary depictions of the lynching of Emmett Till. The positive response to this panel raised the possibility of creating a larger forum for the topic, and the idea for this collection grew.

We thank the Cave Canem Collective, which helped disseminate our call for papers, enabling us to reach numerous writers and scholars interested in and working on our topic.

We want to thank each of our contributors for their commitment to the project. A collection is only as good as its contributors, and we have greatly enjoyed collaborating with this varied and talented group of scholars. We have learned much from them, and we especially admire how their essays combine a passion for literary representation with a commitment to social justice. We believe their work represents a model for the engaged scholar who wants to explore how the literary and the historical shape each other.

In addition to our contributors, we also thank Fred Hobson (UNC) and John Easterly at LSU Press for their interest and encouragement. During very difficult times at the Press in the wake of Hurricane Katrina, John continued to shepherd this book through the review process, offering excellent advice for strengthening the collection and widening its appeal. To all at LSU Press, in particular to Julia Smith, Lee Sioles, and Cynthia Williams, we express our thanks. We owe thanks too to Joseph Flora, who read the book in its early draft and offered his support to the project.

Close to home, we appreciate the support of our colleagues at Samford and

Bucknell. For financial and other support of this project, we thank Dean David Chapman of the Howard College of Arts and Sciences and Provost Brad Creed at Samford University, the Department of English and the Center for the Study of Race, Ethnicity, and Gender at Bucknell University.

EMMETT TILL IN LITERARY MEMORY
AND IMAGINATION

THE EMMETT TILL CASE AND NARRATIVE[S]

An Introduction and Overview

HARRIET POLLACK AND CHRISTOPHER METRESS

In the summer of 1998, a forty-nine-year-old black man was walking down a moonless road in Jasper, Texas. It was late, and three white men in a pickup truck pulled over to offer him a ride. He accepted, and the four men drove out of town. The next morning, James Byrd's naked and dismembered body was lying near the gates of a black cemetery on a lonely stretch of Huff Creek Road in Jasper County.[1]

For many, the echoes of 1955 were strong. While Emmett Till was young and James Byrd old, while Till had risen from the waters and Byrd had been left lying in the morning dew, both black bodies set in full view for an entire nation the implacable intensity of white racism. When authorities later found an *Esquire* magazine article on the Till case in the apartment of one of Byrd's lynchers, the connection between the innocent young boy and the unsuspecting older man was more forcefully made. The fact that many news reports connected Byrd's murder to the lynching of Emmett Till bears testament to a claim that is central to this collection: through its multiple tellings and retellings over the past fifty years, the story of Emmett Till haunts American memory and imagination. That haunting surfaces in the narratives we tell and the realities we live. Whether we are remembering it in the pages of a recent magazine or watching it reenacted again in the dark back roads of East Texas, what happened to Emmett Till is a presence that shapes the way we view and talk about race in America, sometimes wounding us, sometimes urging us to heal.

The essays in this collection explore how the Emmett Till lynching circulates through cultural memory and imagination. To appreciate how the literary artists examined in this collection have explored the meaning of Till's lynching—in explorations that both embrace and diverge from the historical record—it is helpful to understand the case as best we can.[2] The purpose of this historical summary is not to encourage readers to hold these literary artists accountable to the historical record; rather, it is to give readers a better position from which to assess how the workings of memory and imagination enrich that record.

The Case

On August 21, 1955, fourteen-year-old Emmett Till arrived in Mississippi. Earlier that summer, his great-uncle Moses Wright had visited Chicago and invited six-teen-year-old Wheeler Parker, Till's cousin, to come for a stay in the Delta. Till begged his mother to let him join his cousin on the trip, and after some hesitation she relented. Understanding that growing up in Chicago could not prepare her son for what awaited him in Mississippi, she coached him on the ways of the Deep South and warned him to watch his behavior. As Mamie Till-Mobley recalled in her 2003 memoir:

> We went through the drill. Chicago and Mississippi were two very different places, and white people down South could be very mean to blacks, even to black kids. Don't start up any conversations with white people. Only talk if you're spoken to. And how do you respond? "Yes, sir," "yes, ma'am." "No, sir," "no, ma'am." Put a handle on those answers. Don't just say "yes" and "no" or "naw." Don't ever do that. If you're walking down the street and a white woman is walking toward you, step off the side-walk, lower your head. Don't look her in the eye. Wait until she passes by, then get back on the sidewalk, keep going, don't look back. (100–101)

On the evening of Wednesday, August 24, after a few days of swimming and fishing, and a taste of hard-sweat cotton picking, Emmett, along with his cous-ins and a few local black friends, arrived at the Bryant Grocery in Money. Ac-counts of what happened at the grocery vary greatly, and while time has helped to clarify some points of disagreement, many still remain. While some accounts assert that Till had been boasting of his friendships with white people up North and was dared to go into the grocery and say something to Carolyn Bryant (the twenty-one-year-old white woman working the register), Till's cousins and other eyewitnesses at the store say that nothing of the kind happened. Rather, Till simply entered the store in order to purchase some bubble gum. While he was in there alone, something passed between the young black boy and the older white woman, something that flustered Carolyn Bryant. After leaving the store, Till re-portedly let out a wolf whistle in her direction, and Till's cousins—understanding young Emmett's breach of imposed racial etiquette—rushed him into their car and sped away. (For years, Emmett's mother insisted that her son whistled as a result of a speech impediment, but, in the 2005 documentary *The Murder of Emmett Till,* cousins Wheeler Parker and Simeon Wright—eyewitnesses to the event—confirm the wolf whistle.)

For three days, nothing happened. Emmett and his cousins did not tell Moses Wright about the incident. When Wright did learn of it, he considered sending Till home on the first train to Chicago, but he did not. Then, around 2:30 A.M. on Sunday, August 28, Roy Bryant (Carolyn's husband) and his half-brother J. W. Milam arrived at Wright's home, demanding to see the boy from Chicago. Armed with a gun, Milam barged into the house and rousted Till from bed. Although Bryant and Milam would later confess that they had acted alone in kidnapping and murdering Till, reliable early accounts claim that, after taking the boy from Wright's home, they led him to their truck, where they asked an unidentified person if this were the correct boy. He was so identified.

What happened over the next few hours will never be fully known. In their post-trial confession to William Bradford Huie in the January 17, 1956, issue of *Look* magazine, Bryant and Milam claimed that they never intended to kill the boy and spent much of the night driving around looking for a high precipice they could use to scare young Till. But when the Chicago boy started bragging about his white girlfriends—so they claimed—they just had to kill him. Against this account, other reliable witnesses (in particular, an eighteen-year-old black man named Willie Reed) claim to have seen at least two other white men and two other black men in Milam's pickup that morning. According to these accounts, Till was taken to a plantation shed in Sunflower County, and it was here—counter to Bryant and Milam's confession—that Till was beaten, tortured, and shot in the head. His body was taken from the shed in the back of Milam's pickup, weighted with a gin fan, and tossed into the Tallahatchie River.

That morning, the Wrights contacted Leflore County Sheriff George Smith, and he promptly arrested Bryant and Milam on suspicion of kidnapping. (Both admitted to having taken Till but claimed they let him go because they discovered he was the wrong boy.) When Till's body surfaced three days later, the two men were arrested for murder, and the first stirrings of national media attention began. Till's corpse was so badly beaten and decomposed that he could be identified only by his father's ring. When Mamie Till learned that the state of Mississippi was planning to bury her son—and with him the physical evidence of his brutal murder—she demanded that his body be returned home. When the casket arrived in Chicago on September 2, it was sealed with a warning that it was not to be opened. Disregarding the seal, Mamie Till insisted on seeing her son, and what she saw horrified and emboldened her. Wanting "the whole world to see" what Mississippi had done to her boy, she opted for an open-casket viewing, and from September 3 until the funeral on September 6, thousands of Chicagoans viewed Till's battered and bloated corpse. When *Jet* magazine published a photograph of his corpse in their September 15 issue, all of black America saw what those thousands of Chicagoans had seen. To this day that image remains one of the seminal icons of the civil rights movement.

Over the weeks leading up to the trial, the Till case became a national and international sensation. At first, not one of the five lawyers in Sumner, Mississippi, would take the defendants' case. As the story began to be covered in the national press, however, an us-versus-them mentality quickly emerged, and all five lawyers offered their services. The prosecution fell to District Attorney Gerald Chatham, who was aided by former FBI agent Robert Smith (appointed to the case by Governor Hugh White). As both sides prepared their cases, newspaper coverage was intense. When the trial opened on September 19, nearly one hundred journalists and photographers descended upon the tiny hamlet of Sumner (whose oft-noted town slogan was "A Good Place to Raise a Boy"). In addition to print reporters (including such notables as Murray Kempton, Dan Wakefield, John Herbers, James Hicks, and Clark Porteous), all three national news networks had correspondents in town, and each night those networks rushed footage back to their studios for swift broadcast. As David Halberstam has duly noted, the lynching of Emmett Till and the trial of his murderers emerged as "the first great media event of the civil rights movement" (469).

If not fair, the trial was speedy. On Monday, the lawyers sifted through the all-white, all-male jury pool, and by the morning of Tuesday, September 20, a decidedly nondiverse jury was in place. Just as the trial proper was set to open, however, the prosecution surprised everyone by asking for a recess. According to District Attorney Chatham, the prosecution had only recently learned of the existence of missing witnesses to the kidnapping and murder. Against defense objections, Judge Curtis Swango granted the recess, and that night, in a daring manhunt under the cover of darkness, a group of local black civil rights leaders (led by Dr. T. R. M. Howard and including Amzie Moore, Medgar Evers, and Ruby Hurley) joined forces with black and white journalists (among them Hicks and Porteous) to round up four new witnesses who could strengthen the prosecution's case. On Wednesday, Chatham called his first witness, Moses Wright, who, in one of the trial's most dramatic moments, was asked to identify the two men who took Emmett Till from his home. In one of the best-known journalistic accounts of the trial, *New York Post* reporter Murray Kempton told his readers:

> Moses Wright, making a formulation no white man in this county really believed he would dare to make, stood on his tiptoes to the full limit of his 64 years and his 5 feet 3 inches yesterday, pointed his black, workworn finger straight at the huge and stormy head of J. W. Milam and swore that this was the man who dragged 14-year-old Emmett Louis Till out of his cottonfield cabin the night the boy was murdered.
>   "There he is," said Moses Wright. He was a black pigmy standing up to a white ox. J. W. Milam leaned forward, crooking a cigaret [sic] in a hand that seemed as large as Moses Wrights' whole chest, and his eyes were coals of hatred. ("He Went All the Way," 65)

The following day was the most important of the trial. The prosecution's second witness was Mamie Till, who identified the body found in the river as her son's. After her testimony, the prosecution called its first surprise witness, Willie Reed, who told the court that he had seen four white men in the cab (and three black men in the bed) of Milam's pickup on the morning of the alleged murder. He also later saw Milam exit the plantation shed that this pickup had entered, a shed from which, a few moments earlier, Reed had heard screams. After calling two other missing witnesses to corroborate Reed's story, the prosecution rested its case. Immediately, the defense asked for a directed verdict of not guilty, but, when the judge denied their request, they called their first witness: Carolyn Bryant. When the prosecution objected that the defense had not mentioned her name and that the Supreme Court had ruled many times that whatever happens prior to a crime has no legal bearing on a case, the judge decided to allow her testimony but removed the jury from the courtroom. In her testimony, Bryant claimed that Till grabbed her hand, asked her for a date, and, then, when she tried to walk to the back of the store, Till grabbed her again—this time around the waist—and made lewd remarks. After this testimony, the jury was seated again, and the defense called Sunflower County sheriff H. C. Strider, who gave the jury the "out" it needed. Even though Strider, who had been the sheriff on the scene when Till's body was taken out of the Tallahatchie, had called a black undertaker to handle Till's remains, in court that Thursday he claimed that he could not be certain that the body recovered from the river was white or black, thus calling into question whether or not the prosecution had a corpus delicti.

On Friday, the defense rested its case early in the morning, and most of the day was taken up with stirring closing arguments: two by the prosecution, and one from each of the five defense attorneys. According to one reporter, defense attorney John Whitten informed the jury, "There are people in the United States who want to destroy the way of life of the Southern people . . . [And they] would not be above putting a rotting, stinking body in the river in the hope that it would be identified as Emmett Till" (Johnson, 100). As Murray Kempton records, Whitten told the jury in his final appeal that he was confident that "every last Anglo-Saxon one of you has the courage" to acquit these two innocent men ("2 Face Trial," 108). Despite Gerald Chatham's counterplea that the jury not be fooled—that the "killing of Emmett Till . . . was a cowardly act" (Johnson, 100)—the jury followed its Anglo-Saxon instincts, and after a mere sixty-seven minutes of deliberation returned a not-guilty verdict.

Anger at the verdict was swift and furious. The national and African American press attacked the decision, assailing Mississippi justice and warning that the verdict would hurt the interests of democracy at home and abroad. The *Daily Worker* bemoaned that "Good people everywhere—in America and throughout the world—feel a deep sense of horror over the outcome of the murder trial in Mississippi" ("The Shame of Our Nation," 118), and the *Chicago Defender* promised its readers that "this miscarriage of justice must not be left unavenged" ("What You Can Do," 127). While the southern press did not speak with one voice, the consensus was that Mississippi followed the rule of law and prosecuted Milam and Bryant with due and fair vigilance; the acquittal reflected the weakness of the evidence, not the prejudice of the court, the defense team, or the jury. Even those southern papers critical of the happenings in Sumner were quick to temper that criticism and deflect a general condemnation of Mississippi. An editorial in Hodding Carter's moderate *Delta Democrat-Times* put it this way: "it was not the jury that was derelict in its duty, despite the logical conclusions it might have made concerning whose body was most likely found in the Tallahatchie River, and who most likely put it there, but rather must the criticism fall upon the law officials who attempted in such small measure to seek out evidence and to locate witnesses to firmly establish whoever was guilty or was not guilty" ("Acquittal," 115).

In the wake of this acquittal, and a subsequent grand jury's refusal in November to indict Milam and Bryant on kidnapping charges (even though they had publicly confessed to kidnapping), the case stayed very much in the news. Several journalists took up the cause of finding out the "real story" behind the lynching of Emmett Till. For these journalists, important truths had been obscured by the judicial proceedings, and a series of provocative investigative exposés were published in such venues as the *Chicago Defender*, the *Cleveland Call and Post*, and the *California Eagle*. These early "inside stories" were concurrently supplemented by a steady course of literary responses to the case, creative works that, in their own way, were also seeking to express truths about the lynching. Together, these multivalent responses proved early on that no one single narrative could fully claim to capture the truth about the Till lynching—and what his lynching means to our national history.

The Till Narrative(s): Overview of a Genre and Our Essays

Among these many "inside stories" was, most famously, Alabama investigative journalist William Bradford Huie's checkbook journalism, composed after he convinced recently acquitted Roy Bryant and J. W. Milam to sell their story of the murder. "The Shocking Story of Approved Killing in Mississippi," printed in a 1956 *Look* magazine special issue on "The U.S. Teenager," was an early and key performance of the narrative of Emmett Till, a narrative that now has, according to Christopher Metress's annotated bibliography that ends this book, more than 140 literary and popular culture retellings.

There are countless racial atrocities in American history, but this brutal racist murder of Emmett Till, and the narrative that Huie set in motion around it, has entered, set off, and fascinated the literary imagination. Why? What is the special power of this story—which has a basis in history but also in fictional elements belonging to our national vocabulary of American racism? What gives it this place in our cultural consciousness, consequently seeding a legend—a cultural mythology—compelling repeat and varied performance? The eleven essays in this collection suggest various answers. Together, they also suggest the presence of an "Emmett Till narrative" in post-1955 literature, an overarching recurrent plot that is variously performed but builds on recognizable elements and is as legible as the "lynching narrative" or the "passing narrative," or the recently proposed "segregation narrative" (Norman and Kendrix). Individually, these essays document the uses to which writers have put the Till story.

In "On That Third Day He Rose: Sacramental Memory and the Lynching of

Emmett Till," Metress approaches the Till murder as a "cultural trauma" experienced by an entire generation of black men and women coming of age in 1955. One healing response to trauma is to narrate the past—to tell the story of the event in forms that reconcile it with recovery. Metress attends one recurrent trope in these cultural retellings: the manner in which "Till's brutal slaying is reconfigured as a Christlike sacrifice and young Emmett is reconceived as a savior and redeemer." Finding this pattern in responses by writers as diverse as Mamie Till-Mobley (Emmett's mother), Wanda Coleman, Michael Eric Dyson, and Lewis Nordan, he probes the power of this trope to release the "toxicity" of trauma and make visible the promise of a more redemptive future. In the end, Metress argues that such narratives operate as "sacramental memories" that transform the "deep and unsettling wound" of Till's lynching—a wound "so clearly representative of anger, prejudice, and unmitigated hate"—into a site of healing and liberation.

Sharon Monteith's "The Murder of Emmett Till in the Melodramatic Imagination: William Bradford Huie and Vin Packer in the 1950s" examines two initial renderings of the Till narrative. When Huie revised his 1956 *Look* article "The Shocking Story of Approved Killing in Mississippi" for pulp paperback distribution, it became *Wolf Whistle*, a "true story" of "A Race Sex Killing: The Whole Truth of the Emmett Till Murder Mystery." Huie's story is a most influential origin for the Till narrative that would be so many times reinvented, but, as Monteith shows, Huie's story is unsettling to a critical eye. The power of its revelation was that Till's murderers felt so protected by their whiteness that they would sell a confession that established their guilt. In doing so, they seemed to "solve" the mystery that other accounts could only speculate about. But Huie's "report" of the murder and its resulting prominence further screened truths about what happened in the early hours of August 28, 1955. Monteith examines Huie's sensationalist techniques alongside the "sexploitation" of the Till case as dramatized in Marijane Meeker's *Dark Don't Catch Me* (1956). This pulp fiction, published under the pseudonym Vin Packer, was the earliest novel about the murder, "advertised as 'The Peyton Place of the Deep South'" and marketed as a sensational shocker. It receives its first critical attention here. Reflecting on these two opening performances of the Till narrative, Monteith considers the genre of southern melodrama as a lens through which to view representations of the murder. And revealing the manipulation of the Till case in 1950s popular culture, she reminds us that texts located on the margins of the "literary" can be symbolically and culturally central.

In "Flesh That Needs to Be Loved: Langston Hughes Writing the Body of Emmett Till," Myisha Priest examines the depiction of the body in two works by Hughes: the elegiac poem "Mississippi—1955" and *The Sweet Flypaper of Life*, a groundbreaking experimental children's text built around Roy DeCarava's photographs of life in Harlem. Hughes responds to the historical representation of black flesh as pained and punished, dominated and disciplined—a representation reiterated and reproduced in the photographs of Emmett Till's ravished body. As Priest notes, "The black body [had become] . . . a warning against black transgression." But Mamie Till's publication of photographs of her son's corpse altered that meaning of the murdered body, reinscribing it as a site of African American political resistance that transfigured the "the relationship between woundedness, representation, and black political . . . agency." The now nearly forgotten but unique and innovative *Sweet Flypaper of Life*—a project-in-progress when the Till photos made their appearance and impression—is Hughes's transforming response to the overdetermined text of black bodies. In its story and DeCarava's images, the black body is loved as "a site of human pain *and* pleasure, of a bittersweet blues sensibility." This changed signification expresses both African American subjectivity and political possibility.

Brian Norman's "James Baldwin's Unifying Polemic: Racial Segregation, Moral Integration, and the Polarizing Figure of Emmett Till" considers the reception of Baldwin's off-Broadway play *Blues for Mister Charlie* (1964). Norman notes that the play was dismissed, as protest writing frequently is, with the label "polemical." Appearing in the midst of the civil rights movement's tactical disagreements about "the calls to arms" as opposed to nonviolent civil disobedience, the play shifted a cultural "fault line"—factionalizing literary reception just as Emmett Till's trial had polarized Mississippi and the country. But the play's polemic offers a vision of integration through debate between characters who "cross lines of segregation," dramatized by a stage design that cuts the set into racially polarized Whitetown and Blacktown, divided by a ditch that holds a young man's murdered black body. Addressing a racially mixed audience deeply divided along legal, racial, and ideological lines, Baldwin attempts to use the Till narrative to engender a unifying project that draws on integration and self-determination ideologies. Norman suggests that *Blues for Mister Charlie* became principal evidence in a case against Baldwin and polemical art—which now, like the Till trial, needs reconsideration.

In "Maids Mild and Dark Villains, Sweet Magnolias and Seeping Blood: Gwendolyn Brooks's Poetic Response to the Lynching of Emmett Till," Vivian M.

May analyzes two 1960 poems: "A Bronzeville Mother Loiters in Mississippi. Meanwhile, a Mississippi Mother Burns Bacon" and "The Last Quatrain of the Ballad of Emmett Till." Though these two poems are implicitly linked by reference to Emmett Till, they are otherwise so different that readers rarely discuss their connections. However, as May reveals, the two poems are constructed on parallels; they are kitchen revelations that each build to a signifying kiss. Yet the two poems diverge markedly in terms of form and worldview. May discusses Brooks's choice to pair the two poems and to contrast the perspectives of two women: the "milk-white maid" (recognizable as the imagined consciousness of Carolyn Bryant) and "the Bronzeville Mother" (recognizable as the consciousness of Mamie Till). May delineates how Brooks lays bare the politics of the romantic ballad of the "fine prince" and "maid mild," for it hinges on the white supremacist narrative of chivalry, violence, and murder. The maid mild's internal monologue—focused on the "hero" and "heroine" of the "romance" and the "fun" spoiled when the "dark villain" is a child—suppresses the "blood" and writes out the story of the child victim and his mother. By contrast, the sparse ten lines of "The Last Quatrain," which May reads with new attention, imply a consciousness that can find no form adequate to the story. May contends that through juxtaposition, Brooks emphasizes how violence is embedded in narrative and language; focuses on ignorance as a key tool of oppression; demonstrates how passivity and guilt are self-centered forms of complicity; and highlights Till's mother's love and resistance as politically and poetically significant. May concludes that Brooks's poems can be read as instances of political action, crafted to engender in readers the outrage and action that the maid mild never manages while also giving the dead child's mother the last word.

Laura Dawkins, in "It Could Have Been My Son: Maternal Empathy in Gwendolyn Brooks's and Audre Lorde's Till Poems," brings Brooks's "Bronzeville Mother" into dialogue with Lorde's 1981 "Afterimages." Dawkins situates both poems within the theoretical frame of Pierre Nora's discussion of "sites of memory" that form a counterhistory challenging official history. In Dawkins's reading of "Afterimages," the African American speaker who mourns Till's death determines to "withhold pity" for the wife of Till's murderer just as Brooks's white persona initially resists her tie with the "Other Woman," Mamie Till. Dawkins argues, however, that both poems bring the mothers to acknowledge their shared vulnerability, suppressed anger, and "empathic connection" with the other mother. Dawkins shows that Lorde, who consistently avoids the constraints of one-dimensional identity politics, repeatedly envisions a maternal relation to the world as a saving means of communicating "connectedness, arcing across our differences." Black motherhood, not biological or even female, is "a metaphor for empathic awareness." "By claiming the mutilated child as her 'son,' the mother-poet distances herself from a society that either 'forgets' historical child-victims or else sensationalizes their stories. Even as she defines her distance from these disengaged spectators, however, the poet scrutinizes her own motives for dwelling on Till's tragedy . . . 'Afterimages' records an intensive process of self-examination as the speaker assesses her complex and evolving relationship to a martyred child whom she claims as her own." Remembering Emmett Till's tragedy as historical legacy, Lorde reaches toward symbolic kinship with all victims of racial violence.

Kathaleen Amende reminds us that, for Anne Moody, *Coming of Age in Mississippi* in the 1950s meant other things besides school, basketball, church choir, homecoming dances, and a struggle to make good grades. It meant moving off sidewalks so that white people wouldn't have to redirect their steps. It meant asking unanswered questions. It meant not being told about herself, her body, or her race. It meant being surrounded by a protective silence, based in the fear that narratives about her family history or the NAACP or voting rights struggles would get her killed. In "Silence and the Frustration of Broken Promises: Anne Moody's Struggle with the Lynching of Emmett Till and the Civil Rights Movement," Amende suggests that young Moody first fully recognizes the code of silence that her black southern community has internalized when she is disciplined for asking about Emmett Till's murder. Then she finds herself unable to silence or ignore the questions in her head, and subsequently she enters the organizations of the movement where she sees groups of people struggling to address the problems she had been led to try to ignore. Amende argues that *Coming of Age in Mississippi* reveals why Moody eventually left the movement—that she "did not give up her dream of speaking out," but that "she chose an alternative way of finding that voice and attempting to make a difference. That alternative, of course, is art." In autobiography, Moody "claimed her own story—one that didn't always jibe with the story of the movement—and her own voice. And at the nexus of this re-creation is the murder of Emmett Till"—the murder that shattered her semi-safe falsehoods of security.

Sylvie Kandé's "This Corpse So Small Left Unavenged: Nicolás Guillén and Aimé Césaire on Emmett Till's Lynching" concerns international response within the *Negrismo* and *Négritude* movements. Kandé shows us that Till's murder "sent shockwaves throughout the world at large," generating immediate outrage in Africa and the Diaspora, and bringing race relations in the United States under renewed scrutiny. Her particular focus is on Martinican Aimé Césaire and Cuban Nicolás Guillén, two prominent Caribbean poets who wrote almost simultaneous elegies dedicated to Till. Césaire's "On the State of the Union" first appeared in the Paris-based journal *Présence Africaine* and was republished in his 1960 collection *Ferrements*. Guillén's "Elegy for Emmett Till" was composed in France and published in a 1958 collection, *Elegias*. Kandé argues that these publications indicate "the sense of urgency that animated the founders of Negrismo and Négritude," intellectual and artistic movements concerned with black self-assertion and the recognition of black contribution to national and world cultures. Césaire and Guillén, adding to and yet departing from their work in journalism, chose the poetic form as a medium in which to respect Emmett Till and to address racial terrorism, as well as to open up the issue of democracy in the United States. Kandé's careful reading of these poems emerges from her documentation, summary, and translation of the international journalistic coverage and response—to which she newly and economically gives American readers access. This essay importantly reaches beyond the U.S. borders to consider the Till murder in the transnational context of the black Diaspora, a needed effort in civil rights studies.

Suzanne W. Jones, in "Childhood Trauma and Its Reverberations in Bebe Moore Campbell's *Your Blues Ain't Like Mine*," describes the 1992 novel as seeking "to answer the question that black teenagers in Mississippi, and indeed many people from all over the United States, asked after seeing the photograph of Till's mutilated and bloated body: 'How could they do that to . . . a boy?'" Jones points out that unlike other reinventions of the Till story, Campbell's novel opens with the murder and then writes "into the aftermath," moving from Mississippi to Chicago and from the 1950s to the present. This telling explores the relationship between being caught in society's hierarchical divisions and "being psychically abused during childhood." It also emphasizes the "possibilities for reconciliation between blacks and whites, between men and women, and across class lines." Jones argues that writing toward hope, Campbell "simultaneously expresses America's complex racial pain, physical and psychological, and invents a cure for it. In functioning both as a way to express pain and a way to move beyond pain, Campbell's novel sings the blues for readers."

In "Grotesque Laughter, Unburied Bodies, and History: Shape-Shifting in Lewis Nordan's *Wolf Whistle*," Harriet Pollack looks at a 1993 fictionalization of the Till murder "by a white writer who for thirty-eight years felt the story was not his to tell." Four decades after the event, Nordan revisits the incident and writes a comic novel that is "full of strategic shape-shifting." The "surprising choices Nordan makes," particularly his comedy and his "mutations of the presumed events of history . . . focus the central meanings" of the Till narrative, "even while they alter the story." Pollack speculates about the purposes of fibrillating between unsettling comedy and disconcerting tragedy and between history and fiction—felt for example when Bobo puzzlingly manages to shoot Solon. Her inquiry has to do with the "conscious and unconscious" purposes of this shape-shifting. One effect of Nordan's comic erasure of conventional conceptual boundaries is to challenge the untenable insistence on inviolable category divisions—an insistence fundamental to segregation. Among the many shape-shiftings Pollack attends are shifts between the haunting unburied bodies of seemingly unrelated children; we see their witnessing eyes—Glenn Gregg's eyes with their lids burned off and Bobo's demon eye that continues to see after his death. She reads this trope as a coded transformation of the "tale of the . . . downcast eye" in the apartheid South; looking becomes, in the Till case, in 1960s history and civil rights fiction, and in Nordan's *Wolf Whistle*, "an act of defiance, of national education, revelation, and accusation."

Donnie McMahand, in "(Dis)embodying the Delta Blues: *Wolf Whistle* and *Your Blues Ain't Like Mine*," acknowledges that "as two novelized accounts of Emmett Till's murder, Bebe Moore Campbell's *Your Blues Ain't Like Mine* (1992) and Lewis Nordan's *Wolf Whistle* (1993) could not be more dissimilar." Nordan fuses brutal burlesque and unruly telling, while Campbell's "popular realism" chronicles the continuing implication of Till's death on segregation culture in the rural South and urban North long after 1955. But McMahand argues that Nordan and Campbell alike build into their representations of Till—as well as other black bodies—"contradictory symbols of political compliance and social resistance . . . the novels' schismatic presentations of African American bodies as . . . present and absent, . . . bodies vital and dying, abject and rebellious, [are] textual representations" that link "the segregated and violent South with the cathartic and regenerative rhetoric of the blues." McMahand intricately argues that Nordan and Campbell "meld the black body with the musical concept of a silent break, . . . revealing instances in which the white . . . gaze, apart from acts of torture and killing, attains fulfillment through a continuous and pathological overlooking of the black presence."

One of the goals of *Emmett Till in Literary Memory and Imagination* is to explore the complex relationship between history and memory, especially when that memory is played out in literary texts. Although our contributors discuss more than a dozen literary works that memorialize Till's lynching, there currently exist more than 140 works that do so. Christopher Metress's "Literary Representations of the Lynching of Emmett Till: An Annotated Bibliography" is designed to serve two purposes: to call attention to the full extent of Till's presence in literary memory and to encourage further scholarship in the field. This bibliography annotates works not treated in this volume, including some texts lost or nearly lost and some essential archival materials never published. The list itself suggests the special power of the Till narrative, its cultural resonance, and the place of its remembrance and retelling in our recovery from cultural trauma.

NOTES

1. The best resources for understanding the James Byrd lynching are the PBS film *Two Towns of Jasper—Documenting the Aftermath of a Hate Murder* and Dina Temple-Raston's *A Death in Texas: A Story of Race, Murder and a Small Town's Struggle for Redemption*. The film is also accompanied by an excellent website; see www.pbs.org/pov/pov2002/twotownsofjasper/index.html (accessed 10 October 2006).

2. The following summary of events is informed by a careful weighing of many sources. Among those most important to our conclusions are Hugh Stephen Whitaker's 1963 master's thesis "A Case Study in Southern Justice: The Emmett Till Case"; Stephen J. Whitfield's *A Death in the Delta: The Story of Emmett Till*; the documentaries *The Murder of Emmett Till* and *The Untold Story of Emmett Louis Till*; and the many news articles, memoirs, and assorted materials included in Christopher Metress, *The Lynching of Emmett Till: A Documentary Narrative*.

WORKS CITED

"Acquittal." *Delta Democrat-Times,* 23 September 1955. In Metress, 115–16.

Halberstam, David. *The Fifties.* 1993. New York: Ballantine, 1994.

Johnson, Sam. "Jury Hears Defense and Prosecution Arguments as Testimony Ends in Kidnap-Slaying Case." *Greenwood Commonwealth,* 23 September 1955. In Metress, 99–101.

Kempton, Murray. "2 Face Trial as 'Whistle' Kidnaper—Due to Post Bond and Go Home." *New York Post,* 25 September 1955. In Metress, 107–11.

———. "He Went All the Way." *New York Post*, 22 September 1955. In Metress, 65–67.

Metress, Christopher. *The Lynching of Emmett Till: A Documentary Narrative*. Charlottesville: University of Virginia Press, 2002.

The Murder of Emmett Till. Directed by Stanley Nelson. PBS, 2002.

Norman, Brian, and Piper Kendrix Williams, eds. "Representing Segregation: A Special Issue." *African American Review*, forthcoming 2008.

"Shame of Our Nation." *Daily Worker*, 26 September 1955. In Metress, 118–19.

Temple-Raston, Dina. *A Death in Texas: A Story of Race, Murder and a Small Town's Struggle for Redemption*. New York: Henry Holt, 2002.

Till-Mobley, Mamie, and Christopher Benson. *Death of Innocence: The Story of the Hate Crime That Changed America*. New York: Random House, 2003.

Two Towns of Jasper—Documenting the Aftermath of a Hate Murder. Directed by Whitney Dow and Marco Williams. PBS, 2003.

The Untold Story of Emmett Louis Till. Directed by Keith Beauchamp. Velocity / Thinkfilm, 2005.

Whitaker, Hugh Stephen. "A Case Study in Southern Justice: The Emmett Till Case." Master's thesis. Florida State University, 1963. Available at http://etd.lib.fsu.edu/theses/available/etd-05272004-140932/ (accessed 1 August 2006).

Whitfield, Stephen J. *A Death in the Delta: The Story of Emmett Till*. New York: Free Press, 1988.

ON THAT THIRD DAY HE ROSE

Sacramental Memory and the Lynching of Emmett Till

CHRISTOPHER METRESS

I want to begin with a memory. The time is 1955. The place is Louisville, Kentucky. The one who remembers is Muhammad Ali.

> Emmett Till and I were about the same age. A week after he was murdered in Sunflower County, Mississippi, I stood on the corner with a gang of boys, looking at pictures of him in the black newspapers and magazines. In one, he was laughing and happy. In the other, his head was swollen and bashed in, his eyes bulging out of their sockets and his mouth twisted and broken. His mother had done a bold thing. She refused to let him be buried until hundreds of thousands marched past his open casket in Chicago and looked down at his mutilated body. I felt a deep kinship to him when I learned he was born the same year and day I was. My father talked about it at night and dramatized the crime.

> I couldn't get Emmett out of my mind, until one evening I thought of a way to get back at white people for his death. That night I sneaked out of the house and walked down to Ronnie King's and told him my plan. It was late at night when we reached the old railroad station on Louisville's West Side. I remember a poster of a thin white man in striped pants and a top hat who pointed at us above the words UNCLE SAM WANTS YOU. We stopped and hurled stones at it, and then broke into a shoeshine boy's shed and stole some iron shoe rests and took them to the railroad track. We planted them deep on the tracks and waited. When a big blue diesel engine came around the bend, it hit the shoe rests and pushed them nearly thirty feet before one of the wheels locked and sprang from the track. I remember the loud sound of ties ripping up. I broke out running, Ronnie behind me, and then I looked back. I'll never forget the eyes of the man in the poster, staring at us: UNCLE SAM WANTS YOU.

> It took two days to get up enough nerve to go back there. The work crew was still cleaning up the debris. And the man in the poster was still pointing. I always knew that sooner or later he would confront me, and I would confront him. (34–35)

For an entire generation of black men and women—particularly those who, like Muhammad Ali, were coming of age in 1955—Emmett Till's brutal murder represents what Ron Eyerman, writing specifically about the African American slave experience, calls a "cultural trauma." According to Eyerman, "a psychological or physical trauma . . . involves a wound and the experience of great emotional anguish by an individual," but "a cultural trauma refers to a dramatic loss of identity and meaning, a tear in the social fabric, affecting a group of people that has achieved some degree of cohesion" (2). As one of the defining traumatic events of the African American experience in the twentieth century, the lynching of Emmett Till certainly meets this description. Thus it is not surprising to find that Muhammad Ali's response to that lynching is marked by the same dramatic losses and tears that we find in so many memoirs that reflect on the death of Emmett Till. Recall, for instance, Anne Moody's account in *Coming of Age in Mississippi*. "Before Emmett Till's murder," Moody writes, "I had known the fear of hunger, and the Devil. But now there was a new fear known to me—the fear of being killed just because I was black. This was the worst of my fears. I knew once I got food, the fear of starving to death would leave. I also was told that if I were a good girl, I wouldn't have to fear the Devil or hell. But I didn't know what one had to do or not do as a Negro not to be killed. Probably just being a Negro period was enough, I thought" (125–26). An even greater sense of anguish is expressed by Eldridge Cleaver in *Soul on Ice*. According to Cleaver, learning of Till's lynching "turned me inside out" (23). After seeing a picture of Carolyn Bryant, the white woman at whom young Emmett allegedly whistled, Cleaver had a "nervous breakdown" (23). "For several days," Cleaver remembers, "I ranted and raved against the white race, against white women in particular, against white America in general. When I came to myself, I was locked in a padded cell with not even the vaguest memory of how I got there. All I could recall was an eternity of pacing back and forth in the cell, preaching to the unhearing walls" (23–24).

Like Moody and Cleaver—and like so many of his generation—Ali is disoriented by Till's lynching. However, unlike Moody (paralyzed by the question of "what one had to do or not do as a Negro not to be killed") or Cleaver (pacing his cell and "preaching to the unhearing walls"), Ali devises a plan of action that will, he believes, help him to repair the imbalance that Till's murder has brought into his life. When Ali stood on that street corner in Louisville in the late summer of 1955 and saw those photographs of Emmett Till's head "swollen and bashed in, [with] his eyes bulging out of their sockets and his mouth twisted and broken," he responded to them as would many a traumatized person: that is, he tried everything he could to get those images—and the threats to identity they represent—out of his head. What we must note, however, is that in seeking to rid himself of Till's image and thus set things back in order, Ali is driven to create disorder, whether through defacing the poster of Uncle Sam or by derailing the blue diesel engine from its tracks. Although his plan to derail the engine succeeds, we are led to conclude that his overall plan to unsettle things has, in the end, settled nothing: Uncle Sam, despite all the hurled stones, is "still pointing." Instead of ridding his memory of Till's battered face, Ali simply adds another face to that memory, for just as he will never forget Emmett Till's "eyes bulging out of their sockets," he now claims that he'll "never forget the eyes of the man in the poster." Rather than clearing his mind of a traumatic experience, he is now a young man doubly haunted.

I begin with this brief reflection on Muhammad Ali's response to Emmett Till's lynching because of what it both does and doesn't do. First, it represents so well the power of unsettling experiences to produce disorder. Such experiences, by definition, disrupt and disorient. They throw us and our ways of knowing into confusion. To borrow an image directly from Ali's memoir, unsettling experiences derail us. For a powerful poetic expression of this idea in relation to the Emmett Till case, see Gwendolyn Brooks's 1960 poem "A Bronzeville Mother Loiters in Mississippi. Meanwhile, a Mississippi Mother Burns Bacon." Brooks explores Till's story from the perspective of Carolyn Bryant. Bryant is the Mississippi mother, burning the bacon because it is the day after her husband's acquittal and she is distracted, thinking about how and why her husband killed the young black boy from up North. At the beginning of the poem, she attempts to understand the events through her conventional ways of knowing. "From the first it had been like a / Ballad," she thinks.

> Herself: the milk-white maid, the "maid mild"
> Of the ballad. Pursued
> By the Dark Villain. Rescued by the Fine Prince.
> And the Happiness-Ever-After.
> That was worth anything.
> It was good to be a "maid mild."
> That made the breath go fast. (313)

The more she thinks about what happened, however, the more her certainties disintegrate—she cannot make Till fit into the role he was supposed to have played:

> But there was something about the matter of the Dark Villain.
> He should have been older, perhaps
> The hacking down of a villain more fun to think about
> When his menace possessed undisputed breadth, undisputed height
> And a harsh kind of voice
>
> . . .
>
> The fun was disturbed, then all but nullified
> When the Dark Villain was a blackish child
> Of fourteen, with eyes too young to have lost every reminder
> Of its infant softness. (314)

Unsettled by these eyes of infant softness, the white woman's ballad collapses. She is left, in the end, with nothing but disorder:

> The one thing in the world that she did know and knew
> With terrifying clarity was that her composition
> Had disintegrated.
> That, although the pattern prevailed,
> The breaks were everywhere. That she could think
> Of no thread capable of the necessary
> Sew-work. (314–15)

   What Ali's response does not do is the same thing that Brooks's "milk-white maid" is unable to do; neither can find a way to reorder the chaos produced by the senselessness of Till's lynching. That is, neither can find the threads capable of repairing the breaks that are now everywhere around them. However, in order to heal the wounds of trauma, such reorderings are necessary. As Eyerman has observed, "a traumatic tear evokes a need to 'narrate new foundations,' which includes reinterpreting the past as a means of reconciling present/future needs" (4). There are, of course, as many ways to reorder traumatic experiences as there are needs both present and future. Not surprisingly, then, when memoirists, historians, and poets explore the personal and cultural traumas generated by

Emmett Till's lynching, all sorts of diverse reorderings emerge. As Elizabeth V. Spelman has argued in a different context, "whether or not it is our lot as humans to suffer, it often seems as if it is our lot to attempt to give form to suffering—be it our own, that of those close to us, or that of strangers near and far" (2). In this essay, however, I want to explore one of the most frequent means by which we have sought to give form to the insufferable events of August 28, 1955, and thus turn our unsettling memories of that day into something from which we can draw strength. While I agree with Eyerman's observation that traumatic tears do indeed evoke the need to narrate new foundations, sometimes that need for a new foundation is met by resurrecting an older one and using that as the thread capable of doing the "necessary / Sew-work."

As my title suggests, that capable thread upon which many have seized is the figure of Jesus. Time and again in memoirs, essays, histories, poems, and novels, Till's brutal slaying is reconfigured as a Christlike sacrifice and young Emmett is reconceived as a savior and redeemer. In one way, then, he has become the literal incarnation of the anonymous "Black Christ" that marks so much of African American lynching literature. Recall, for instance, the opening lines of Claude McKay's "The Lynching" ("His Spirit in smoke ascended to high heaven. / His father, by the cruelest way of pain, / Had bidden him to his bosom once again" [190]) or, even more directly and more fully, Countee Cullen's long poem "The Black Christ." However, these earlier representations of the lynched Black Christ do not insist upon the redemptive power of the victim's horrible death. McKay and Cullen employ the image of the Black Christ as a means of drawing our attention to the decidedly nonredemptive nature of the lynching. In McKay's poem, for instance, the victim may have been "bidden to [his father's] bosom once again," but "The awful sin remained still unforgiven." To emphasize this, McKay has the lynchers return the next morning to the scene of their crime: "Day dawned, and soon the mixed crowds came to view / The ghastly body swaying in the sun: / The women thronged to look, but never a one / Showed sorrow in her eyes of steely blue; / And little lads, lynchers that were to be, / Danced round the dreadful things in fiendish glee" (190). The ascending "Spirit" of the poem's opening line—a Spirit that initially possesses all the redemptive possibilities of Christ's sacrifice—degenerates into "a ghastly body" and then into "dreadful thing" that produces "fiendish glee" instead of amazing grace. As we shall see, however, the Black Christ image serves a markedly different purpose for those seeking to draw meaning from Emmett Till's death.

Of course, not all representations of Till's lynching rely on the figure of Jesus as a sense-making trope that discovers redemption amid the horror. Often, Emmett Till appears not as a redeemer who saves but as a restless ghost who condemns and disrupts, a young man whose death is given meaning and purpose by the power it has to haunt and destroy those who allowed that death to happen. We see this kind of reconfiguration in James Baldwin's play *Blues for Mister Charlie* (1964), Audre Lorde's poem "Afterimages" (1982), Bebe Moore Campbell's novel *Your Blues Ain't Like Mine* (1992), and, of course, in Brooks's "Bronzeville Mother." In *Blues for Mister Charlie*, for instance, Richard Henry—Baldwin's stand-in for Till—is anything but an innocent redeemer. Unlike Till, Richard is a born southerner and a grown man, a local preacher's son who, after eight years in New York City, returns South as a rehabilitated drug-addict with militant ideas about race, integration, and equality. Moreover, he expresses a deep hatred of white people, repeatedly brags about his sexual conquests of white women, and is ultimately murdered not for wolf whistling at a white woman but for knocking down the husband of a white woman and then mocking that man's sexual impotency in front of his wife. As one of the play's white characters observes, Richard's "effect was—kind of unsettling" (111).

In fact, we can read the many liberties that Baldwin has taken with the details of the Till case as intended to produce a similar kind of unsettling, and one of the main ideas that Baldwin wants to unsettle is the notion that nonviolent Christian love is the best way to respond to racial violence. When Richard tells his grandmother that "the only way the black man's going to *get* any power is to drive all the white men into the sea," she tells him that he is going to make himself "sick with hatred." Richard responds, "I'm going to make myself *well* with hatred" (21). When she objects that "It can't be done . . . Hatred is a poison," Richard insists, "Not for me. I'm going to learn to drink it—a little every day in the morning, and then a booster shot late at night . . . and I'll get well" (21). Although Baldwin is certainly not endorsing hatred as the only effective tool for political change, he is—through his unsettling stand-in for Emmett Till—suggesting that the African American community must question the redemptive power of Christian suffering as a political tool. This point is best exemplified by Richard's father, Meridian Henry, a Christian minister who at the beginning of the play conducts workshops in nonviolent resistance but at the end places his son's gun "in the pulpit. Under the Bible. Like the pilgrims of old" (120). For Baldwin, the Emmett Till story serves to challenge our conceptions of redemption and hope for the future, leading us away from the model of undeserved Christian suffering, represented by "all that turn-the-other-cheek jazz" (100), and toward a more violent form of engagement with hatred and oppression.

As *Blues for Mister Charlie* suggests, not all writers reinscribe Emmett Till's lynching within the familiar pattern of Jesus's atoning sacrifice (and some, like Baldwin, write directly against that gesture). However, that pattern of atonement has certainly been the most persistent means for coming to terms with this particular collective trauma. Not surprisingly, Emmett Till's mother, Mrs. Mamie Till-Mobley, appears to have been the first to insist upon the redemptive power of her son's death. According to a front-page article in the September 10, 1955, issue of the *Chicago Defender*, Till-Mobley, upon meeting her son's casket at Illinois Central Station, cried out, "Lord you gave your only son to remedy a condition, but who knows, but what the death of my only son might bring an end to lynching!" (29). Similarly, in an interview she gave to the *Defender* the following year, she recounted her experience the night following the discovery of her son's death. In this recollection, we can see both the disorientation the trauma of her son's brutal lynching caused her and the means by which she found reorientation through that death's similarity to the crucifixion.

> While I was lying there, wide awake, I pondered over the whole chain of events leading up to that fateful day. My mind went back and forth over my life like a roving camera searching, searching, for some reason why this had happened to me.
>
> I was angry with God that He had let Bo be kidnapped and slain so brutally and aloud I demanded, "Why did you do this[?] Why are You so cruel that You would let this happen? Why do you allow this kind of persecution?"
>
> . . .
>
> Then began one of the strangest experiences of my whole life. It was just as though someone had entered the room and we were carrying on a conversation. It was as real to me as though we were both flesh and blood.
>
> The presence said to me, "Mamie, it was ordained from the beginning of time that Emmett Louis Till would die a violent death. You should be grateful to be the mother of a boy who died blameless like Christ. Bo Till will never be forgotten. There is a job for you to do now."

I sat up in bed and stretched out my hand. I was praying hard that nobody would come up front before the conversation was completed, because I wanted the answer and I wanted to finish talking this thing out . . .

"What shall I do?" I asked.

The voice replied, "Have courage and faith that in the end there will be redemption for the sufferings of your people and you are the instrument of this purpose. Work unceasingly to tell the story so that the truth will arouse men's consciences and right can at last prevail."

The Voice died away and the Presence left the room. I lay down and slept peacefully. (232–33)

Although Mamie Till-Mobley was alone in the presence of this comforting voice that night in Chicago, she was not alone in her understanding of how to give meaning to her son's death. For many others at the time, the best way to grasp the significance of the events in Money, Mississippi, was to read them through the lens of Christ's redemptive suffering. For instance, a reader of the *Pittsburgh Courier* contributed a short poem to the October 8, 1955, issue:

> Bow thy head O state of Mississippi
> Let tears of shame course down thy cheek
> Ravished the standard of humanity,
> A boy's body floats in a creek.
> God so loved the world, He gave His son,
> To teach the Brotherhood of Man,
> What now, unrelenting state[,] will be done
> To wash the boy's blood from your hand? (Skelton)

An editorial in the *California Eagle* echoed this sentiment: "These state officials and rich farmers and prosperous business men and self righteous clergymen and spineless editors and whimpering liberals are all on record as being horrified at the murder . . . They are the Pontius Pilates of 1955, washing their hands clean of Emmett Till's blood" ("There Stands Mississippi"). In addition, the *Atlanta Daily World* proclaimed that "every door-post in the nation is sprinkled with the blood of Emmett Till, that ill-fated lad who allegedly 'wolf-whistled' up a breeze whose chilly listing will doubtless blow the world good" ("Till Time Finishes the

Till Case"), and a subscriber to the *Cleveland Call and Post* warned his fellow citizens not to forget the young boy who was "sacrificed on the cross of ignorance" (Lee). In what was perhaps the most widely disseminated reinscription of Till's lynching as echoing the redemptive power of Christ's suffering, *Life* magazine reminded its readers that "the soul of Emmett Till himself was known but to few, but it was a thing of value. It was fashioned on July 25, 1941, by the Lord God Almighty who placed on it this distinctive seal: *This is my son, akin to all others, but unlike any one of them. Like each of My children he is unique, irreplaceable, immortal. I hereby send him among other men, who are his brothers.* He went and was slain" (48). This image of Emmett Till as a slain son of God even found its way into the visual arts of the day. David Driskell's impressionistic oil painting of 1956, entitled "Behold Thy Son," shows a woman—presumably Mamie Till-Mobley—holding her dead son, his arms outstretched in imitation of the crucifixion, the positioning of the two bodies echoing the familiar form of the pieta. In addition, that same year a California artist named Yucca Salamunich crafted a bronze statue of Mamie Till-Mobley, which she entitled "The Negro Madonna."

Emmett Till is still being remembered today as a Christ figure who died for our sins. Wanda Coleman's poem "Emmett Till" (1986) opens with the image of the River Jordan, describes Emmett's mother as a "black madonna / bereft of babe" (331), speaks of the young Till as being "crucified" for his alleged whistle, characterizes his submergence in the Tallahatchie River as a baptism, and ends with the lines: "*on that third day / he rose*" (332). In 1994, historian Cleanora Hudson-Weems published *Emmett Till: The Sacrificial Lamb of the Civil Rights Movement* (a chapter of which is devoted to the "Spiritual Force of Till's Lynching"), and in 2000, musician William Roper premiered a violoncello solo, "A Poem for Emmett Till: A Freedom Song," an eight-movement piece that begins with young Till in the womb and includes a penultimate movement devoted to "Emmett's Ascension." In "Emmett Till's Open Casket as *La Pietà*" (2004), Quan Barry laments the news of Mamie Till-Mobley's passing, beginning his poem with an image of her "breaking the coroner's seals, prying her way" to her son, and concluding with the reflection that "When Mary holds the dead Christ in her arms / she has seen everything / but the Resurrection" (44). Moreover, Mamie Till-Mobley continued throughout her life to speak of her son's death in all its redemptive possibility. As she told Studs Terkel in a 1992 interview, "He's never far from my mind. I was reading in Scriptures where the Lord Jesus Christ

Emmett Till and his mother, Mamie Till-Mobley.

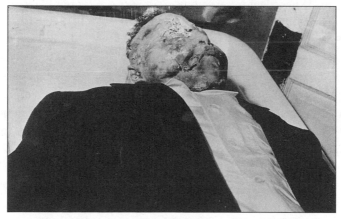

Emmett Till's open casket, 1955. Courtesy *Chicago Defender*.

was scarred. His visage, his face was marred beyond that of any other man, and Emmett came to me. I said, 'Oh my God, what a comparison.' The spirit spoke to me as plainly as I'm talking to you now. And the spirit said, 'Emmett was race hatred personified. That is how ugly race hatred is.' I said, 'Oh.' I had to sit down. It struck me really hard. If Jesus Christ died for our sins, Emmett Till bore our prejudices, so . . ." (Terkel 26).

But perhaps the most passionate correlation of Emmett Till with an atoning Jesus in recent times occurred on July 25, 1991, the day on which the city of Chicago renamed parts of Seventy-first Avenue in honor of Emmett Till. That day also marked what would have been Emmett Till's fiftieth birthday. Speaking at the dedication ceremony, Michael Eric Dyson opened by noting that "the meaning of Emmett Till's brief life and tragic death is so monumental we can scarcely grasp hold of it" (267). But, like so many before him, Dyson is able to find a capable thread from which he can weave a pattern of meaning. After acknowledging Mamie Till-Mobley, who was "without consent called upon to sacrifice her only-begotten son" (267), Dyson implores his audience not to forget "the old and deep wounds" of racial conflict. Although calling the circumstances of Till's murder "undeniably absurd" (268), Dyson insists that this death "galvanized a people perched on the fragile border between heroism and fear to courageously pursue meaningful and complete equality" (268). It is clear that Dyson believes that Till's death can continue to perform this function today for a new generation, but that it can only do so if that generation is willing to take up the "sacrament of remembrance" (269). It is through this sacrament, so much like that other sacrament, that we make "communal choices to remember . . . and renew our hearts and illume our minds" (269). In a concluding sentiment that permits us to grasp firmly the profound meaning behind what at first appeared so "undeniably absurd," Dyson urges the following: "if we continue to recall his life and death, the memory of Emmett Till will continue to open doors of painful truth and [a] tragic but redemptive history for all of us" (270).

In calling attention to the persistence of this trope of Christian redemption in representations of Emmett Till's life and death, I do not mean to suggest that it is the best or only way to pay homage to his memory. Yet this trope is helpful in reminding us of the potentially sacramental power of memory. For memory to be sacramental, it needn't be specifically Christian. Rather, a sacramental memory takes the deep wounds and unsettling traumas of our fallen world and discovers in them the presence of things unseen, the presence of meaning, purpose, and—above all else—hope. Few wounds have been as unsettling as the face of Emmett Till. Ask anyone who remembers seeing that picture in the late summer of 1955. Watch anyone who sees it for the first time today. Few images seem less likely to open doors to a redemptive history. How to get to the hope unseen when what we see is so brutal, so awful, so clearly representative of anger, prejudice, and unmitigated hate. By most any account, Emmett Till's broken and battered face should be one of the most "unholy" wounds, one of the most divisive images in American history. That this image has also come to have a "holy" meaning—one that holds out the promise of transformation and redemption—bears testament to the power of sacramental memory to give form to our suffering and release the toxicity of old wounds.

Since I began this essay with a memory, let me end with one. Like Muhammad Ali, the novelist Lewis Nordan was the same age as Emmett Till in the summer of 1955. But, unlike Ali, Nordan is white, a Mississippian, born and raised among the very kind of people who sanctioned the taking of Emmett Till's life. In 1991, Nordan was in Atlanta promoting his second novel. While speaking to a television talk show audience of mostly black people, he was asked what his next novel would be about. According to Nordan, his response was totally unexpected: "It will deal with the death of Emmett Till" ("Growing Up White," 271). A year later, he completed his novel *Wolf Whistle*, and a year after that he sat down to explore why—after nearly forty years—he was driven to tell the story of Emmett Till. "Just before I appeared on that television show in Atlanta," he confessed, "I chose a necktie from my suitcase and knotted it so tight around my neck that my face turned blue. My hair I plastered into place with great globs of a product called Mega Gel. (The tube advises, Extreme Hold for Design and Control.) My shoes were shined. My beard was trimmed . . . My belt was pulled to the last hole . . . Mega Gel had the idea: Extreme hold for control" (274). He continued:

> Never mind the details, and don't imagine that I am asking for sympathy, but only believe that one week before this television interview, my own personal life had fallen into chaos. Everything was haywire, helter-skelter, inside out. Unlike Mega Gel, I had lost control, and could discern no design in the scheme of things.
>
> Looking back now I understand a few things better. All my cosmetics and my strict adherence to a self-imposed dress code were attempts to

gain control of a world flying off it axis. When that anonymous woman at the microphone asked me about my next book, I reached down to the core of myself for something substantial to answer her with.

What I found there was Emmett Till. As soon as I spoke his name, I knew that I had found a buried chunk of my self's permanent foundation, the granite cornerstone of something formative and durable and true. . . . On that television program, Emmett emerged suddenly as the unshakeable ground of *me*, where I could stand and watch in safety the rags and tags of my personal life flying away in the whirlwind, in confidence that they would all return or that what did not return could be lived without.

In *Wolf Whistle*, Emmett, Bobo, holds the same position in the novel as he held in my heart. He is the fixed center, in the midst of other lives that have been turned inside out. In the directionless fictional histories of the characters of *Wolf Whistle*, there are hints of what happened in my own history, and perhaps in the history of all human beings—death, heartbreak, betrayal, lost love, and lost hope.

Emmett, though, is *terra firma*. He is the reality, he is the rock. (274–75)

Although there is nothing distinctly Christian about Nordan's characterization of Emmett Till, the young boy certainly possesses redemptive power. A figure of "safety" amid the "whirlwind," Till helps Nordan to find a "fixed center" from which he can gain control. Before he committed to telling Emmett Till's story, Nordan was like Gwendolyn Brooks's "milk-white maid": the one thing that he "did know and knew / With terrifying clarity was that [his] composition / Had disintegrated / That, although the pattern prevailed, / The breaks were everywhere." However, whereas Brooks's Mississippi mother can "think / Of no thread capable of the necessary / Sew-work," Nordan finds Till, his rock. The irony here is that young Till, the very person who allows Nordan to discover design in the scheme of his own life, is the same figure who breaks up the composition that gave such a false design to the life of the Mississippi mother. Not surprisingly, Till serves a similarly redemptive function for several characters in Nordan's novel. In fact, the novel, unlike Nordan's memoir, makes explicit the connection between Till and Christ, thus placing *Wolf Whistle* directly within the narrative tradition we have been exploring. For one character in particular, the schoolteacher Alice Conroy—whose life, like Nordan's, is marked by "death, heartbreak, betrayal, lost love, and lost hope"—the power of Till's atoning sacrifice is most explicit and transformative. At the trial, she has an epiphany much like the one Nordan had when he, in the midst of his own turmoil, "reached down to the core" of himself and found Emmett Till:

> People brought church fans with them and were fanning their brains out. On one side the fans showed Jesus with a lamb sitting on his lap . . . On the other fans Jesus was suffering the little children to come unto him, which made Alice think of herself, with all these innocent children around her and all, even if she didn't feel very much like Jesus, since she had excellent reason to believe that Jesus never would in a million years have slept with a married man. And there were even pictures of Jesus on the Cross with some thorns and the water and the Blood, which made Alice think of the little boy who'd got murdered, and this broke poor Alice's heart and made her believe that forevermore she would love the weak and draw them into her heart. (240–41)

In *Wolf Whistle*, just before the dreadful deed is done, Emmett Till's murderer sees "a little bit of Jesus" in the young boy's face. At first, the murderer is confused by the similarity—"colored child like [Till] was and Jesus white as the day is long"—and this leads him to wonder if "anyone else [had] noticed the resemblance" (169). As we now know, that resemblance was noticed from the very beginning and has remained strong for the past fifty years. The evening after she first learned of her son's death, Mamie Till-Mobley was visited by a presence, one as "real to [her] as flesh and blood." It not only told her that her son's death had "been ordained since the beginning of time," but it also urged her to have courage and faith, and to work unceasingly to tell the truth so that right could at last prevail. Ever since, Emmett Till has been a similar presence in America's cultural and literary imagination, a voice that has called out to many to speak the truth of his story. It is a truth that, at first glance, would appear to speak only of "death, heartbreak, betrayal, lost love, and lost hope"—and thus many see no reason to re-open such deep and unsettling wounds. But we know better: we know that wounds—coupled with a little faith—have the power to set people free.

WORKS CITED

Ali, Muhammad, with Richard Durham. *The Greatest: My Own Story.* New York: Random House, 1975.

Baldwin, James. *Blues for Mister Charlie.* 1964. New York: Vintage, 1995.

Barry, Quan. "Emmett Till's Open Casket as *La Pietà.*" In *Controvertibles,* 44. Pittsburgh: University of Pittsburgh Press, 2004.

Brooks, Gwendolyn. "A Bronzeville Mother Loiters in Mississippi. Meanwhile, a Mississippi Mother Burns Bacon." In Metress, *Lynching,* 313–17.

Cleaver, Eldridge. *Soul on Ice.* New York: Dell, 1968.

Coleman, Wanda. "Emmett Till." In Metress, *Lynching,* 328–33.

Colin, Mattie Smith. "Mother's Tears Greet Son Who Died a Martyr." *Chicago Defender,* 10 September 1955. In Metress, *Lynching,* 29–30.

Dyson, Michael Eric. "Remembering Emmett Till." In Metress, *Lynching,* 266–70.

Eyerman, Ron. *Cultural Trauma: Slavery and the Formation of African-American Identity.* New York: Cambridge University Press, 2001.

Hudson-Weems, Cleanora. *Emmett Till: The Sacrificial Lamb of the Modern Civil Rights Movement.* Troy, MI: Bedford, 1994.

"In Memoriam, Emmett Till." *Life,* 10 October 1955, 48.

Lee, Marvin E. "Rope and Faggot" (Letter to the editor). *Cleveland Call and Post,* 22 October 1955.

McKay, Claude. "The Lynching." In *Witnessing Lynching: American Writers Respond,* edited by Anne P. Rice, 190. Foreword by Michele Wallace. New Brunswick, NJ: Rutgers University Press, 2003.

Metress, Christopher. *The Lynching of Emmett Till: A Documentary Narrative.* Charlottesville: University of Virginia Press, 2002.

Moody, Anne. *Coming of Age in Mississippi.* New York: Dell, 1968.

Nordan, Lewis. "Growing Up White in the South: An Essay." In Metress, *Lynching,* 270–74.

———. *Wolf Whistle.* Chapel Hill, NC: Algonquin, 1993.

Payne, Ethel. "From 'Mamie Till Bradley's Untold Story.'" In Metress, *Lynching,* 226–35.

Roper, William. "A Poem For Emmett Till: A Freedom Song." Unpublished musical score.

Skelton, T. R. Untitled poem. *Pittsburgh Courier,* 8 October 1955.

Spelman, Elizabeth V. *Fruits of Sorrow: Framing Our Attention to Sorrow.* Boston: Beacon, 1997.

Terkel, Studs. *Race: How Blacks and Whites Think and Feel about the American Obsession.* New York: New Press, 1992.

"There Stands Mississippi." *California Eagle,* 22 September 1955.

"Till Time Finishes the Till Case." *Atlanta Daily World,* 30 October 1955.

THE MURDER OF EMMETT TILL IN THE
MELODRAMATIC IMAGINATION

William Bradford Huie and Vin Packer in the 1950s

SHARON MONTEITH

If the facts as stated in the *Look* magazine account of the Till affair are correct, this remains: two adults, armed, in the dark, kidnap a fourteen-year-old boy and take him away to frighten him. Instead of which, the fourteen-year-old boy not only refuses to be frightened, but, unarmed, alone, in the dark, so frightens the two armed adults that they must destroy him.
—WILLIAM FAULKNER, "On Fear" (1956)

Anything that comes out of the South is going to be called grotesque by the Northern reader, unless it is grotesque, in which case it is going to be called realistic.
—FLANNERY O'CONNOR, "Some Aspects of the Grotesque in Southern Fiction," in *Mystery and Manners* (1961)

Emmett Till was murdered in 1955 just three months after *Brown II* mandated that schools should be integrated "with all deliberate speed," a contradictory statement that could be read by the white segregationist South as license to stall integration indefinitely. The phrase itself was imbued with a tinge of melodrama—occurring as it does in Sir Walter Scott's popular novel *Rob Roy* (1817), in which a lawsuit suffers interminable delays—and the trial of Till's killers was, like the *Brown v. Board of Education* ruling, a focal event for segregationists who harnessed the state apparatus to ensure that post-*Brown* retaliatory violence would receive public approbation. When the verdict was announced in Sumner, Mississippi, on September 23, 1955, and Till's self-confessed abductors were absolved of his murder, northern journalists dubbed the day "Black Friday," a direct counter to "Black Monday," the anti-*Brown* epithet for the day of the school decision.

Following the original *Brown* decision of May 17, 1954, the National Associa-

tion for the Advancement of Colored People (NAACP) had filed petitions to de-
segregate schools across some 170 school boards in seventeen states. Early resistance to school desegregation was embodied by the Citizens' Councils, the first
of which was formed in July 1954 in Sunflower County in the Mississippi Delta,
precisely where Till's murder would take place a year later. In turn, the councils
were aided by the Mississippi State Sovereignty Commission, created in 1956
to prevent federal encroachment on states' rights and to spy on anyone deviat-
ing from the segregated norm as underlined by local law and the Ku Klux Klan.
According to historian Numan V. Bartley, in the year separating the two *Brown*
decisions, "the Deep South sank deeper into hysterical reaction, while border
states cemented their psychological identification with the nation, and the peripheral South, like an unstable planet, swayed between the magnetic attraction
of North and South. And the long hot summer of 1955 lay ahead" (81).[1] One of
the effects of the "hysterical" reaction to *Brown* was that in the Deep South and,
specifically, Mississippi—where the volume of lynchings had led to the state's
reputation as "the land of the tree and the home of the grave"—racist violence
became more covert as small bands of white men on nighttime raids superseded
public lynching parties. As that summer waned, one race crime would become
the "inside story" of vigilante "justice" and would contain all the ingredients of
a shocking and lurid thriller, so much so that the three Delta counties around
which Till's killers apparently roamed on the night of his murder would become
known as "Till Country" or "Terror Country" (Levine, 93–95).[2]

Till would be commemorated in poetry and prose as a troubling moral presence, a ghost unable to rest, and, if one of the first and most influential accounts
was to be believed, an enigma. William Faulkner forcefully captured this aspect
of the Till story in his essay "On Fear": how could an unarmed child so unnerve
"two armed adults that they must destroy him"? (Meriwether, 100). In its first
literary incarnations, Till's murder formed the core of a pulpy melodrama typical
of the paperback revolution, a mass medium for the mass generation. Quickly
tagged the "wolf whistle case," the murder and the acquittal of the two killers
was a tragedy told by white writers from 1956 through 1959 as a racial melodrama, a popular and populist narrative mode. The melodramatic form charac-
teristically coincides with periods of social crisis and in its southern incarnation
reflects the region's obsession with race mixing and the nation's vilification of
the region as morally degenerate. For example, at the Till trial, defense attorney
J. W. Kellum, in a swirl of rhetoric, invoked his clients' constitutional rights

to commit racist murder: "If Roy [Bryant] and J. W. [Milam] are convicted of murder . . . where under the shining sun is the land of the free and the home of the brave?" (Wakefield). The core of melodrama is conflict between villains and their victims, who often become symbolic heroes. Violence and tragedy—real or imagined—are integral to popular melodrama, and both are often characterized by sensationalism.[3] Usually, however, violence and suffering are a means of testing and ultimately demonstrating the "rightness of the world order," so that "evil rides high but is, in the end, overcome" (Cawelti, 46, 261). The Till case was denied a moral resolution in the 1950s. However, the melodramatic formula is also a collective ritual that demonstrates how a culture embodies mythical archetypes and its own particular preoccupations, as in the southern gothic of Faulkner's *Sanctuary* (1933)—which the National Organization of Decent Literature included in its 1954 list of disapproved books.

In contemporary melodramatic representations of Till's murder, tragedy and guilt were auxiliary to the investigation of the peculiarly southern circumstances out of which the violence occurred and according to which it could be understood. The case was a national and international sensation, and the punishment Till suffered before his death was displayed for all to see when his grieving mother refused to let him be buried in Mississippi and allowed his tortured body to be viewed by the public in Chicago over Labor Day weekend. Mamie Till was the first to strategically deploy her son's murder as melodrama precisely for the political shock she knew it could inflict. She was not the first to recognize the power of the expressively tragic in the service of civil rights; W. E. B. DuBois had used the cover of the *Crisis* to display a gruesome picture of Jesse Washington castrated and burned in Waco, Texas, in 1916. Yet her painful declaration that "it just looked as though all the hatred and all the scorn the world ever had for a Negro was taken out on that child" moved whites as well as blacks in its moral certitude. Via a single photograph, Till's mother compelled the world to look on the evidence of racist cruelty that would otherwise have been buried with her son in Mississippi; it was a warning that those white men protecting a moribund tradition of southern race relations would inevitably turn to violence in order to do so.[4]

Peter Brooks goes so far as to claim that melodrama is "the principle mode for uncovering, demonstrating and making operative the essential moral universe in a post-sacred era" (15), and the Till case, with its dramatic plot, sudden revelations, sparse facts, and lurid speculations, can best be understood within the metaphysical universe that was the divided South mired in a racial dilemma. If "reality" was a Middle American, middle-class vacuum in the 1950s, the distance and darkness of the barbaric rural South set it apart as alien. The region was the key problem; "The Sahara of the Bozart" for H. L. Mencken, it was central to Gunnar Myrdal's "American Dilemma." For some outspoken southerners too, the region into which Emmett Till descended in 1955 was the national site of violent excess. In 1949, one of the most vocal white southern opponents to segregation, Lillian Smith, had closed *Killers of the Dream* with an apocalyptic denunciation of hatred, beginning with its peculiarly "southern" forms before panning out to show a cyclorama of immoralities in the atomic age: "our times are blazing with sex murders, rapings, KKK, cruelty in marriage relations, bombings of children in war" (253). Smith disdained "stained-glass writing" that "shuts out the glare and the turmoil in man's soul and his world" to present the "official daydream," preferring bold and clear-sighted representations of the South (215). In 1944 her instant best-seller *Strange Fruit* had been celebrated in some quarters and banned in others for its taboo-busting depiction of small-town Georgia, a setting Smith chose "as a symbol of man's brokenness in this modern world, man's deep split, man's alienation from himself and his God. I chose it, too, because I felt that in this small space I could catch both God and the Devil, that I could hold for a little while both good and evil" (Cliff, 217).

By the 1950s the "South" had become entrenched as the nation's abject, with stories exploiting small-town violence and stereotypes of steamy southern sex and miscegenation the order of the day. Erskine Caldwell's *Trouble in July* (1940) told a powerful tale of mob violence and lynching, and W. L. Heath's pulp fictions *Violent Saturday* (1955) and *Ill Wind* (1957) became popular film noirs. *Phenix City Story* filmed in 1955 told the "true story" of "a modern Pompeii and Sodom and Gomorra" in Alabama. In 1956 *Rose Tattoo* was described as "the boldest love story you have ever been permitted to see," and *Baby Doll* dramatized a new openness to explicit sexuality. The wider implication was that sex and depravity lurked behind every racial encounter in the South.

Two writers, both white, were among the first to represent the story of Chicago-born Till's murder, and they pitched their stories as racial melodrama. William Bradford Huie's journalistic "Wolf Whistle" was first published in *Look* magazine in January 1956 and reworked in 1959 as a "true story." Vin Packer's *Dark Don't Catch Me* (1956) was the first novel to use the murder as a dramatic trigger, its title probably deriving from Faulkner's personal essay "Mississippi"

(1954), in which he described feuding whites who band together only to repel outsiders: "No Negro ever let darkness catch him in Sullivan's Hollow" (Meriwether, 33). Huie and Packer were known as prolific tellers of pulp stories—as fiction, as journalism, and always as melodrama. *Melodrama* is a sufficiently capacious term to encompass the pejorative connotations it has earned and the serious social concerns it has generated. As a mass cultural form it always gravitates toward what is topical or "news," taking up issues that "spring up with the turns of history and consciousness," as Robert Heilman emphasizes; its salient discovery is "the local habitation of evil" (93–94), whereby those who commit evil deeds are representative of the times rather than eternal or elemental villains. These elements in the murder of Emmett Till attracted Huie and Packer.

Huie was a novelist and journalist, known for *The Klansman* (1967), a "hotly controversial novel about sex and segregation," and *The Revolt of Mamie Stover* (1951), a glamorously sinful story about a "six-foot tall yellow-haired whore" from Mississippi, both of which were made into risqué movies. But he is also remembered for *Three Lives for Mississippi* (1965), his investigation of the murder of civil rights workers Michael Schwerner, James Chaney, and Andrew Goodman in Neshoba County in 1964, a book for which Martin Luther King Jr. wrote a laudatory introduction. Hailing from Alabama, Huie stated that "racial anguish" in the South was his natural subject, believing himself to be a "truth-seeker" in whom whites could confide ("most of us old-time Southerners are kin") and to whom blacks would respond because he could "put Negroes at ease by using their four-letter words" ("Wolf Whistle," 32–33).[5] Huie was celebrated as an iconoclastic investigative reporter; *Time* magazine assured readers that "he is an aggressive, blunt-spoken reporter who makes it clear that no one is going to put anything over on him . . . And few facts in Huie's exposés have ever been disproved."[6] However, he was also labeled a yellow journalist and was called the original "checkbook journalist" for paying Milam and Bryant around $4,000 for the "true story." Milam asserted that he killed fourteen-year-old Till because "he had a white girl's picture in his wallet" and refused to repent his "crime": "Well, what else could I do? . . . He thought he was as good as any white man . . . I just decided it was time a few people got put on notice" (Huie, "Wolf Whistle," 36). Those people were so-called outside agitators: "Chicago boy . . . I'm tired of 'em sending your kind down here to stir up trouble. Goddamn you, I'm gonna make an example of you—just so everybody can know how me and my folks stand" (Huie, "Wolf Whistle," 36). Huie headlined his article, published because the law of double jeopardy disallowed further prosecution, "The Shocking Story of Approved Killing in Mississippi." It appeared in *Look*, a magazine that, while it successfully competed with *Life*, also published a fair proportion of sensational-ist revelations and exposés.[7]

A year later Huie followed up the story with "What's Happened to the Em-mett Till Killers?" tracing the way notoriety had impacted Milam and Bryant's lives. When he reworked both articles as "Wolf Whistle" in 1959, the story be-came a "true crime original." "A Race Sex Killing: The Whole Truth of the Em-mett Till Murder Mystery" was told in a collection of "factual stories . . . more shocking than fiction," bringing together "stories of greed and deception by a fearless reporter."[8] He chose to take the "wolf whistle," a motif he castigated other journalists for employing in their "yearning for simplicity" ("Wolf Whis-tle," 43), as the title not only for his story but also for the collection in which it appears. In this way, Huie created a parable of the "race sex struggle" with the available facts and used techniques that are virtually indistinguishable from literary strategies. For Huie, history and psychology were intermeshed in the popular Freudianism of the 1950s; he posited the southern environment and its bloody history as a paradigmatic psychological landscape determining both the crime and the criminals. Store owner Roy Bryant, Huie stated, had no choice but to act on "the talk" about his wife and Till; "in the opinion of his Negro cus-tomers—for him to have done nothing would have marked him a coward and a fool" (22). The murder that ensues is presented as the inevitable consequence of breaking racial codes in the post-*Brown* Mississippi Delta.

Huie intended to tell the Till story yet again in a motion picture contracted to RKO, a natural choice of Hollywood studio for this racial-legal thriller, clearly hoping that a current event that had already aroused public interest could be translated into a provocative mix of Old South clichés and sensationalism, a natural exploitation film. Huie's melodramatic field was, he allowed, "tremen-dously sensational," a phrase he deployed to describe the effect of his *Look* story (Raines, 389). But Huie's film option was shelved, and he admitted later that, "given the style of movies at the time, there seemed no way to make a film about two men who casually murder a boy and then escape punishment with the bless-ing of their peers" (Raines, 388–89). No feature film about Till has yet been made because, although the story has all the ingredients of a social melodrama, it still lacks the morally satisfying ending that the form demands, just as in the 1950s it lacked the basic moral and sentimental legibility of the classical Hol-lywood narrative.

Huie's twenty or so books sold around 25 to 30 million copies by his death in 1986, and Vin Packer remains the bestselling author of some sixty "genre fictions" under various pseudonyms and her own name, Marijane Meeker. Packer is best known for crime fiction, "lesbian pulp," and "gay noir," and, most recently, for having written a memoir about her relationship with crime writer Patricia Highsmith. She is one of very few women to have secured success in the world of mass paperback fiction, a fact she satirized in *The Girl on the Best Seller List* (1960) after her lesbian novel *Spring Fire* (1952) outsold Erskine Caldwell's *God's Little Acre* (1933).[9] In *Dark Don't Catch Me,* Packer re-creates the South as popularized in 1950s melodrama, especially those movies about the South from which the Motion Pictures Association of America (MPAA) withheld its seal of approval, citing their emphasis on taboo subjects such as sex, violence, and interracial relationships. Despite—or because of—the dwindling Production Code, novels and films with "adult themes" were rapidly assimilated into American popular culture. In his 1956 *New York Times* review of *Dark Don't Catch Me,* Anthony Boucher wondered whether "The Problem of the South" was made "purely sexual in origin" thereby situating the novel even more firmly in what Kenneth C. Davis has referred to as the "two-bit" paperbacking of America in the 1950s (Boucher, 12).

Huie and Packer could have hardly been more different in background. He was a celebrity investigative journalist often described as a folk hero by those who knew him, while she hid behind various noms de plume.[10] He was a seventh-generation southern conservative, and she grew up in New York, only spending time in the South when as a teenager she attended boarding school in Staunton, Virginia. These differences were reflected in their approaches to Till's murder. Huie's body of work includes a number of southern stories, while *Dark Don't Catch Me* is one of only two literary forays Packer has made into the South over a very long career. (Her second venture, *3 Day Terror* [1957], is also set in a small town and tells another story of murder and mayhem fueled by the post-*Brown* moment.) In different ways, both writers succeeded in tapping into the supposedly "closed" southern society for the mass market: Huie by interviewing two of Till's killers and publishing the story, and Packer by imagining the sordid secrets of a small town and what happens when gossip is overtaken by vicious violence in a murder that recalls Till's. Huie and Packer caught the mood of the popular 1950s crossover between family melodrama / true confession and "adult" material but modified the formula according to the contemporary dangers of "race mixing" in the South. In this they each contributed to a southern literary genre, the black-white sex and murder thriller. One version has the black man cross the color line, come to the attention of angry whites in search of a scapegoat, and face murderous consequences, as in *Light in August* (1932) and *Strange Fruit* (1944). The other version focuses on the wrongly accused black man, as in *The Marrow of Tradition* (1901), *Intruder in the Dust* (1948), or *To Kill a Mockingbird* (1960). However, in the case of Emmett Till, contrary to the regional formula, whites not blacks were on trial—and on the defensive. Packer played on that defensiveness in a fictional exposé of a divisive and hypocritical southern town, and Huie, ostensibly, fought against it: "Whatever our racial sins down here, I like to think we are less hypocritical than some of our enemies. I like to think that the truth serves decent purposes better than mystery or propaganda" ("Wolf Whistle," 33).

Huie was a version of William Randolph Hearst's idea of the journalist as hero-protagonist of his own stories, epitomized in novelist Richard Harding Davis's coverage of the Spanish-American War of 1898 and later by Hearst journalists Lee Mortimer and Robert Ruark. Indeed, the tough no-nonsense newsman was a durable construct as a Hollywood romantic lead over the decades. At his most obsessive the go-getting newsman was parodied in Billy Wilder's disturbing *Ace in the Hole* (1951), in which reporter Kirk Douglas conspires to stage a great "story" at the expense of a man's life. The investigative reporter is a very masculine type, especially as performed by Clark Gable in such films as *It Happened One Night* (1934) and *Teacher's Pet* (1958), and as personified by CBS's Edward R. Murrow throughout the 1950s. Huie aligned himself with masculine icons: "If anybody tells me a lie, when I ask them a relatively simple question, it sets me afire. I can't help it. Like Hemingway, I have a built-in bullshit detector, and if I smell it, I'm off and running. I have to get to the bottom of whatever the situation might be" (Greenhaw, 243). Huie was arbiter of what made a "good" story, just as Hearst shifted the imperative driving news reporting from information giving to storytelling. Reviewing the Till case in 1959, Huie called it a "spectacular" story, saying that "it brewed more excitement in Europe, Asia, and Africa than had the Scottsboro case twenty-four years earlier" (Huie, "Wolf Whistle," 16). He differentiated himself from other less-inspired reporters: "The day of the initiating newspaper and the resourceful reporter is fast going if it isn't gone" (32).[11] In the 1960s he signaled his skill even more definitively, "I went to Mississippi and dealt with the murderers of Emmett Till" (Huie, *Three Lives*, 10). Interviewed in 1977 by Howell Raines, Huie persisted in his claim that "court trials don't usually establish the truth. It takes a reporter to establish the truth"

(Raines, 389). Nevertheless, it is clear that in nosing out the story, Huie failed to scent all the bullshit in Milam's account of events, perhaps because it fulfilled his expectations that the victim would be guilty of being "uppity" and reckless and that the killers would be Snopeses.

Huie set up the typology of characters such that the Till case would be read as a southern social melodrama trammeled with violence, at once simplifying and intensifying the racially polarized society in which the protagonists played out facets of the "southern" psyche. In Huie's story, Carolyn Bryant becomes "The Woman," Milam "The Taboo Enforcer," and Till simply "The Young Negro" ("Wolf Whistle," 17, 22, 19). It is a formulation that Gwendolyn Brooks satirized in a 1960 poem, in which the Carolyn Bryant figure imagines herself as a "milk white maid" pursued by the Dark Villain and rescued by the "Fine Prince" until her hatred for the prince who would kill a child overwhelms her.[12] Huie enfolded Till's story into a disquisition on the complex code of (racist) "honor," leaving Carolyn Bryant the silent symbol of segregation. In this way, he recalled, consciously or unconsciously, Tom. P. Brady's warning in the segregationist tract *Black Monday* (1955) that in Mississippi trouble would inevitably follow if ever a "supercilious glib young Negro who has sojourned in Chicago or New York" made "an obscene remark, or a vile overture or assault upon some white girl" (Estes, 44).

In Huie's "Wolf Whistle," the Till trial plays out according to the design for segregated living that Lillian Smith outlined in her parable "Two Men and a Bargain" (1949), in which Mr. Poor White is Mr. Rich White's henchman, a "Tobacco Roader" based on postslavery archetypes reinforced through segregation. Huie quoted defense lawyer J. J. Breland as saying, "Hell, we've got to have our Milams and Bryants to fight our wars and keep our niggahs in line," the irony of which Huie seemed to relish as much as the populist disapproval of the legal profession. In Huie's tale Mr. Rich White may be read as the team of defense lawyers ("Ole Miss and Princeton alumni") and Mr. Poor White as the "niggah-hating rednecks," echoing one of Milam's lawyer's comments that labeled his client as akin to "slavery's plantation overseer." Huie described the trial as "a play" performed for the world's press, its ending already written and its performers well rehearsed in southern etiquette and bemused by outsiders in the audience who "strangely, believed that a Negro youth who tries to 'mess around' with a white woman should be allowed to live" ("Wolf Whistle," 28–29). Moses Wright's accusatory finger pointing out Milam and Bryant in court epitomized the "drama for the prosecution." Of course, the defendants were never called upon to testify in their own behalf, the play having been staged to protect their role as "Mr. Poor White," but J. J. Breland and the other Sumner defense lawyers championed openly the "fine young soldiers" who were only "protecting the womanhood of Mississippi from defilement" (31).

Huie replaced speculation with a convincing history of the Till murder, a "controversial documentary exposé" according to the cover of the first Signet edition of *Wolf Whistle*. But why was he so influential? First, he presented himself as telling the brutal truth whomsoever it might offend, rich or poor, white or black, and he fortified that "truth" by describing how he had been castigated by detractors in the North and South for what he uncovered. He took pride in being a conservative rather than a liberal; he was "looking for a story, not a cause" (Halberstam, 434). Second, Huie "scooped" Milam's story; for those studying the trial there were no extant court transcripts from which to quote until they were rediscovered in 2005. Nor was there a transcript of Huie's interviews with Milam and Bryant, and, having spoken to Huie, the self-confessed murderers would not speak to others. Third, like Walter Benjamin's storyteller, Huie recognized two important qualities: that a great storyteller should be rooted in the people and that he should recognize the importance of reiteration and echo. By telling the story in a repetitive loop from 1956 to 1959, and by returning to it as a touchstone in subsequent books, Huie's version assumed the status of the primary "account" of Till's murder for a very long time. While he exposed a paranoid South and deviant segregationist ideology in which violence and murder were appropriate if they prevented racial change, and while he exposed the minds of two of Till's killers to reveal their poor white prejudices, Huie also generated the image of fourteen-year-old Till as a rebellious youth who "got fresh" with the "responsible—and extraordinarily pretty—young woman" who tried to let the incident lie ("Wolf Whistle," 42).[13]

Huie's creative intervention into the events around the murder risked dispensing with the sympathy that accompanies the murder of any child: "You can call him a child—if you call 160-pound boys who have had sexual experience *children*" ("Wolf Whistle," 41, emphasis in original). So when Huie relayed what Milam said were the boy's last words, "What you white bastards don't know is that evah white girl wants us Negroes," they could be deemed "in character." "Some readers may find this difficult to believe," he wrote, "But, I have heard Negro rapists do it [brag] to their white captors. It's hate bursting the dykes—the doomed creature's last desperate kick at his tormentor's genitals" (Huie, 36).

Huie's expert knowledge of the segregated South put him at the scene when black rapists—the staple character in the southern racial melodrama from *Birth of a Nation* to *The Green Mile*—taunted their white subjects; and in Huie's story, Till is rendered less than human, a "doomed creature" in its final throes. In short, Milam's explanation of Till's death was verified in "Wolf Whistle"—"Bobo's speech is in character with what he had been telling his Negro cousins. In Chicago the Negro cousins later showed me the white girl" (Huie, 36)—and the fear Till would have felt in the face of racist brutality is airbrushed out of the text. Huie did ask why Till did not make a break for freedom while in the back of Milam's pickup but posited the wraparound rear window and a watchful Bryant as reason enough. By continuing, "But the real answer is the remarkable part of the story. Bobo wasn't afraid of them! He was tough as they were. He didn't think they had the guts to kill him," Huie accepts Milam's rationale. That the boy may have been paralyzed by fear is a possibility never broached.

This version of Emmett Till as a braggart has usually been accepted by novelists and literary and cultural critics. In sensationalist language that angered Angela Davis, Susan Brownmiller asserted that the wolf whistle that Till supposedly blew was a "deliberate insult just short of physical assault, a last reminder to Carolyn Bryant that this black boy, Till, had it in his mind to possess her" (Brownmiller, 247). Literary critic Jerry H. Bryant states that Huie "discovers that Bryant and Milam undertook their defense of their southern honor reluctantly and killed the black youngster only after he refused, with the same cockiness with which he had whistled at Bryant's wife, to acknowledge their superiority as white men" (Bryant, 164–65). It should be noted, however, that Jerry Bryant's explicit intention is to present a defiant, pugnacious Till so that the "conventional smarty aleck symbolizes a political movement that cracks the old forms." In his powerful meditation on Till, "The Killing of Black Boys," John Edgar Wideman, the same age as Till in 1955, also accepts Milam's (and Huie's) image of the boy: "I was a bit of a smart aleck like Emmett Till. I liked to brag. Take on dares like him." And although he privileges Till's cousin's (Curtis Jones) story of what happened outside the Bryants' store, when he quotes Huie quoting Milam, Wideman concurs with that version of events: "To the very end, Emmett Till didn't believe the crackers would kill him . . . Milam found the boy's lack of fear shocking" (Metress, 283–84).

The literary status of Huie's version of the murder seems to confound some historians too. Raines refers to "Wolf Whistle" in notes without reference to its genre or veracity. James C. Cobb cites Huie only generally as the journalist who paid for Milam and Bryant's story but makes repeated reference to Hugh Whitaker's 1963 master's thesis, in which Huie is quoted. Although the thesis referred to the court transcript that disappeared and to interviews with more witnesses than Huie pursued in 1955–56, Milam's story, "as told by" Huie, is, inevitably, incorporated into Cobb's historical account of the events of Sunday, August 28 (Cobb, 119).[14] For those piecing together what happened to Emmett Till, there was little choice but to return to Huie. Stephen Whitfield in *A Death in the Delta*, the first and best study of the Till case by the first historian to challenge Huie's primary account, still acknowledges Huie as the most significant source for Toni Morrison's play *Dreaming Emmett* (1986): "Insofar as the drama presents historical evidence, it is accurate; for Morrison has read the indispensable William Bradford Huie" (Whitfield, 120).

The thriller and romance framework often provides popular cover when the objective is to expose racism and injustice in conscience-shaking stories. By publishing the story as a mass-market paperback original, Huie exposed racism and explained its cause, but he spent limited time on the victim. He risked seeming a talented exploiter of the topical rather than a commentator. Although Huie described his eliciting of a murderer's story as a libel settlement for portrayal rights rather than a payoff ("others . . . find this sort of thing distasteful and I have not found it particularly *pleasing*"), he does not condemn the murder unequivocally until later (Raines, 393; Halberstam, 435). Nor in emphasizing the predictability of the murder does he critique the failure to control the mob mentality, a problem that so vexed Lillian Smith, for example, in *One Hour* (1959). The southern racial paradigm wherein a black boy should know his place or suffer the consequences remains in place in "Wolf Whistle" with Huie as its translator. Thus Huie seemed to prove W. G. Sumner's old aphorism in *Folkways* (1907) that legislation cannot make mores, and led the reader to the impasse that C. Vann Woodward described as lending credence to "the existence of a primeval rock of human nature upon which the waters of legislation beat in vain" (Woodward, 103). However one characterizes Huie, the Till story was his raw material, and his version dominated subsequent historical and imaginative responses to the murder. The murderers' silence, even at their own trial, was broken only by Huie's investigation, but Milam's story as told to Huie also acted as a screen for many years; instead of only revealing the truth, as he claimed, Milam concealed the possibility that others were involved in the murder.[15] Huie's "bullshit meter"

failed to register that clinging to that primeval rock on which civil rights legislation foundered were more individuals than the two men arraigned in court.

J. W. Milam described himself to Huie as Till's sole killer. Milam's "account"
does not veer from "I" to "we" until after Till has been shot dead. "I shot him
. . . Then me and Roy wired the fan to his neck and rolled him into the water"
("Wolf Whistle," 38). In fact, his statement that, "We were never able to scare
him [Till]" in Huie's original 1956 article (Metress, 206) shifted by 1959 to "I
couldn't scare the niggah" (Huie, "Wolf Whistle," 36). Milam's story is privileged
over other possible versions: Bryant is "pathetic," a "scrapper and no killer,"
and his testimony is never cited. Huie acted, in effect, as Milam's interlocu-
tor. Carolyn Bryant's possible involvement is also elided from the 1956 *Look*
article through subsequent refinements. Huie wrote that the press was trying
to "make her into a Tennessee Williams or Erskine Caldwell character" ("Wolf
Whistle," 21). In telling Milam's story, Huie removed her from the truck where
witnesses had seen or heard her waiting when Till was forcibly removed from
Moses Wright's home, and he rehabilitated her as a sensible and sensitive young
woman who was not involved on the night Till was murdered.

Most importantly, in Milam's story, the boy is cast as the architect of his own
fate, and the Signet paperback version of Huie's "Wolf Whistle" was publicized
as the tale of a "brash Negro boy from Chicago" murdered for "accosting a white
woman." Huie was adamant that he was preparing material for the "objective"
reader ("Wolf Whistle," 41) to accept that a brazen youth taunted his abductors into murdering him: "There is no reason to believe that Milam and Bryant
intended to kill. Had Bobo acted as they expected him to act, he would have
escaped with a 'whipping' . . . The murder resulted from coincidence . . . Bobo
showed the girl's picture once too often. He showed it in the wrong place to
the wrong man, too soon after the Supreme Court had decreed a change in the
Delta 'way of life'" (42–43). Huie followed Milam in his avowal that Till pulled
from his wallet three pictures of three white girls, "Chicago sluts, I guess" (36),
and that while undergoing a pistol whipping, "Bobo never hollered—and he
kept making the perfect speeches to insure martyrdom." In following up Milam's
"lead" in Chicago with Till's friends, Huie became convinced that, "With no suggestion from me, they told me about 'Bobo's white girl.' They showed me where
the girl lived . . . I was tempted to talk with her but prudence restrained me. Her
father might resent a Kinsey inquiry" (40). The reader understands that some
witnesses' stories do not need to be heard. Milam gets the last word in Huie's

story; he has no regret, only shock that the community that let him get away with murder should shun him so decidedly afterwards: "Crazy goddamn situation, ain't it?" (51). That Huie re-creates Milam's idiosyncratically rural southern speech invites the reader's disdain of Milam's "truth," but there is evidence to suggest that Huie was, nevertheless, utterly convinced by his source: "I published the complete truth about a story that certainly the situation demanded . . . It was good for the country" (Raines, 389).

Packer's novel, on the other hand, never sets itself up as objective in any way. It was advertised as "The *Peyton Place* of the Deep South," as "sensational," and "a shocker."[16] Grace Metalious's *Peyton Place* published earlier in 1956 was a runaway success that spawned a film in 1957, four sequels and a long-running television series. Its taglines—"The explosive bestseller that lifts the lid off a respectable New England town," "A skeleton in every closet," and "The scandalous book that everyone's talking about"—are reworked southern-style for *Dark Don't Catch Me*. Packer builds her story on the Emmett Till "plot" as supplied by popular journalism, including those articles by Huie that preceded "Wolf Whistle," and she is cavalier with the facts in her reconstruction.[17] The one unchangeable fact is the death of the Till character (Millard Post). The crime that leads to his murder (which Packer disdains to describe) is the culmination of the sexual and racial tensions between blacks and whites that foreshadow his arrival in the ironically renamed and relocated Paradise, Georgia. The choice of Georgia over Mississippi may not simply be a displacement of the Till story but also a nod to Lillian Smith's influence in establishing the mass paperback appeal of the small southern town mired in ignorance but enlivened by sexual desire. Clearly, Packer's novel also required a larger setting—Paradise is a town of one thousand—than the crossroads that is Money, Mississippi. Her exploration of the racialized small-town setting is made much of in publicity for the Fawcett Gold Medal paperback: "Paradise, Georgia USA where black and white have lived together, and in secret loved together for three hundred years; where the white man knows that the dark-skinned man is his blood brother and hates him for it; where the white woman looks on the dark-skinned man with lust and longing . . . Out of this shared and silent intimacy, compounded of fear, hatred, sexual guilt and carnal knowledge, springs this startling novel which lays bare the secrets behind the violent deeds of the South."[18] Packer writes as if uncovering a "secret" South through characters with murky pasts. This is a trait of the melodramatist who typically offers "the dirt beneath the rug . . . the corrupt motives behind the scenes" (Cawelti, 262) and succeeds in making entertainment out of even the most tragic of circumstances.[19] A nonsoutherner, Packer could easily be read as an example of the "hit-and-run" school of popular writing whereby a northerner parachutes in to "hit," that is to say, expose, the "savage" South.

She deploys a heady mix of steamy southern stereotypes. One white character, Hollis Jordan, is an Old South cliché. Heir to a plantation, he has renounced his inheritance out of guilt after kicking his pregnant black wife in the stomach and killing their child because he didn't want a "nigger" son. Twenty years later he is discovered in Paradise's Awful Dark Woods with a young white woman, Ada, gazing upon her naked body in awe. After the scandal, Ada marries another man, turns to drink, and later commits suicide, but not before her son has taken up with a black girl (daughter of the local doctor) who has been raped by the county coroner, Doc Sell (Packer's stand-in for J. W. Milam). One married neighbor (a northern woman come South) fantasizes about her black gardener, and Vivie Hooper (Packer's version of Carolyn Bryant) displays such evident enjoyment of sex that her husband is shocked, "There's something in you that's got to be bridled" (Packer, 94). In a bizarre twist, or doubling of the point, a small black child is named Marilyn Monroe Post; Carolyn Bryant had been described by journalists as "a crossroads Marilyn Monroe." Black Marilyn is called a "bitch" and sexually abused by Little Thad, a white boy. The black child requires medical attention, but the white father, Thad Hooper (Roy Bryant), is dismissive about his son's violent act: "She's a nigger . . . heck, they're born with their motors running. Now, you know that!" (67). Hooper's reaction is placed in stark contrast to his concern that his daughter may have witnessed what happened ("Little white girls got no business ever in their life seeing naughty things") and to his volcanic reaction when young Millard Post approaches his wife. The southern town that Packer's "Till" enters is mean and aggressive in its virulent racism, and almost as monstrous in its patriarchal repression of a white woman's sexuality as in its exploitation of a black child.

Millard Post leaves Harlem in New York City for Paradise, having received the kind of lecture from his father on how to behave in the segregated South that Till's mother expressly remembered giving her son (Payne, 228). By the second page of the novel, Packer has set up the terms in which his youthful innocence should be understood: "Bye, bye Baby-O" (the words a cousin of Till's said he used to Carolyn Bryant) is simply a childish slogan. Millard luxuriates in his appearance, "cuttin' out now in sweet, sweet style," bemoaning that each time he does "something big" his friends never see him; he is a child seeking approval from his peers. Although he is quietly afraid of flying, Millard "never punked out yet; not on anything; not on anyone; no deal ever made him chicken" (Packer, 6). The time it takes for Millard to journey south, by plane rather than train, is played out across chapters that alternate diachronically with those set in Paradise so that the collision of the boy with the place is swift, inevitable, and momentous. During the journey Millard fails to become sensitized to even the most banal features of Jim Crow etiquette and on arrival is "caught" and shocked by the dark and forbidding warning of a white man of whom he asks a polite question: "They say around here a nigger with a pocket handkerchief better be looked after. Same with neckties I reckon" (109). The man is only too willing to explain Millard's new status: "I'm just saying some places don't cotton to pocket-handkerchief niggers . . . All you gotta do down here to get along, boy, is remember you're a nigger. We got nothin' against niggers" (110). Millard's sharp city clothes distinguish him as different, but the language is also saturated with imagery of his impending death; a "necktie" party is a hanging or lynching.

The poverty his southern relatives endure is equally shocking, and as Millard's tears of "child-lost loneliness" lull him to sleep in a Paradise shack, he tries to hate the South: "Don't sound like nothing; south . . . Can't hate South like he can hate jew, spic, mick, wop; they all got guts in their names. South. Just a fuggin direction" (Packer, 136). The following day before he has even begun to acclimatize, he steels himself to play the role of "up-North cousin" with a younger cousin building up that image for each Paradise child they meet: "He sleeps in pyjamas . . . He belongs to a club [a gang] . . . He came down here by air-o-plane," and, finally, he "had him white tail lotsa times!" (146–53). Packer imagines a situation that bears on Till's own as Millard is dared to "cluck his tongue" at Vivie Hooper, a woman so beautiful that "she's like irrigation to these drought-swollen parts" (13). The prank leads to his murder before he has spent three days in the South.

There are two moments in *Dark Don't Catch Me* when the deus ex machina slows. Millard Post's eldest cousin suddenly realizes his vulnerability: "dumb kid's probably scared, strange place, kin carrying on like he's the Fuller Brush man staying overnight or something. Ought to do more for your own kin" (Packer, 155). But, tired and overworked, he decides to leave discussion until later, sending Millard on his way with a prescient comment that, again, confuses Millard's sharp dressing with funeral garb, "Don't get the burying clothes dirty"

(156). In another scene Thad Hooper (Roy Bryant) controls his temper when challenged by that same cousin; the confrontation is defused. Packer shows that it is together with other men that the decision to act violently is taken, "as though their instincts had merged together" into a single animal. Carson McCullers described this mob mentality resonantly in *The Ballad of the Sad Café* (1951): "whether the matter will be settled peaceably, or whether the joint action will result in ransacking, violence, and crime depends on destiny" (15–16). By turning to other white men, Hooper is locked into committing the violent crime. The first words that "runty" county coroner Doc Sell (J. W. Milam) says to Hooper are an accusatory joke in which Hooper is a "coon-coddler," and his "guffawed" response makes the racist consensus clear (Packer, 12). Similarly, when a friend of Hooper's chooses his wife's caution over loyalty to Hooper on that murderous night, it becomes clear that what Hooper has set out to do will, nevertheless, prove unforgivable in the wider community. Kate Bailey is adamant: "I don't approve of this kind of midnight justice . . . We have courts of law . . . it isn't right to take the law into your own hands." When her husband retorts, "We got to keep them in line! If that smart nigger gets away with what he does—," she holds up a mirror for him to face the mob mentality: "It isn't likely he will . . . if he's in Doc Sell's hands" (171).

Doc Sell, with whom the less rabid Hooper joins to pursue Millard, is a virulent racist and a rapist, renowned for his cruelty: "Yeah, burn him for it! Nervy black ape! Doing his dirty things to a pure, pure white woman" (Packer, 177). Hooper and Sell's segregationist mantra reworks the same post-*Brown* "explanations" that Huie put forward for the murder in "The Shocking Story" and later in "Wolf Whistle": "A white's got to treat a nigger like a nigger, or the nigger will lose respect for the white . . . and show his shoulder to the white and sass him. And if enough of them got away with it, if enough whites dropped their guards, the niggers could just *take over*" (Packer, 99). In *Dark Don't Catch Me*, Doc Sell yokes the murder indisputably to the *Brown* decision, torturing the boy inside the deserted shack that serves as the black school in Paradise. At a desk in a run-down classroom, Millard half confesses to a crime he did not commit, "feeling up" Vivie Hooper. Packer ensures that the punishment is out of all proportion to any possible "crime" and in so doing injects her story with a level of social criticism that Huie pushes to the background of his attempt to explain the criminals rather than the crime. Doc Sell is manic in his racial hatred, but he never loses sight of the Supreme Court order that congeals that hatred in this historical moment. He is "the only one" opposed to building a new school for black children even as a move to prevent integration because he disapproves of their being educated at all: "Burn everything nigger in sight. Smelly nigger books smell from niggers reading them!" (177). Millard's charred body is discovered in the ruins of the school, and Sell and Hooper, like Milam and Bryant before them, declare that they only took the boy for a ride and let him out to return to his uncle's house alone. The men, "two of our leading citizens, family men . . . men who have knelt with us to pray, fought for us and with us in war and peace for the ideals we hold to be godly" are taken at their word (179).

Huie and Packer fulfilled audience expectations and demands for representations of rabid white supremacists resisting the *Brown* decision and of the national racial crisis as irredeemably "southern." If Huie hoped that his no-nonsense style would demystify the sensational South, he should not have chosen a mass market potboiler of a short story as his primary format. While melodrama often acts as a safety valve, "siphoning off ideological contradictions and deliberately leaving them unresolved" (Cook, 175), Huie's "Wolf Whistle" is both fiction and the document to which those who study the tragedy of Emmett Till continue to return most often, precisely because it provided such a convincing "resolution." In the aftermath of the case, Packer dramatized the racial paranoia upon which Huie's story rested. Between them, Huie and Packer successfully exploited the story of Till's murder in ways that Flannery O'Connor understood very well: "Anything that comes out of the South is going to be called grotesque by the Northern reader, unless it is grotesque, in which case it is going to be called realistic" (O'Connor, 41). Even if Huie aimed to be the consummate realist, the mixture of horror and fascination, guilt and desire that animates the "true crime" story has always overwhelmed the reader's criticism of social values. That is to say, the moral aesthetic that traditionally governs any social melodrama and the punishment of evil that closes it are not the overriding effect that the reader carries away from "Wolf Whistle"—or indeed, from *Dark Don't Catch Me*. Even when shocked by the grotesque immorality of the crime, readers of pulp fiction traditionally gain pleasure from the fantasy of identifying with the victimizers as well as the victims of violence, a melodramatic device successfully exploited in early representations of Till's tragic murder.

NOTES

1. Bartley calculates that by August 1955 when Till was murdered there were 60,000 members of White Citizens' Councils in Mississippi dominating the state's politics. In his memoir about the impact of the *Brown* decision, Derrick Bell refers to *Brown* as "a long-running racial melodrama" and wryly describes his role while working for Thurgood Marshall as "the briefcase-carrying counterpart of the Lone Ranger."

2. Bayard Rustin remembered Amzie Moore, head of the NAACP in the Delta, using these terms when in the fall of 1956 he toured the area before writing "Terror in the Delta." Till was abducted in LeFlore County, according to his killers and witnesses; he was murdered in a barn in Sunflower County, and his body was dumped in Tallahatchie County.

3. Brustein asserts, "Any work inspired by the Emmett Till case is almost automatically destined to be melodrama," by extension equating the melodramatic mode with oversimplification and provocation, stereotype and cliché (161–65).

4. The image of Till's mutilated body also provided an emotive real-life intertext for African American writers engaging with the racial struggle in the 1950s. In Richard Wright's *The Long Dream* (1958), whose working title was "Mississippi," Till is a potent symbol behind the description of Chris's mutilated body, with its "bloated head" and the "mass of puffed flesh that had once been Chris's cheeks; there was no expression on those misshapen features now; not only had the whites taken Chris's life, but they had robbed him of the semblance of the human" (75).

5. Civil rights journalist David Halberstam described Huie as "somewhat roguish," an "eccentric" journalist (434).

6. See the cover publicity for *He Slew the Dreamer*. In 1968, Huie also paid James Earl Ray and his lawyers around $40,000 to talk in his bid to establish who killed Martin Luther King Jr. Like the FBI, he paid for information about civil rights murders.

7. For example, *Look* published Kingsley Davis's "How Much Do We Know About Divorce?" 26 July 1955, 65–69; the 18 March 1958 edition was the lowdown on alcoholism that included a priest's confession. Cary Grant's LSD-style psychotherapy was the subject of the 1 September 1959 issue. In 1961 John F. Kennedy, as he was being interviewed by the magazine, became aware that the writer was digging around for information about his brief first marriage to Durie Graham in 1947; see Hersh, 331–34.

8. Huie prefigures the New Journalism of the 1960s such as Truman Capote's *In Cold Blood* (1965), although as Raymond Williams pointed out in 1961, the popularity of journalistic accounts of murderers' confessions can be traced back to James Catriach, who sold 1,666,000 copies of his confession (Williams, 186).

9. Packer remembers Roger Fawcett, executive of the Gold Medal (Fawcett) paperback empire, wanting to shake the hand of the writer who had finally managed to outsell the 1933 novel; see Server, 206.

10. Packer's real name is Marijane Meeker, and she also wrote as M. E. Kerr and Ann Aldrich.

11. This statement recalls Hearst's declarations such as "The *Journal*, as usual, ACTS While the Representatives of Ancient Journalism Sit Idly By and wait for Something to Turn Up."

12. Gwendolyn Brooks, "A Bronzeville Mother Loiters in Mississippi. Meanwhile, a Mississippi Mother Burns Bacon," in *Selected Poems* (New York: Harper, 1963). Huie is derisive about Till's mother, whom he describes as three-times married, "a divorcee with a steady friend"; he is openly skeptical about what he sees as her money management of her son's death ("Wolf Whistle," 26). Once her full name has been noted, she swiftly becomes "Mamie," and when referring to Emmett, Huie uses her nickname for her son (Bobo) in order, it is assumed, to seem closer to the boy and to have penetrated to the heart of the events that caused his death.

13. Mamie Till-Mobley stated that she filed a million-dollar lawsuit against Huie and *Look*, arguing that the story had defamed her son, but the charge was dismissed because only the victim of libel—Till himself—could have brought such a charge (Till-Mobley and Benson, 215–16).

14. Cobb states that Milam and Bryant "described" their crimes to Huie (220). Whitaker's unpublished thesis "A Case Study in Southern Justice: The Emmett Till Case," was undertaken at Florida State University.

15. Moses Wright, Willie Reed, Wheeler Parker, and black reporters, notably, Jimmy L. Hicks of the *Cleveland Call and Post*. Stephen Whitfield made this point as long ago as 1988, arguing that the number of murderers involved "affects not only the issue of legal culpability, but also the extent of the communal guilt and the character of the crime itself" (55–57).

16. See the cover of Packer's book.

17. One critic seems completely unaware of the novel's basis in the Till case: "the eventual crime and its aftermath could have been treated in greater detail—indeed, the story could support a book twice its length" (Breen, 60).

18. The *Peyton Place* analogy is not generally deployed around novels about race relations although Morris Dickstein refers to Baldwin's *Another Country* as "a *Peyton Place* of interracial bohemia" (189).

19. William Darby has said that in order to enjoy Packer's novels, "the reader must delight in being a snoop" (151).

WORKS CITED

Bartley, Numan V. *The Rise of Massive Resistance: Race and Politics in the South During the 1950s.* Baton Rouge: Louisiana State University Press, 1969.

Bell, Derrick. *Silent Covenants.* New York: Oxford University Press, 2004.

Boucher, Anthony. "Criminals at Large." *New York Times Review of Books,* 21 December 1956.

Brady, Tom P. *Black Monday.* Winona, MS: Association of Citizens' Councils, 1955.

Breen, Jon L. "The Novels of Vin Packer." In *Murder off the Rack,* edited by Jon L. Breen and Martin Harry Greenberg. New Jersey: Scarecrow, 1989.

Brooks, Peter. *The Melodramatic Imagination.* New Haven, CT: Yale University Press, 1976.

Brownmiller, Susan. *Against Our Will: Women and Rape.* London: Secker and Warburg, 1975.

Brustein, Robert. "Everybody's Protest Play," 161–165. In *Seasons of Discontent: Dramatic Opinions, 1959–1965.* London: Jonathan Cape, 1966.

Bryant, Jerry H. *Victims and Heroes: Racial Violence in the African American Novel.* Amherst: University of Massachusetts Press, 1997.

Cawelti, John G. *Adventure, Mystery, and Romance: Formula Stories as Art and Popular Culture*. Chicago: University of Chicago Press, 1976.

Cliff, Michelle, ed. *The Winner Names the Age: A Collection of Writings by Lillian Smith*. New York: W. W. Norton, 1978.

Cobb, James C. *The Most Southern Place on Earth*. New York: Oxford, 1992.

Cook, Pam. *The Cinema Book*. London: British Film Institute, 1985.

Darby, William. *Necessary American Fictions*. Bowling Green, OH: Bowling Green University Popular Press, 1987.

Davis, Kenneth C. *Two-Bit Culture: The Paperbacking of America*. Boston: Houghton Mifflin, 1984.

Davis, Kingsley. "How Much Do We Know About Divorce?" *Look*, 26 July 1955, 65–69.

Dickstein, Morris. *Leopards in the Temple*. Cambridge: Harvard University Press, 2002.

Estes, Steve. *I Am A Man: Race, Manhood, and the Civil Rights Movement*. Chapel Hill: University of North Carolina Press, 2005.

Faulkner, William. "Mississippi." *Holiday Magazine*, April 1954. In Meriwether.

———. "On Fear: The South in Labor: Mississippi." In Meriwether.

Greenhaw, Wayne. "The First Great Checkbook Journalist." Afterword to *He Slew the Dreamer: My Search, with James Earl Ray, for the Truth About The Murder of Martin Luther King, Jr.*, by William Bradford Huie. Montgomery: Black Belt Press, 1997.

Halberstam, David. *The Fifties*. New York: Villard, 1993.

Heilman, Robert. *Tragedy and Melodrama: Versions of Experience*. Seattle: University of Washington Press, 1968.

Hersh, Seymour M. *The Dark Side of Camelot*. New York: Little Brown, 1997.

Hobson, Fred C. "The Savage South: An Inquiry into the Origins, Endurance and Presumed Demise of an Image," 133–46. In *Myth and Southern History*, edited by Patrick Gerster and Nicholas Cords. Urbana-Champaign: University of Illinois Press, 1989.

Huie, William Bradford. *He Slew the Dreamer: My Search, with James Earl Ray, for the Truth About The Murder of Martin Luther King, Jr.* Montgomery: Black Belt Press, 1997.

———. "The Shocking Story of Approved Killing in Mississippi." In Metress, 200–207.

———. "Wolf Whistle." *Wolf Whistle and Other Stories*. New York: Signet, 1959.

Levine, Daniel. *Bayard Rustin and the Civil Rights Movement*. New York: Rutgers University Press, 2000.

McCullers, Carson. *The Ballad of the Sad Café*. New York: Bantam, 1971.

Meriwether, James B., ed. *William Faulkner: Essays, Speeches, and Public Letters*. New York: Modern Library, 2004.

Metress, Christopher, ed. *The Lynching of Emmett Till: A Documentary Narrative*. Charlottesville: University of Virginia Press, 2002.

O'Connor, Flannery. "Some Aspects of the Grotesque in Southern Fiction." In *Mystery and Manners*, edited by Sally and Robert Fitzgerald. New York: Farrar, 1961.

Packer, Vin. *Dark Don't Catch Me*. New York: Paperback Library, 1965.

Payne, Ethel. "Mamie Bradley's Untold Story." *Chicago Defender*, May 1956. In Metress, 226–34.

Raines, Howell. *My Soul is Rested: The Story of the Civil Rights Movement in the Deep South*. Harmondsworth: Penguin, 1977.

Rustin, Bayard. "Terror in the Delta." *Liberation* 1 (9 October 1956): 17–19.

Server, Lee. "Vin Packer (1927–)." *Encyclopedia of Pulp Fiction Writers,* edited by Lee Server. New York: Checkmark, 2002.

Smith, Lillian. "Extracts from Three Letters." In Cliff, 212–18.

————. *Killers of the Dream.* New York: W. W. Norton and Co., 1949.

Till-Mobley, Mamie, and Christopher Benson. *Death of Innocence: The Story of the Hate Crime That Changed America.* New York: Random House, 2003.

Wakefield, Dan. "An Hour and Seven Minutes: Justice in Sumner in September 1955." *Nation* 1 (October 1955).

Whitfield, Stephen. *A Death in the Delta: The Story of Emmett Till.* Baltimore: Johns Hopkins University Press, 1988.

Wideman, John Edgar. "The Killing of Black Boys." In Metress, 278–88.

Williams, Raymond. *The Long Revolution.* London: Hogarth, 1992.

Woodward, C. Vann. *The Strange Career of Jim Crow.* Oxford: Oxford University Press, 1966.

Wright, Richard. *The Long Dream.* New York: Harper and Row, 1987.

FLESH THAT NEEDS TO BE LOVED

Langston Hughes Writing the Body of Emmett Till

MYISHA PRIEST

I propose that we view the whole of American Life as a drama acted upon the body of a giant Negro, who . . . forms the stage and scene upon which and within which the action unfolds.
—RALPH ELLISON, "Twentieth-Century Fiction and the Black Mask of Humanity"

In the *Crisis* magazine records, a white reporter's dispassionate account of a 1915 lynching reads: "Hundreds of kodaks circled all morning at the scene of the lynching. People in automobiles and carriages came from miles around to view the corpse dangling from the end of a rope . . . picture card photographers installed a portable printing plant at the bridge and reaped a harvest in selling the postcards showing a photograph of the lynched negro" (quoted in Allen, 11). Grounded in the centering figure of the black corpse, the article concentrates on the hanging body as the site of text making. The text is the story of American self-creation vested in the deconstruction of black subjectivity. By pairing automobiles with carriages, harvesting with selling, and the modern phenomenon of the printing press with the pastoral setting, the text-in-creation derives rhetorical power by linking domination of the ravaged body to fundamental markers of American identity. The article tells us how the ambiguities of Americanness—commercial prosperity and rusticity, modernity and history, popular sentiment and official justice—are resolved in the black body that has been marked by a violent ritual of power, and then displayed to symbolically reproduce that power. The crowd, the writer, and the reading public are all witness-participants in the enactment of a primal scene, the gruesome dramatization of the origin of American subjectivity in black woundedness and subjection.

Until the Emmett Till case, newspaper reports like this one routinely described lynchings, including grisly details of the victims' pained utterances, the means and duration of the attacks, the variety and gruesomeness of the injuries, the location(s) of the victim(s) display, and the number, ages, and genders of witness-participants. The use of cameras was customary, highlighting the blunt shamelessness of the lynching bee and underscoring its importance as a public spectacle. Newspapers provided detailed accounts of the events; postcards and photographs, body parts, articles of clothing, and pieces of the killing tools also circulated as talismanic texts that memorialized lynching beyond the boundaries of the original stage. Readers, like the collectors, participated in possessing the body and deploying it as a cultural text, for after the body circulated at the crime scene it was disseminated through the social body in the distribution of the newspaper. Writing about the event, the reporters restaged the spectacle, offering up the anonymous ravaged black figure for cultural consumption and appropriating this violent elaboration of power to writing.

The link between the lynched black body, writing, and the making of text was often dramatized by the presence of notes posted on the corpse, sometimes pinned to the very skin. For example, after a well-attended lynching in Alabama, the crowd harvested souvenirs of ears, fingers, and toes as trophies, then left a memento of its own:

> On the chest of the Negro was a piece of blood stained paper, attached by an ordinary pin. On one side of this paper was written:—
> "We must protect our ladies."
> The other side of the paper contained a warning to the Negroes of the neighborhood. It read as follows:—
> "Beware all darkies! You will be treated the same way." (Ginzburg, 5)

This palimpsest is a central text of American writing: the ideals of liberty, property, and power underwritten and underscored by the domination and discipline of black flesh. Writing about lynching emerged, like the bloodstained note above, from its grounding within the wounded black body. The black body became a sign of material and textual power, and a warning against black transgression. Ralph Ellison theorizes in his 1953 essay "Twentieth-Century Fiction and the Black Mask of Humanity" that white American writing is indeed founded upon the black figure "drained of its humanity." Lynching is the spectacular display of power "upon and within" the black body, and the "stage and scene" of American self-making. Lynching enforces material domination upon black persons by asserting the certainty of physical pain and suffering at the hands of an overwhelming, terrifying power. Lynching also functions as a "symbolic instrument" that reiterates the spectacular staging of the event well beyond the original moment (Patterson). Lynching is not simply a moment of violent power but the making of a *text* of white power based on the spectacle of black suffering.

The black body therefore proved to be an unwieldy instrument in the hands of black reporters who endeavored to employ it in the service of their own writing, and to generate black resistance to violent control. The *Crisis* noted of a contemporaneous lynching that the black-owned *Topeka Plaindealer* had tried to take photographs and distribute them so that "the world may see and know what semi-barbarous America is doing," but that the distribution inexplicably failed (Allen, 11). As far back as the earliest African American writings, such spectacles had proved a difficult location for the representation of the African American subject or the development of political power. For example, Ida B. Wells's antilynching campaign illumined the widespread use of lynching as a coercive tool, and, by using newspaper articles as documentary evidence, showed how newspaper accounts were a mechanism of lynching's power. The NAACP founded its campaign on her work and tactics, especially her strategy of publishing accounts of lynching to rouse black audiences, yet even the more widespread and institutional support represented by the NAACP failed to generate substantial political power; their proposed antilynching legislation failed to become law in 1922, 1937, and 1940 (Markovitz, 23).

Wells's exposure of lynching's utility as a mode of political and economic control did not counteract the symbolic force of the black body as a text of subjection. Writing about the spectacle of the despoiled black body as an avenue to self-representation has proved at least as impracticable as using it to generate political power. If the representation of black suffering means one is a nameless "corpse hanging from a rope," and rejection of it means the erasure of the historical and contemporary forces that bind, shape, and define freedom, then where could the violent act of rupture that was the genesis of the African American subject be represented? Even so eloquent a voice as Frederick Douglass reminds us that though the spectacle of black suffering is a "primal moment," it shatters the project of self-making, and "deprive[s] me of the powers of description" (53). Instead of words, Douglass leaves us with the lingering image of the pen laid in the cracked and scarred flesh to stand in for a hoped-for synthesis between materiality and textuality wherein the most buried aspects of the African American subject might emerge. This famous image might be the countersign to the ravaged body with writing pinned into its flesh, a form of text-making emerging from the sentience of the wounded body, an act of remembrance that transforms the body from the "blood stained gate" to a site of transformation.

Employing the display of the riven body as a resistant strategy complicates the enterprise of self-representation. Mamie Till reinscribed the cultural text that her son's ravaged body became, and insisted that the ravaged text of blackness could be a site of resistance and transformation. Her willed and ritualized act of mourning altered the meanings associated with the text of the ravaged black body. Publicly disputing the dominant reading of her son's lynching, Mamie Till reelaborated the act of ravishment and recast it as a means of humanizing black pain and suffering. By displaying her son's body and disputing its legal and cultural significations, she illustrated a new mechanics of black self-representation in the face of subjection and negation. Mamie Till's enduring gift to the project of black self-representation has been the performance of reading the text of black woundedness that links black suffering with black political power, and with the assertion rather than the silencing of a black voice. By claiming his ravishment as a righteous symbol of personal and collective power, she made of the black body a site of transfiguration.

Mamie Till changed the meaning of the black body on the cultural landscape, and that change registered throughout African American cultural production. I want to argue that Mamie Till's insistence on expanding the meaning of black ravishment influenced literary production, and, in light of that, read Langston Hughes's experimental text *The Sweet Flypaper of Life*. It is a well-accepted critical assertion that Langston Hughes's opus focuses on unearthing folk forms and language and using them to redefine African American literature. Here I read that intention as a struggle against the problematic form that was the black body as cultural text, epitomized by the difficult poem "Mississippi—1955." As Christopher Metress argues, "Mississippi—1955" is riddled by unsatisfactory changes that "erase" the body of Emmett Till from history ("Langston," 1). Till's erasure from the poem crafted in his honor dramatizes how efforts at humanizing the black body can be thwarted by the forms of its representation. Instead of memorializing Till, "Mississippi—1955" memorializes and personifies the act of his destruction. In contrast, *The Sweet Flypaper of Life* builds upon Mamie Till's reading of the black body as a means of transforming cultural narratives about black woundedness. *The Sweet Flypaper of Life* envisions the formal transformations enabled by this shift in the ravaged text of blackness. Hughes focuses on the body as a site of human pain but also of pleasure, finding in the redeployed body a bittersweet blues sensibility that widens the terrain of African American subjectivity.

Words That Dripped with Blood

"The first words that entered this case were literally dripping with the blood of Emmett Till."

—District Attorney Gerald Chatham

The fate of the murderers was never at stake during the trial. What *was* at stake was the continued efficacy of the black body as an instrument of terror, and the dissimulation of black ravishment as a text of power. Therefore, utilizing and controlling the uses of the text of ravaged blackness was the foundation of the prosecutorial strategy. Sheriff Harold C. Strider indicated in initial newspaper accounts that the body found in the Tallahatchie River had been conclusively identified as Emmett Till, that he had in fact been murdered, and that the murder had occurred two days prior to the discovery of the corpse. Yet on the most crucial day of the trial—the day of Mamie Till's testimony—Strider testified that he could not identify the body. "It was in mighty bad shape," he testified. "The skin was slipping on the entire body" (Metress, *Lynching*, 97). Mamie Till had testified that she "looked at the eyes, the forehead, the nose, and the chin" and established through that catalogue of features that she "knew definitely that was my boy, beyond a shadow of a doubt"(Kempton, 85). Strider employed such gruesome detail to refute Mamie Till's "tender" testimony and to reify the legal meanings of the body in the face of her unauthorized bodily knowledge. Seeking to dismantle the authority of her voice and deny the bodily knowledge that grew out of the shattered remains of her son, the sheriff's final contention was that the body was damaged beyond "recognition." He asserted that its only recognizably "Negro" characteristic was "kinky hair" and that the erasure of identifying racial features meant that he could not tell whether the body was that of a white or black man. "At the time I saw the body," he alleged, "He was as white as I am!" (99). This queer and contradictory testimony, which substituted the menaced white southern male body for the known racial text of the black one, was the foundation of the defense strategy: to erase the humanity of the black body and to make that disavowal a bridge binding black ravishment to the administration of law.

The "slipperiness" of Till's body was central to the defense's claims to power, and the methods used to establish meaning in the ruined flesh were numerous, contradictory, and powerful. Mrs. Bryant, Till's accuser, testified that the four-teen-year-old Till was a man, hulking, menacing, and unafraid to put his hands on her or to proclaim his "knowledge" of white women. Rumors abounded that Emmett Till had slipped away to California, having escaped punishment while causing the "punishment" of the state of Mississippi; the body in the water was a plant slipped in by black conspirators, or a black man from another county. All of the various stories worked to establish the legal meanings of blackness, which centered on the criminality of the black body, the threat embodied by Till, and the necessity for violent regulation. The sheriff's claims derived their power from this aggregate text. In his final testimony, Sheriff Strider asserted that while the body in the river might be "white" and therefore could not be identified as a lynch victim, the picture of Emmett Till on the mortician's block was "black" and therefore could not implicate a white man in a crime. "I hand you here a photograph and I ask you if this picture represents a true likeness of the body that you saw," asked Defense Attorney John Whitten. "It doesn't" replied the sheriff, further asserting that "the body in the picture is darker than the body I saw at the river" (Metress, *Lynching*, 99). The sheriff's command of the slippage between these bodies exemplifies how power resides in and is gen-erated from the establishment of meaning in the text of the broken black body. While Till's body was not physically displayed during the trial, the operations of power on his body made his absent corpse the central figure in the courtroom.

The black body was the originating source of the illicit black voice, and it was that voice that was also on trial in Sumner. Even as the defense claimed power from Till's body, it also utilized the broken body to silence the black voices raised in outrage against Till's murder. Despite the defense's "color blind" perspective, the lynched body was a racialized one, the site of a communal rite of passage, marking the boundary between black and white, free and unfree. Yet this prac-tice remained "unspeakable." Lynching was horrifying violence embodied as text, but it also made a text of the moment in which speech stops, when human articulation gives way to moans and screams, when the speaking voice of the body renders the sentience of the victim incoherent, or when that voice is har-nessed to the production of the "fiction of power" of the white tormentors. To protest against it, to resist against it by even naming the victim was to invite an often fatal violence to oneself.[1] Yet, the black press sought to remake that text, to give black pain another voice. By the time of the trial, the black press had widely published the grisly picture of Emmett Till and made him the focus of efforts to force federal intervention to secure the protection and legal support of black citizens. The body as represented in court was meant to fortify Mississippi's defense against social change, to stop "the organized hate campaign" that black voices represented (Ethridge, 22).

To establish the criminality of black speech acts, the trial focused consistently on establishing the danger of black voices, and illuminating the relationship between the black voice and the black body. The defense openly accused the prosecution of "flaunting the Negro press before the jury" (Kempton, 85), as if the mere existence of a black written voice speaking of black pain could infiltrate the inviolable space of the courtroom to menace the jury. The proposed solution, according to Mississippi's *Delta Democrat Times,* "would have been for all NAACP mass meetings to have been banned, all NAACP representatives ousted from the courtroom, and all Negro publications censored" (137–38). Moreover, the defense regularly invoked Emmett Till's subversive, inappropriate, "northern brogue" as the originating act, the crime that set all other crimes in motion. As did many lynchers, Till's killers emphasized the necessity of quelling eruptions of "smart speech," "wise remarks," "talking big," and "impudence" (Ginzburg, 7). Criminal speech was second only to rape as an incitement to lynch, on odd doubling that suggests that crimes of the voice were akin to rape in their power to violate, and bore a peculiar relation to the violation of white manhood. The defense repeatedly invoked Till's voice as a dangerous "wolf whistle" to demonstrate how the black voice breached the sexual boundaries dividing black from white. The white reading public widely authorized the murderers' desire to look for and punish "the boy who done that talk," emphasizing the cultural consensus about the danger of black speech acts and endorsing violence against the body as a means of containing it (Johnson, 69).[2] Defense attorneys and reporters alike consistently characterized Till's crime of speech against white womanhood as "unprintable," illuminating the way that boundary-violating black speech acts threatened the (written) word. Till's murder was punishment for an illicit speech act, for deploying the black voice as a dangerous, unbounded force. His murderers silenced the individual expression of voice by destroying the body from which it issued and then used the destruction of that body as a threat against collective outrage and a warning against any response.

The trial of the killers took place in "Sumner, A Good Place to Raise a Boy," as the town's welcome sign claimed (Feldstein, 98). The technical basis for the acquittal was the jury's contention that the black mother could not, because of the condition of the body, identify her son. The body of Emmett Till was invoked in the courtroom to reiterate that the exposure of the black body signified black subjection, and that white power was reproduced in the act of its display. We must wonder how Mamie Till escaped participating in the continued ravishment of the black subject that seemed attendant upon its exposure. While her power centered on her insistence that we witness the effects of ravishment against the body of a child, her reading of his image was much more complicated than simply proclaiming that the tragedy of his lynching was more brutal because the violence was perpetrated against a child, for as Langston Hughes reminded, "Mississippi must lead the world in the lynching of children" (Metress, *Lynching*, 125). The image of the brutalized black child was not a rare one. Rather, it was Mamie Till's response to it, her skill in reinscribing that sign, which made it a locus of change. Though Sumner's sheriff had ordered a quick and clandestine burial of Emmett Till's body, his uncle rescued him from his nameless grave at Mamie Till's behest. They acted quickly to deliver the body to Chicago for an open-casket funeral, and this unintended slipping away produced a curious and oppositional effect to the killers' attempt use his body to reify black subjugation. When Mamie Till placed her son on display because she wanted to let everyone "see what they have done to my boy" and thousands viewed him, she claimed his pained and ravaged body in front of an audience of witnesses. She gave his muted pain a voice, a voice that was willing "to go everywhere, to speak anywhere, to get justice" (Hirsch, 32). The state of Mississippi meant the quick burial of Till's body to prevent rituals of mourning and to erase the memory of his personhood. In its place the specter of his pain at the hands of "unspeakable" racial violence and its affirmation by the courts were meant to effect a symbolic mutilation consonant with the physical. Instead, when his mother claimed his body—"[her] son"—and displayed it for thousands to see, she made unassailable claim to ties of kinship, to memory, to his humanity. His body, identified by a catalogue of features, became a symbol of ravishment which, at the same time, was sacred and impenetrable. He was an unassailable heart, sacred and vulnerable, exposed and of the flesh, a "heart encased in glass [where] no arrow can pierce it" (Bradley, 227).

The black press echoed Mamie Till's claim that the cultural text of black woundedness could be reclaimed. The pictures of Emmett Till lying in state decenter the point of view of the lynch mob photographs. Most photographs show the body hanging, isolated from a high point in a town square or town center, or conversely surrounded by crowds of white people looking directly into the camera, smiling, pointing at and posing with the body. The pictures of Emmett Till published by the black press, focused on shots of the grieving mother approaching the casket, the young Till dressed in Sunday finery, and the somber crowds in the sacred space of the church. Lynching purportedly had no black witnesses, only "dark whispered rumors of fleeing men who saw the crime committed" (Wakefield, 120). Yet the pictures covering the funeral show the large, unregulated crowd of black witnesses gathered in front of the church, crossing and filling the street, a mirror of the shaping and reshaping of black political subjectivity which would occur in the wake of Till's death. In that context, he was not an anonymous black boy, an oxymoronic figure with little social currency. He was a son, he was "hers," and theirs. When she claimed him as her child, she swathed his injured body within the terms and signs of belonging, creating a bodily discourse outside the discourse of rights and legalities, one privileging remembrance. She gave the disembodied catalogue of parts and the "slipping" skin a wholeness by stealing him away into the arms of love. When she claimed her child she subverted the idea of his dispossession. Her display of his disfigured body, accompanied by pictures of his living form, made his death legible because it was motivated by the desire not to erase but to establish and confirm the existence of love. When she affirmed that his body belonged to a natal family and a larger community of outraged kin, that it was not a "dark secret" but a source of outrage, she spoke in a language of agency wherein the articulation of pain became political praxis.

They Raised Figures Against Me in Place of Wire

After the murder of Emmett Till, Langston Hughes lamented in his weekly column in the *Chicago Defender* that "I have never heard or read about any Congressional committee investigating lynching" (Metress, *Lynching,* 125). In his most in-depth essay examining the Till case, Hughes, just two years after his own investigation by Joseph McCarthy's House Committee on Un-American Activities, makes this assertion no less than three times. At the same time, Hughes decries the willingness of House Committee to investigate black people for subversive activities against the United States. He links the history of lynching as well as its contemporaneous manifestations with the suppression of black crimes of political insurgency and with destructive reprisals against the expression of a black political voice. Yet his distant irony contains the persistent specter of the failure of black voices to stop the violence against black bodies, a fear of those reprisals turning against him, and a fear that the word might fail to articulate the pained constitution of the African American subject.

Within his column Hughes imagines that an antidote to black silencing and the failures of American writing itself might be found by "showing just one lynched body" (Metress, *Lynching*, 125). In light of the legal debacle that was the Till trial, what did Hughes want from the lynched body? Although Hughes seeks a partial remedy in constitutional investigation, his real hope lies in less institutionalized, less colonized, even unimagined responses that might make whole the pained reality of black life, might make visible "what has never been recorded [and] nobody knows" (125). The column Hughes penned in response to the not-guilty verdict, like the poem "Mississippi—1955," arises from the memory of the dead, several of whom appear within its pages. The first half functions like an abbreviated "roll call," an act of remembrance in which the dead are counted and named, their absences registered, and their stories told. There are "Charlie Lang and Ernest Green . . . young Negro boys like Emmett Till, too only 14 years old when they were lynched in Mississippi on Oct. 1942"; there are also the "5,000 recorded [lynchings] since Tuskegee Institute began keeping a list of lynchings"; there are also the unnamed "Negroes who have been murdered, beaten to death by individual whites, or simply shot down by southern police"; and the victims of "lawless killing of Black men and women" that is an "old southern custom going back to slavery days" (125). Hughes calls for the named and unnamed dead to stand forth in the body of his column addressing the political utility of the lynched body. Linked with this roll call are images of resistance bound by the reality of violent reprisal. Hughes's column locates resistance within the ravaged black body and yet is stymied because the bodies have been ravaged in acts of resistance. For example, one story tells of a man who told his "master," "I never had a whipping and you can't whip me." In spite of his b(l)ack talk and because of it, "he died," creating a silence within the column. Attempts to create a black political subjectivity only produce the threat of death and the certainty of violent containment. "Because nobody wants to die," he writes, "thousands of Negroes stayed away from the polls at the last election in Mississippi" (125). Though the success of such a display had not yet been actualized, for Hughes, "showing one lynched body" was central to the development of black political subjectivity. It is this possibility that Hughes hopes the lynched body will break open, and yet his column is defined by the historical failures of this body to achieve such radical change.

The poem "Mississippi—1955" precedes the column and is a product of and a response to those contradictions. In a recent essay on Langston Hughes, Christopher Metress has argued that Hughes's poem "written in memory of a dead boy, Emmett Till," one of the first literary responses to the lynching, suffers from the 'purg[ing]' of the memory of Till from the text." Metress shows how Hughes's successive revisions illuminate an ambiguity about how to represent Till, a sense of the danger and power of the historical moment from which Hughes moves farther and farther away. Metress's essay argues that we must return the poem to its original version and place that version in the context of Hughes's writing for the *Chicago Defender* in order to make contact with the memory of Emmett Till that lies buried within the poem. I am highly persuaded by his argument and would extend it by arguing that Till never appears in the poem, not even in its original version. Rather, it is the specter of terror that actually appears, leaving the remembered body, the lynched body that Hughes saw as a site of rupture and resistance, haunting the edges of the text. It was this problem, the fundamental tension standing between the black body and the word, which Hughes sought to address in his many unsuccessful revisions. As Metress argues, the erasure of Emmett Till from the poem has helped bring about his erasure from our collective memory; Till's erasure is one individual and very specific instance of the erasure of the humanity of the wounded black body from the larger cultural text, and this poem in his memory is one place where we can see what the greater inability to translate those wounds into present meaning has meant for us all.

The original version of the poem precedes the column and reads as follows:

> OH, WHAT SORROW!
> OH, WHAT PITY!
> OH, WHAT PAIN!
> THAT TEARS AND BLOOD
> SHOULD MIX LIKE RAIN
> AND TERROR COME AGAIN
> TO MISSISSIPPI.

Come again?
Where has terror been?
On vacation? Up North?
In some other section of the nation,
Lying low, unpublicized?
Jaundiced eyes
Showing through the mask?

OH, WHAT SORROW,
PITY, PAIN
THAT TEARS AND BLOOD
SHOULD MIX LIKE RAIN
IN MISSISSIPPI—
AND TERROR, FETID HOT,
YET CLAMMY COLD,
REMAIN

Even in this first version of the poem, there is only a bare trace of Till; the poem does not reveal the humanity of a murdered person but an event, the "com[ing]" of terror, the march of violent power against unnamed black victims. In the first stanza, figures of horror—tears and blood—signify the ruptured, abject body. Sorrow and Pity and Pain are the markers of trauma, the means by which we recognize loss and by which we recognize an essential silence. These exclamations come through the breached boundaries signified by the rain of blood and tears, marking the body's crossing of the broken border between sentience and ravishment, from subject to abjection. Markers of the body's destruction stand in for experience that is beyond articulation. Even the capital letters denote a kind of futile increase in volume, an emphasis that can be gestured to rather than expressed.

What does have a "body" or a physical presence in the poem is terror. First suggested by the path of rupture left in its wake, terror gains in the second and third stanza a material presence. Where the injured body shows up in the free flow of blood and tears signify the impotence of the silently outraged, terror acts. Terror has eyes and the power to survey; terror has and transmits sensation, omnipresently reproducing its "fetid" heat across the landscape of Mississippi.

Terror has permanence. It is intractable, ubiquitous. Terror "remain[s]." Even if we can argue that Emmett Till's drowned and spoiling body can be seen in the final figure that is "fetid hot, / Yet clammy cold," he appears as the embodiment of terror, which wears his corpse as a mask, or the shattered "remain[s]" that terror has left behind.

"Mississippi—1955" can be read as a poem in which the history of the wounded body of Emmett Till gets written out. It can also be read as a narrative enactment of that writing out. That is, Hughes's inability to get Till into the poem written in his memory is itself a demonstration of the effacement of the wounded black body from African American texts. Though Hughes's call for calculated display suggested that the body could be a site for institutional and cultural change, the poem does not inscribe the humanity of Emmett Till within its stanzas. Rather, the poem relies on extratextual knowledge—the collective memory of Emmett Till's body and Mamie Till's assertion of his humanity—to suggest the sentience of the wounded body in the face of terror's overwhelming power to erase it. The memory of the bloodied words accounts for the fact that, though Hughes longs to see "one lynched body" as a means of breaking open the discourse of black ravishment, the body or person of Emmett Till never appears in the poem. Since his column and poem appeared in print one week after the not-guilty verdict had been rendered, Hughes was rightfully skeptical about the value of the black body as a means to officially recognized power. But the nuances of Mamie Till's reading of her son's death left a lingering suggestion that, though the articulation of the body as legal text had not changed its basic meaning as a result of Emmett Till's display, there was an extralegal residue that could be harnessed. There was a power in the reinterpretation of the body that could be a foundation for the collective act, the origin of tactics and strategies that would change the workings of power. Perhaps the poetic form was simply too "bloody," linked too strongly with the history of mutilation that occurred in language. In response, I would argue, Hughes turned to the experimental children's text *The Sweet Flypaper of Life* and used its enactment of rituals of remembrance to create a form in which the black body might be represented, scarred by the presence of wounds, but beautiful in its humanity. At stake in Hughes's experimental form is uncovering a structure that will enable the articulation of the primal moment of blackness—the moment of formation that destroys the power of words—by making of that very pain a new avenue of articulation.

Principles of Pleasure

Out of Mamie Till's reinterpretation of the wounded body comes Langston Hughes's fictionalized life story of Sister Mary Bradley, a combination of words and photographs grounded in the altered cultural currency of black bodies. To construct the text, Hughes selected 140 pictures from a group of over 300 photographs by Roy DeCarava. DeCarava was the first African American photographer awarded the Guggenheim, and he spent his fellowship year (1952–53) making the Harlem photographs that would eventually accompany the written text of *The Sweet Flypaper of Life*. During his fellowship, DeCarava took over two thousand pictures capturing the daily life of Harlem, and in early 1954, he sought Hughes out to show him a selection of the pictures. In DeCarava's work Hughes found a sensibility akin to his own, one that valued what was beautiful and ugly about black life. Hughes sought out a publisher for DeCarava's photographs, and with the encouragement of that same publisher, agreed to write a text to go along with them (Rampersad, 249; Parr, 242).

At the time of their collaboration, DeCarava was considered a groundbreaking photographer, depicting what Alain Locke saw as an unrepresented "spiritual freedom" among African Americans (Stange, 65). The spiritual freedom depicted in his Harlem photographs emerged from DeCarava's efforts to capture the quotidian, the everyday practices wherein "the desires and longings that exceed the frame of civil rights and political emancipation find expression" (Hartman, 13). These daily practices assert selfhood within but also against the constraints of pain. DeCarava's belief in the cultural and political efficacy of exposing the everyday shaped the practice of his work. For example, he avoided encumbering his photographs with lighting or staging. He valued the "creative expression[s]"of his subjects and wanted not to change the way people looked but to expose what was there (Stange, 61). What was there was the body, black and human, wounded but resistant.

The result of their collaboration was the first fictional phototext by and about African Americans, hailed as the first photographic text of black life that did not pathologize its subjects. *Sweet Flypaper of Life* was widely regarded as an extraordinary and original work in its form and content. Hughes's biographer recounts that "no book by Hughes was ever greeted so rhapsodically" (Rampersad, 249); the book rapidly sold out of it first printing of 3,000 clothbound volumes and 22,000 paperbacks, and a second printing of 10,000 copies was ordered. Contemporary critics like Lewis Gannett recognized and praised the radical formal qualities of the text. He described the work as "a harmony which is more than poetry or photography alone, but its own kind of art" (Rampersad, 249). Despite its lush critical praise and the enthusiasm of the buying and reading public, in the years after its publication *The Sweet Flypaper of Life* has been lost to reading audiences and to critical consideration. The original work has long been out of print and is found mostly in the rare book collections of research libraries. Even more telling is its absence from many critical biographies and bibliographies of Hughes's work. *Sweet Flypaper of Life* has not been anthologized in the many collections of Hughes's works and does not appear in several major bibliographies of Hughes's opus. When it does appear, the text can often be found in the "miscellany" section of his bibliography.

The disparity between the praise to which the book emerged and its subsequent loss is telling. In the same way that the black body has been difficult to write into the narrative of black humanity, this text about the black body has found a precarious purchase within the history of the works of Langston Hughes and the larger body of African American literature. The "value" or "merit" of this book is without question. The problem is not that the book is "minor" or less masterful but that the meaning of its labor and its relationship to the rest of Hughes's works needs to be uncovered. The recovery of this text involves recognizing its effort to redeem the black body to black writing. Viewed that way, this work becomes a centerpiece, even a turning point, in a long history of African American writers seeking a way to use ravished black flesh to open up the possibilities of writing black subjectivity. As Hughes's column demonstrates, he was well aware of and highly invested in the political stakes of "showing" the black body. Though the text did not start out as a statement on the lynching of Emmett Till, we can still see *The Sweet Flypaper of Life* as a radical experiment undertaken to transform the text of ravaged blackness, a project akin to that of Mamie Till. That the black body was "pained" Hughes did not deny, but his work asserts the redemptive value of the effort toward redress for that pain, and of representing a selfhood scarred but not wholly defined by ravishment.

Claimed as a means of revealing black humanity, the ravaged body opens up new possibilities for black cultural production. The process of DeCarava and Hughes's form-breaking collaboration exemplifies this dynamic, with the written text evolving in response to images. With this combination of words and pictures, the text seeks a frame of reference that focuses on black bodies as sites of humanizing pain, and more importantly, of pleasure. The title of the work suggests that the text produces and is produced by such doubling of black pleasure and pain. "I done got my feet caught in the sweet flypaper of life," remarks the central and centering figure, Sister Mary Bradley. Though the pained and bound space of black subjectivity is the trap she gets caught on, she reminds us "it is sweet, ain't it?" (Hughes and DeCarava, 92). That sweet and sour place might be the black body itself poised at the moment between social death and the possibility of freedom, a body that, though threatened, can now be "read" as a potential text of liberation.

The structure of the text invites us to read it as a story about the black subject in making and about the changed relationship between the black body, self-making and the word. The original version of the book begins on the front cover with a picture of the clear eyes of a child, staring out and bearing witness to the rest of the text. Her face takes up the largest portion of the cover, and bracketed between the title and the first paragraph of written text, her eyes regard the viewer from the very center of the frame created by words. Words are decidedly underprivileged in relation to the child's face and, later, to the represented body. The cover contains one of the very few big blocks of words in the book, which uses them instead to frame the stories that the pictured bodies tell. The child's face is a kind of dark center, a "loophole of retreat" in which the subject is bound and from which it also emerges. Beginning with the child's picture, the loopholes expand, as photographs press against the boundaries of the printed word until they are literally at the edge of the page. The light and dark pattern of the words on the first page create the effect of an unfettered space where the child's eyes stare out and establish the core meanings of the work: it is to these eyes that we are beholden, these eyes that initiate and enable construction of the adult subject who narrates the book. The transformation of the text of the body arises from the redeemed flesh of the children who populate the story. Just as Mamie Till emerged into political visibility and expanded the boundaries of her own subjectivity by claiming the body of her son, Sister Marie Bradley of Hughes's work is freed into narration by her ties to children: Ronnie Bell, who faces us on the front cover; Louetta, Sister Mary's tenth grandchild; and the troubled grandson Rodney, whose story is central to Sister Mary's description of the streets of Harlem. In many of the pictures of children, they stand, literally, in the vestibules and borders within the pictures—in doorways, windows, and on stoops, or as with Ronnie Bell, on the very threshold of the text—because they are the gateway between the discovery of the flesh both pained and beloved. The impulses behind the work are manifested in the figures of children; the desire to

protect their exposed flesh releases the black voice and encourages the development of a politicized adult subjectivity.

In its unconventional form, *The Sweet Flypaper of Life* posits that forms of
representation change as black humanity becomes legible within them, that the
voice released to express the "tortuous constitution of agency" will alter the
boundaries of text (Hartman, 7). The book also models that dynamic moment
of change, where the humanized black body bursting the bounds of literary form
offers to American text making "transcendence in the form of ritual" (Ellison,
39). By using the pained black body to open up narration, the text reimagines
the primal moment of blackness, one that emerges from the moment of wounding into verbal expression of its sentience, the articulation of pain wrenching
from "black, beaten but unbeatable throats" (Hughes, "Songs"). Echoing Mamie
Till's act of redeeming the scarred body by claiming it in love, *The Sweet Flypaper
of Life* represents ties of the heart, and even heartbreak, as potentially liberating.
Love and intimacy assume great political significance because they arise from
a radical political act of self-claiming. The text is defined by numerous pictures
of mothers, fathers, and children in states of pleasure and possession, which are
the framework for agency. We are privy to the "daily practices" of Harlem life
which are spaces of freedom. Hair braiding, eating, dressing, and hugging all
become visible as acts of self-claiming and self-possession, all practices "coun-
terinvesting in the body as a site of possibility" (Hartman, 51). The compressed
frames of the photographs produce subjects who are borne down by what men-
aces them (the picture frames often rest right on top of the subjects heads) and
at the same time show subjects free inside of intimate, tender, shadowed places
where they are uncontested in their humanity. Images of dancing, a paradigmatic scene of the performance of black subjection *and* resistance, are the lynch-
pin linking images of familial intimacy and the rearticulation of the pained body
(Hartman, 51). Though bracketed by the pain of Harlem—economic repression,
backbreaking domestic work—the family "has a party every Saturday night, usually not no big party: just neighbors and home folks. But they balls back and
stomps down" (Hughes and DeCarava, 47). Even in pleasure, these are bodies in
pain, for the phrase "balls back and stomps down" connotes aggressive, force-
ful, even destructive acts against and also by the body. Yet, this set of pictures
also suggests escape—not from the ravished body but into its pleasures. These
few sentences take up several pages of text because they are the background for
pictures of dancers. The dancers' movements are slightly blurred, so that the

pictures suggest escape, flight, a visual "stealing away" beyond the boundaries of woundedness (Hartman, 72–73). Rather than reifying subjection, this private dancing becomes a site of pleasure, a group act that, though shaped by the constraints of mastery and domination, cannot be pierced by them.

The pained but pleasured bodies, broken by ravishment or from the strenuous exercise of pleasure, invoke a ritual of transcendence wherein the black voice emerges from within this nexus of pain and pleasure. The climax and ritual close of the evening of dancing, Sister Mary's singing, is also the generative moment of power in the text. She sings a blues song of unlikely power: "My Blues ain't pretty / My Blues don't satisfy— / But they can roll like thunder / In a rocky sky" (Hughes and DeCarava, 49). Her blues, like the rest of the words in the text, "mean" as they are juxtaposed with the signifying black body. In the context of humanized black pain, Sister Mary's blues echo, with a difference, the cry of pain that could not find material expression in Hughes's poem "Mississippi—1955." The disembodied voice of "Mississippi—1955," lost in its litany of apostrophes (OH WHAT SORROW! / OH, WHAT PITY! / OH WHAT PAIN!) gives way to a blues about "my" pain. These blues are claimed as a mode of expressing the sentience of pain; *because* they are of the body, they are of the voice. As Mamie Till claimed of Emmett Till's pained body, these blues are "mine," and ours. Like the poem, Sister Mary's blues are centered in the trope of the rainstorm. In "Mississippi—1955," the rain signifies blood and tears, the opened and draining body, and the coming of terror. Sister Mary's storm may threaten her, but it also encodes a reciprocal threat or act of resistance; her thunder is a coming thing, a cleansing, even an apocalyptic force. It is the storm of political change on the horizon. Harnessing the voice of the wounded body, her remembered song, to borrow a phrase from *Beloved*, "searched for the right combination, key, the code that broke the back of words" (Morrison, 261). In the moment of her song the past speaks in the present, claiming a painful and dangerous continuity—ugly like wounds but mighty like thunder.

This verbal claim for the sentience of black pain assumes the weight and authority of the written word, becoming a material artifact as a part of the body of the book. Sister Mary's blues are a primal moment within this text, one that establishes the origins of the speaking subject in pain. In this moment, pain does not deprive the subject of the powers of articulation but grants them. Speaking its pain, the black body becomes legible in writing as a political subject. *The Sweet Flypaper of Life* suggests that the creation of intimate and private political autonomy in the pained body is a transformative act that has its counterpart in collective and public expression. After the ritual at the Saturday night party, the pictorial text takes us out of the private space of black life and into the Harlem streets, where "No matter which way you look . . . something is happening" (Hughes and DeCarava, 64). The last half of the text focuses on a vigorous sense of mobility and change in the streets, the unregulated bodies of individual black people traversing the wide-open spaces created by the wide frames. The photographs of the streets culminate in the nighttime "street meetings on the corner," the beginning of a set of four photographs depicting a black political gathering (80).

The pictures of the private dancers and the libratory space of kinship and intimacy give way to pictures of the political gatherings, which are the only other pictures that include large groups of people, and where the frame and lighting of the pictures also emphasizes their group rather than individual identity. The pictures of the political gathering are dark, almost black; the central figures stand out starkly, and figures behind them remain in the dark as if they, too, might soon be drawn forth from the shadows. Though the people gather on the street, the darkness lends them an intimacy that blurs the boundaries between indoors and outdoors, and links the political autonomy associated with the interior spaces to the gatherings in the street. The most crucial of these photographs is the first, which shows a black man raised above the streets on a block; though he stands high above the implied crowd as he would in the photograph of a lynching, he stands on a street platform used to transmit and project his voice. That he is in the process of vehement speech is expressed by his body, captured with its wide-open mouth, stern look, and expanded chest. His accusatory finger points up and away, outside of the frame of the picture, showing that this speech act addresses the crowd inside and indicts those outside. The written text reports that his voice is the voice of black resistance "talking about 'Buy Black': 'Africa for the Africans': And Ethiopia shall stretch forth her hand'" (80–81). The Harlem streets depicted here are an explicitly political space, poised between surveillance and revelation. Made visible to us by the revelation of autonomy in the intimate body, these pictures do what Hughes's column had not been able to do: link the display of the black body to black freedom struggles.

As Mamie Till's act of public mourning and her use of the body as a political text forced Hughes to reckon with the impact of the body on his own narrative voice, Sister Mary's narration of the emergence of the black political voice from within the private body informs her self-making. The text's movement from the child's staring eyes to the intimate freedoms of the body to the transformation of the social body marks out Hughes's reimagined trajectory of black self-making. Thus the work concludes by showing how Sister Mary Bradley, who comes into the text as a disembodied voice whose speaking produces the subjectivities of others, can then appear in her own text, as voice and as image. *The Sweet Flypaper of Life* ends with Sister Mary's healing, her redemption from the gates of death, her assertion that flesh does not mean subjection, even though it is "cut up by life" (91). "Still good as new," she vows not to "sign" any messages to "come home." Instead, she places her (sign)ature on the text itself, the word-picture of her own selfhood. The last words in the text are "here I am" beneath the picture of her staring straight out at the viewer. Her look disturbs the readers' ability to read her, reiterating instead the power of her reading as performed in the text, and the capacity of black subjectivity to emerge from within the wound.

Many argue that the Emmett Till case gave birth to the civil rights movement because thousands were urged to action by the clarity with which they were able to read the narrative of his humanity and their own.[3] If that is true, then one version of that movement must maintain that African American resistance arose out of overt politicization of the display of the body of a ravaged black child. Mamie Till established the increasing significance of the pained bodies of children in formulating ideas of black resistance which reiterated themselves in the school desegregation campaigns, the student sit-ins, the Children's Crusade in Birmingham, and, finally, in political and cultural change. This body was an expression of injury—the power of the perpetrators—and a site of agency asserting the power of the wounded. When Hughes harnesses this text in his own work, it changes the boundaries of form. By making of text a radical spoken and written act of remembrance that illuminates the body in pain *and* pleasure, Hughes suggests that when we hold the contradictions of black self-making simultaneously within our view, we hold out of the possibility of transformation. By honoring that hope, Hughes makes text a place where black selfhood becomes visible, where black flesh can finally be/loved.

NOTES

1. The reports of African Americans killed after protesting against a lynching are legion. A particularly well-known example involves the murder of a pregnant woman, Mary Turner, who

was lynched and her baby trampled after vowing to bring the law to bear against those who had lynched her husband.

2. Emmett Till's voice was also a focus of the prosecution's case and an abiding interest of the black media. The evidence of the prosecution and the interest of the black media lay in the possibility that Till had a speech defect as a lingering effect of childhood polio. It was claimed that Till stuttered and that his speech impediment made for an unusual whistling sound in his speech. Unfortunately, even the idea that Till stuttered provided the defense with another means of demonizing Till's speech act. His stutter became beastly speech, devoid of reason, brutish and dangerously unknowing.

3. See Anne Moody, *Coming of Age in Mississippi* (New York: Dell, 1968), 123–29.

WORKS CITED

Allen, James, et al. *Without Sanctuary: Lynching and Photography in America*. Santa Fe: Twin Palms, 2003.

Barthes, Roland. *Camera Lucida: Reflections on Photography*. Translated by Richard Howard. New York: Hill and Wang, 1981.

Bradley, Mamie Till, as told to Ethel Payne. "Mamie Bradley's Untold Story." *Chicago Defender*, April–June 1956. In Metress, *Lynching*, 226–35.

Davis, Thadious. "Reading the Woman's Face in Langston Hughes's and Roy DeCarava's *The Sweet Flypaper of Life*." *Langston Hughes Review* 14, no. 1 (Spring 1993): 23–36.

Douglass, Frederick. *Narrative of the Life of Frederick Douglass, an American Slave, Written by Himself*. Edited by Houston A Baker Jr. New York: Penguin, 1982.

Ellison, Ralph. "Twentieth Century Fiction and the Black Mask of Humanity." *Shadow and Act*. New York: Random House, 1953.

Ethridge, Tom. "Mississippi Notebook: Our State a Target for Hate Campaign." *Jackson Daily News*, 4 September 1955. In Metress, *Lynching*, 22–24.

Feldstein, Ruth. *Motherhood in Black and White: Race and Sex in American Liberalism, 1930—1965*. Ithaca: Cornell University Press, 2000.

Ginzburg, Ralph. *100 Years of Lynchings*. Baltimore: Black Classic Press, 1988.

Hartman, Saidiya V. *Scenes of Subjection: Terror, Slavery and Self-Making in Nineteenth-Century America*. New York: Oxford University Press, 1997.

Hirsch, Carl. "50,000 Mourn at Bier of Lynched Negro Child." *Daily Worker*, 10 September 1955.

Hughes, Langston. "Langston Hughes Wonders Why No Lynching Probes." *Chicago Defender*, 1 October 1955. In Metress, *Lynching*, 124–26.

———. "Songs Called the Blues." In *Selected Poems of Langston Hughes*, 107. New York: Knopf, 1959.

———, and Roy DeCarava. *The Sweet Flypaper of Life*. New York: Hill and Wang, 1955.

Ings, Richard. "A Tale of Two Cities: Urban Text and Image in *The Sweet Flypaper of Life*." In *Urban Space and Representation*, edited by Maria Balshaw and Liam Keene, 39–54. London: Pluto, 2000.

Johnson, Sam. "Uncle of Till's Identifies Pair of Men Who Abducted Chicago Negro." *Greenwood Commonwealth,* September 1955. In Metress, *Lynching,* 68–75.

Kempton, Murray. "The Future." *New York Post,* 23 September 1955. In Metress, *Lynching,* 84–87.

Markovitz, Jonathan. *Legacies of Lynchings: Racial Violence and Memory.* Minneapolis: University of Minnesota Press, 2004.

Metress, Christopher. "Langston Hughes's 'Mississippi—1955': A Note on Revision and an Appeal for Reconsideration." *African American Review* 37, no. 1 (2003 Spring): 139–48.

———, ed. *The Lynching of Emmett Till: A Documentary Narrative.* Charlottesville: University of Virginia Press, 2002.

Morrison, Toni. *Beloved.* New York: Knopf, 1987.

Parr, Martin, and Gerry Badger. *The Photobook: A History.* Vol. 1. New York: Phaidon, 2004.

Patterson, Orlando. *Rituals of Blood: The Consequences of Slavery in Two American Centuries.* New York: Basic Civitas, 1998.

———. *Slavery and Social Death: A Comparative Study.* Cambridge: Harvard University Press, 1982.

Rachleffe, Melissa. "The Sounds He Saw: The Photography of Roy DeCarava." *Afterimage* 52, no. 2 (Summer 1998): 6–12.

Rampersad, Arnold. *The Life of Langston Hughes.* Vol. 2. New York: Oxford University Press, 1986.

Stange, Maren. "Illusion Complete Within Itself: Roy DeCarava's Photography." *Yale Journal of Criticism* 9, no. 1 (Spring 1996): 63–92.

Wakefield, Dan. "Justice in Sumner." *Nation,* October 1955. In Metress, *Lynching,* 120–24.

Wells-Barnett, Ida B. *On Lynchings.* New Hampshire: Ayer Company Publishers, 1991.

JAMES BALDWIN'S UNIFYING POLEMIC

Racial Segregation, Moral Integration, and the
Polarizing Figure of Emmett Till

BRIAN NORMAN

In any case, white people, who had robbed black people of their liberty and who profited by this theft every hour that they lived, had no moral ground on which to stand.
—JAMES BALDWIN, "Letter from a Region in My Mind," 1962

Some years ago, after the disappearance of civil rights workers Chaney, Goodman and Schwirner [sic] in Mississippi, some friends of mine were dragging the river for their bodies. This one wasn't Schwirner. This one wasn't Goodman. This one wasn't Chaney. Then, as Dave Dennis tells it, "It suddenly struck us—what difference did it make it wasn't them? *What are these bodies doing in the river?*"
—JAMES BALDWIN, *The Evidence of the Things Not Seen*, 1985

Writings in the protest mode, even those by established novelists or poets, are often considered nonliterary on the grounds that they are too polemical or polarizing. During the civil rights movement, however, James Baldwin navigated his dual roles of famed literary artist and political spokesman by writing a polemical play based loosely on the lynching of Emmett Till. The product, *Blues for Mister Charlie* (1964), appeared at a crucial time in the civil rights movement when racial polarization and calls to arms increasingly displaced integration strategies of nonviolent civil disobedience. In the play, Baldwin uses the polarizing figure of Till for an integration strategy: bring together segregated factions of society onto the same stage. Baldwin thus addresses division rather than represses it. Against the racially segregated stage of Whitetown and Blacktown, Baldwin provides a vision of integration amid polarization. He raises ideological debates about religion, self-determination, violence, and justice between those characters who cross a dreadfully visible line of racial segregation.

During a famous 1963 meeting with Robert F. Kennedy, Baldwin convened other leading black celebrities to demand a federal response to southern white violence against black citizens, especially black children, on behalf of a nation-wide civil rights movement. For Baldwin, it was important to say that not only was desegregation legal but it was right. The group urged a presidential escort of a black student across the lines of segregation at a school in the South. In the absence of such a symbolic commitment to civil rights, the group argued, the nation would deplete totally the national record of morality. Baldwin's biographer reports, though, that in the end "Kennedy rejected [the escort] as a 'meaningless moral gesture'" (Leeming, 222). While Baldwin's previous two novels had been widely praised by literary critics, after the meeting he increasingly adopted a protest mode and so ran the risk of charges of polemicism and nonliterariness. Writers who cash in their literary celebrity for political advocacy are often reclaimed in literary studies by readings that insist upon the aesthetic complexity of the overtly political. But this move would erase some of the fine edges of moral indictment tendered by polarization and polemics in *Blues*. Calls for integration and Black Power are often posed as opposites, but Baldwin rejects this opposition in a play where characters cross racial lines in a project directed at an equally divided national audience. Baldwin conjures the deeply polarizing figure of Till in order to join integration goals with calls for armed resistance so that his readers can see how state-sponsored justice and self-determination are not mutually exclusive.

Given the historical import and galvanizing effect of Till's story, many writers employ Till as a barometer of the limits of American democratic institutions, a trope of the perils of interracial sexuality, and a marker of the origins of the civil rights movement in the Jim Crow South. In his 2003 essay "'No Justice, No Peace': The Figure of Emmett Till in African American Literature," Christopher Metress notes how, against the acquittals in the court case, literary artists have often retried the case in the "court of literature" (101), thereby allowing Till to reemerge as a figure that condemns as well as catalyzes. This is why, after more than fifty years, critics, historians, and the American public return to Till's story in order to resolve a fractured, painful, and unsettled past that is out of alignment with the highest hopes of the civil rights movement. So, courtroom scenes are especially prominent in depictions of Till, though in Baldwin's play such a scene is just one more manifestation of Whitetown and Blacktown. While the Civil Rights Act of 1964 promised a just future that would leave behind the pain and violence of the segregated South, writers like Baldwin rekindled the event to underscore a still polarized America that was slow to connect the southern pulpit of Martin Luther King, the Harlem podium of Malcolm X, and widespread black civil unrest into a national movement. It is this simultaneous racial polarization and national unification that Baldwin enacts and dissects as he reanimates the figure of Till.

Racial Segregation and Baldwin's Vision of Integration

In the social and political upheavals of the 1960s, Baldwin and many other writers reassessed traditional institutions of power, which questioned not only state hypocrisy but also the basic tenets of the civil rights movement. Baldwin examined his own commitment to integration in response to the crescendo of criticisms by a younger, more militant generation. For instance, in *The Fire Next Time* (1963), Baldwin asserts,

> What it comes to is that if we, who can scarcely be considered a white nation, persist in thinking of ourselves as one, we condemn ourselves with the truly white nations, to sterility and decay, whereas if we could accept ourselves *as we are,* we might bring new life to the Western achievements, and transform them. The price of this transformation is the unconditional freedom of the Negro . . . He is *the* key figure in his country, and the American future is precisely as bright or as dark as his. And the Negro recognizes this, in a negative way. Hence the question: Do I really *want* to be integrated into a burning house? (108)

Baldwin's commitment to integration—underscored by his insistent use of "we" to describe a segregated nation—is necessarily ambivalent. Tethering the fate of two segments of a segregated populace into one future (be it an integrated nation or humanity more generally) requires the commitment of those on both sides. In his protest essay, Baldwin joins other civil rights leaders by drawing on his history in his father's Harlem storefront church. As a young Pentecostal preacher, Baldwin learned that metaphorical depictions of the racial situation, such as his famous use of Noah's rainbow sign and the one-hundredth anniversary of emancipation, allow both a removal from and a claiming of lofty American promises of equality for all. As theologian and civil rights scholar James Cone argues, "Optimism about blacks achieving full citizenship rights in America has always been the hallmark of integrationism. This optimism has been based not only on the political ideas of America but also upon its claim to be founded on Christian principles. Blacks believed that the Christian faith requires that whites treat them as equals before God" (6). But the figure of the Christian preacher was losing currency with a younger generation, and Baldwin addresses this tension in his protest essay and later in *Blues*. While the nation's television cameras captured the political successes and controversies of the twin pulpits of Martin Luther King Jr. and Malcolm X, Baldwin's pulpit became his best-selling writings. He accepted two difficult tasks: to examine a racially polarized nation and to address the seemingly immiscible poles of nonviolence and militancy which threatened to fracture two generations of African Americans with seemingly divergent strategies of protest. In *Fire*, "*the* key figure" that allows the audience to examine its segregated nation (its "house") is Baldwin's own speaking "I" and personal experience; in his play, it is the Till figure that can unlock the promise and the danger of integration.

Those at the center of the civil rights movement drew upon the tactics of both nonviolence and militancy; its activists and spokespersons, in fact, often refused to dissociate the two. At the height of the movement, King railed against the situation of "Negro brothers smothering in an airtight cage of poverty in the midst of an affluent society" (292). He saw that the inescapable conditions of injustice rendered violence—however wrongheaded—a logical reaction. So, too, as we see in *Blues*, Baldwin rails against the constraints of a legal system insidiously bereft of moral authority. Nevertheless, in this period, Baldwin consistently draws upon discourses of right and wrong in order to carve out a space for moral action *within* the purview of the state (i.e., the courtroom) but from a moral or religious tradition *beyond* its jurisdiction. So, too, from King's "I Have a Dream" (1963) to Malcolm X's "The Ballot or the Bullet" (1964), civil rights rhetoric takes state promises—equal access, full citizenship, natural rights, racial parity—at face value in order to transform a society that practiced discrimination while announcing equality. In a national landscape polarized by racial segregation and institutional poverty, doctrines of non-violence emerged amid a political environment where violence was seen not as a last resort but as a rational reaction to racism. Nonetheless, dominant depictions of civil rights tend to set up a polarity between militancy and nonviolence. In response to threats of violence from a nascent Black Power movement, nonviolence was often heralded as the moral twin to immoral militancy. But, as Baldwin contends in *Fire*, "The real reason that non-violence is considered to be a virtue in Negroes . . . is that white men do not want their lives, their self-image, or their property threatened" (73). Attempts to render nonviolence and militancy as polar opposites often served the self-interest of those in power, even though their tenuous hold on the language of democracy could not weather extended interrogation with stories of injustice like Till's.

Taken collectively, the divergent, numerous, and often contradictory depictions of Till manifest Baldwin's dilemma in the protest mode: how to address division without reinscribing it? To solve this predicament of representing segregation from within a vision of integration, Baldwin deploys strategies of polarization but not as a means to stand alone in righteousness. Rather, Baldwin's strategy of "love" seeks to transform the system for the betterment of all. Baldwin never presents himself or representative figures like Till as exclusively ethical or divorced from the sins of fellow citizens. In his essay "Words of a Native Son" (1965), he explains to his readership why "that dead boy is my subject and my responsibility. And yours" (401). Baldwin declares, "It's a terrible delusion to think that any part of this republic can be safe as long as 20,000,000 members of it are as menaced as they are . . . I know you didn't do it, and I didn't do it either, but I am responsible for it because I am a man and a citizen of this country and you are responsible for it, too, for the very same reason: As long as my children face the future that they face, and come to the ruin that they come to, your children are gravely in danger, too" (400). Baldwin draws upon civic discourse to ask the nation as a whole to confront the lesson of Till, while he also recognizes the divergent positions and experiences of his mixed audience. Baldwin's work inhabits a polarized world in order to imagine the equitable, integrated state of democratic discourse, if not practice. In a polemical mode, Baldwin can analyze a landscape of national inequity (racial segregation) from which the audience must collectively push toward national change in the form of racial desegregation or cultural integration.

Minister Henry's Gun: Integration Strategies of Racial Polarization in Blues

In 1964, just as Black Power began to denounce integrationism as racial nihilism or self-hatred, Baldwin wrote *Blues,* in which the religious discourse of nonviolence comes into direct conflict with calls for armed resistance. Baldwin based his play "very distantly indeed" (*Blues,* xiv) on the murder of Till and the racially segregated milieu that promulgates such an act. Though the play culminates in a courtroom drama where the white murderer is acquitted—a fact already inscribed within the historical record—the play centers on moral crises of the characters, the searing persistence of racial divides, and the changed consciousnesses of black and white community members. Most noticeably, Baldwin's play rejects a chronological narrative structure in favor of present scenes laced with overlapping flashbacks in a structure more akin to the genre of court testimony. Many reviewers found the structure unnecessarily confusing or distracting. For instance, in the *Saturday Review*, Granville Hicks deemed the play propaganda and added that it was "difficult to follow at the beginning" (27). Henry Hewes praised the play a week later but still rejected the structure because "the total pattern is erratic, with numerous flashbacks that do not seem necessary to the relatively simple narrative of the play" (36). But the complicated flashback structure is central to Baldwin's call for his audience to confront the nation's history in its inequitable present; further, the structure is able to resurrect Richard (the Till figure) so that he can participate in the story that culminates in his lynching.

To portray systems of violently enforced racial segregation, Baldwin vivisects the stage along a municipal chasm: a racial divide runs through the middle separating Blacktown from Whitetown (see stage diagram). By segregating the stage, he runs the risk of reinscribing the very racial divisions he protests. Yet by not addressing real racial division, he would have courted accusations that he subscribed to a naïve integration vision. By confronting the audience with Blacktown and Whitetown, the play makes visible the site at which Baldwin painstakingly yokes religious nonviolence to calls for violent resistance. The racial divide suggests visibly that calls for violence emerge at the moment when, and the site where, democratic institutions of justice stop short—in this case, the courtroom.

Very few characters cross this heavy-handed manifestation of W. E. B. DuBois's racial veil. Further, the divide manifests as an actual ditch in which an actor playing Richard lies, "face down in the weeds!" (*Blues*, 2), after having been murdered by Lyle in the opening scene. The ditch separates the two halves of the stage, thereby imagining municipal segregation as an open grave traversed by only a few characters: the murderer, a black minister, and Parnell, a white liberal journalist invited equally into the homes of black and white families. Though Parnell's eventual alliance with Lyle extinguishes naïve faith that white liberalism will surpass racial lines, Baldwin fuses religious nonviolence and mili-

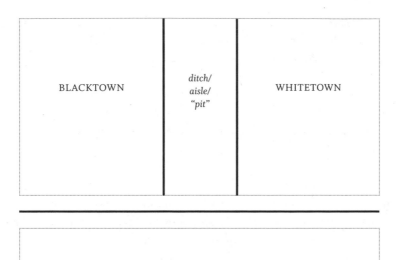

The staging for *Blues for Mister Charlie*.

tancy to offer the promise of connecting the black church of stage right to stage left—that is, to Whitetown's side of the segregated courtroom. This move suggests the possibility for, but not yet the attainment of, justice in the Till case.

In the climactic scene of the murder trial, Richard's father, the minister Meridian Henry, takes the witness stand and interrogates the ability of The State to pass judgment, hear a confession, or even allocate responsibility because "the truth cannot be heard in this dreadful place" (105). Meridian's extemporaneous speech is not a beleaguered plea transplanted from an apolitical pulpit. That interpretation would confirm accusations of myopic fatalism leveled at the black church by Black Power in the 1960s or by an earlier generation of communists, as in Richard Wright's *Native Son* (1940). Instead, when The State turns the courtroom into a forum to indict black militancy instead of the murderers, Meridian realizes that he is just "beginning to become" a minister (105) when he abandons the exhausted, politically removed religious rhetoric of "good and evil." In its stead, Meridian invests his theological rhetoric with the state's language of democracy, which is the strategy of civil rights, *and* with the language of self-determination, which is the dominant strategy of Black Nationalism:

> THE STATE: Perhaps the difficulties your son had in accepting the Christian faith is due to your use of the pulpit as a forum for irresponsible notions concerning social equality, Reverend Henry. Perhaps the failure of the son is due to the failure of the father.

> MERIDIAN: I am afraid that the gentleman flatters himself. I do not wish to see Negroes become the equal of their murderers. I wish us to become equal to ourselves. To become a people so free in themselves that they will have no need to—fear—others—and have no need to murder others. (102)

The State fails to understand the generational and ideological rifts within the community of Blacktown by imagining a homogeneous continuity between Meridian and his son, the pulpit-borne integration doctrines and northern-imported militancy, and the versions of justice imagined by Blacktown and Whitetown. Meridian, however, recognizes the limits of both the integration and Black Nationalist projects and seeks to bridge nonviolence and militancy. In his testimony, Meridian harnesses the church's moral vocabulary and the violent threats of racial self-determination in order to question the state's moral and judicial authority. Neither integration nor militancy displace one another; Meridian *incorporates* his dead son's militant stance into his theology and community leadership. The result is a vision of equality possible only in a transformed nation able to indict racist fantasies instead of the victims of racist violence. Further, to articulate such a vision of racial equality, Meridian directs his gaze internally to Blacktown; his is not a vision of integration where justice arises when a segregated community moves toward middle ground. Rather, Meridian seeks to heal fissures within Blacktown and reject the racial fantasies that lead to Richard's lynching.

Capitalizing on the sexual panic that undergirded much of American race relations, the members of Whitetown offer as "evidence" Richard's assumed sexual depravity: their fantasy of his desire for white women. Rather explicitly, Richard invokes the racialized sexual anxieties that infuse the Till case, as well as the violent interracial sexual plot informing the key novel of Richard's namesake: Wright's *Native Son*. For Whitetown and The State, Richard is a gun-toting maniac with no social responsibility. In order to bolster their own moral outrage, the defense for Whitetown references a gun and "lewd" pictures of white women supposedly smuggled into the South by Richard, the wayward son gone North. Just as The State is unable to prove these allegations of sexual depravity, it is unable to produce the alleged gun and pictures. Juxtaposed to the absent evidence of Richard's lewd nature, however, Baldwin offers the very present possibility of what might best be called *moral violence:* tucked inside Meridian's Bible rests Richard's missing gun, hidden from the policing gaze of The State. As his name suggests, Meridian is a figure that cleaves apart and together the ideological divides within and between Blacktown and Whitetown. To the history of the doctrine of nonviolent love and "all that turn-the-other-cheek jazz" Baldwin adds an arsenal (101).

Integration, Black Nationalism, and the Polemical Mode

Baldwin's work in general is suffused with simultaneous commitments to the hope of American democracy and to eliminating America's violent inconsistencies in race relations. From this side of the 1960s, when progressive morality has fallen out of favor, it is difficult to appreciate the power of tethering religion, morality, and militancy. Political theorist Lawrie Balfour reflects on an American political landscape in the wake of Baldwin's death by mourning the loss of what she calls Baldwin's "supple moral vocabulary" (xi). Balfour adds that Baldwin "would have insisted, furthermore, that women and men interested in disparities of power not cede the language of moral passion to conservatism" (xi–xii). Indeed, the grounds upon which Baldwin first assumed cultural icon status were the same grounds upon which black militants consigned him to generational irrelevance and, contradictorily, white liberals consigned him to "race hatred" (Spender, 256): Baldwin may have left the pulpit at seventeen but the pulpit never left him. By superimposing the black pulpit and the white judicial bench in the Till story, Baldwin creates a fiery polemic for a polarized nation, writ large upon a starkly segregated stage, in order to provoke a moral crisis where characters must traverse lines of segregation to escape the political or legal status quo. Baldwin juxtaposes democratic promises and the experience of blacks in America, which is a common strategy of 1960s social movements. In addition to speeches by Martin Luther King Jr. and Malcolm X, for instance, the Students for a Democratic Society's Port Huron Statement proclaims, "The declaration 'All men are created equal . . .' rang hollow before the facts of Negro life in the South and the big cities of the North" (1).

In 1964, shortly after appearing on the cover of *Time,* Baldwin's fame stagnated as his ability to speak on behalf of a silenced black population rapidly eroded. Dismissals of Baldwin came from across the political spectrum, from Black Nationalists to literary élites to COINTELPRO (the FBI counterintelligence program to repress political dissent). Collectively, these judgments sunk Baldwin's career as political advocate into a literary-political quagmire. The widespread rejections of Baldwin do not reflect a change in the quality or ferocity of his work; rather the dismissal resulted from the dry rot of the moral platform upon which those who came to be labeled integrationists stood as they argued for state-sponsored social justice. To wit, legal scholar Patricia Williams revisits an epicenter of the integration age, *Brown v. The Board of Education,* in order to rekindle the project that the anemic term *integrationist* belittles: "Jerome Culp, a Duke University law professor, has observed that the litigators and activists who worked on *Brown* in the early 1950s assumed at least three things that have not come to pass: (1) that good liberals would stand by their commitment to black equality through hard times (2) that blacks and whites could come to some kind of agreement about what was fair and just—that there *was* a neutral agreed-upon position we could aspire to; and (3) that if you just had enough faith, if you just wished racism away hard enough, it would disappear" (21–22). Williams brilliantly traces the fate of national "race dialogues" in the absence of a progressive moral currency, and I defer to her analysis of the distortion of integration into an apolitical national "conversation" about race. For this essay, though, we can revisit the progressive connotation of "faith" in Williams's third assumption. Even Williams suspends her skepticism in the discourse of faith in order to take seriously Baldwin's religiously inflected project of integration. Williams juxtaposes the "neutral ground" sought by integration to the racial balkanization (separatism) prized by Black Nationalists. This common juxtaposition forestalls Baldwin's integration strategy of polarization. Further, Baldwin explicitly refuses the idea of neutral ground in integration because Till's murdered body lies in the ditch at stage center, the middle ground. To cross lines of segregation, characters must cross over Till's unhallowed grave.

The fulcrum of Baldwin's reception and dismissal is bound up with our changing relationship to the value and appropriateness of the moral, or more specially, polemical mode in literature. Typically, critics distrust or reject polemical work on the grounds that it renders complex problems as having two easy and unimaginative opposing sides. In such a view, if Baldwin is a polemicist, all he can do is offer simplistic renditions of the race problem. Blacktown and Whitetown are simplistic, and therefore uninteresting from a literary standpoint. Baldwin's work, however, is known for its complexity, and *Blues* is no exception. The polemical is anything but simple.

Etymologically, *polemic* pertains to controversy, that which is disputatious.[1] The capacious definition could, of course, render anything polemical given the current truism that everything is political. So, *polemic* marks writers and arguments that spark what the *Oxford English Dictionary* (OED) describes as "aggressive controversy"—the writer being the aggressor, not the normative system that crushes dissenters and dissent. The *OED* also offers a more specific context: *polemic* has origins in the early seventeenth century in the long wake of the Great Schism and the rise of Protestantism. As such, *polemic* originally referred to theological debates, specifically to the author who "writes or argues in opposition to another . . . especially in theology" (*OED*, sb. def. 2). By 1680, authors of polemics risked punishment for invoking dissent by offering "The same thing to be true and false at once" in theological debates (sb. def. 2). Polemics, then, work by invoking a crisis by bringing together incommensurable evidence or ideas—Till's story and inclusive doctrines of American justice, for example. By the time of Baldwin's polemic, the source of authority (truth) is not necessarily theological; rather, in the twentieth century, authority lies in the modern nation-state and its doctrines of representative democracy. Yet the Church is not totally displaced by the nation-state; the Church becomes churches. And for Baldwin, his was the marginalized Harlem storefront church where preachers dissented from or reversed the too-familiar American correlation of racial identity with the Christian religious vocabulary of light and dark, good and evil, black and white.

The *OED* traces how the modern nation-state rose to power and *polemic* shifted from theological controversy to a weapon of war, the ultimate polarization of *us* and *them*. By the late eighteenth century, *polemical* pertained to that which is militaristic. Further, the term gained flexibility because one could be a professional polemicist by the mid-nineteenth century. Writers could "wage war" by "polemizing." In the wake of World War I and at the apex of the nation-state, we added *polemology*: the bona fide science of war. In addition to the fascination with a science of war, polemics are also a weapon of *rhetorical* war because writers can "polemize" or "polemicize."

So, Baldwin's polemic may be seen as a weapon of rhetorical war in the ongoing struggles for racial justice in the United States. Conservative as well as Black Nationalist responses to the fiery polemics of polarized nations explicitly reject the possibility of national collectivity in integration and instead embrace separatism or balkanization. Meanwhile, Baldwin refused to see the world as divided neatly into camps along the veil of race or any other identitarian concern. Instead, he employed his "supple moral vocabulary" to address the complexities of class, gender, age, ideology, and religion on the segregated stage housing Till's murdered body. But critics were quick to dismiss what they saw as Baldwin's "wishy-washiness," which they regarded as indicative of integrationist "impotence," a "problem of identification," or, as the young Eldridge Cleaver claimed in 1968's *Soul On Ice*, simply a symptom of Baldwin's "diseased" love for white men.[2] Yet, before his dismissal, Baldwin sought continuities between integration and Black Power. His efforts are not a version of liberal humanism in blackface; rather, he uses Till in an integration project where the audience must locate itself in the segregated cartography of Blacktown and Whitetown connected by Till's makeshift grave.

Exhuming Emmett Till: James Baldwin's Polemoscope

In addition to the broad etymology of *polemic*, it is interesting to note the invention of the polemoscope: a sort of land-based periscope that uses the technology of mirrors to convert the human gaze into a multiplanar weapon of war against the enemy caught in the subject's high-tech sights. Like the polemoscopes used in foxholes, Baldwin's polemical strategies are elaborate technologies that allow the reader or viewer to understand segregation, which Baldwin considered a national race war. Baldwin's polemic engages the polarizing story of Till to examine violent American segregation from the vantage afforded by a moral or religious vision of racial reconciliation. I describe Baldwin's use of Till as an exhumation in order to underscore the great feat Baldwin attempted at the height of the civil rights movement to keep the solution of integration alive for a younger militant generation, a complacent northern audience, a generally exasperated nation, and the decade-old murder case.[3] In a complicated structure of flashbacks and changing scenery atop a steady racial fault line, Baldwin exhumes Till's body to offer his multiracial audience a return to the moral clarity of an earlier moment in civil rights. This moral clarity and a segregated stage allows Till to address the seemingly more equitable present moment of legal desegregation and a seemingly integrated multiracial audience.

The post–civil rights dismissal of Baldwin buries his complex response to desegregation in *Blues'* psychological study of the rather unexceptional white supremacist, Lyle, generalized in the title as Mister Charlie. As Adrienne Rich recalled in 1982, "Reading James Baldwin's early essays in the fifties had stirred me with a sense that apparently 'given' situations like racism could be analyzed and described and that this could lead to action, to change" (118).[4] But Rich consigns Baldwin to the wrong side of a generational rift (Rich protests his inattention to gendered oppression), even though she embraces Baldwin's influential insight that race is a fantasy we can analyze and escape. Contrary to the more pragmatic goals of civil rights, such as inclusion into existing governmental or economic systems, Baldwin asked his audience to accept the moral challenge of confronting the nation's racial fantasies. According to Baldwin, American racism was rooted primarily in a psychological terror of each other. In *The Fire Next Time,* for example, Baldwin identifies the "Negro" as a white invention and argues, "Therefore, a vast amount of the energy that goes into what we call the Negro problem is produced by the white man's profound desire not to be judged by those who are not white, not to be seen as he is" (109). In *Blues,* Baldwin places whiteness itself, as well as integration and self-determination, on trial—inverting the historical scene of the Till trial and the acquittal of the murderers. In his response to The State's accusations that he caused the death of his son, Meridian proclaims, "Do you accept this answer? I am a man. A *man!* I tried to help my son become a man. But manhood is a dangerous pursuit, here. And the pursuit undid him because of *your* guns, *your* hoses, *your* dogs, *your* judges, *your* law-makers, *your* folly, *your* pride, *your* cruelty, *your* cowardice, *your* money, *your* chain gangs, and *your* churches!" (103). Conjuring familiar civil rights images (hoses, dogs), Meridian portrays the masculine posturing of Black Power as a deadly response to equally deadly White Power. By underscoring the distance between "you" and "us" in the courtroom, Meridian addresses the audience, not The State, with his polarizing but ultimately redemptive rhetoric of achieved manhood.

Though many criticize Baldwin for his seeming refusal to make sexuality a category of analysis like race—a pressing criticism given the hypersexualized justifications for Till's murder—Baldwin's central contribution to civil rights and to 1960s social movements was to make race a subject of social analysis. In the inaugural essay of *The Fire Next Time,* Baldwin argues, "And if the word *integration* means anything, this is what it means: that we, with love, shall force our brothers to see themselves as they are, to cease fleeing from reality and begin to change it" (23–24). One hundred years after the emancipation from slavery, Baldwin argues for a second emancipation—this time psychological—on a national scale. To do this, Baldwin employs a language of "love" as a moral "duty." Baldwin exhorts, "If we—and now I mean the relatively conscious whites and the relatively conscious blacks, who must, like lovers, insist on, or create, the consciousness of the others—do not falter in our duty now, we may be able, handful that we are, to end the nightmare and achieve our country, and change the history of the world" (119). Baldwin's polemic embeds within a polarized national landscape an image of collectivity—a "we"—that employs a language of civic responsibility to save us from racial nightmare.

Melvin Watkins considers the curious cultural influence Baldwin garnered as a political advocate in the 1960s. Watkins concludes, "Baldwin's point of focus was not the surface dilemma—fascinating enough in itself—but the festering ambivalency, the personal, moral quandary that lay beneath the surface" (112). In *Blues,* the courtroom scene is a constricting plane upon which to engage the complexities of a racially segregated nation whose stark dividing lines could shadow power inequities *within* Blacktown and Whitetown. By plumbing beneath the surface of interracial relations in jurisprudence, Baldwin presciently critiques how lines of segregation can morph into lines of balkanization for Black Nationalism. In Baldwin's play, integration and Black Power coexist. Richard adopts postures associated with doctrines of self-determination (militancy, youthful defiance, seeking confrontation with Whitetown) and Meridian espouses views associated with integration (nonviolence, faithful meditation, interracial camaraderie), but the two characters congregate in a play protesting racial segregation. Whereas Whitetown depicts Richard as out of control and dangerous, Richard is central to Meridian's conversion to a real minister by play's end.

Baldwin underscores debates within and between Blacktown and Whitetown in order to insist upon the complexity of the segregated world that witnesses Till's murder. Baldwin, for instance, does not latch onto the sympathetic journalist Parnell as the enlightened character who crosses boundaries to bring the doctrine of liberal humanism and equality to an overlooked African American population. Rather, Parnell fails to interrogate the paradoxical nature of his project: the privilege of movement upon which he relies is a result of the divisions he attempts to erase. So, Parnell ends his testimony in alliance with his source of full citizenship: Whitetown. In the courtroom scene, Baldwin maps a crisis of mutually existing truths onto Whitetown and Blacktown, both of which demand simultaneously "Make him [Parnell] tell the truth!" (113). Under The State's interrogation, Parnell verifies the story of Richard's advances on a white woman. In complacent relief, Whitetown collectively asserts, "It took him long enough! . . . We been trying to tell him—for years!" (114). In court, Parnell becomes white once again and fails to straddle any boundaries, just as he fails to topple the divisions of Whitetown and Blacktown. This is why Juanita, Richard's girlfriend, says, in response to Parnell's request to join the black protest march leaving the courtroom, "Well, we can walk in the same direction" (121). Baldwin does not prematurely announce the end of racial division nor does he celebrate Parnell's belated alliance; instead, he addresses the persistence of racial division even among those espousing integration. Whereas Baldwin's project *begins* in racial polarization to articulate the need for racial equality, The State and Whitetown *end* in racial polarization to prove they were right all along. It remains purposefully unclear if the protest march walks away from racial inequality in a white-owned American justice system, or from the justice system altogether.

The success of Baldwin's play does not lie in any one particular character, so Parnell's alliance with one side of the town or the other does not determine the point of the play—or Baldwin's political orientation. The responsibility shifts to the audience to traverse the second line of segregation: the line between the stage and the viewers, between the polarized characters and the multiracial theatergoers, between Richard's exhumation and Till's grave (which often marks the beginning of the civil rights movement). Baldwin asks the audience to recognize, analyze, *and change* the system. The work of the play lies in the difficult process of creating real collectivity through the polemical tool of a deceptively simple segregated town. Baldwin must move the heterogeneous American populace from the seeming picture of equality in the multicolored audience of a theater in New York's Greenwich Village to the scene upon the stage of racial division and intraclass strife. Baldwin's ditch calls our attention to the municipal, legal, and social history of segregation—an inevitable result of the naturalization of racial polarization. The ditch can serve as a bridge to traverse, just as readily as it serves as an open grave for those like Richard (or Till) who cross lines of power. So, too, the line between stage and audience separates social analysis from dumb voyeurism. If the audience accepts Baldwin's invitation to see the nation in terms of Whitetown and Blacktown, a new future may be possible.

In an early criticism of the play, Joe Weixlmann considered the negative responses to Baldwin's stage and noted that much of the "assailing" of *Blues* saw the play's structure as a failed vehicle for Baldwin's considerable talents as novelist and essayist. Weixlmann questioned Baldwin's choice to borrow a roundly criticized stage technique from Eugene O'Neill's *All God's Chillun Got Wings*. Yet Baldwin's use of the theater to tell Till's story provided a new opportunity to confront directly the relationship between his audience and his subject—the seemingly integrated and the municipally and culturally segregated. Baldwin's polemical play was not pure aesthetic invention divorced from the trenches of real racial war. In fact, Baldwin's play served as the latest lightning rod for the persistent phenomenon of divorcing political writing from literary realms. Or, as Calvin C. Hernton insisted in 1970, "The question of whether *Blues for Mister Charlie* was artistically a bad play is about as relevant to the real issue as saying that *Crime and Punishment* is artistically a bulky, sloppy novel, which it certainly is" (114).

The etymology of *polemic* again helps us because it joins polarization and militarism explicitly in the venue of the theater. In addition to its association with war, *polemic* stands for a specifically literary technique. The polemoscope also served as a device for theater patrons in the late eighteenth century. Amid the camouflage of omnipresent opera glasses, aristocrats donned small polemoscopes not to watch the stage but to observe—from a discrete ninety-degree angle—their fellow audience members. So, too, Baldwin's polemoscopic play forces the viewers to regard and reflect upon each other through the lens of polarization on the stage. For, to fail to cross lines of segregation on the stage and between the stage and audience would only result in more dead bodies lying in ditches. To raise Richard's discarded body, the audience must leave the flattening legal field of the courtroom on stage and use the polemoscope to analyze the diverse audience in an unequal America. But was the postintegration generation amenable to such a complex project?

"Unfocused Anger": The Unraveling of Baldwin's Integrative Vision of Polarization

The short-lived off-Broadway run of *Blues* is infamous, and the play's reception provides a glimpse at later generations' rejection or misinterpretation of Baldwin's moralism. Watkins succinctly reports, "Baldwin's blunt portrayal of the hatred stirred in blacks because of white racism shocked critics and audiences alike and, after the initial uproar, the play foundered at the box office" (112). The unprofitability of Baldwin's starkly segregated world is not terribly surprising. But the vehemence, speed, and drama with which progressive critics and writers dismissed the polemical theatrical experiment deserve attention. For Watkins, the value of the piece is nearly synonymous with its box office performance. He accounts for the success of Baldwin's earlier work in a Manichean description of Baldwin as black polemicist and white romantic: "This dual approach, the ability to assume the voice of black as well as white Americans, accounts, in great part, for his popularity and acceptance among Americans on both sides of the racial issue" (117). If those committed to integration praised Baldwin's ability to assume both black and white voices, those committed to self-determination or racial separatism might view with skepticism or disdain Baldwin's success with a mixed audience. If Baldwin's success or decline was related to the political climate of the day, this may account for Baldwin's floundering cultural influence after the early 1960s.

Watkins's characterization of Baldwin's "dual role" also describes the divergent reception of the play. Much of the initial reaction against *Blues* accused Baldwin of setting up camp on one side of the racial line or the other. Darwin Turner neatly consigned the play to the "protest tradition," concluding that it was written for an exclusively white audience.[5] Tom F. Driver noted that Robert Brustein of the *New Republic* and Howard Taubman of the *New York Times* echoed Turner's charge of exclusively addressing a white audience. In the review, though, Driver concludes that Baldwin had severed politics and economics from civil rights in favor of ahistorical racial stereotypes. Driver, however, lauds Baldwin's polemical stance toward what he imagined to be an exclusively white audience because Baldwin "alienated a large part of the liberal intelligentsia." By ignoring socialist theory and prevailing liberal discourse about unemployment, job training, and the ballot, Driver argues, "Baldwin has taken what will seem to many a reactionary step: he has described racial strife as *racial* strife, warfare between black people and white people" (292). And so began the misreading of Baldwin's stage production as naturalizing race instead of questioning segregation and the false dichotomy between integration and black self-determination. For many critics, though, *Blues* failed because he fused two separate plays: one addressing a white audience, one a black audience.

As *Blues* took the stage, prominent white liberals were beginning to distance themselves from the ambitious moral challenges first cultivated in the pulpit of the optimistic 1960s. The rhetoric of protest was falling out of literary favor. Calls for compromise disguised as political pragmatism displaced Baldwinian moral challenges and utopian visions. Baldwin's polemical play is unsteadily situated at this salt point. Baldwin's decline, especially in literary circles, was explicitly framed in terms of a zero sum game between art and politics. In a

1968 critical review, Irving Howe castigates Baldwin when he "opens wide the spigot of his rhetoric" (Howe, 103) and begins to look less like Jane Austen and more like Richard Wright. In another review, poet-critic Stephen Spender likewise grows tired of polemics that demand too much of their imagined readers and not enough of their subjects. Spender notes that such work "is the tragedy of [Baldwin's] race" (256). Presaging a post–civil rights schism in the uneasy moral alliance between white liberals and black protest writers, Spender asserts, "[Baldwin] has, as a Negro, a right, of course, to despise liberals, but he exploits his moral advantage too much" (257). These reviews point to the general trend by Baldwin's white critics to pull away from black writing during the rise of Black Power. By 1969, Joseph Keller described in the pages of *Negro American Literature Forum* white critics' anxiety that they could not properly approach Baldwin's play—nor, black writing generally—because they do not share his experience.

In the turn away from Baldwin's work after the early 1960s, the border between serious writings and polemical ones, between morality and career building, or between personal feelings and political process often fell along the color line. This is especially ironic given Baldwin's suggestion that Till's murder is an inevitable product of the American color line. Spender inscribes a literary color line by abandoning the rhetoric of morality: "Although Mr. Baldwin considers love is the only answer to the American race problem, it is not all evident from [*Fire*] that he loves white Americans, and at times it is even doubtful whether he loves his own people. Not that I blame him for this. What I do criticize him for is postulating a quite impossible demand as the only way of dealing with a problem that has to be solved" (258). Spender empties "love" of its history in the civil rights movement, and he portrays it as meager, possibly naïve. Instead of connecting Baldwin's complex analysis of segregation to other struggles, Spender dismisses Baldwin's work entirely on the grounds that he stood for mere race hatred and is therefore no more helpful than the Black Muslims: "[Baldwin] quite rightly resents the claims of whites that they are superior to colored people. But in fact he thinks that the colored are superior" (Spender, 257). In response, Baldwin insists, "I do not hate white people. Because I can't afford to. Just because I want to live . . . I think people mistake my vehemence—and, you know, this becomes so sad. I'm vehement and indignant. That's not the same thing as hatred. Or even the same thing as bitterness" (Eckman, back flap).

Despite Baldwin's own attempts to convince his audience of the value of indignation in integration works, Spender plays the trump card of infrapolitics: "Moreover, color prejudice is not confined to white Americans and Europeans. It exists between colored people themselves" (259). Though insights about the heterogeneity of political classes were central to social movements like antiracism and feminism in the late 1970s in the birth of coalitional politics, Spender's gesture toward internal difference functions to implode the work of Baldwin, not to understand multiple groups' oppression. Like Spender, many critics ascribed the political failure of *Blues* to Baldwin's aesthetic inadequacies, not to a literary environment where polemicism had lost favor. Rejecting Baldwin's vehemence, critics positioned themselves in the deserted middle ground of what they portrayed as rational compromise between segregated races.

But to stake out a stable middle ground in Baldwin's play requires burying Till's body. Baldwin's polemicism relies upon the extremes created by segregation, racially meted democratic justice, and militant rejections of integration; Till's body lies between these. Baldwin's polemical work is able to convene, if not reconcile, Parnell, a white liberal; Lyle, a racist murderer; Meridian, a nonviolent preacher; and Richard, a northern militant. These characters question themselves and their racial attitudes in the privacy of flashbacks that counter their official courtroom testimony. Each character *suggests* an integrated and honest future: Parnell joins Meridian's protest march (121), Lyle confesses his guilt to Meridian (120), Meridian retains Richard's gun "like the pilgrim's of old" (120), and Richard is afforded the chance to posthumously deliver his own story via Lyle's flashback (118). But the goal of integration remains purposefully unfinished. The polemical mode asks the audience to translate these possibilities into an integrated society off the stage.

What is most compelling about the reprimands and rejections of Baldwin's play is that a knee-jerk rejection of disdaining the polemical serves as their fulcrum. In a representative review of Baldwin's subsequent fiction, Mario Puzo complains about Baldwin's reputation as a political writer: "Yet it would seem that such gifts [of lingual dexterity], enough for critics and moralists and other saintly figures, are not enough to insure the writing of good fiction" (155). Puzo's dismissal cements the separation between art and politics by tossing Baldwin's fiction on the rubbish pile of mere propaganda. Puzo contends, "It is possible that Baldwin believes this is not tactically the time for art, that polemical fiction can help the Negro cause more, that art is too strong, to [sic] gamy a dish for a prophet to offer now. And so he gives us a propagandistic fiction, a readable book with a positive social value" (34). Puzo accepts Baldwin's famous self-descriptions as a witness or prophet only to hollow out such rhetoric on the basis that it is inartistic. For Puzo, Baldwin's polemicism fails to elevate his characters into the pantheon of the literary, whereas Baldwin is interested in elevating Till into the realm of justice.

In addition to dismissal by white liberals, Baldwin's complex polemics no longer held much interest by the early 1970s in literary circles allied with Black Nationalism. In a review of *The Devil Finds Work* (1976), Black Arts writer Orde Coombs dismisses Baldwin's nonfiction as messy compendiums of "tortured speculations" held together by "passion that is all reflex" (6). Coombs eulogizes the passing of Baldwinian moral challenges such as those in *Fire*, and he laments Baldwin's "unfocused anger" in essays filled with "ideas that jump around and contradict one another" (6). Coombs concludes that Baldwin's "possible force, then, is scattered willy-nilly, to the winds, and all that vision and moral weight that fortified a generation, becomes as disturbing as the memory of a hurricane on a placid summer's afternoon" (7). For Coombs, it is integration itself, not American race relations, that is a torrential nightmare from which one must awake in the clear dawn of Black Nationalism. Whereas an earlier generation sought moral clarity to solve segregation, a younger Black Nationalist generation articulated a doctrine of racial self-determination by rejecting integration and naturalizing racial polarity.

By the 1990s, Coombs's contention that Baldwin was not able to package the "moral weight" of one generation for the next was reversed by Henry Louis Gates Jr. In his 1993 elegiac essay, Gates places some blame on Baldwin himself for the loss of moral force in the 1970s and for what Gates describes as Baldwin's artistic "decline." According to Gates, Baldwin dumbed down his work after the success of the early 1960s as the price of becoming a public intellectual: "The connoisseur of complexity tried to become an ideologue" (58). Again, the figure of the artist-spokesperson is an impossible marriage. For Gates, political analysis and theory—as well as good art—have no use for moral polemics. Editor and collaborator Sol Stein echoes this sentiment and notes, "In both his fiction and his nonfiction, as time went on Baldwin allowed the preacher in him to overtake the writer" (13). In another eulogy, Amiri Baraka also contends that Baldwin's later work lacks complexity—only Baraka praises this shift as necessary to a post-integration Black Arts movement. At Baldwin's funeral, where Kendall Thomas witnessed the willful forgetting of Baldwin's queer and white characters,[6] Baraka's eulogy stages a postmortem reclamation and celebrates Baldwin's post–civil rights dismissal: "The celebrated James Baldwin of earlier times could not be used to cover the undaunted freedom chants of the Jimmy who walked with King and SNCC or the evil little nigger who wrote *Blues for Mr. Charlie*. For as far as I'm concerned, it was [*Blues*] that announced the black arts movement, even so far as describing down to minute fragments of breath the class struggle raging inside the black community—even as it is menaced by prehuman maniacs" (132). In order to claim Baldwin as father to the very movement that buried him, Baraka lops off the left half of the stage of *Blues* where Whitetown lives. However, the power of the polemics of *Blues,* and its moral challenge to its audience to claim responsibility for racial violence, resides in Baldwin's consistent demand that we address the complexities of religion, violence, and class *within* each side *and across* the ditch separating the two races. Baraka reclaims Baldwin, but this is a balkanized Baldwin. Baldwin is dissected, and Baraka only retains those parts that he brands the "real" Baldwin. The "tainted" parts join the rubbish pile. And, in the process, Till's grave may be covered over in the rush to erase or not cross lines of segregation, the line that connects as well as divides Blacktown and Whitetown.

NOTES

1. *The Oxford English Dictionary,* 2d ed., 1989.

2. Bluefarb dismisses Baldwin's 1963 homosexual story "Previous Condition" because Baldwin seeks "identification in the white world, but ironically he also fails to find even a place for himself in the black world" (26). See Field, Reid-Pharr, and Thomas for direct studies of the politics and sexuality of Cleaver's attack on Baldwin.

3. See also Ishmael Reed's *Reckless Eyeballing* (1986), in which Till's accusers exhume his body to stand trial. Metress notices the trope of exhumation and discusses Baldwin "rais[ing] the ghost of Emmett Till" (95) and Till "haunting" African American literature generally. Conversely, on Till as a figure of loss, see Moten.

4. For analyses of Baldwin's relationship to the women's movement and women, see Harris, Norman, and Kaplan.

5. The actual crowd was relatively diverse in part because Baldwin kept ticket prices low to allow Harlem's poor to attend (Leeming, 231–34; Eckman 222–35). The play survived three months with help from three white southerners and substantial donations from some Rockefellers—an irony considering Baldwin's assertion, "I'm not writing this play for people from *Scarsdale*" (Eckman, 235).

6. Thomas reports that there was little to no mention of *Giovanni's Room* or *Another Country* in the eulogies.

WORKS CITED

Baldwin, James. *Blues for Mister Charlie.* New York: Dial, 1964.

———. *The Evidence of Things Not Seen.* New York: Holt, Rinehart, and Winston, 1985.

———. *The Fire Next Time.* New York: Dial, 1963.

———. "Words of a Native Son." 1965. In *The Price of the Ticket,* 395–402. New York: St. Martin's, 1985.

Balfour, Katharine Lawrence. *The Evidence of Things Not Said: James Baldwin and the Promise of American Democracy.* Ithaca: Cornell University Press, 2001.

Baraka, Amiri. "*Jimmy!*" In Troupe, 127–34.

Bluefarb, Sam. "James's Baldwin's 'Previous Condition': A Problem of Identification." *Negro American Literature Forum* 3, no. 1 (1969): 26–29.

Cleaver, Eldridge. *Soul on Ice.* New York: Dell, 1968.

Cone, James H. *Martin and Malcolm and America: A Dream or a Nightmare.* Maryknoll, NY: Orbis, 1991.

Coombs, Orde. "The Devil Finds Work." *New York Times Book Review,* 2 May 1976, 6–7.

Driver, Tom F. "The Review that was Too True to Be Published." *Negro Digest* 13 (1964): 34–40. Reprinted in *Critical Essays on James Baldwin,* edited by Fred L. Standley and Nancy V. Burt, 291–95. Boston: G. K. Hall and Co., 1988.

Eckman, Fern Marja. *The Furious Passage of James Baldwin.* Philadelphia: Lippincott, 1966.

Field, Douglas. "Looking for Jimmy Baldwin: Sex, Privacy, and Black Nationalist Fervor." *Callaloo* 27, no. 2 (2004): 457–80.

Gates, Henry Louis, Jr. "The Welcome Table." In *English Inside and Out: The Places of Literary Criticism,* edited by Susan Gubar and Jonathan Kamholtz, 47–60. New York: Routledge, 1993.

Harris, Trudier. *Black Women in the Fiction of James Baldwin.* Knoxville: University of Tennessee Press, 1985.

Hernton, Calvin C. "A Fiery Baptism." 1970. In Kinnamon, 109–19.

Hewes, Henry. "Change of Tune." *Saturday Review,* 9 May 1964, 36.

Hicks, Granville. "A Gun in the Hand of a Hater." *Saturday Review,* 2 May 1964, 27–28.

Howe, Irving. "James Baldwin: At Ease in the Apocalypse." 1968. In Kinnamon, 96–108.

Kaplan, Cora. "'A Cavern Opened in My Mind': The Poetics of Homosexuality and the Politics of Race in James Baldwin." In *Representing Black Men,* edited by Marcellus Blount and George P. Cunningham, 27–54. New York: Routledge, 1996.

Keller, Joseph. "Black Writing and the White Critic." *Negro American Literature Forum* 3, no. 4 (1969): 103–10.

Kenan, Randall. *James Baldwin.* New York: Chelsea House, 1994.

King, Martin Luther, Jr. "Letter from Birmingham City Jail." 1963. In *A Testament of Hope: The Essential Writings and Speeches of Martin Luther King, Jr.,* edited by James M. Washington, 289–302. San Francisco: Harper Collins, 1986.

Kinnamon, Kenneth, ed. *James Baldwin: A Collection of Critical Essays.* Englewood Cliffs, NJ: Prentice-Hall, 1974.

Leeming, David. *James Baldwin: A Biography.* New York: Penguin, 1994.

Metress, Christopher. "'No Justice, No Peace': The Figure of Emmett Till in African American Literature." *MELUS* 28, no. 1 (2003): 87–103.

Moten, Fred. "Black Mo'nin'." In *Loss: The Politics of Mourning,* edited by David Eng and David Kazanjian, 59–76. Berkeley and Los Angeles: University of California Press, 2003.

Norman, Brian. "Crossing Identitarian Lines: Women's Liberation and Baldwin's Early Essays." *Women's Studies* 35, no. 3 (2006): 241–64.

———. "Duplicity, Purity, and Politicized Morality." In *James Baldwin's Go Tell It on the Mountain: Historical and Critical Essays,* edited by Carol E. Henderson, 13–18. New York: Peter Lang, 2006.

Puzo, Mario. "His Cardboard Lovers." *New York Times Book Review,* 23 June 1968, 5, 34.

Reid-Pharr, Robert. "Tearing the Goat's Flesh: Crisis, Abjection, and Homosexuality in the Production of a Late-Twentieth-Century Black Masculinity." In *Novel Gazing: Queer Readings in Fiction,* edited by Eve Kosofsky Sedgwick, 353–76. Durham: Duke University Press, 1997.

Rich, Adrienne. "Split at the Root: An Essay on Jewish Identity." 1982. In *Blood, Bread, and Poetry: Selected Prose 1979–1985,* 100–123. New York: Norton, 1986.

Spender, Stephen. "James Baldwin: Voice of a Revolution." *Partisan Review* 30 (1963): 256–60.

Stein, Sol. *Native Sons.* New York: Ballantine, 2004.

Students for a Democratic Society. "The Port Huron Statement." 1962. Mimeographed at 1608 W. Madison St., Chicago, 3d printing, 1966.

Thomas, Kendall. "'Ain't Nothin' Like the Real Thing': Black Masculinity, Gay Sexuality, and the Jargon of Authenticity." In *Representing Black Men,* edited by Marcellus Blount and James Cunningham, 55–69. New York: Routledge, 1996.

Troupe, Quincy, ed. *James Baldwin: The Legacy.* New York: Simon and Schuster, 1989.

Turner, Darwin T. "James Baldwin and the Dilemma of the Black Dramatist." In *James Baldwin: A Critical Evaluation,* edited by Thurman O'Daniel, 189–94. Washington, DC: Howard University Press, 1977.

Watkins, Mel. "An Appreciation." In Troupe, 107–23.

Weixlmann, Joe. "Staged Segregation: Baldwin's *Blues for Mister Charlie* and O'Neill's *All God's Chillun Got Wings.*" *Black American Literature Forum* 11, no. 1 (Spring 1977): 35–36.

Williams, Patricia. "Pansy Quits." In *The Rooster's Egg: On the Persistence of Prejudice,* 15–41. Cambridge: Harvard University Press, 1995.

MAIDS MILD AND DARK VILLAINS, SWEET MAGNOLIAS AND SEEPING BLOOD

Gwendolyn Brooks's Poetic Response to the Lynching of Emmett Till

VIVIAN M. MAY

In 1960, Gwendolyn Brooks published a pair of poems about Emmett Till's 1955 murder: "A Bronzeville Mother Loiters in Mississippi. Meanwhile, a Mississippi Mother Burns Bacon," and "The Last Quatrain of the Ballad of Emmett Till."[1] Set in Mississippi, the first poem focuses primarily on the character and consciousness of Carolyn Bryant, wife of one of the accused murderers, while the second, set in Brooks's fictional black Chicago neighborhood of Bronzeville, focuses on the story of Mamie Bradley, Till's mother. Despite these differences, Brooks sets both poems in the domestic space of the kitchen, suggesting that racialized and eroticized violence are part of the fabric of everyday life. Thus, the color red, particularly images of seeping blood, "a red that had no end" ("Bronzeville," 79), creates a thread between the two poems. Brooks clearly participates in a long-standing African American literary tradition in which black authors write about lynching as a means of critiquing "the innate character of white society, its destructive nature and brutality" (Harris, 69). Her poems can be read as examples of political protest and ethical critique: through poetry, Brooks appeals to her readers to "take a stand against injustice" by daring "to question the myths" that shape our imaginations (Molina, 331).

First, by demystifying the "magnolias and chivalry of the south" (Ottley, 131), Brooks illustrates how romanticized notions of southern decorum comprise what philosopher Charles W. Mills would characterize as "an invented delusional world, a racial fantasyland" (*Racial*, 18). She thoroughly discredits the idealized veneer of gentility and debunks any pretense to heroic achievement of the archetypal southern love story to reveal its brutality. Moreover, Brooks emphasizes how the Carolyn Bryant character's flights of fancy are a key component of the cognitive "opacity" Mills describes as necessary to maintaining and unifying a "white polity" (*Racial*, 19). Brooks underscores how, rather than being a passive observer or unwilling participant in the murderous white supremacist narrative of chivalry, adventure, and marriage that led to Till's murder, the Carolyn Bryant character is an active accomplice, even if she refuses to acknowledge her agency in this regard.

To better illustrate the willful opacity of the powerful, Brooks juxtaposes the two mothers' narrative points of view. By placing these different points of view and settings side by side, but not collapsing the two poems into one, Brooks offers a complex portrait of the interplay of race, gender, and region on one's person and one's life circumstance. She also deconstructs overly simplistic oppositions between black and white, North and South, and self and other. In fact, Brooks's strategy is suggestive of an "apposite" narrative technique, a key mode of black feminist inquiry. Valerie Smith maintains that, as a method, apposition is flexible and destabilizing, capable of "reading" the politics of race and gender concurrently ("Black," 671–72). She further contends that this approach is significant because it "provides strategies of reading simultaneity" (*Not Just*, xv); it is dynamic, rather than static.

Through juxtaposition, Brooks emphasizes how violence is embedded in narrative and language, focuses on ignorance as a key tool of oppression, demonstrates how passivity and guilt are self-centered forms of complicity, and highlights Till's mother's love and resistance as politically and poetically significant. Moreover, by pointing to an unacknowledged "metaphysics of interconnectedness" (Keating, 521), Brooks invites readers to face their "conjoined history" (Violet, 488); she calls for accountability to the past and to each other in ways that envision change without obscuring differences in power, collusion, and privilege.

Epistemologies of Ignorance: Guilty of the Sins of Omission

In a series of interviews with journalist Ethel Payne, published in the *Chicago Defender* from April to June 1956, Mamie Till Bradley addresses the nation's massive self-deception about its history. She describes continual efforts at evasion and criticizes the refusal to face the truth of racial injustice and violence at the collective and individual levels. Bradley states, "The large class of decent people in this country are guilty of the sins of omission when they fail to speak out for the right and take a stand against injustice. These are the people I am appealing to" (233). Till's mother identifies this unjust way of interpreting the world as a practice of domination that must be challenged and changed—a practice that Mills names an "epistemology of ignorance."

Mills maintains that the "racial contract" in the United States has two components. One, exploitation and coercion, has been somewhat recognized, although the desire for collective "amnesia," to erase this history, is a constant threat (Mills, "White"). The second element of the racial contract, the epistemological, he argues has not been adequately recognized. Mills describes an "inverted epistemology of ignorance" or "an agreement to misinterpret the world." One is taught "to see the world wrongly," he argues, "but with the assurance that this set of mistaken perceptions will be validated by white epistemic authority" (*Racial*, 18). It is this agreement to "see the world wrongly" that Brooks challenges, echoing Bradley's call to stop participating in the "sins of omission."

However, Brooks takes Mills's insights one step further, for she demonstrates that the racial contract coexists with other coercive social contracts. As the first poem illustrates, the white racial contract intersects with a binary gender contract and a heterosexual marriage contract. Brooks therefore emphasizes that the "rewards" and validation for learning to "see the world wrongly" are simultaneously racialized, gendered, and heteronormative. These apparently disconnected sets of "mistaken perceptions" are, in the poems as in real life, validated together. Brooks's attention to the interdependence of race, gender, and sexuality reveals a nuanced understanding of coercion that is unavailable when each factor is accounted for separately.[2]

Brooks also underscores how evasion and ignorance have been encouraged and continue to be rewarded, individually and structurally. For example, the Mississippi mother consciously *knows* it is "good to be a 'maid mild.' / That made the breath go fast." Willing to be "Pursued" then "Rescued," she tells us, is "worth anything," for it leads to the elusive but penultimate fantasy, "The Happiness-Ever-After" ("Bronzeville," 75). At the same time, Brooks points to the structural rewards available to the husband/murderer. For instance, when he comes downstairs to eat his breakfast and starts ranting about white power, Brooks writes: "Nothing could stop Mississippi. / He knew that. Big Fella. / . . . And, what was so good, Mississippi knew that" (78). In other words, he knew all along that the state would reward him, or at least not punish him, for murdering Till. Like the ballad, the law has been structured with him in mind. Brooks shows how these seemingly separate structural and narrative inequalities interdepend to maintain a supremacist polity.

Speech vs. Silence: Brooks's Use of Form

Many accounts suggest that Carolyn Bryant was in her husband's truck to identify Till the night he was killed.[3] Since she never testified to this fact, whether
she was in the truck or not remains unknown. Nevertheless, it is as if Brooks
tries to push this silent witness into speech by creating a verbose interior monologue in the first poem. Moreover, the marked contrast in length between the
two poems highlights differences in power and subject-position between the
Mississippi mother and the Bronzeville mother. Rather than occupying a democratic, equally available "rhetorical space,"[4] Brooks suggests that black women's
voices and stories have been silenced and pushed to the margins. Thus, the second poem is sparse and almost painfully silent.

Although the first poem's title names the Bronzeville mother first, she exists in the poem paratextually as "That sassy, Northern, brown-black—" (78).
She is the nameless and bodiless "Other Woman's eyes" (80) watching from the
margins of the white characters' consciousnesses. The Till character, also nameless, enters the narrative first as the stereotypical and ominous-sounding "Dark
Villain" (76), but immediately becomes more diminutive, "a blackish child / Of
fourteen, with eyes still too young to be dirty" (76). He soon shrinks to "That
little foe," only to become, just prior to his death, the "*little-boyness* in that barn"
(77).

Instead of being outraged at Till's murder, the Carolyn Bryant character is
more disturbed by the gap between fiction and fact, between the myth of the
black rapist / dark villain and the reality of Till's "eyes still too young to be dirty"
(76). By invoking the romance plot / ballad tradition of princes, "fair" maidens,
and "Dark Villains," Brooks highlights the embedded racial politics of supposedly neutral or ostensibly universal narrative conventions. She suggests it is
no accident that darkness signifies a threatening and violent predator whereas
whiteness signifies purity, princely qualities, and a (narrowly defined) womanhood "worthy" of rescue. Thus, despite its title, the first poem's primary focus
is the Mississippi mother's fate, guilt, desires, family, and future. Sickeningly,
it explores how "The fun was disturbed, then all but nullified / When the Dark
Villain was a blackish child" (76) rather than the "lecherous brute" (Harris, 26)
he was *supposed* to be, at least according to the dominant cultural mythology.

The Carolyn Bryant character's egocentric focus on the "hero" and "heroine"
of the "romance," and their spoiled "fun" and games, makes the victim, Emmett

Till, and his family disappear almost entirely. This disappearing act stems from "boomerang perception" (Spelman, *Inessential*, 12) wherein the "other" serves merely as a mirror back to oneself (Narayan, 138)—but not in a way that requires any accountability or reflexivity. Moreover, at the collective level, by shifting attention away from the murder victim and his mother and back to the "Fine Prince" and his wife, Brooks points to the possible dangers of characterizing Till's lynching a "national tragedy." As Elizabeth V. Spelman explains vis-à-vis the historical uses of a rhetoric of tragedy in the United States, framing slavery as democracy's "tragic flaw" all but erases the suffering of the victims by focusing instead on the mistakes and shortcomings of the perpetrators. "Slavery as tragedy" is a rhetorical vehicle by which the primary focus of attention once again becomes the founding fathers (and *their* tragic flaws and mistakes) rather than slaves' lived experience, silenced knowledge, and suppressed history. African Americans remain marginalized as historical agents whereas whites magically return to the center of attention as flawed but redeemable creators of democracy (*Fruits*, 34–58).

Brooks's implication is that, like tragedy's perverse function in maintaining a white-centered history and guilty national imagination, the ballad convention of the fair maiden, fine prince, and dark villain plays a similar role—hence the Mississippi mother's focus back to herself, her spoiled fun, and her own passive guilt. Determined not to participate in this poetic legacy, Brooks challenges prevailing "literary histories and traditions" (Smith, *Not Just*, xiv). Not only do these conventions uphold the virtues of the fine prince and fair maiden, they also stifle Bradley's and Till's stories, erasing the role of racial and gender domination in the nation's past and present. In Brooks's poems, therefore, the murder of Emmett Till is specific (such that he and his mother are both named in the second poem) and metonymic (hence the namelessness of all characters in the first poem)—the burning ("Bronzeville," 75), "scorching," the "hack[ing] down (unhorsed)," the "whimpering," "cramped cries" (77), and the endless blood demand that Till's individual story be remembered as well as the violent collective history behind it.

This long history of stifled stories and subjugated lives also helps to explain the brief and spare structure of "The Last Quatrain." Brooks's form emphasizes the "silences that structure the social hierarchy in which we live" (Smith, *Not Just*, 21)—the unspeakable crimes, the violent past that shapes our nation's present. In other words, it comes as no surprise that the second poem is comprised of ten short lines. Although also set in a kitchen, Emmett's mother's kitchen, a "red room" in Chicago's "windy grays" ("Last," 81), readers do not have access to any details of the mother's life or interior thoughts. Moreover, Brooks surrounds each line on the page with visual space: her use of white negative space surrounding sparse black lines highlights the racially structured silences, the absences in the story.

These large white spaces surrounding spare, short lines, considered alongside Brooks's calling the second poem a "quatrain"—when, in fact, it is not—suggest that she is writing against "a prevailing mode of being, a white frame of reference" (Anzaldúa, xxii). This "embedded contradiction" (Davies, 340) between the title and the form of the second poem, and the title (presence) and content (absence or peripheral lurking) in the first poem, illustrates that there are few genres or spaces in which black women can articulate their ideas. In other words, it symbolizes what Carole Boyce Davies describes as a "tension . . . between the limitations of spoken language and the possibility of expression" (346). Brooks points to how little has been heard from black women.

Simultaneously, through silence, Brooks indirectly calls to mind Bradley's *Chicago Defender* interviews with Payne. There, Bradley explains that "people wonder why I am so calm, and some even think that I am cold . . . No tears came, only a deep lonely feeling that time and space had crushed me" (227). Later, she tells Payne, "I am alone now . . . I am alone with my thoughts and my heart buried in a pine box underneath glass" (234). In an almost impressionistic manner, Brooks emphasizes Bradley's deep sadness and utter loneliness:

> She sits in a red room,
> > drinking black coffee.
> She kisses her killed boy.
> > And she is sorry. ("Last," 81)

Unlike the Carolyn Bryant character's wordy self-pity in the first poem, the brevity of the second poem evokes the Bradley character's grief, her sense of disembodiment and disconnection. This emptiness also suggests that no form is adequate to telling the story. Yet the inadequacy of form does not stem from the fact that Till's death is "unthinkable." To frame it as "unthinkable" potentially denies the historical ubiquitousness of lynching, reinforcing a "collective amnesia" (Mills, "White") of the "red prairie," or heartland soaked with blood, at the close of "The Last Quatrain of the Ballad of Emmett Till" (81).[5]

Instead, I interpret Brooks as implying that Bradley's story has been violently "annihilated"—like Till himself. As Dori Laub explains with regard to holocaust testimony, the "absence of an empathetic listener . . . who can hear the anguish . . . annihilates the story" (in Boler, 168). Thus, the starkness and silence in "The Last Quatrain of the Ballad of Emmett Till" underscore how the act of speaking and the reciprocity of being heard are not universally available and, in fact, belong to a long tradition of domination in which only certain stories and voices predominate. The double annihilation—of Till's body and of his mother's story, almost of her entire person, reduced to "Decapitated exclamation points" in the first poem ("Bronzeville," 80)—suggests that physical violence and epistemic or narrative violence are interdependent components of domination, the "one-two" punch of social control.

Blood on White Shoulders, Her Own Shoulders: Violence, Language, and Love

A key "contractual" feature of epistemologies of ignorance is an agreement to forget the ugly past and to ignore the problematic present. Brooks's poems work against the collective will to block out Till, for cognitive erasure goes hand in hand with his murder—a literal blocking or snuffing out. The omnipresent blood in both poems demands that Tills's murder be remembered, but not in a sensationalist way. Through countermemory, Brooks seeks to interrupt the ritual forgetting connected to ritual, collective violence. It is also significant that the blood, "a red ooze" that is "spreading darkly, thickly, slowly," begins to cover the Mississippi mother's "white shoulders" (79)—symbols of seduction and white femininity. Here, Brooks overtly links the romance and murder plots.

The red gash of Carolyn Bryant's lipstick (77),[6] the "lengthening red" hand imprint on the Bryants' baby's face (79), and the red of Till's spreading blood all culminate in the Fine Prince's suffocating kiss. His kiss is "close close"—so close that Brooks leaves out the comma—and "His mouth, wet and red, / So very, very, very red, / Closed over hers" (80). Both his wet red lips and her red lipstick evoke blood: their kiss seals the white, heterosexual contract and emphasizes how *both* Bryant characters are complicit in the murder. Brooks deromanticizes the romance plot and invokes the real-life courtroom scene when Bryant and Milam made a gross performance of kissing and groping their wives to "celebrate" their acquittal (Kempton, "2 Face," 107; Kilgallen, 106).

Additionally, Brooks suggests that language is part and parcel of the seeping "blood." She writes, "From the first it had been like a / Ballad. It had the beat inevitable. It had the blood. / A wildness cut up, and tied in little bunches" ("Bronzeville," 75). In the first poem, punctuation becomes decapitated, ballads have the regulatory "beat inevitable," and the pages are filled with allusions to tortured and murdered bodies—the "retaliatory killings" (Mills, *Racial*, 85) required to maintain the status quo. Brooks emphasizes that understanding race supremacy and violence requires understanding domestic coercion and the conventions of "romantic love." The "ballad" of chivalrous romance is completely intertwined with the story of Till's lynching—this ideology of love cannot be rescued. Language, metaphor, and narrative convention reflect and reinforce larger cultural narratives: stories and ballads, quatrains and sentences, verbs and punctuation are all sites of social acculturation, even control.

For example, in the first poem, the Mississippi mother learns in segregated schools the heterosexual romance ideology of passive white womanhood and of the perfect, supportive wife. She performs this part repeatedly, from hiding burnt bacon ("Bronzeville," 75) to putting on lipstick for her "prince" (77). Similarly, the Fine Prince has learned a vicious form of southern white masculinity, a role he plays out first by "Rushing" (76) to "hack down" and murder the Till character, then by hitting his child (78), and, finally, by grabbing his wife and kissing her violently (79–80). All that is left to the Till character is the role of predator—the Dark Villain. And all that remains for him, plot-wise, is mandatory death.

In this context, the word play of the "'maid mild'" (75) who was *made* mild is important: it points to the "subtle . . . ways racist societies shape subjectivities" (Aanerud, 75). The Mississippi mother is "the milk-white maid, the 'maid mild' / Of the ballad"—the "ballads they had set her to, in school" ("Bronzeville," 75). She learns to become, and find reward in being, the direct object of other people's verbs: she is, passively, "Pursued / By the Dark Villain. Rescued by the Fine Prince" (75), and, at the end, kissed by her husband even though "She heard no hoof-beat of the horse and saw no flash of the / shining steel" (80). Later, we learn about the Mississippi mother "that her composition / Had disintegrated" (77); apparently, she has nothing to do with this breakdown. Once again, the passive verb construction reinforces the notion that the Carolyn Bryant character is simply a blameless bystander, even when it comes to her own disintegration.

We see the holes in the fabric, the metaphysical threat to her person, as does she, but "she could think / Of no thread capable of the necessary / Sew-work"

(77). In all four cases (pursued, rescued, distintegrated, kissed), the Mississippi mother claims no agency, no role in the whole murder and acquittal. Linda Martín Alcoff argues that ignorance is a carefully structured part of oppression ("Are There"). Likewise, Brooks shows, through the Mississippi mother, a particular instance of structured ignorance. She demonstrates that language, grammar, and narrative help to make the unacceptable (lynching, murder) acceptable; simultaneously, she illustrates that part of the structuring pattern of willful ignorance, and part of its violence, is grammatical and narrative. Ignorance and opacity, violence and coercion, happen even at the level of the sentence, the verb tense, the "decapitated" punctuation.

She Did Not Scream. She Stood There: Complicity and the Labor of Ignorance

In addition to illustrating language's role in structured inequality, the first poem highlights the Mississippi Mother's "labor of ignorance" (Spelman, "Labor"); maintaining dominance and, simultaneously, denying responsibility for inequality, requires continual work. Brooks therefore documents the Mississippi mother's psychological and physical efforts at ignorance. For example, although passive verbs predominate, showing the Mississippi Mother to be apparently helpless and lacking in agency, Brooks occasionally uses active verbs to show how, in fact, the Carolyn Bryant character works hard to comply with all that she has been "set to." To make the racist romance plot work, she "hastened to hide" her burned bacon and prepared a perfect breakfast ("Bronzeville," 75), "made the babies sit in their places at the table," and, "before calling Him, she hurried / To the mirror with her comb and lipstick" (77).

Despite the impossibility of hiding the smell of burned bacon, the fact that she even tries to cover up her mistake reveals the depth of her investment in the role of the perfect wife / fair maiden. Similarly, by capitalizing "Him," Brooks suggests that the Mississippi mother still respects her man as if he were God. By ascribing total power to "Him," she can better deny her own role as a participant in the murder. Moreover, it is significant that the "lipstick necessity was something apart" from "Whatever she might feel or half-feel" (77), for the Carolyn Bryant character insists that "He must never conclude / That she had not been worth It" (77).

Here Brooks points to the Mississippi mother's complicity in two ways: first, by describing her "half-feeling" that "there was a something about the matter of the Dark / Villain" (76)—an incongruity that, remarkably, she cannot name—

and secondly, by capitalizing "It" in the Mississippi mother's head. The Bryant character cannot even bring herself to call Till's murder a murder—she diminishes its ostensible significance (via capitalization) by using an unclear referent. If she speaks the unspeakable, names the truth, she will have to face "It," so she doesn't. Consider also her thinking, appallingly, "He should have been older, perhaps" (76), as if the murder of the Till character would then be justifiable. A few lines later, we read that her "fun was . . . all but nullified / When the Dark Villain was a blackish child" (76). The fact that the "fun" was, passively, "all but" nullified suggests that the murder was still somewhat "fun"—as if it were all a game, not a brutal murder. In the next stanza, she thinks tentatively that "there *may* have been something / Ridiculous" (76, emphasis added) in the two large, white men killing "that little foe" (or, may not have been!), despite the fact that she "could not remember now what that foe had done / Against her, or if anything had been done" (77).

In other words, although she shows moments of uncertainty, which could be read as promising signs of change, glimmers of critical consciousness, the fact remains that she only "half-feels" any doubt and still reveres and performs well for Him. Brooks therefore reminds us "That, although the pattern prevailed, / The breaks were everywhere" (77). The pattern prevails in large part because of the Mississippi mother's willingness to make it continue. Even near the end of the first poem, she chooses complicity instead of resistance. For example, the "sickness" she feels when her husband kisses her occurs passively, for it "heaved within her" and "Pushed like a wall against her" (80). This disgust is not her own—it is akin to an alien force outside herself. Even when a "hatred for him burst into glorious flower, / And its perfume enclasped them—big, / Bigger than all magnolias" (80), she just stood there and "did not scream" (80). Although the hatred is "Bigger than all magnolias"—and hence larger than the state of Mississippi ("the magnolia state") and southern womanhood ("steel magnolias")—Brooks suggests that hatred alone is not enough: there must be outrage, action, and accountability, on an individual and collective level, for real change to occur, not tentative, pallid critiques, silent hatred, and guilty self-pity.

The Mississippi mother's chosen complicity, her continual labor of ignorance—standing there despite the hatred—is therefore "The last bleak news of the ballad" (80). Even when her doubts persist and grow, even when hatred bursts within her and sickness heaves in her body, she chooses quiet compliance—she chooses to make it appear that all is well. Here Brooks illustrates brilliantly what Audre Lorde would assert twenty years later: that "white women face the pitfall of being seduced into joining the oppressor under the pretense of sharing power" (118). These differences in position and asymmetries of power must be acknowledged in meaningful ways by white women if transformative coalitions across the lines of race and gender are to occur.

She Kisses Her Killed Boy: Strategic Resistance

Excoriating the Mississippi mother's role in maintaining white supremacist patriarchy is one way that Brooks's poems can be read as examples of political resistance. Even though the Carolyn Bryant character does not act out or resist, Brooks encourages her readers to do so: in critiquing the Mississippi mother, Brooks invites us to act differently. Brooks employs other tactics as a means of resistance. For instance, she ascribes the negative "Color of the paste in her paste-jar" ("Bronzeville," 79) to the Mississippi mother's white child and the positive "tint of pulled taffy" ("Last," 81) to Emmett's mother.

Brooks also uses reversal to implicitly challenge Carolyn Bryant's testimony. Thanks in large part to this testimony (before the judge, journalists, and public, but not the jury; see Metress, 89–97), prosecutors cast Till as a sexual predator who whistled at Carolyn Bryant and grabbed her so hard around the waist that she felt threatened. Brooks turns this tired trope of the sexually violent black male aggressor on its head. She suggests, instead, that it is the Fine Prince who is debased and threatening, for it is in *his* hands, the killing hands, that the Mississippi mother finds herself "Gripped" ("Bronzeville," 79). It is her husband who "followed her," who "whispered something to her . . . / About love, something about love and night and intention." It is he, not Till, who makes her feel "The fear, / Tying her as with iron," and it is readers who also find themselves afraid when "Suddenly she felt his hands upon her" (79).

Moreover, in contrast to Till's supposed "wolf-whistle," Brooks describes "the cramped cries, the little stuttering bravado" uttered by Till "in that barn" (77). Rather than raise the stereotypical specter of sexual aggression, she focuses on how Till was tortured and killed in the barn—his last cries, his last breath.[7] She ascribes predatory brutality, in terms of sexual and killing desire, to the Roy Bryant character. By suggesting that white masculinity is murderous, destructive, and dangerous, Brooks counters William Bradford Huie's influential, stereotypical, and inflammatory 1956 "exposé" about J. W. Milam, Roy Bryant, and Emmett Till in *Look* magazine.

In addition to using inversion and reversal, Brooks's juxtaposing the Mississippi mother and the Bronzeville mother is telling. Unlike the passive Mississippi mother, the Bronzeville mother is agential in the face of brutality. For example, in the first poem, the Bradley character hovers at the edges of white consciousness in the heart of the deep South: loitering ("Bronzeville," 75) and looking (80), she refuses to disappear. In the second poem, the Bronzeville mother's agency and resistance become clearer. The red wet kiss between the Mississippi mother and her husband is coercive, whereas "Emmett's mother" lovingly "Kisses her killed boy" ("Last," 81). Brooks names the fact of Till's murder here, unlike the indirect allusion to "It" by the Carolyn Bryant character, and the kiss itself signifies an act of love and resistance on Emmett's mother's part (for she would have been kissing her son's disfigured corpse).

In stark contrast to the Mississippi mother's acquiescence to her husband's kiss and all it stands for, Emmett's mother's kiss evokes her fight, in real life, against all efforts to cover up her son's story and, literally, his body. As is well known, Bradley refused to have her son buried by the sheriff in Mississippi. Instead, she brought him home to Chicago, where he lay in state in an open casket for the world to see—in defiance of the sheriff's order that his casket remain closed (Metress, 225; Williams, 43–44). She rebuffed all efforts to cast her son as the villain and instead showed that he was the victim of a gruesome murder. Brooks's two poems do the same.

Tactical juxtaposition, or apposing but not collapsing these two poems, helps Brooks to demonstrate how language and violence intimately interdepend, particularly within the conventions of the romance plot; to critique white privilege and willful ignorance; and to delineate the inadequacies of guilt and passive complicity when outrage and action are needed. Finally, Brooks's apposition allows the Bronzeville mother's resistance and courage to shine through. By having "The Last Quatrain" serve as the second in the pair of poems, Brooks gives Mamie Till Bradley, Emmett's mother, the last word.

AUTHOR'S NOTE

I would like to thank Professor Trudier Harris for first encouraging me to write about Brooks's poetry and for her words of advice which have continued to inspire me. I would also like to thank Christopher Metress and Harriet Pollack, as well as LSU Press's anonymous reviewers, for their insightful feedback.

NOTES

1. Brooks originally published these two poems in *The Bean Eaters*. All page references here refer to Brooks's 1963 *Selected Poems*.

2. For an excellent discussion of the intersectional politics of gender, race, and sexuality, see McBride.

3. For example, see Adams.

4. For a more detailed discussion of rhetorical space and the politics of speech, see Code.

5. In arguing that Till's lynching is not "unthinkable" or, rather, is thinkable, I do *not* mean that I condone or accept it. Moreover, I acknowledge that to name such an event unthinkable could signify its status as a "limit event" (La Capra, 133), or an "excess" of trauma (Boler, 166) beyond easy comprehensibility. I concur with this analysis within trauma theory of the "unthinkable" but do not agree with the everyday connotation of "unthinkability," which often entails a refusal to remember how very ordinary, thinkable, and doable such gross acts of violence toward other persons are.

6. Her lipstick in the poem evokes her noticeable lipstick in the courtroom. For example, journalist Murray Kempton describes Bryant's "lower jaw scarred with lipstick" ("Baby," 54).

7. She also alludes to the fact that he had a speech impediment (which could account for a stuttering whistle-like sound). See Adams, 218.

WORKS CITED

Aanerud, Rebecca. "Thinking Again: *This Bridge Called My Back* and the Challenge to Whiteness." In *This Bridge We Call Home,* edited by Gloria E. Anzaldúa and Analouise Keating, 69–77. New York: Routledge, 2002.

Adams, Olive Arnold. Excerpts from *Time Bomb: Mississippi Exposed and the Full Story of Emmett Till.* In Metress, 214–24.

Alcoff, Linda Martín. "Are There Epistemically Disadvantaged Identities?" Presented at the Ethics and Epistemologies of Ignorance Conference, State College, PA, 26 March 2004.

Anzaldúa, Gloria E. "Haciendo caras, una entrada." In *Making Face, Making Soul Haciendo Caras,* edited by Gloria E. Anzaldúa, xv–xxviii. San Francisco: Aunt Lute, 1990.

Boler, Megan. "The Risks of Empathy: Interrogating Multiculturalism's Gaze." In *Feeling Power: Emotions and Education,* 155–74. New York: Routledge, 1999.

Bradley, Mamie Till. From "Mamie Bradley's Untold Story," as told to Ethel Payne, *Chicago Defender,* April–June, 1956. In Metress, 226–35.

Brooks, Gwendolyn. "A Bronzeville Mother Loiters in Mississippi. Meanwhile, a Mississippi Mother Burns Bacon." In *Selected Poems,* 75–80. New York: Harper and Row, 1963.

———. "The Last Quatrain of the Ballad of Emmett Till." In *Selected Poems,* 81. New York: Harper and Row, 1963.

Code, Lorraine. *Rhetorical Spaces: Essays on Gendered Locations.* New York: Routledge, 1995.

Davies, Carole Boyce. "Other Tongues: Gender, Language, Sexuality and the Politics of Location." In *Women, Knowledge, and Reality: Explorations in Feminist Philosophy,* 2d ed., edited by Ann Garry and Marilyn Pearsall, 339–52. New York: Routledge, 1996.

Harris, Trudier. *Exorcising Blackness: Historical and Literary Lynchings and Burning Rituals.* Bloomington: Indiana University Press, 1984.

Huie, William Bradford. "The Shocking Story of Approved Killing in Mississippi." *Look,* 24 January 1956. In Metress, 200–208.

———. "What's Happened to the Emmett Till Killers?" *Look,* 22 January 1957. In Metress, 208–13.

Keating, Analouise. "Forging El Mundo Zurdo: Changing Ourselves, Changing the World." In *This Bridge We Call Home,* edited by Gloria E. Anzaldúa and Analouise Keating, 519–30. New York: Routledge, 2002.

Kempton, Murray. "The Baby Sitter." *New York Post,* 20 September 1955. In Metress, 53–55.

———. "2 Face Trial as 'Whistle' Kidnapers—Due to Post Bond and Go Home." *New York Post,* 25 September 1955. In Metress, 107–11.

Kilgallen, James L. "Defendants Receive Handshakes, Kisses." *Memphis Commercial Appeal,* 24 September 1955. In Metress, 104–7.

Lorde, Audre. "Age, Race, Class, and Sex: Women Redefining Difference." In *Sister Outsider: Essays and Speeches,* 114–23. Freedom, CA: Crossing Press, 1984.

McBride, Dwight A. "Can the Queen Speak? Racial Essentialism, Sexuality, and the Problem of Authority." In *Black Men on Race, Gender, and Sexuality: A Critical Reader,* edited by Devon W. Carbado, 253–75. New York: NYU Press, 1999.

Metress, Christopher, ed. *The Lynching of Emmett Till: A Documentary Narrative.* Charlottesville: University of Virginia Press, 2002.

Mills, Charles W. *The Racial Contract.* Ithaca: Cornell University Press, 1997.

———. "White Ignorance." Presented at the Ethics and Epistemologies of Ignorance Conference, State College, PA, 26 March 2004.

Molina, Papusa. "Recognizing, Accepting and Celebrating Our Differences." In *Making Face, Making Soul Haciendo Caras,* edited by Gloria E. Anzaldúa, 326–31. San Francisco: Aunt Lute, 1990.

Narayan, Uma. *Dislocating Cultures: Identities, Traditions, and Third World Feminism.* New York: Routledge, 1997.

Ottley, Roi. "Southern Style." *Chicago Defender,* 8 October 1955. In Metress, 131–33.

Smith, Valerie. "Black Feminist Theory and the Representation of the 'Other.'" 1989. In *The Woman That I Am: The Literature and Culture of Contemporary Women of Color,* edited by D. Soyini Madison, 671–87. New York: St. Martin's, 1994.

———. *Not Just Race, Not Just Gender: Black Feminist Readings.* New York: Routledge, 1998.

Spelman, Elizabeth V. *Fruits of Sorrow: Framing Our Attention to Suffering.* Boston: Beacon, 1997.

———. *Inessential Woman: Problems of Exclusion in Feminist Thought.* Boston: Beacon, 1988.

———. "On the Labor of Ignorance." Presented at the Ethics and Epistemologies of Ignorance Conference, State College, PA, 26 March 2004.

Violet, Indigo. "Linkages: A Personal-Political Journey with Feminist-of-Color Politics." In *This Bridge We Call Home,* edited by Gloria E. Anzaldúa and Analouise Keating, 486–94. New York: Routledge, 2002.

Williams, Juan. *Eyes on the Prize: America's Civil Rights Years, 1954–1965.* Introduction by Julian Bond. New York: Viking Penguin, 1987.

IT COULD HAVE BEEN MY SON

Maternal Empathy in Gwendolyn Brooks's and Audre Lorde's Till Poems

LAURA DAWKINS

In *History and Memory in African-American Culture,* Robert O'Meally and Geneviève Fabre describe the French historian Pierre Nora's concept of *lieux de mémoire*—"sites of memory"—as "products of [the] interaction between history and memory, of the interplay between the personal and the collective" (7). According to Nora, "*Lieux de mémoire* originate with the sense that there is no spontaneous memory, that we must deliberately create archives . . . maintain anniversaries . . . pronounce eulogies . . . [W]e buttress our identities upon such bastions" (289). Elaborating upon Nora's thesis, Werner Sollors maintains that such "sites of memory" gain particular importance in minority cultures, since "what is called 'memory' (and Nora's *lieux de mémoire*) may become a form of counterhistory that challenges the false generalizations in exclusionary 'History'" (O'Meally and Fabre, 8). Within African American culture, certainly, the "will to remember . . . to limit forgetfulness" has produced a "commemorative vigilance" (O'Meally and Fabre, 7) in the form of poetry, fiction, drama, essays, speeches, and sermons that re-create or interpret crucial events in black history. These "sites of memory" not only bear lasting witness to the African American past but also serve as a corrective to narrowly focused mainstream accounts of the American heritage.

Perhaps no single incident in African American history has inspired such "commemorative vigilance" as the tragedy of Emmett Till. Although Till's story has generated numerous literary treatments by African American authors across the country,[1] one of the earliest and most powerful responses was Gwendolyn Brooks's "A Bronzeville Mother Loiters in Mississippi. Meanwhile, A Mississippi Mother Burns Bacon" (1960). The poem daringly focuses on neither the lynched teenager nor the outraged black community but on Carolyn Bryant, the young southern wife of one of the boy's killers and the ostensible target of Till's alleged "wolf whistle." Twenty-one years after the publication of Brooks's poem, the black poet and activist Audre Lorde conversely chose to center her haunting "Afterimages" (1981) on an African American speaker who mourns Till's death and determines to "withhold pity" for the wife of Till's murderer. Yet the two poems are linked in their preoccupation with Bryant's identity both as the mother of two sons and the wife of a child-killer. If "A Bronzeville Mother" records the white mother's devastating realization of her husband's capacity for violence against a powerless child, "Afterimages" imagines the costs of such knowledge for this mother over the years since Till's death. More importantly, "A Bronzeville Mother" and "Afterimages" suggest that motherhood potentially creates a bond transcending racial and cultural differences. Initially resisting her tie with Till's mother—the "Other Woman," Mamie Till Bradley—Brooks's white persona ultimately acknowledges their shared vulnerability and suppressed anger, just as Lorde's black speaker moves toward a recognition of her empathic connection with the defeated white mother for whom she at first denied compassion.

According to Joanne V. Gabbin, no other major American poet besides Brooks "has given such consistent treatment to [the] themes [of] motherhood and children" (263). "A Bronzeville Mother," one of the poet's best-known treatments of these themes, was sparked—as Brooks herself acknowledged—by her deeply personal response to the story of Emmett Till. In a 1967 interview with Roy Newquist, Brooks explained that the Till murder outraged her maternal sensibilities and led her to speculate about the white mother's response to her husband's violence:

> I wrote about the Emmett Till murder because it got to me. I was appalled like every civilized being was appalled. I was especially touched because my son was fourteen at the time, and I couldn't help but think that it could have been him down there if I'd sent him to Mississippi. That was a very personal expression. I tried to imagine how the young woman, the one who was whistled at, felt after the murder and after the trial, after her sight of the boy's mother. What it was like to live with a man who had spilled blood. I imagined that she would have certain cringing feelings when he touched her—at least I would. (Gayles, 35–36)

Inhabiting the consciousness of Carolyn Bryant as she broods upon Till's murder, Brooks re-creates the terror and revulsion that perhaps lurked behind the young woman's public pose of loyalty to her husband. The poet imagines Bryant as an effaced and passive figure, who "say[s] not a word" (79) during the course of the poem, yet who silently wrestles with the horror of her husband's act, painfully—and fruitlessly—attempting to reconcile the grim reality of child murder with the romantic southern mythology ingrained in her since girlhood.

As Gertrude Reif Hughes has demonstrated, Brooks's poem is an "anti-ballad" that traces the white woman's bitter awakening to the "killing romance" that has shaped her life (193). Casting herself as the "maid mild" and her husband as the "Fine Prince" who rescues her from the "Dark Villain," the woman initially believes that she can place the event within a satisfying artistic frame:

> From the first it had been like a
> Ballad. It had the beat inevitable. It had the blood.
> A wildness cut up, and tied in little bunches.
> Like the four-line stanzas of the ballads she had never quite
> Understood—the ballads they had set her to, in school. (75)

Yet, in contemplating Till's murder, the wife continually runs up against rifts and contradictions that threaten the shapeliness of the reassuring "composition" she has constructed: the "Dark Villain" is not a sinister stalker of "undisputed breadth, undisputed height," but a "blackish child / Of fourteen, with eyes still too young to be dirty, / And a mouth too young to have lost every reminder / Of its infant softness" (76). Acknowledging that "the breaks were everywhere," that "her composition / Had disintegrated" (77) under the pressure of reality pushing against the borders of her narrative frame, the wife is forced to relinquish her faith not only in the "Fine Prince" but also in the chivalric myths of her homeland.

Once the wife's consoling narrative has collapsed, her husband's image metamorphoses in her eyes from "Prince" to predator. Accordingly, when her young son misbehaves at the breakfast table and the "Fine Prince lean[s] across the table and slap[s] / The small and smiling criminal," she transposes the image of Till's mutilated face on to her own child's visage: "She could think only of blood. / Surely her baby's cheek / Had disappeared, and in its place, surely, / Hung a heaviness, a lengthening red, a red that had no end." Similarly, when her husband kisses her, murmuring "something about love and night and intention," she sees "no flash of the shining steel," but instead "a red ooze . . . seeping, spreading darkly, thickly, slowly." "Gripped in the claim" of her husband's hands, the wife succumbs to the same coercive force wielded against the adolescent black child. Ironically, the "Fine Prince" who had ostensibly "protected" her from Till assumes the role of sexual intimidator himself. As "his mouth, wet and red, / So very, very, very red, / Closed over hers," the mother implicitly links her own destiny as the killer's wife—her "fear / Tying her as with iron"—to Till's fate as a bound, doomed captive (78).

Significantly, the young white woman identifies not only with the victimized black child but also with that child's grief-stricken mother. She cannot dispel her image of the bereaved Mamie Till Bradley:

> Then a sickness heaved within her. The courtroom Coca-Cola,
> The courtroom beer and hate and sweat and drone,
> Pushed like a wall against her. She wanted to bear it,
> But his mouth would not go away and neither would the
> Decapitated exclamation points in that Other Woman's eyes. (80)

The white woman's attempt to distance herself from the black mother, evidenced by her mental reference to Bradley as "that Other Woman," will not make her memory of the grieving mother's eyes "go away," nor will it efface her unwilling recognition that, like the black mother, she has no power to shield her sons from the violence of the "Fine Prince": "The children were whimpering now. / Such bits of tots. And she, their mother, / Could not protect them" (78). Believing that "the Hand" of her husband has become a deadly weapon menacing her children, the white mother's maternal terror and sense of helplessness implicitly connect her with the bereft black mother, whose stunned gaze—her pupils like "decapitated exclamation points"—continues to haunt her. Indeed, the title of Brooks's poem tellingly links the two mothers in postures of impotence: the "Bronzeville mother" Bradley "loiters in Mississippi," her courtroom testimony useless in securing justice for her slain son, while the "Mississippi mother" Bryant "burns bacon" as she dutifully (if distractedly) prepares breakfast for her child-killer husband.

The white mother's subtle alignment with the black mother insidiously undermines the husband's self-proclaimed invincibility. Unaware that his wife's idealized image of him has been irrevocably shattered, the husband swaggers for his wife's benefit, declaring his own and the South's triumph:

> Still, it had been fun to show those intruders
> A thing or two. To show that snappy-eyed mother
> That sassy, Northern, brown-black—
> Nothing could stop Mississippi.
> He knew that. Big fella
> Knew that.
> And, what was so good, Mississippi knew that.
> They could send in their petitions, and scar
> Their newspapers with bleeding headlines. Their governors
> Could appeal to Washington . . . (78)

Even as the "Fine Prince" crows about his acquittal, his "maid mild" implicitly reaches a different verdict. Her disturbed thoughts while preparing breakfast and her revulsion within her husband's embrace culminate in a final silent repudiation of her "protector":

> She did not scream.
> She stood there.
> But a hatred for him burst into glorious flower.
> And its perfume enclasped them—big,
> Bigger than all magnolias. (79)

As the miasma of the white mother's hatred "enclasp[s]" the couple, overwhelming the seductive scent of "magnolias"—the masking "perfume" of southern mythology—the last components of the wife's unstable "composition" crumble.

Described not as a corrosive and injurious emotion but as a "glorious flower," the wife's hatred for her husband signals her blossoming awareness—the potentially redemptive awakening of her social consciousness. Indeed, the "ballad" of one woman's emergent recognition of southern brutality and injustice parallels the dawning of national awareness for which Till's murder was a catalyst.[2] In Brooks's poem, maternity creates a bridge between "Bronzeville" and "Mississippi," between the bereaved black mother and the white mother who fears for her children's safety at the hands of a violent husband. Although Till's mother is physically absent from "A Bronzeville Mother," her voiceless grief links her with the similarly silent but mentally rebellious Carolyn Bryant. The poet suggests that maternal empathy, providing a counterforce "bigger than" the white patriarchal power that it contests, will ultimately find a voice in the political arena.

Tellingly, the penultimate stanza of "A Bronzeville Mother" contains an ambiguous pronoun that serves to confuse—and fuse—the identities of the black
mother and the white mother. The wife of Till's killer, visualizing the nightmarish courtroom scene of "beer and hate and sweat and drone," remembers
"Decapitated exclamation points in that Other Woman's eyes," an image immediately followed by the lines, "She did not scream. / She stood there. / But
a hatred for him burst into glorious flower" (79). Does the pronoun "she" refer
to the "Other Woman" Mamie Till Bradley or to the white mother haunted by
the black woman's eyes during the trial? The ambiguity underscores that Till's
mother and the mother of Roy Bryant's own children are victims of this man's
brutality. The "hatred" that "burst[s] into glorious flower" thus implicitly encompasses the two women, constructing an empathic bond founded upon a
fierce maternal passion.

Insisting on the submerged but powerful connections between the white
mother Carolyn Bryant and the black mother Mamie Till Bradley, "A Bronzeville
Mother" prefigures "Afterimages," a late twentieth-century work in which Audre
Lorde—reversing perspectives—centers upon a black woman's reluctant recognition of her empathic ties with an abused white mother. Lorde, a writer
whom Brooks admired, shared her precursor's preoccupation with themes of
motherhood and children, and specifically viewed the reverberating effects of
Till's violent death through the lens of an African American maternal figure.[3] Set
many years after the lynching, "Afterimages" portrays a black female speaker's
anguished memories of the incident as well as her emotionally fraught present-
day view of a haggard Carolyn Bryant. The lingering horror of Till's fate haunts
the speaker—who calls Till her "son"—and the beaten-down white mother
whose husband took the boy's life.

A self-proclaimed "Black, Lesbian, Feminist, warrior, poet, mother doing my
work," the writer and activist insisted throughout her career on the connections
and the differences among her multiple roles. Acknowledging that she "had to
learn to hold on to all the parts of me that served me, in spite of the pressure
to express only one to the exclusion of all others," Lorde clearly recognized and
consistently avoided the constraints of single-axis identity politics. Many of her
poems record her self-conscious struggle to integrate "all the parts" that consti-
tute an evolving sense of self. However, Lorde frequently assumes the persona of
a mother as a way to speak across differences, to span the gulf between disparate
identities. "Now That I Am Forever with Child," Lorde's most celebrated poem
about motherhood, describes the speaker's childbirth as the creation of a "new

world" (8), an image that encompasses not only the emerging infant but also the new mother's enlarged consciousness. Yet, biological motherhood, as Lorde makes clear in several works, is not a prerequisite for a maternal perspective; indeed, the speakers of her poems often serve as "symbolic mothers" of the individuals or groups they address. Drawing upon the African American tradition of "othermothering" or "symbolic kinship," Lorde envisions a maternal relation to the world as a potentially redemptive means of communicating "the knowledge of our real connectedness, arcing across our differences" (*Sister Outsider*, 133).

Lorde frequently invokes the figure of the "Black mother"—whom she equates with the poet—as a trope for empathy or emotional attunement:

> The white fathers told us: I think, therefore I am. The Black mother within each of us—the poet—whispers in our dreams: I feel, therefore I can be free. (*Sister Outsider*, 38)

> The Black mother who is the poet exists in every one of us. (100)

> I personally believe that the Black mother exists more in women; yet she is the name for a humanity that men are not without. But they have taken a position against that piece of themselves, and it is a world position, a position throughout time. (101)

Restricted neither by race nor gender, the identity of the Black mother, as Lorde defines it, functions within any individual who engages empathically with other human beings. Although Lorde affirms that a maternal relation to the world is not a race-specific perspective, since the Black mother "exists in every one of us," she nevertheless draws on historical precedent to connect an all-inclusive maternal engagement with African and African American ideologies of motherhood—specifically, the concepts of "symbolic kin" and "othermothering."

In *Black Feminist Thought*, Patricia Hill Collins has demonstrated that, in African American culture, "fluid and changing boundaries often distinguish biological mothers from other women who care for children . . . othermothers—women who assist bloodmothers by sharing mothering responsibilities—traditionally have been central to the institution of Black motherhood . . . In African-American communities these women-centered networks of community-based child care often extend beyond the boundaries of biologically related individuals and include 'fictive kin'" (119–20). As Herbert Gutman has documented in *The Black*

Family in Slavery and Freedom, the "othermother" tradition was an essential adaptive strategy for African Americans during enslavement and afterwards. Gutman maintains that the creation of surrogate kin groups among violently disrupted black families began with the Middle Passage: "African slaves cut off from very different West African social settings continued to view kinship as the normal idiom of social relations, and on slave ships, according to Orlando Patterson, it was customary for children to call their parents' shipmates 'uncle' and 'aunt' and even for adults 'to look upon each other's children mutually as their own'" (217). Gutman explains that "kin titles" among unrelated slaves "bound them to fictive kinsmen and kinswomen, preparing them in the event that sale or death separated them from parents and blood relations" (219). The development of quasi-familial relations thus served to "further group solidarity" and to "order a community regularly disordered by the choices owners made" (222).

Contending, "We are [all] jointly responsible for the care and raising of the young," Lorde affirms the tradition of "symbolic kinship" as an essential ideal in twentieth-century American society as well. In several poems, she adopts the persona of "symbolic mother" in relation to black child-victims of racial hatred. In "Power," for example, the poet refers to Clifford Glover, a ten-year-old African American boy shot by a white police officer, as "my dying son"(215); similarly, the speaker of "New York City 1970" calls the four little girls killed in the Birmingham church bombing "my children" (102). In "A Woman / Dirge for Wasted Children," a poem dedicated to Clifford Glover, the speaker claims a maternal connection that transcends temporal boundaries: "Centuries of wasted children / warred and whored and slaughtered / anoint me guardian for life" (228). For Lorde, the African American mother's knowledge of her children's endangerment within a racist society imbues her with the responsibility to battle racial oppression on behalf of all the world's children. Whereas traditional Western societies encourage mothers to narrow their loyalties and limit their public role, the black woman's experience of motherhood—whether biological or symbolic—necessarily expands her global awareness and redefines her authority within the community. The "Black mother in all of us," therefore, represents attentiveness to others' pain and an active engagement with issues of social injustice—one's internalized awareness of what black motherhood has historically encompassed.

"Afterimages" centers upon a black maternal figure's intense moral conflict as she attempts to articulate her response to Emmett Till's murder. Declaring that, when Till's mutilated body was thrown into a Mississippi river, he was "baptized my son forever" (340), the poet assumes the persona of a "symbolic mother" as a strategy by which to legitimize her right to speak and establish the authenticity of her emotional engagement. By claiming the authority to mourn and memorialize the murdered child, the mother-poet distances herself from a society that either "forgets" historical child-victims or else sensationalizes their stories. Even as she defines her distance from these disengaged spectators, however, the poet scrutinizes her own motives for dwelling on Till's tragedy, and struggles to find an appropriate and efficacious response to his suffering. The poem records an intensive process of self-examination as the speaker assesses her complex and evolving relationship to a lost child whom she claims as her own.

Perhaps forestalling charges of poetic vampirism—a feeding on others' pain as material for poetry—the speaker compares her "hungry eyes" with "dragon-fish that learn / to live upon whatever they must eat" (339). Self-reflexively interrogating her own enterprise as a writer, the poet suggests that she can neither construct nor speak about other, more nourishing visions because these violent, nightmarish images are the food she has been given, the reality she inhabits. Although she separates her own meditation on Till's murder from graphic tabloid descriptions and photographs of the young boy's mutilated body, the poet nevertheless laments that her visual image of a "black boy hacked into a murderous lesson" has become a recurring nightmare, "recalled in me forever / like a lurch of earth on the edge of sleep / etched into my vision":

> His broken body is the afterimage of my 21st year
> when I walked through a northern summer
> my eyes averted
> from each corner's photographies
> newspapers protest posters magazines
> Police Story, Confidential, True
> the avid insistence of detail
> pretending insight or information
> the length of gash across the dead boy's loins
> his grieving mother's lamentation
> the severed lips, how many burns
> his gouged out eyes
> sewed shut upon the screaming covers
> louder than life
> all over

the veiled warning, the secret relish
of a black child's mutilated body
fingered by street-corner eyes
bruise upon livid bruise (340–41)

Revealing an intense moral revulsion against media treatments of Till's murder, the poet indicates that the journalists' motives are exploitative—an appeal to a voyeuristic public for commercial gain—and implicitly racist, uncovering the white media's desire to control the black population through horrific cautionary tales ("veiled warnings"). Significantly, the speaker draws attention to her geographical location ("I walked through a northern summer"), perhaps to suggest that northern journalists depicting southern barbarity are ironically complicit in the racial violence they expose: they offer forth Till's body in lurid photographs to be "fingered" and covertly "relish[ed]" by "street-corner eyes."

In *Regarding the Pain of Others*, Susan Sontag maintains, "there is shame as well as shock in looking at the close-up of a real horror. Perhaps the only people with the right to look at images of suffering of this extreme order are those who could do something to alleviate it . . . or those who could learn from it. The rest of us are voyeurs, whether or not we mean to be" (42). Indeed, Sontag continues, "Most depictions of tormented, mutilated bodies do arouse a prurient interest . . . Images of the repulsive can also allure" (95). The poet of "Afterimages," claiming that "wherever I looked that summer / I learned to be at home with children's blood / with savored violence / with pictures of black broken flesh / used, crumpled, and discarded" (341), similarly suggests that consumers of tabloid journalism during the summer of Till's murder assumed a cannibalistic relation to the dead child, devouring gruesome newspaper images with their eyes before crumpling up and discarding them, implicitly from mind as well as sight. Stumbling across these abandoned newspapers as she "walked through a northern summer," unable always to "avert" her eyes, the poet—unlike the casual consumers who throw the "used" papers on the street—becomes permanently haunted by the battered face of the child victim.

Yet how can the speaker, recording this disturbing image for the reader—recalling the "gouged out eyes," the "severed lips," and the "gash across the dead boy's loins"—separate herself from the voyeurs she deplores? How can she ensure that her own relation to Till is not vampirish, that she is not using an historical atrocity as food for her poetry, gaining an empty aesthetic object (the poem) from a young boy's suffering? The poet's anxiety about her own motives for dwelling on Till's murder, evidenced by her early comparison of her poetic vision to the dragonfish that "learns to live upon whatever it must eat," also registers in the closing stanzas, in which she returns to the image of the adaptable dragonfish in order to explain her ability to survive and write about "the horrors we are living / with tortured lungs / adapting to breathe blood" (342).

However, the most effective means by which the speaker defines the distance between her own response to Till's lynching and that of the "street-corner" voyeurs is by establishing a maternal relation to the murdered boy. An inescapable part of her historical legacy as an African American woman, Emmett Till's tragedy reinforces the poet's sense of symbolic kinship with victims of racial violence:

> I inherited Jackson, Mississippi.
> For my majority it gave me Emmett Till
> his 15 years puffed out like bruises
> on plump boy-cheeks
> his only Mississippi summer
> whistling a 21-gun salute to Dixie
> as a white girl passed him in the street
> and he was baptized my son forever
> in the midnight waters of the Pearl. (340)

By claiming the mutilated child as her "son," the narrator bridges the gulf between poet-spectator and victim, and validates her right to speak of Till's unspeakable fate. As the boy's "mother," the poet assumes the roles of public mourner and guardian of Till's memory, "forever" bearing witness to her maternal loss.

Yet the complexities of the poet's self-defined identifications don't end there. More than half the lines of "Afterimages" focus not on the poet's memories of the summer that Till was murdered but upon her recollections of another summer and another suffering figure, that of a white woman left destitute by a devastating flood:

> The Pearl River floods through the streets of Jackson
> A Mississippi summer televised.
> Trapped houses kneel like sinners in the rain
> a white woman climbs from her roof to a passing boat

her fingers tarry for a moment on the chimney
now awash
tearless and no longer young, she holds
a tattered baby's blanket in her arms.
In a flickering afterimage of the nightmare rain
a microphone
thrust up against her flat bewildered words
    "we jest come from the bank yestiddy
    borrowing money to pay the income tax
    now everything's gone. I never knew
    it could be so hard."
Despair weighs down her voice like Pearl River mud
caked around the edges (339–40)

The speaker reveals early in the poem that the images of "a black boy hacked into a murderous lesson" and "a white woman [who] stands bereft and empty" have become "fused" in her mind; during the remainder of the poem, she teases out—and complicates—the connections between these two figures. The poet implicitly identifies the working-class southern white woman with Carolyn Bryant. Imagining that the Pearl River has avenged Till's murder by striking back at this woman whose "costly honor" was protected at the expense of the boy's life, the poet grimly approves the river's "muddy judgment" and accordingly "withholds pity" (341) for the despairing woman whom she believes is indirectly responsible for her "son"'s death. The "fused images" of Till's mutilated body and the woman "adrift in the ruins of her honor" form a parable of cosmic punishment that becomes "etched into [the poet's] visions."

However, "Afterimages" clearly records a process of emotional struggle on the speaker's part as she witnesses the woman's pain. By assuming a maternal role toward the child-victim, the poet also opens herself to an identification with the sorrowing white mother, whose "tow-headed children hurl themselves against her / hanging from her coat like mirrors" (340). She acknowledges that "the white girl besmirched by Emmett's whistle" was "never allowed her own tongue" (342), and she recognizes that this "protected" white woman is also a victim of the child-killer's violence. When the woman attempts to speak of her pain, her husband "with ham-like hands pulls her aside / snarling, 'She ain't got nothing more to say!' / and that lie hangs in his mouth / like a shred of rotting meat" (340). Silenced, the woman "stands adrift" as the "man with an executioner's face / pulls her away"; while she "wrings her hands" helplessly, the man, in an image that recalls Brooks's portrait of the "Fine Prince" with "his hands upon" his wife, lays claim to her children: "crying and frightened / her tow-headed children cluster / like little mirrors of despair / their father's hands upon them" (342). The speaker joins the images of Till and the white woman again in the last stanza, linking "the ghost of a black boy / whistling" with the woman who "measures her life's damage"; however, the poem's final image of a woman who "begins to weep" (342) is not racially marked, inviting the reader's question: is the weeping woman the grief-stricken speaker—Till's symbolic mother—or the "bereft and empty" white woman? As in "A Bronzeville Mother," the two women have become "fused" into one keening figure at the poem's conclusion, suggesting a potentially healing empathic identification between the black mother and the white mother.

To be sure, empathic identification between women—as Lorde insists in another context—should not obscure one's recognition of the differences among forms of oppression: "Some problems we share as women, some we do not. You [white women] fear your children will grow up to join the patriarchy and testify against you, we [black women] fear our children will be dragged from a car and shot down in the street, and you will turn your backs upon the reasons they are dying" (*Sister Outsider*, 119). The white woman whose husband claims her children and authoritatively silences her inhabits a different realm of suffering from the black mother whose son has been "hacked into a murderous lesson." Yet Lorde contends that women must develop "patterns for relating across our human differences as equals," differences that have been "misnamed and misused in the service of separation and confusion." In "our world," Lorde continues, "divide and conquer must become define and empower." Coalition-building across differences ideally creates not a fusion of identities but a "mutual empowerment":

I am a lesbian woman of Color whose children eat regularly because I work in a university. If their full bellies make me fail to recognize my commonality with a woman of Color whose children do not eat because she cannot find work, or who has no children because her insides are rotted from home abortions and sterilization; if I fail to recognize the lesbian who chooses not to have children, the woman who remains closeted because her homophobic community is her only life support, the woman who chooses silence instead of another death, the woman who is terrified lest my anger trigger the explosion of hers; if I fail to recognize them as other faces of myself, then I am contributing not only to each of their oppressions but also to my own, and the anger which stands between us then must be used for clarity and mutual empowerment, not for evasion by guilt or for further separation. I am not free while any woman is unfree, even when her shackles are very different from my own. (*Sister Outsider*, 132–33)

Reflecting the essayist Lorde's progression from defining differences to building coalitions, the speaker of "Afterimages" moves from a separation of herself from the white woman's pain to recognition that she (the poet) and the white mother are connected through their maternal emotions. The indeterminacy of the weeping woman's identity at the end of the poem compels the reader to view her as a raceless symbol of female grief, of "ancient and familiar sorrows."

Maternity in "Afterimages," as in Brooks's "A Bronzeville Mother," heals the breach between divided sensibilities. The historical legacy of "symbolic motherhood" in African and African American communities functions in Lorde's poetry as a compelling metaphor for an inclusive empathy extending beyond one's home and one's community to encompass oppressed peoples across the globe. If, "for the embattled / there is no place / that cannot be / home / nor is" ("School Note," 217), then the "Black mother in all of us" must define the entire world as her "home front" from which to battle for human rights—even while she recognizes that no place can truly be "home" until social injustice is eradicated. Like Brooks, Lorde suggests that motherhood provides a lens through which disparate perspectives can become a unitary vision. For both poets, the brutal murder of a young black boy in 1955 became a "site of memory" that stirred maternal outrage and inspired powerful poetic meditations. Every mother's nightmare, the story of Emmett Till demands "commemorative vigilance" and serves as a call to action among "symbolic mothers" worldwide. Certainly, "A Bronzeville Mother" and "Afterimages" not only bear witness to a historical tragedy but also testify to the empathic power of the awakened maternal consciousness.

NOTES

1. See Christopher Metress, "No Justice, No Peace," for a valuable discussion of African American literary treatments of the Emmett Till case. His *The Lynching of Emmett Till* contains a selection of primary texts about the Till lynching and aftermath, including a generous sampling of literary works.

2. As Ruth Feldstein and others have noted, the outrage generated by the Emmett Till case served as a spark for the civil rights movement: "The political mobilization of blacks that the open-casket funeral and subsequent rallies helped generate was neither local nor short-term . . . The world did see and the 'war on Dixie' did escalate. As the famous and the ordinary alike construct their own memories of that period, the case often figures as a pivotal moment" (108).

3. In an interview with Haki Madhubuti in 1974, reprinted in Gayles, *Conversations with Gwendolyn Brooks,* Brooks stated: "I admire and respect Audre Lorde. Her work many Black people find exceedingly difficult. And so a lot of our people are not going to buy her books. But she's an excellent poet" (80).

WORKS CITED

Brooks, Gwendolyn. "A Bronzeville Mother Loiters in Mississippi. Meanwhile, A Mississippi Mother Burns Bacon." In *Selected Poems,* 77–80. New York: Harper, 1963.

Collins, Patricia Hill. *Black Feminist Thought: Knowledge, Consciousness, and the Politics of Empowerment.* New York: Allen and Unwin, 1990.

Feldstein, Ruth. *Motherhood in Black and White: Race and Sex in American Liberalism.* Ithaca: Cornell University Press, 2000.

Gabbin, Joanne V. "Blooming in the Whirlwind: The Early Poetry of Gwendolyn Brooks." In *The Furious Flowering of African American Poetry,* edited by Joanne V. Gabbin, 252–73. Charlottesville: University Press of Virginia, 1999.

Gayles, Gloria Wade, ed. *Conversations with Gwendolyn Brooks.* Jackson: University Press of Mississippi, 2003.

Gutman, Herbert George. *The Black Family in Slavery and Freedom, 1750–1925.* New York: Pantheon, 1976.

Hughes, Gertrude Reif. "Making it *Really* New: Hilda Doolittle, Gwendolyn Brooks, and the Feminist Potential of Modern Poetry." In *On Gwendolyn Brooks: Reliant Contemplation,* edited by Stephen Caldwell Wright, 186–212. Ann Arbor: University of Michigan Press, 2001.

Lorde, Audre. "Afterimages." In *Collected Poems,* 339–42.

———. *Collected Poems.* New York: Norton, 1997.

———. "New York City 1970." In *Collected Poems,* 101–2.

———. "Now That I Am Forever with Child." In *Collected Poems,* 8.

———. "Power." In *Collected Poems,* 215–16.

———. "School Note." In *Collected Poems,* 217.

———. *Sister Outsider: Essays and Speeches.* Freedom, CA: Crossing Press, 1984.

———. "A Woman / Dirge for Wasted Children." In *Collected Poems,* 228–29.

Metress, Christopher. "'No Justice, No Peace': The Figure of Emmett Till in African American Literature." *MELUS* 28 (Spring 2003): 87–103.

———, ed. *The Lynching of Emmett Till: A Documentary Narrative.* Charlottesville: University of Virginia Press, 2002.

Nora, Pierre. "Between Memory and History: *Les Lieux de Memoire*." Trans. Marc Roudebush. In O'Meally and Fabre, *History and Memory,* 284–300.

O'Meally, Robert, and Genevieve Fabre, eds. *History and Memory in African-American Culture.* New York: Oxford University Press, 1994.

Sollors, Werner. "National Identity and Ethnic Diversity: 'Of Plymouth Rock and Jamestown and Ellis Island'; or, Ethnic Literature and Some Redefinitions of America." In O'Meally and Fabre, *History and Memory,* 92–121.

Sontag, Susan. *Regarding the Pain of Others.* New York: Farrar, 2002.

SILENCE AND THE FRUSTRATION OF BROKEN PROMISES

*Anne Moody's Struggle with the Lynching of Emmett Till
and the Civil Rights Movement*

KATHALEEN AMENDE

In classrooms around the world, Anne Moody's 1964 autobiography *Coming of Age in Mississippi* has become almost a staple text for studying the Jim Crow South of the early twentieth century as well as the inner world of the civil rights movement of the 1950s and 60s. Moody was one of the early members of the Congress of Racial Equality's (CORE's) student division, SNCC (Student Nonviolent Coordinating Committee), and she was part of one of the earliest Woolworth's lunch counter sit-ins. Her understanding of the movement and its everyday workings has led numerous educators to present her text as an inspiring and inspired book about the strength of the movement. Onita Estes-Hicks argues further that Moody's text is especially valuable for its depiction of the "extraordinary spiritual bonds which existed in the segregated South and which emboldened long-suppressed locals to make a stand for freedom" (12). I would argue, however, that these bonds, if and when they exist in Moody's life as she presents it in her writings, are neither strong enough to spur her into the movement nor strong enough to sustain her work once there. Instead, Moody seems to be seeking in the movement the fulfillment of a promise that she has heard all her life, a promise that has been made so often that it has become, as Gertrude Stein might have pointed out, nothing but meaningless words. It is a promise of safety and security—a promise that, while it is threatened over and over during her life, is radically altered and broken with the violence of Emmett Till's lynching. After Till's lynching, Moody seeks out first one and then another escape from her daily life and the glaring incongruities between "normal" life and what she knows is happening. Over and over again, she tries to find ways to silence the noise in her head—or at least ways to ignore it. When nothing else works, she finally turns to a group of people she sees struggling to deal openly with the same problems she has been attempting to ignore. Thus, Moody's entrance into the organizations of the movement, instead of being an example of the bonds that sustain her, is an attempt to find those bonds and seek safety by mixing her voice with those of other African Americans who find it impossible, after the murder of Till, to remain silent and inactive any longer.

In a sad but poignant statement, Myrlie Evers posits that Till's lynching was an impetus "to help a people become stronger and to eliminate the fear so that they have to speak out and do something" (Hampton, et al., 15). But, unlike many texts that claim a similar legacy of action resulting from the Till murder, *Coming of Age in Mississippi* shows that Moody is unable to remain an active member of the movement when her need for action is frustrated over and over again. In fact, shortly after the events she describes in her book ended, Moody left the movement and went to the North. Since then, she has worked as an artist-in-residence in Berlin, Germany, and at Cornell University and, now, she works as a legal counselor in New York City. But she has never returned to the South, and she almost never agrees to talk about her time in the movement. However, that she wrote her memoir the year after leaving the movement, while it was still in full swing, tells us that Moody did not give up her dream of speaking out, of having a voice loud enough to silence the "noise" of society. It shows us that she chose an alternate way of finding that voice and attempting to make a difference. That alternative, of course, is art. Through creating an autobiography, Anne Moody re-created not only her own identity but also the movement and her place within it. Through this re-creation, she claimed her own story—one that didn't always jibe with the story of the movement—and her own voice. And at the nexus of this re-creation is the murder of Emmett Till. This autobiography, as Christy Rishoi points out, is (like all autobiographies) selective and self-manipulated.[1] Moody paints herself as the woman whose voice will not be silenced, whose voice is too strong even for the movement, but who cannot choose violence as a form of expression. In the end, she chooses for herself the expression of creativity and art where perhaps she can see, in herself if nowhere else, the fulfillment of the false promises that the murder of Emmett Till exploded.

Moody's departure is certainly telegraphed by the last lines of her text. As she is on her way to Washington to testify at the Council of Federated Organizations (COFO) hearings, she listens, depressed, as her fellow movement workers are singing "We Shall Overcome":

"I wonder. I wonder."
We shall overcome, We shall overcome
We shall overcome some day.
I WONDER. I really WONDER. (384)

Even before the movement is officially declared dead in the mid- to late 1960s, Moody has realized that nonviolence is doomed to failure. After the Birmingham bombing, she argues with her friend George that "nonviolence is through and you know it . . . After this bombing, if there are any more nonviolent demonstrations for the mere sake of proving what the rest of them have, then I think we are overdramatizing the issue" (318). She further believes that "if Martin Luther King thinks nonviolence is really going to work in the South as it did for India, then he is out of his mind" (319). This moment of disavowal is not spontaneous, however; it has been long coming. From the moment that Till was killed, eight years earlier, Moody has faced nothing but one frustration after another. The action that Till's death calls for is impossible, and because she cannot reconcile her unwillingness to commit violence with her lack of belief in nonviolence, Moody becomes sick, agitated and, eventually, too frustrated to continue. The frustrations and silences that accompany her new knowledge are worse, in many ways, than the silence that existed before she joined the movement. This new frustration is the silence that Tillie Olsen calls the "thwarting of what struggles to come into being, but cannot" (6). It is a silence borne of the knowledge that every avenue has been taken, and none have proven fruitful. For Moody, this silence is no longer one of necessity but one of resignation.

Recently, at one of the Modern Language Association's annual conferences, a paper presented by Christopher Metress addressed the multiple legacies of the Emmett Till lynching. Using examples such as Eldridge Cleaver, Metress pointed out that there are multiple paths, all of them originating with the Till lynching, that lead toward resistance and that not all are nonviolent. While his presentation specifically addressed an avenue of violence, I would add that, with Anne Moody as a prime example, many paths simply stopped in frustration and silence. While reviewers, admiring readers, and teachers want to preserve Moody as a paragon of the nonviolence movement, I would argue instead that Moody is an example of its failure. Furthermore, I would argue that, for Moody, although she was moved to action as a result of the Till lynching, the genesis of this failure was also born in her reactions to that event.

From the time of her earliest childhood, Moody recalls the conscious and purposeful silencing enacted by her community, in the form of her family, her neighbors, and the white people for whom she works. Neither black nor white people are safe in questioning racial inequalities, discussing interracial relationships of any sort, or attempting to actively address or correct wrongdoings. In her essay, "Representing Whiteness in the Black Imagination," bell hooks examines and explores what may be part of the mindset behind this silence that oppresses both black and white communities, but especially black ones. Hooks discusses a "black gaze," referring to the ability of blacks to see or assess white people and to understand what is going on around them: "In white supremacist society, white people can 'safely' imagine that they are invisible to black people since the power they have historically asserted, and even now collectively assert over black people accorded them the right to control the black gaze" (340). She continues: "Black slaves, and later manumitted servants, could be brutally punished for looking, for appearing to observe the whites they were serving as only a subject can observe, or see. To be fully an object then was to lack the capacity to see or recognize reality" (340). I would add to hook's formulation the capacity to speak about that reality.

An example of this silence comes when Moody's mother tells Anne, after Emmett Till's death, to go on to work like nothing has happened (123). Anne does so, seeing and hearing her employer Mrs. Burke talking about and holding "guild" meetings in response to the Till situation, but not acknowledging that Mrs. Burke does so. By having such meetings in the first place, Mrs. Burke is making clear that she does not expect Anne to hear what is going on or speak of it—even though Anne is in the house and nearby. She takes for granted that she can control not only the black gaze but also the black voice.

Throughout hooks's study, this idea of a "voice" becomes predominant. Rather than romanticizing this voice, hooks attempts to examine the historical forces that have traditionally silenced African American's actual physical voices. Hooks argues that first slaves and later free African Americans "learned to appear before whites as though they were zombies, cultivating the habit of casting the gaze downward . . . To look directly was an assertion of subjectivity, equality. Safety resided in the pretense of invisibility" (340). Blacks, hooks writes, are taught to be invisible as well as silent, and generations of African Americans perpetuated that silence and invisibility in the name of safety and security. Certainly, Anne's mother was a victim of such a cycle. When Anne, as a teenager, insists that she enjoys spending evenings talking with a young white couple who are employing her, her mother incredulously demands, "What you gotta talk about with them white folks?" (50). She further insists that, by talking to Anne as at least somewhat equal, the white employers "done ruined" Anne (50). This same inability to understand Anne's need to speak occurs when, after Anne has joined the movement, her mother begs her numerous times to quit, even pointing out how she is destroying her family as well as herself.

It comes as no surprise that Anne, like many girls, learned the lessons taught to her by her family, and by her mother in particular. The assimilation process was so complete that Anne, like most children, was unaware for a long time that it was even happening. She learned not to leave the house when her parents were not home, she learned to always look out for her little sister, and she learned to watch, every day, for her mother coming up over the hill from the fields. But these rather innocent and innocuous lessons came side by side with a less innocent and much more insidious one—the imposition of silence, especially regarding racial issues.

As an example of this silencing, Anne explains her first instance of meeting, at age five, the two light-skinned boys, Sam and Walter, who are introduced as relatives. Ed, her mother's dark-skinned brother, tells Anne that Sam and Walter are his brothers, and thus her mother's brothers as well. She becomes confused, noting that "how Ed got two white brothers worried me" (30). Back at home that night, Moody begs her mother to explain, but when Moody's mother finally answers, it is with an angry assertion that she and Ed have a different father than do Sam and Walter, their half-brothers. She silences Moody, telling her to "shut up" and demanding to know why Anne wants to know so much. Readers cannot help but be reminded here of Richard Wright's questioning of his mother in his seminal *Black Boy*, to which Nellie McKay has drawn attention in an essay for the *Southern Review*: "Moody's recollections of black adult reactions to her questions were similar to those Richard Wright, asking the same questions a quarter of a century earlier, received. Out of fear that the children might speak out of turn in racially dangerous situations and thus endanger themselves and the community, frustrated adults refused to discuss these problems with their children" (119).

Both Wright and Moody are creating a type of civil rights narrative wherein the younger generation of African Americans rebel against the silencing of their grandparents and parents. It isn't easy for Anne, who first embraces her mother's silence out of fear: "Mama was so mad that I was scared if I asked her anything else she might hit me, so I shut up. But she hadn't nearly satisfied my curiosity at all" (31). Although Moody has been brought up knowing that she is different from white children, she has been, until this point, carefree in this knowledge. It simply has not occurred to her that there is anything to question. What Moody does not (perhaps *can not*) clarify, however, is that this moment is also undoubtedly troubling to her mother, who is forced to break the silence and who, instead of attempting to explain what must have occurred in order for Sam and Walter to be conceived, simply demands silence. Perhaps what Moody does not see is that her mother's silence is another form of the promise that the naïve child believes in—a promise of security. Only through silence is her mother able to keep her daughter safe. Should she answer Moody's questions, perhaps her answers and the situations that would be revealed would inculcate Anne's movement into the racially dangerous world of African American adulthood. Or perhaps Anne's mother is simply unable to face the spiral of questions that would undoubtedly result from one explanation—a spiral that would lead (for both Anne and herself) into the traditions, lies, fears and hypocrisies at the bottom of the southern racial situation. The choices are all troubling. In her essay, "Sisters Under Their Skins: Southern Working Women, 1880–1950," Dolores Janiewski explains some of the nature of these troubling choices. She writes that the systems at work in the South were hardest on black women like Moody's mother because "the intersection between two systems of domination—race and class—forced black women to the bottom of the rural hierarchy" (18). Being at the bottom of this hierarchy, according to Janiewski, was hard because black women were forced "to socialize children into their subordinate place" (18). She reminds readers that white women's position in the South was predicated on black women's continued subordination—another silent prearrangement that kept the black women in an inferior position. Anne's mother is incapable of breaking this pattern, and she chooses silence as the alternative to any sort of explanation.

What complicates her position, however, is the promise of normalcy and safety that she has, perhaps even unconsciously, made to herself and to Anne. Anne's mother seeks over and over again to provide her children with a stable family life. She works multiple jobs, she marries multiple times, and she continues to reinstate her role as "mother" by having multiple children *for* her husbands. But the promise of a stable family life is constantly threatened—first when Anne's home is burned down, threatening the physical necessities of life,

then when her father leaves, threatening what she sees as the normal structure of a family. When Raymond, her step-father, threatens her physically and,
more obliquely, sexually, the threat to her physical body and to her definitions
of "father" push her to run away from home and live with cousins. Even before
explicitly racial problems threaten her stability, racially affected situations leave
her floundering for a sense of security. Anne knows that her family is not stable,
but because of the silence imposed upon her by that family, she is unable to express her own feelings until years later when she writes the autobiography that
allows her an individual voice.

Despite her mother's desire to keep Anne safely naïve, it is not long after the
incident with Sam and Walter that Moody realizes that the differences between
blacks and whites go beyond the structure of the family unit and seem to lie in
the larger social privileges that whites possess. She has become friends with
the little white children who live across the street, and one Sunday afternoon
when her mother takes her to the theater, she sees her friends. When Anne
makes an attempt to run into the white section of the theater to visit with them,
Mrs. Moody drags her, crying, out of the theater and home. After this incident,
Moody begins to realize the racial differences between blacks and whites. Her
realization comes from what she begins to notice, not what anyone tells her; it
is as if the silence and inability to speak has somehow honed her other senses,
including her sense of sight, or observation: "I had never really thought of them
as white before. Now all of a sudden they were white and their whiteness made
them better than me. I now realized that not only were they better than me
because they were white, but everything they owned and everything connected
to them was better than what was available to me. I hadn't realized before that
downstairs was any better than upstairs. But now I saw that it was. Their whiteness provided them with a pass to downstairs in that nice section and my blackness sent me to the balcony" (38). Once she "realizes" that white people are
assumed to be better than she is, Anne decides there must be a reason "besides
being white" (39). She tries for a while to discover this secret by examining
different parts of the white anatomy. But even though she convinces her white
friends to play "doctor" with her, she can find no difference. When she once
more asks her mother about the situation, her mother is "mad" (40). As a last
ditch effort, she asks her white employer, and the white woman refuses to answer as well, merely smiling at the seeming simplicity and naiveté of the question. Although her employer does not get angry, her refusal to answer Anne's
question has the same silencing effect.

The biggest shock for Moody, and a solid indication for her that the silence in the community around her is purposeful and self-imposed, comes with the brutal murder of Emmett Till in 1955 (the same year that Moody enters high school). It is quite possible that Anne would have continued, like others in her community, in silence and self-denial, had Emmett Till been an adult. When Emmett Till is murdered, the wall between the adults who comprise a system of authority and the children and teenagers who represent her peer group becomes glaringly obvious. Instead of creating docility, the adult world's attempt to silence Moody and her young friends creates agitation and even outright terror. When she asks her mother about the murder, Anne sees that her mother is afraid. Rather than getting angry, her mother answers in a terrified whisper, directing Moody to go on to work and to "let on like you know nothing about that boy being killed and just do your work like you don't know nothing'" (123). In one of the more revealing moments of her autobiography, Anne realizes what her readers have known all along—that her mother's silencing has been due to fear.[2] Such fear, especially when unexplained and voiced in a terrified whisper, undoubtedly creates a vague but powerful fear in the listener. Anne finds it hard to think about anything other than this fear, even though she definitely follows her mother's advice and falls silent in the presence of her white employer, Mrs. Burke.

Mrs. Burke, a leading member of a "guild" that is a forerunner to the White Citizen's Councils, is also passionate about the Till murder. She is passionately angry that Till came down to Mississippi and "put a whole lot of notions in the boys' heads here and stirred up a lot of trouble" (125). When she realizes that Anne is the same age as Till, she turns "so red in the face, she looked as if she was on fire" and insists that it is a "shame he had to die so soon" and that "a boy from Mississippi would have known better than that" (125). While it is no surprise to Anne that the white community would defend its own, she is shocked and flabbergasted by the woman's insistence that Till *had* to die, despite his being no older than Anne. Even if Mrs. Burke feels some sympathy for the death of a child, marking it as a "shame," she still insists that it is Till's own fault that he is dead, refusing to place blame where it truly lies. Anne writes that "for the first time out of all her trying, Mrs. Burke had made me feel like rotten garbage. Many times she had tried to instill fear within me and subdue me and had given up. But when she talked about Emmett Till there was something in her voice that sent chills and fear all over me" (125). Anne is suddenly aware that whatever innocence childhood holds, it is not enough to protect her. The promise of security and normalcy that her mother desperately wanted to give her is exploded. In what is perhaps the most oft-quoted passage from her autobiography, she explains: "Before Emmett Till's murder, I had known the fear of hunger, hell, and the Devil. But now there was a new fear known to me—the fear of being killed just because I was black. This was the worst of my fears . . . I didn't know what one had to do or not do as a Negro not to be killed. Probably just being a Negro period was enough, I thought" (126). And when a local African American teacher, Mrs. Rice, who tells her what the letters "NAACP" stand for, is soon after fired by the African American community, she realizes that it isn't just the white authority figures who can instill fear in her.

It is, in fact, partly the silencing of a black authority figure by other black authority figures that drives Anne to hate both white *and* black people. "I was fifteen years old when I began to hate people. I hated the white men who murdered Emmett Till and I hated all the other whites who were responsible for the countless murders Mrs. Rice had told me about and those I vaguely remembered from childhood. But I also hated Negroes. I hated them for not standing up and doing something about the murders. In fact, I think I had a stronger resentment toward Negroes for letting the whites kill them than toward the whites" (129). Although she feels this disgust and this anger, internalizing a sort of self-hatred, she is unable to say anything to anyone. She is well aware of the repercussions of saying too much about anything related to race.

Ironically enough, however, it is as a result of Emmett Till's murder that many in the African American community find voices to at least whisper about things formerly taboo. They do not speak of the murder, though. Instead, they talk about the things in their own community that Till's murder brings to the forefront. Gossip, rumors, and kitchen-table conversations become increasingly more focused on interracial sexual relationships in town. If Emmett Till was murdered for supposedly whistling at and/or flirting with a white woman, then, although no one will say it, the underlying message seems to be that such a death can and most likely will take place at any time for any African American in their community who involves him or herself with a white person. Something, however, has changed in the tone and nature of these conversations. Although people have always discussed what black *woman* was sleeping with which white *man*, Moody writes that there was now "new gossip . . . about what Negro man was screwing which white woman" (131). The new form of gossip, she argues, "created so much tension, every Negro man in Centreville became afraid to walk the streets. They knew too well that they would not get off as easily as the white man who was caught screwing a Negro woman. They had only to look at a white woman and be hanged for it. Emmett Till's murder had proved it was a crime, punishable by death, for a Negro man to even whistle at a white woman in Mississippi" (131).

Such a discussion would have been completely taboo prior to the Till murder. Although lynching had been going on for a very long time, and it was more than likely that people talked about the mingling of race and sex, these discussions would have been conducted by adult African Americans behind closed doors in the privacy of their own homes. Anne would have had no access to such conversations and would have been punished for attempting to have one herself. Perhaps, in part, this was a result of the dogma and propaganda—generated by white southerners but upheld even among black communities, if only through a refusal to negate such things—that a white woman would not, nay, *could* not agree to sexual relations with a black man. We know, of course, that such relationships did happen but to suggest openly such a thing would traditionally have meant ostracism at the least for a white person and quite conceivably death for a black person.

Almost as if to prove this death threat correct, a few weeks after the Till murder, white people in Moody's hometown of Centreville burn down the home of a poor black family; nine people, including children, are killed in the fire. It is later learned that white community members set this fire to get rid of a mulatto man who has been living next door to the family and who is having an affair with a poor white woman. Such a burning proves not only that death *is* the punishment for such an affair but also that the talk about affairs between white women and black men has spread through the African American and white communities. This burning was, undoubtedly, meant as an example of white justice—the punishment of a black man who could ruin a white woman's reputation. In effect, however, it was the silencing of a truth that could, if it were voiced loud enough, shatter the base upon which southern racial philosophies rested. If white women were consenting to sexual relations with black men, then the prevailing southern ideology that a white woman would never willingly have sex with a black man—and needed to be protected from black men—was proved false. And if black men could be seen as mature sexual partners in relationships, then such a vision, along with the idea of a consenting white woman, challenged the stereotypes of the innocent and asexual black boy and the overly sexualized, aggressive, male rapist.[3]

Eventually, these conversations die down, but Anne is unable to forget them.

After the burning of the house, the conversations become even louder in her head, and she finds herself wishing that she could drown out the noise or cover it up. She figures that if the people in her community had seen the burnt buildings and smelled the burning stench in the air, "they wouldn't be talking so much" (136). And when she goes home the first afternoon after the burning, a moment of understanding passes between her and her mother regarding the silence of the African Americans in the town. "She just looked at me," Moody says, "And for the first time I realized she understood what was going on within me, or was trying to anyway" (136). The silence between Moody and her mother, and between Moody and her community, suddenly becomes an understandable and purposeful thing. She recognizes that silence is necessary not only for survival but also for her own sanity. Christy Rishoi argues that Moody "represents her mother as a repressive force on a roughly equal level as that of whites, but she never explicitly recognizes the likely reasons for her mother's behavior" (100). I would counter that even if this is so during the rest of the work, in this one moment, Moody does seem to understand the promises to which her mother has clung and that have been shattered by the Till murder.

Moody decides that she needs to find something to do to help maintain silence or else to turn her attention away from the noise. She immerses herself in basketball, piano lessons, and church choir—all activities that are loud. Perhaps they keep her from having to *hear* that whistle that sings out from Bryant's Grocery and Meat Market, the scream from J. W. Milam's tool shed, the burning of paper on the walls of her neighbor's home, or even the sounds of her own dissatisfaction and disgust. When none of her activities manage to drown out these sounds, she leaves home and heads first to Baton Rouge and then, a summer later, to New Orleans, where she can earn more money and isn't surrounded by the memories of the violence that filled her hometown. It is worth noting that, for Anne, working in a chicken factory in New Orleans—surrounded by blood, guts, disease, and chicken corpses—is a more satisfying experience than working in her hometown for any of the rural white families. Perhaps the chicken corpses are more appealing than the human ones. In fact, she says, seeing all those corpses around her all the time, while it turns her "off chicken," turns her "on to life" (169).

Unfortunately, every time that Anne comes back to Centreville, she has to face the same violence and death she has tried so hard to leave behind. After her first summer away, she hears, immediately upon her return, that a member of her own family has been run out of town for supposedly "messing with" a white girl. And later her classmate Jerry is beaten viciously for allegedly calling up and talking to a white telephone operator, calling her *baby*. When, eventually, she hears that Samuel O'Quinn, a local man, has been shot in the back for being an NAACP member, she experiences an internal moment of resistance that she knows she must quell:

> His death brought back memories of all the other killings, beatings, and abuses inflicted upon Negroes by whites. I lay in bed for two days after his death recalling the Taplin burning, Jerry's beating, Emmett Till's murder, and working for Mrs. Burke. I hated myself and every Negro in Centreville for not putting a stop to the killings or at least putting up a fight in an attempt to stop them. I thought of waging a war in protest against the killings all by myself, if no one else would help. I wanted to take my savings, buy a machine gun, and walk down the main street in Centreville cutting down every white person I saw. Then, realizing that I didn't have it in me to kill, I slowly began to escape within myself again. (187)

The anger and violence of this early fantasy is a foreshadowing that the philosophy of nonviolence will not be convincing to Moody. Here, Moody's autobiography more closely resembles Frederick Douglass's *Narrative*—wherein Douglass swore he would not let his master beat him any longer and fights back—than some of the other slave and civil rights narratives that embrace nonviolence. However, this fantasy represents for Moody a realization about the necessity of silence and brings with it the pain of being unable to escape her inferior status and of suffering from the racial divide. During her childhood and teen years, she learns how to live with this painful realization. She tries to learn not to notice, not to care so much, and not to "mind," by focusing her attention on those areas within her black culture where she has relatively free entry: her religion, her schooling, the high-school basketball team, and her church choir. And when she returns from one of her summer trips to Baton Rouge, Anne takes the advice of a teacher who tells her, "You gotta find something to do . . . that will take your mind off some of this. It's not good for you to concern yourself too much about these killings and beatings and burnings" (145). For the next two years, although the world around her does not change and she herself has many encounters with racism, she concentrates on basketball, music, school work, and jobs. She retreats into the communal solitude that so many of her family and friends have already found and becomes a member of the silent black majority.

It is only when she enters the academic community of Tougaloo College that Anne realizes that she can either continue to run from the sounds in her head or she can face them head on and fight them or give expression to them. The agitation that begins with the murder of Emmett Till finds release and even some relief when she enters the civil rights movement during her junior year in 1962. When one of her roommates asks her to attend an NAACP meeting, much of what has been buried just below the surface of her thoughts springs to the forefront, and readers are reminded, linguistically, of the moment when, after O'Quinn's murder, Moody must choose whether to give in to the silence around her:

> I promised her that I would go to the next meeting. All that night I didn't sleep. Everything started coming back to me. I thought of Samuel O'Quinn. I thought of how he had been shot in the back with a shotgun because they suspected him of being a member. I thought of Reverend Dupree and his family who had been run out of Woodville when I was a senior in high school, and all he had done was to get up and mention NAACP in a sermon. The more I remembered the killings, beatings, and intimidations, the more I worried what might possibly happen to me or my family if I joined the NAACP. But I knew I was going to join, anyway. I had wanted to for a long time. (248)

When she first hears of O'Quinn's murder, she reconsiders these same events and knows that, because she is unwilling to embrace violence, there is nothing she can do. But here she reexamines that choice in favor of nonviolence. She reverses the decision that had made it marginally possible to exist peacefully within her community. It is worth noting, however, that when Moody later *leaves* the movement, it is because she believes that nonviolence has failed. While she does not necessarily retreat back into silence, her decision to leave and go North (written about in online biographies and reviews, but not depicted in the book) does bring to mind the dichotomy of violence/silence that exists for her earlier in her youth.

Moody, in her quest for a voice and her desire to break the unnatural silences that surround the African American community, becomes part of what

John Dittmer calls "the Emmett Till generation" (58), a generation of civil rights workers including Amzie Moore, Sam Block, and Joyce and Dorie Ladner. He identifies this group as "the young women and men who became the vanguard of SNCC and CORE in the 1960s . . . who . . . later identified the Till lynching as the beginning of the modern civil rights movement in Mississippi" (58). But if Moody is one of this generation, and she most certainly is, she is also one of those whose voice was effectively silenced by the failure of nonviolence as an efficient method of speaking. In her history of CORE, Inge Powell Bell writes that among African Americans during this time, there was "frustration born of the realization that none of the established political channels would enable the Negro to make any significant progress. One by one they had failed to deliver. The small increases of status won through equalization of school expenditures and northward migration did not even begin to fill the growing gap between expectation and reality. A new outlet for the push toward equality had to be found. It was direct action" (7).

In the end, Moody turns to art as the "new outlet" of expression and re-creates herself and her time in the movement through her autobiography. Through art she manages to find a toe-hold for expression about her youth and the movement. But, much like her expression through the movement, it is no more than a toe-hold. Even though she later worked for Cornell as a civil rights project coordinator, and spoke once more in an interview (lost among the archives of Tulane University and Jackson State's shared Tom Dent Collection and unable to be recovered for use in this essay), she has otherwise refused to grant interviews or make public appearances. Unfortunately for Moody, whose desire for nonviolence seems tied in many ways to the fate of CORE itself, thwarted expectations and hoped-for promises, borne with the death of Emmett Till thirteen years earlier, were too much. Ultimately, like Wright, she moved North, leaving behind Mississippi and her hopes for equality in that state.

NOTES

1. Christy Rishoi's *From Girl to Woman: American Women's Coming-of-Age Narratives* (2003) examines how Anne Moody's autobiography purposefully presents Moody as the rugged individual at the center of a modern slave narrative in which the most powerful form of resistance is the "resistance to external definitions" (93).

2. In *Womenfolks, Growing Up Down South*, Shirley Abbott speaks on the systems that are passed

down through generations of women. According to Abbott, "to grow up female in the South is to inherit a set of directives that warp one for life" (3). She describes these inherited directives: "The legacy passed from mother to daughter is everywhere ambivalent and complex, full of unconfessed wishes and unadmitted bequests, woven with demands and admonitions, some of which contradict the rest" (148). Although Abbott was writing about white southern women, it is easy to see that this "legacy" is one that black women pass down to their daughters as well.

3. This image of asexuality and innocence can be seen in caricatures of young black children as "pickaninnies" from the time of slavery through the early twentieth century and in the reduction of older black men to what Rosemary Ruether, in "Black Theology vs. Feminist Theology," calls "an asexual beast of burden, denied any self-affirmation through sexual identity."

WORKS CITED

Abbott, Shirley. *Womenfolks: Growing up Down South.* New Haven, CT: Ticknor and Fields, 1983.

Bell, Inge Powell. *CORE and the Strategy of Nonviolence.* New York: Random House, 1968.

Dittmer, John. *Local People: The Struggle for Civil Rights in Mississippi.* Urbana: Illinois University Press, 1994.

Estes-Hicks, Onita. "The Way We Were: Precious Memories of the Black Segregated South." *African American Review* 27, no. 1 (Spring 1993): 9–18.

Hampton, Henry, Steve Fayer, and Sarah Flynn. *Voices of Freedom: An Oral History of the Civil Rights Movement from the 1950s Through the 1980s.* New York: Bantam, 1990.

hooks, bell. "Representing Whiteness in the Black Imagination." In *Cultural Studies,* edited by Lawrence Grossberg, Cory Nelson, Paula Treichler. New York: Routledge, 1992.

Janiewski, Dolores. "Sisters Under Their Skins: Southern Working Women, 1880–1950." In *Sex, Race, and the Role of Women in the South: Essays by Jean E. Friedman [et al.],* edited by Johanna Hawks and Shelia Skemp. Jackson: University Press of Mississippi, 1983.

McKay, Nellie Y. "The Girls Who Became the Women: Childhood Memories in the Autobiographies of Harriet Jacobs, Mary Church Terrell, and Anne Moody." In *Tradition and the Talents of Women,* edited by Florence Howe, 105–24. Urbana: Illinois University Press, 1991.

Metress, Christopher. "Forgotten Sparks: Rethinking Emmett Till and the Beginning of the Civil Rights Movement." Paper presented at the Modern Language Association National Conference, Philadelphia, 28 December 2004.

Moody, Anne. *Coming of Age in Mississippi.* New York: Dell, 1968.

Olsen, Tillie. *Silences.* New York: Dell, 1978.

Rishoi, Christy. *From Girl to Woman: American Women's Coming-of-Age Narratives.* New York: SUNY Press, 2003.

Ruether, Rosemary. "Black Theology vs. Feminist Theology." *Christianity and Crisis,* 15 April, 1974. Available at www.religion-online.org/showarticle.asp?title=433 (accessed 15 June 2005).

THIS CORPSE SO SMALL LEFT UNAVENGED

Nicolás Guillén and Aimé Césaire on Emmett Till's Lynching

SYLVIE KANDÉ

Negrismo and *Négritude,* two intellectual and artistic movements concerned with black self-assertion, paradoxically owe much of their longevity in the history of ideas to their detractors' renewed criticism throughout the twentieth century. Since their inception in the 1920s and the 1930s, these two related movements were meant to challenge the colonial status quo through a controversial stand on the richness of the African past, the fundamental importance of African input to European and American modernity, and the need for people of African birth or descent to mine their collective historical experiences in order to contribute to the edification of a truly "New World" in which everyone would be equally entitled to freedom. All along, the *Négritudes,* in all of their local variants, have been accused of romanticizing an atemporal Africa merely in reaction to Western biases, of deflecting the political aspirations of colonized people, and even of subscribing to the tenets of nineteenth-century scientific racism and far-right nationalism (Dash, 73–81). With their "mood of heightened racial awareness" (Cobb, 133) and their strident dissent in sociopolitical affairs, the *Négritudes* have also become easy prey for certain postmodern and/or postcolonial preferences for identity indeterminacy and political evasiveness. Interestingly, then, the *Négritudes* are being reproached for being ahistorical in their static definition of blackness and, at the same time, excessively historical. That is, they have embarked on the self-imposed mission to uncover the time and space-governed reality of the downtrodden, who have been continuously obliterated in the dominant discourse, while ignoring the more subtle exploration of the "peculiar intimacy" (to borrow Sara Suleri's expression) between dominant and dominated.

With two elegies written almost simultaneously to pay homage to Emmett Till, the respective founders of *Negrismo* and *Négritude,* Cuban poet Nicolás Guillén and Martinican poet Aimé Césaire, display their concomitant engagement with the past, present, and future African American condition in an effort to ascribe meaning to "this mourning, this crime / this corpse so small left unavenged / this cadaver colossal and pure."[1] They register— Guillén in Spanish and Césaire in French—their pain and bitter rage at this blatant demonstration of racial hatred and assign guilt in lieu of the judicial institution that staged a mock trial that eventually acquitted the murderers. This essay explores the intertextual relation that links "Elegy for Emmett Till" and "Message on the State of the Union" to their sources—a series of newspaper articles, selected from the many French publications devoted to the lynching. Although Guillén and Césaire had previously written numerous essays and articles, they chose the poetic form and the elegiac voice to honor Emmett Till and the way that African Americans, despite lynching and other forms of internal terrorism, have contributed to the American founding narrative. In doing so, they anticipate philosopher Jacques Derrida's aphorism "What cannot be said should not be hushed, but written," and they merge with African American protest literature, enriching it with their own African-derived imagination, their memory of the Caribbean plantation, their intuition of the culture of the Old South, and their vision of a depleted, violent, and mute postslavery world that only the most oppressed can rejuvenate.

The news of Emmett Louis (a.k.a. Bobo) Till's murder found the two Caribbean poets in Paris. Their similar artistic and political sensibilities suggest that they may have learned of this event from the same sources. Partly under the influence of Langston Hughes, whom he met in Cuba in 1930 and with whom he maintained a correspondence,[2] partly under the influence of *Négritude* (Sardinha, 64), and partly on the basis of his own "mulatto" experience, Guillén began extolling in his poetry the African matrix of Cuban culture, using Afro-Cuban rhythm (*son*) for formal innovations. With the publication of *Motivos de Son* (1930) and *Songoro Cosongo* (1931), he was immediately recognized as a major poet and became the voice of *Negrismo*. His passionate interest in folk culture led him to join the Communist Party around 1937. Guillén did not personally participate in the attack led by Fidel Castro on the Moncada barracks in Santiago de Cuba in 1953. However, as a leader of the National Anti-Fascist Front since 1939, and as a journalist of *Hoy,* the Front's newspaper, Guillén thought it safer to avoid Batista's widespread repression against suspected supporters of the insurrection and left the country. He spent a long and painful period of political exile in Eastern and Western Europe as well as in Latin America, until the Cuban revolution enabled him to return home in 1959. From 1953 to 1958, Guillén lived intermittently in France, due to the temporary nature of the residency status granted to him by the French immigration services.

Meanwhile, two collections of his poems were translated into French and published in Pierre Seghers's bilingual collection "Autour du Monde" (*Chansons cubaines* and *Élégies antillaises*); other poems appeared in French or Francophone periodicals, such as *Les Temps Modernes, Europe,* and *Présence Africaine. Présence Africaine* was at the time a dynamic publishing house, journal, and cultural center around which gravitated most of the important black intellectuals, artists, and writers established in or passing through Paris, including Césaire, Richard Wright, Jacques Roumain from Haiti, and Léopold Sédar Senghor of Senegal. Indeed, while being celebrated by French writers, Guillén had established a strong relationship with *Présence Africaine,* which he acknowledged in a 1955 postcard to his wife, Rosa: "My friendships here are: . . . Manolo and Margot, as I told you, and some young people from Latin America and Africa, the latter are the editors of the journal *Présence Africaine,* where two of my poems have been published" (Augier, 419). In that period, he received African writers from the *Présence Africaine* group at his home more than once a week.

After another European tour, Guillén came back to Paris on August 26, 1955 (two days before Till's murder), where he stayed until the end of the year. In February 1956, he sent his wife a copy of "Elegy for Emmett Till," with the following comment: "a poem dedicated to Emmett Till, a black boy who was lynched in the south of the United States a few months ago." To trace the sources Guillén may have relied upon for this information, one can refer to his comments on the confusing press accounts in France of Castro's 1956 return to Cuba from Mexico. Noting that "in Paris, I left the most contradictory news concerning the situation in Cuba," Guillén lamented that, depending on which newspaper one read, Castro was either dead or alive, either hidden in the Sierra Maestra or still in Mexico. Reports by the U.S. press were, in his opinion, as confusing: "I do not believe that the news of Castro's death, published by a North American newspaper, the *New York Herald Tribune,* is confirmed" (Augier, 409–26). Significantly, his "Elegy for Jesus Menéndez" incorporates allusions to the *Wall Street Journal,* the *New York Times* and the *New York Herald Tribune* (Marquez and McMurray, 108–36). Guillén may have learned of Emmett Till's fate from the *Présence Africaine* group, and as a Communist intellectual, he certainly read about him in French newspapers (probably in *L'Humanité* and *Le Monde*). He also probably read the available American press on the subject, including the African American magazine, the *Crisis.*[3]

Aimé Césaire's election as a Communist deputy to the French National Assembly in 1945, followed by his victory in the 1946 plebiscite that turned Martinique into a French department, made it necessary for him to spend extensive periods of time in Paris. In his student years there, he had launched the *Négritude* movement, along with two other poet-politicians, Léopold Sédar Senghor and Léon Gontran Damas from French Guyana. Co-founder in 1947 of the publishing house and its journal, *Présence Africaine*, Césaire remained in close contact with this center. Acting as a Pan-African magnet, *Présence Africaine* seems to have been the privileged site where breaking news, such as the lynching of an African American teenager, was formally and informally discussed. Yet, from September 1955 to January 1957, no essay on the subject appeared in the journal. W. E. B. Dubois, at the time chairman of the Peace Information Center, does not mention the case in his paper "Africa and the American Negro Intelligentsia," published in the December 1955–January 1956 issue (no. 5, pp. 34–51). Nor does William Fontaine—an African American philosopher and former classmate of Nigerian nationalist Nnamdi Azikiwe—mention the lynching in his essay "Segregation and Desegregation: a Philosophical Analysis," published in the June–November 1956 issue (no. 8–9–10, pp. 155–73). James W. Ivy, the editor of the *Crisis* (1946–66) and a multilingual scholar who, out of interest for black cultures worldwide, translated and republished in the NAACP magazine articles originally written in French, Spanish, and Portuguese, also failed to mention the case. In "The National Association for the Advancement of Colored People as an Instrument of Social Change"—also published in the June–November 1956 issue of *Présence Africaine* (330–35)—Ivy reports that the NAACP's vigorous campaigns have altogether eradicated lynching. "Obliteration of lynching from American life," Ivy wrote, "is one illustration of the effectiveness of the NAACP as an instrument of social change . . . Now lynching has diminished to the vanishing point" (332). Ivy's omission of the Till case is all the more striking given that he had published in the *Crisis* a series of editorials pertaining to it in 1955 and 1956. Consequently, the only text ever published by *Présence Africaine* in the wake of Emmett Till's murder was "Message on the State of the Union" (n.s. no. 6, February–March 1956, pp. 119–20), the elegy written by Césaire and republished with substantial revisions in his 1960 collection *Ferrements*.

As a Francophone leftist intellectual, Césaire also likely turned to *Le Monde*, a top-quality newspaper with moderately leftist views, and *L'Humanité*, the organ of the Communist Party, for the information he gathered prior to writing this poem,[4] in addition to probable discussions in the *Présence Africaine* circles. Both newspapers covered the event approximately from September 1, 1955 (one day after Emmett Till's mutilated and decomposed body was pulled from Mississippi's Tallahatchie River) to January 31, 1956 (one week after the official publication by W. B. Huie of "The Shocking Story of Approved Killing in Mississippi" in *Look* magazine).⁵ *Le Monde*'s September 27 article, although not devoid of paternalism, virulently indicts the investigators, the defense, the jury, and even the poorly prepared accusation: in a nutshell, the whole judicial process and, moreover, "the white order [that] still rules in Mississippi."⁶ But the reporter also hints at a significant change in the "Faulknerian climate": a trial for the murder of a black person, though a pretense, did take place in Sumner, Mississippi, and Emmett's great-uncle, Moses Wright, a poor sharecropper, dared testify against the "white brutes." *Le Monde*'s opinion echoed the mounting protest of several organizations in France, such as M.R.A.P. (Movement against Racism, Anti-Semitism and for Peace) and L.I.C.R.A. (International League against Racism and anti-Semitism), which immediately organized a large meeting in Paris, with the participation of expatriate Josephine Baker, to denounce the racist murder (Fraser 238). However, by November 11, all hope for change had died with Bryant and Milam's acquittal for the murder and "kidnapping." *Le Monde*'s correspondent, Henri Pierre, blamed the parochialism and "the passivity of the American public opinion toward an event that elsewhere generates so much emotion and disgust" (11 November 1955).

A September 20 article relates the history and circumstances of the murder, and the quick degradation of the initial consensus on the tragedy across racial lines. The intervention of the NAACP had reminded Mississippi white supremacists to urgently and locally fight against the *Brown v. Board of Education* decision that was leading to national school desegregation. *Le Monde*'s anonymous correspondent, possibly Henri Pierre, closes the article with advice to American critics of European colonialism, most notably of French colonialism in Algeria, whose foundations had begun to shake under the first onslaught of an upcoming eight-year liberation war (1954–62). "In any case, the situation of Black people [in America] should call for more reserve and modesty from those who denounce the 'colonialism' of others. America, too, has her *medinas* [segregated native quarters in North Africa] and her ghettos." Such remarks may have triggered the comments of the American embassy in Paris quoted by historian Cary Fraser: "The trial broke at a time when French sensitivities were aroused over foreign criticism of the French handling of the North African situation. [The acquittals] gave the French an opportunity, which was eagerly seized, to point to racial problems in the United States and to indulge in an outraged sense of indignation and innocence" (McBride dispatch to the Department of State, 5 October 1955, quoted in Fraser, 248). It is, however, worth mentioning that *Le Monde*'s last article to deal directly with the Emmett Till case in January 1956 does not merely describe Milam as an ex-plantation overseer, "straight out of *Uncle Tom's Cabin*" but also compares him to the "gendarme auxiliaire of Ain-Abid," a French policeman who, paid by a photojournalist eager to document French repression, cold-bloodedly killed one of his Algerian prisoners for a sensational photo (11 January 1956, 30 December 1955).

The Communist newspaper *L'Humanité* was as outraged by "a southern state committed to the subjugation of black Americans" (to borrow Fraser's terms) as by a French government committed to the subjugation of Algerians. The coverage of the Emmett Till affair began on September 3, 1955, and kept the readership aware of each new development with a vivid terminology that opposes "the racists of Mississippi" to "the murdered 14 year-old child" (3 September 1955), his "unfortunate mother" (13 November 1955), and "the quiet boldness of Uncle Moses who never gets to be called 'Sir' in court" (23 September 1955). Using a variety of resources (pictures, cartoons, quotes by prominent personalities, poems, and rhetorical devices) the newspaper endeavors to render the general climate of the trial—for instance, the picnic-like ambiance of the Sumner court, where the four rowdy children of the suspects deafened the jury by their screams and were only soothed by toys and plastic guns (21 September 1955). *L'Humanité* also insists on describing the background and larger context of the case, such as the call for a crusade "against all the evils threatening the white man" that was launched by the Ku Klux Klan "Grand Maji" a few days before the murder (3 September), and the "latent civil war" that opposed African Americans fighting for civil liberties and was committed to the Old South status quo (9 January 1956).

But parallels with the situation in Algeria are quickly drawn, first with comments by Algerian-born French writer Robert Merle, who wrote: "[This ruling] is an important victory for racism, and racism sooner or later turns into fascism . . . We too, should be very careful in North Africa where the settlers' anti-Arab racism is as deplorable as the anti-Black racism in the American southern states" (28 September 1955). This theme is developed by French writer and journalist André Wurmser in his editorial entitled, significantly, "Where the Somme River runs into the Mississippi River." Wurmser publishes a dismissal letter supposedly written by an American Jiu-Jitsu club to an African American member, only to reveal that the letter was in fact sent by the French Federation of Judo and Jiu-Jitsu to two of its members, who happened to be Algerian. His straightforward conclusion is that "one version of colonialism equals another" (1 October 1955). The series of articles on Emmett Till published by *L'Humanité* ends with a review of Huie's piece in *Look* magazine and the effects (or absence thereof) of Milam's revelations (9 January 1956).

The speedy and extensive coverage of these revelations in the French press, which occurred before Guillen's and Césaire's elegies were completed, affected to some extent the content of both poems, but it definitely played an important role in Césaire's piece. The insertion of expressions taken from the partial translation of Milam's "confession" provided by *Le Monde* and *L'Humanité* indicates that Césaire completed his elegy to Emmett Till shortly after January 10, 1956, in time to be published in the February/March 1956 issue of *Présence Africaine*. For instance, the repeated address "Hey Chicago boy," featured in the 1956 and the 1960 versions of the poem, along with the rhetorical question asked by Milam ("Is it still true that you're worth / as much as a white man?") reproduces lines printed in both newspapers (*Le Monde*, 11 January 1956; *L'Humanité*, 9 January 1956) We know that Guillén had also completed his poem by February 1956 (Augier, 424), and that it appeared in Spanish and French that year.[7]

The writing and publication dates of "Elegia a Emmett Till" and "Message sur l'Etat de l'Union" are a strong indication of the sense of urgency that animated the founders of *Negrismo* and *Négritude*. Their common desire to express their grief and outrage in a fuller, bolder, and more unpredictable way is evidenced by their preference for free-verse poetry over prose. In fact, Césaire, to define poetry, has often used the *noria* as a metaphor. To him this water wheel with multiple buckets around its circumference, used to raise and lower water, represents the word that scrapes the depths of the subconscious, bringing pieces back to the surface of the mind (Leiner, xii). Indeed, poetry, like psychoanalysis, can probe into the subconscious and bring back into consciousness uncensored material to be molded by language. Guillén and Césaire saw the elegy as the most appropriate poetic form to pay homage to the child-martyr, a teenager full of life yet full of innocence "[whose] eyes were a sea conch in which the heady battle / of [his] fifteen-year-old blood sparkled"; an "adolescent angel on whose shoulders / had not yet healed the scars / of where there once were wings." Throughout literary history, the ancient genre of elegy has been consistently devoted to the expression of sorrow on the occasion of an individual death or collective catastrophe, although some elegies also lament the pains of love or deal with religious subjects. Even though some literary critics have defined the successful elegy as a natural vehicle for refined feelings, the success of Guillén's and Césaire's elegies to Emmett Till can rather be attributed to the poets' intense and simultaneous engagement with the tragedy and with language.

Both poets recognized in Emmett Till a tragic hero entangled with other characters—his tormenters, the Mississippi River—in a web of preordained forces at work against him. They also opted to give their narration of the murder a tragic treatment. The "story" in itself matches the Aristotelian definition of the "perfect plot," which "must have a single, and not (as some tell us) a double issue; the change in the hero's fortunes must be not from misery to happiness, but on the contrary from happiness to misery; and the cause of it must not lie in any depravity, but in some great error on his part" (Cuddon, 984). The swift "action" happens in one place—the town of Money, Mississippi (now erased from the map) and its vicinity. It might have happened in one day had Roy Bryant not been traveling at the time of the alleged "wolf-whistle." The sequences of the murder are predictably aligned according to a primal logic: a black male trespasses the color line that guarantees the perpetuation of the southern segregated order; the transgressor is put to death in a ritualized way that reinforces the status quo. In fact, in journalistic and poetic narrations of the event, Emmett Till reveals himself to be, in spite (or because) of his young age, a tragic hero who, placed at a crossroads with his life at stake, chooses to act in a disturbingly risky way. The first instance occurs when he rushes into the "truth-or-dare" game proposed by the other children at the store and addresses Carolyn Bryant in a flirtatious way. Many overloaded the moment with sexual connotations, his murderers and their supporters, of course, but also some journalists who managed to obtain from family members that Emmett, at barely fourteen, looked like a grown man. Others downplayed it as a child's prank, regardless that written and unwritten rules of segregation were well understood even by children. Yet the game takes on an important meaning if we accept Milam's rendition of Emmett's last words, most notably his mention of his white grandmother. Black grandson of a white grandmother, Emmett challenged his arbitrary confinement within racial borders by hopscotching the color line, a transgressive movement well depicted by a series of chiasmata linking opposite colors and genders, life and death, in the following lines of Guillén's *Elegy:* "*Black, murdered,* alone: this *boy* who tossed *a rose of love* / at a passing *girl* / who was *white*" (emphasis is mine).

The second tragic turn in Emmett's last moments occurs when he decides to stand up to his tormenters. During his interview with Huie, "Big" Milam recalled that with the help of his half-brother Bryant, he dragged Emmett out of his great-uncle Moses Wright's house and beat the child. Aggravated that Emmett remained defiant despite his beating, Milam lashed out: "Chicago boy, I'm tired of 'em sending your kind down here to stir up trouble. Goddam you, I'm going to make an example of you—just so everybody can know how me and my folks stand." On their way to the Tallahatchie River, the men stole a metal fan used in ginning cotton, ordered Emmett to carry it to the water and undress: "He stood there naked. It was Sunday morning, a little before 7. Milam: 'You still as good as I am?' Bobo: 'Yeah.'" In fact, the various journalistic narratives all seem to subtly confirm a link of causality between Emmett's attitude, which Milam attributed to Northern antisegregationist propaganda, and the child's subsequent assassination.[8]

Although Emmett's arrogance is one of the least credible elements in Milam's confession,[9] this second "great error" (in Aristotle's terms) has provided Césaire with core poetic material. Again, both versions of his elegy noticeably incorporate the address and rhetorical question used by Emmett's kidnappers to challenge him: "Hey Chicago boy / is it still true that you're worth / as much as a white man?" In the 1956 version, Césaire devotes four full lines to Emmett's credo: "He believed. Even at the edge of the night / at the edge of the Mississippi carrying its bars, its barriers, / its tomb-like avalanche between the high banks of racial hatred, / He believed. He believed that a black man was worth as much as a white man." In the 1960 version, the emphasis switches from the strength of Emmett's belief—marked by the repetition of the verb *believed*—to the nature of his credo, that is, the end of "the high banks of racial hatred" represented by the slightly surrealist allegory of the spring ("Spring, he believed in you") with an anaphoric reappearance of the term in the three following lines. In the poet's eyes, Emmett's tragic "error"—his refusal to humble himself in front of his enemies, even to save his life;[10] his claim to belong equally to humankind; and his belief in the advent of the "spring," a truly new and better world—makes him the authentic hero of the "new *Négritude*." In his *Notebook of a Return to My Native Land* (1936–38), Césaire distinguishes the dying "old *Négritude*," a behavior characterized by submissiveness and self-depreciation, from the "upright and free" new *Négritude* (Irele, 30–31), which he celebrates. His new *Négritude* is obviously tied to the African American concept of the "new Negro," immortalized by the 1920 portrait of a Harlem man carrying an antilynching sign that reads "The New Negro Has No Fear." Through Guillén and Césaire's works, *Negrismo* and *Négritude*, two intellectual and artistic movements that have ardently worked at grounding black self-assertion in an Africanized imagination (Feracho), could recognize in Emmett Till the young fearless and loving prophet of a new age in which enslavement, Jim Crow laws, and local forms of segregation and colonization would be banished.

Although the legal triumph of the murderers was largely supported by the local white community,[11] a significant segment of U.S. and world opinion remained implacable in their condemnation of the culprits. Guillén and Césaire, in the manner of the fifth-century Greek tragedians who staged legends taken from the ancient mythological pool, used the biblical parable of Abel and Cain to evoke the case's unequivocal polarization of the forces of hatred and the promises of tomorrow. Césaire refers explicitly to this metanarrative of fratricidal strife to depict Emmett's entrapment on that ill-fated day. Fourteen-year-old Emmett must face barehanded his five-hundred-year-old "brothers," men as old as the violence which presided over the birth and growth of the Americas: "They were five centuries old EMMET TILL [sic] / five centuries is the ageless age of Cain's stake." They are men of stubborn hatred and bigotry; "But They / they were invulnerable, dense as they were, / and mounted, massively, on bizarre immemorial billy goats."[12] Guillén, on the other hand, makes the murderers' silhouettes disappear into a larger group of "white men dancing / in a cannibal light" around "nocturnal bonfires / with a black man always burning" somewhere on the bank of the river: they emblematize the South, "the alcoholic South, . . . the South of insult and lash." In "Elegia," the brothers locked in a deadly embrace are Emmett and the treacherous Mississippi River, three times invoked by Guillén as "(O) ancient river, brother of the Black." Of the Mississippi that flows immutably, indifferent and blind to the "mute trees with ripened moans for fruit" and even to "a fragile youth, / a flower from your banks / . . . scarcely a child, / a dead child, murdered, alone, / black," the poet demands adamantly that it stop being a silent accomplice of his young brother's killing: "Look, and in the night made bright, speak . . . Mississippi!" The poet demands that the river be like the *Negrismo* and the *Négritude* leaders, that is, the voice of the voiceless, and not like Cain asking "Am I my brother's keeper?"

Guillén's and Césaire's poetic talent enables them to blend this biblical imagery with a strong indictment of the political system that supported the murderers, providing an adequate context for their impunity. For Guillén, the Mississippi River is the artery of the Old South that clings to its plantation economy, the ancillary tradition of white supremacy, and the commodification of the black body for labor and entertainment. Guillén depicts the scene "with a black man always burning: / the obedient Black, / his torn bowels wrapped in smoke, / his guts choked with fumes, his abused sex." He bitterly denounces the perverted process of the integration of African Americans in American society. In a striking enumeration, he describes Emmett as a typical American boy who goes to school, church, and the movies; who plays with friends in the neighborhood; and who likes sports, especially baseball and boxing. This boy, who thinks of himself as part of the nation, carrying with him "his picture of Lincoln, a U.S. flag," is brutally reminded of his difference: "black." His mutilated body reveals the vehement refusal of the nation to imagine itself as a multicultural and (in Guillen's terms) "mulata" entity that could transcend the oppressive racial divisions inherited from the past:

> Feel the absent contour of this brow,
> smashed by stone and stone,
> by lead and stone,
> insult and stone.
> Look upon this gaping breast
> where once-warm blood is hard and caked.(Marquez and McMurray, 95)

In his contextualization of the murder, Césaire emphasizes the slow attrition of the roots of American wealth through figures that any president could emphasize in his annual speech, the "State of the Union" address. Increasingly depleted of its mineral resources, the nation has long lost its most important treasure—humanity: "in the heart, what? / Nothing, zero, / mine without ore, / cavern in which nothing prowls, / of blood not a drop left." This emptiness has been filled with the tradition of patriarchy, bigotry, and violence imported five hundred years ago with Columbus. Yet America's exsanguine heart needs new blood and will suck it out of youthful, lively, and proud people such as Emmett Till: "Then night remembers its arm / a vampire's flabby flight suddenly hovering / and BIG MILAM's Colt 45 / wrote the verdict and the State of the Union in

rust letters / on the living black wall."[13] The 1956 version of the poem directly in-
dicted the peculiar metabolism of the capitalist system, by which the flesh of the
lower classes feeds the machines and their sweat makes skyscrapers, banks, and
churches surge from the ground. The 1960 version keeps to the consequences
of the system; since the eighteenth century, the political and administrative ma-
chine functions on its own, and people's hearts are bleached out: "and the 180th
year of these states / but in the heart unfeeling clockwork / what, nothing, zero /
of blood not a drop / in the white heart's tough antiseptic meat?" Big Milam is
the product of this system—along with "the clots of hatred swollen with age,"
and "five centuries of torturers, / of witch burners . . . / . . . of cheap gin of big
cigars / of fat bellies filled with slices of rancid bibles / a five century mouth bitter with dowager sins"—just like Emmett is its victim.

With their impassioned elegies, Guillén and Césaire "turn outward from
the[ir] circumscribed world to voice black experiences as symbol for the de-
valuation of human life by modern man,"[14] and their work merges with American protest literature. Since the end of the nineteenth century, social protest
has represented a strong undercurrent in American literature, and, not surprisingly, some American writers did take a stand on Emmett Till's murder. William
Faulkner's statement on the case stands out as a remarkably powerful one, not
only because of the author's literary stature but also because of his southern
origin. He declared: "Because if we in America have reached that point in our
desperate culture when we must murder children no matter for what reason,
or what color, we don't deserve to survive and probably won't" (UPI press dispatch written in Rome, Italy, September 1955). Yet it is African American writers and poets, whose life and work have been shaped by the oppressive legacy of
slavery and subsequent segregation, who have come to dominate the discourse
on U.S. race relations. From Langston Hughes to Wanda Coleman, their literary responses to the child's murder have been indeed numerous and fervent.
Guillén and Césaire, who have long attempted to align themselves with African
American writers and poets out of racial and political solidarity, succeeded with
their respective elegies in transcending linguistic and cultural barriers. Fully
identifying with the African American condition and struggle had evidently
been a major concern for Guillén and Césaire, especially as promoters of a pan-
African theory of identity and as critics of U.S. capitalistic choices. Guillén's
famous journalistic essay "Road to Harlem" (1929), written to warn Cuba about
the dangers of racial ghettoization, was followed by a seminal series of conversa-

tions with Hughes and the production of numerous poems on African American ordinary folks as well as political figures such as Martin Luther King and Angela Davis. Guillén consistently berated the American brand of freedom that, according to him, was the monopoly of the white majority (White, 68–74). He saw as the only solution an international front against racism and capitalism under the banner of Communism. As critic Clement White writes, "For Guillén, this is the only hope for the Black race—the hope intertwined with the myth that Communism holds the answers to hate and oppression" (129). In that, Guillén was close to African American writers with Marxist sympathies, including Dubois, Hughes, and Wright.

Aimé Césaire had also developed an early interest in African American literature, as shown by his doctoral thesis on African American poetry. In Paris in the 1930s, he, along with Senghor, met Hughes, Claude McKay, and Countee Cullen, whose works were, as he confided, "part of our personal 'essentials'" (Leiner, viii). In July 1941, Césaire published an introduction to a French translation of poems by James Weldon Johnson, Jean Toomer, and McKay in his notorious journal, *Tropiques*. Contrary to critics Clayton Eshelman and Annette Smith's assertion (2), his own poetry, and "On the State of the Union" specifically, do draw on these African American poets' form of expression. Undoubtedly, Césaire chose the elegiac mood to match as closely as possible the "blues" form, though his lexical register remains extremely sophisticated. His Emmett Till, like the narrator of McKay's poem "America," seems to say: "Yet as a rebel fronts a king in state, / I stand within [America's] walls with not a shred / Of terror, malice, not a word of jeer" (Gates, 985–86). While Césaire concurred with Guillén that racism can only be cured by a radical redistribution of economic wealth, by the time he wrote his elegy to Emmett Till he had already begun questioning Marxism's ability to incorporate racial issues into a class analysis and to deal with the nationalistic aspirations of ethnic minorities. In fact, he resigned from the Communist Party in 1956, shortly after the Bandung Conference and the Soviet invasion of Hungary (which was approved by the French Communist Party). His resignation was also a response to Guy Mollet, the head of the French Section of the Workers' International (SFIO), who in his new capacity as president of the Council of Ministers had decided to intensify France's involvement in the Algerian war.

Through their identification with African American voices and figures of dissent, Cuban Nicolás Guillén and Martinican Aimé Césaire asserted themselves as American (and ultimately transnational) poets who "sought to awaken among Blacks a consciousness of the importance of their history and their presence in the Americas" (Cobb, 137). Inscribed in an already established "historical connection for a Pan-American identity" (Feracho, 4), Guillen and Césaire's stance reflects their historico-cultural solidarity as Caribbeans with other Americans of African heritage. That stance can also be explained by their shared awareness of a mounting U.S. military presence in the Caribbean. But foremost their desire to identify with oppressed blacks in the United States reveals the empowering dimension, for the rest of the black world, of the African American struggle for democracy and of the new spirit and aesthetics that were born from it. Martin Luther King Jr., and Emmett Till and his mother, emerge not only as "metaphors for tragic marginality" (Kubayanda, 90) but also as promises for a new global ethics. Mamie Till Bradley's paramount importance in that regard is fully acknowledged by Cornel West, who wrote: "The high point of the black response to American terrorism is found in the compassionate and courageous voice of Emmett Till's mother, who stepped up to the lectern at Pilgrim Baptist Church in Chicago in 1955 at the funeral of her fourteen-year-old son, after his murder by American terrorists, and said: 'I don't have a minute to hate. I'll pursue justice for the rest of my life'" (21). For West, Mamie Till Bradley's attitude best exemplifies the potency of the blues tradition in the face of white supremacist powers (19, 21).

Recent historiography has identified Emmett Till's murder in 1955 as one of the major sparks of the U.S. civil rights movement and a powerful catalyst for irreversible change in twentieth-century American social dynamics. Yet it is important to keep in mind that this horrendous event also sent shockwaves throughout the world at large, generating immediate outrage abroad and bringing U.S. race relations under renewed scrutiny. The lynching of this child compelled poets Nicolás Guillén and Aimé Césaire, who were already alerted to the oppressive circumstances of African Americans under Jim Crow laws, to immediately write a tribute to the martyr. This murder indeed resonated with the poets' personal and collective experience. It is well known that Césaire's great-grandfather was executed for allegedly stirring up a revolt, and in 1917, Guillen's father, a typographer and lawyer, was assassinated for political reasons (Kubayanda, 136). Moreover, as Caribbeans, Guillén and Césaire shared with other Americans of African heritage the legacy of the plantation complex system, and they could intuitively envision "the South of insult and lash" that the infamous Mississippi River constantly nourished. Dedicated to promoting another world order where justice and equality would prevail, they underlined in their respective elegies the economic roots of a racial violence that was tacitly tolerated by complicit institutions. But as Guillén and Césaire rewrote the story of Emmett's reality, reframing his "corpse so small left unavenged" into biblical and American foundational narratives, they aimed above all at reempowering the victims (and themselves) against five long centuries of economic, physical, and discursive violence. Violence, as journalist Philip Gourevitch defines it in the context of another fratricidal tragedy—that of the Hutus against the Tutsis in Rwanda—consists "in the ability to make others inhabit your story of their reality—even, as is so often the case, when that story is written in their blood" (48). By highlighting the victim's ability to ultimately change, if only poetically, the binary order of segregation that crushes him, Guillén and Césaire have sublimated Emmett's death into a Negritude moment, one that encapsulates the past, the present, and the future of humankind.

NOTES

1. I am indebted to Gérarde Magloire-Danton for the translation of this expression.

2. See Mullen, 26. Hughes was introduced to Guillén in February 1930 and interviewed by him for the newspaper *Diario de la Marina* on March 9, 1930: "Hughes' early contact with Guillén was to have a profound effect on the young Cuban, who had not yet written his landmark collection *Motivos de Son*. Guillén sent a copy of the book to Hughes, who replied with a letter of praise on 17 July 1930" (30).

3. An excerpt from an article on Emmett Till published in the *Crisis*, October 1955, appears in the margin of "Elegy for Emmett Till" (Marquez and McMurray, 87).

4. A memorandum addressed by the Paris office of the American Jewish Committee to its National Office on October 7, 1955, reviews the reaction to the Emmett Till case in the European press. "Surprisingly, on this occasion the Communists were less vociferous than many of the liberal and conservative elements" (1). It also mentions *Le Monde's* moderate tone (2). Press clippings, Sc Micro-F 1. 005, 268–1–2–3, New York Public Library.

5. Although W. B. Huie's article was officially published on January 24, 1956, the story had already "hit the newsstands on Tuesday" (10 January), as stated by the *New York Post* on January 15, 1956, and as shown by reviews published in *Le Monde* and *L'Humanité* on January 10 and 11. On January 10, 1956, W. B. Arthur, managing editor of *Look* magazine, issued a statement attesting the accuracy of the information included in Huie's article, in response to Milam and Bryant's recent retraction.

6. "Le procès des assassins présumés d'un jeune noir est suivi avec une attention passionnée

par l'opinion américaine," *Le Monde,* 20 September 1955; "Les deux assassins présumés du jeune noir sont acquittés . . . mais seront poursuivis pour kidnapping," *Le Monde,* 25–26 September 1955; "La ségrégation aux Etats-Unis. Le procès de Sumner marque peut-être le début d'un réveil des consciences," *Le Monde,* 27 September 1955; "Demande d'enquête sur la disparition de deux témoins du meurtre d'Emett [*sic*] Till," *Le Monde,* 2–3 October 1955; "L'oncle d'Emmett Till a dû fuir le Mississippi," *Le Monde,* 6 October 1955; "Les ravisseurs d'Emmet [*sic*] Till ne seront pas inculpés pour kidnapping," *Le Monde,* 11 November 1955; "Le gouverneur de l'Illinois demande une enquête fédérale sur l'affaire Emmett Till," *Le Monde,* 12 November 1955; see also "Nouveau meurtre raciste dans le Mississippi," *Le Monde,* 10 December 1955; "Le Magazine 'Look' publie un récit détaillé de l'assassinat du jeune noir Emmett Till—La culpabilité des meurtriers présumés ne fait aucun doute," *Le Monde,* 11 January 1956. See also "Les Etats du Sud contre l'interdiction de la ségrégation," *Le Monde,* 19 January 1956, and "La question raciale accentue la division du parti démocrate américain," *Le Monde,* 11 February 1956.

7. "Elegy for Emmett Till" did appear in the review *Propósitos,* Buenos Aires, 21 August 1956 (see Augier, 427) while the collection *Elegias* was first published in 1958. The poem appeared in French in the journal *Les Temps Modernes* 124 (May 1956): 1579–82, and in Couffon, 165–68.

8. Available at www.pbs.org/wgbh/amex/till/sfeature/sf_look_confession.html (accessed 2003). In his narrative, Milam blames Emmett for the murder he was "forced" to perpetrate: "Well, what else could we do? He was hopeless. I'm no bully; I never hurt a nigger in my life."

9. See "Bomb Shell in the Till Case" *New York Post,* 11 January 1956: "Many of the quotations attributed to Milam in this article ["The Shocking Story" in *Look*] offer the picture of Emmett Till that Milam would like the country to accept. It is a portrait of provocation and arrogance." See also "Milam, Bryant Talk Movie Deal," *New York Post,* 18 January 1956: "[Emmett's mother, Mrs. Mamie Bradley] will not permit her son to be portrayed, she said as he was in the current issue of *Look Magazine* . . . 'I know the kind of boy that Emmett was' she said 'and he was nothing like he was pictured in that article. Those were Milam's words on how Emmett acted, and I don't believe that part of his story, although I believe his confession. But Emmett was no Superman, and saying that he took all that beating without begging for mercy or that he kept talking back to them to the very end just isn't true. The[y] were only trying to justify why they did it.'"

10. *Le Monde* (11 January 1956) and *L'Humanité* (9 January 1956) curiously suggested that Emmett did not try to run away and continued talking back because he did not believe Milam would dare kill him. There were apparently in the truck other (black and white) men, a report scrutinized when the FBI investigated the case 2005–7; see Beito and Royster Beito and the FBI report, which is now online.

11. According to John N. Popham, the community raised $10,000 to bail them out and hired five defense lawyers; see *New York Times,* 24 September 1955.

12. Translated by Clayton Eshleman and Annette Smith, with one modification. "Mais Eux / eux étaient invulnérables, tardifs qu'ils étaient, / et montés, massifs, sur de louches boucs immémoriaux."

13. Translated by Clayton Eshleman and Annette Smith, with one modification. "Alors la nuit se souvient de son bras / mou vol de vampire qui tout soudain plana / et le gros colt de BIG MILAM / sur le noir mur vivant / en lettres de rouille écrivit la sentence et l'état de l'Union."

14. Martha Cobb's remarks refer to Nicolás Guillén, Langston Hughes, and Jacques Roumain but could apply to Aimé Césaire as well (134).

WORKS CITED

Augier, Angel. *Nicolás Guillén. Estudio Biografico-critico*. Havana, Cuba: Ediciones Union, 1984.

Beito, David T., and Linda Royster Beito. "Why it's unlikely the Emmett Till murder mystery will ever be solved." 26 April 2004. Available at http://hnn.us/articles/4853.html (accessed 26 April 2004).

Césaire, Aimé. *Ferrements*. Paris: Seuil, 1960.

———. "Introduction à la poésie nègre américaine." *Tropiques* 2, no. 3 (July 1941): 37–50.

Cobb, Martha. *Harlem, Haiti and Havana: A Comparative Critical Study of Langston Hughes, Jacques Roumain and Nicolás Guillén*. Washington, DC: Three Continents Press, 1977.

Couffon, C., ed. *Nicolás Guillén*. Paris: Seghers, 1964.

Crisis. 1955–56.

Cuddon, J. A. *Dictionary of Literary Terms and Literary Theory*. New York: Penguin, 1991.

Dash, Michael. *The Other America: Caribbean Literature in a New World Context*. Charlottesville: University Press of Virginia, 1998.

Eshleman, Clayton, and Annette Smith, eds. *Aimé Césaire: The Collected Poetry*. Berkeley and Los Angeles: University of California Press, 1983.

Feracho, Leslie. "The Legacy of Negrismo/Negritude: Inter-American Dialogues." *Langston Hughes Review* 16, nos. 1 and 2 (Fall/Spring 1999): 1–8.

Fraser, Cary. "Crossing the Color Line in Little Rock: The Eisenhower Administration and the Dilemma of Race for U.S. Foreign Policy." *Diplomatic History* 24, no. 2 (Spring 2000): 233–64.

Gates, Henry Louis, Jr., and Nellie Y. McKay, *The Norton Anthology of African American Literature*. New York: Norton, 1997.

Gourevitch, Philip. *We Wish to Inform You That Tomorrow We Will Be Killed with Our Families: Stories from Rwanda*. New York: Farrar, Straus, and Giroux, 1998.

Hutton, James, ed. *Aristotle's Poetics*. New York: Norton, 1982.

Irele, Abiola, ed. *Aimé Césaire—Cahier d'un retour au pays natal*. Ibadan, Nigeria: New Horn Press, 1994.

Kubayanda, Josaphat Belunuru. "Nicolás Guillén and Aimé Césaire: A Universalist Approach to the Poetics of Africanness in Latin America and the Caribbean, 1929–1961." PhD diss., Washington University, St. Louis, Missouri, 1981.

Leiner, Jacqueline. "Entretien avec Aimé Césaire." *Tropiques 1941–1945*. Paris: Jean-Michel Place, 1978.

Le Monde. September 1955 to February 1956.

L'Humanité. September 1955 to February 1956.

Marquez, Robert, and David A. McMurray, eds. *Man-Making Words: Selected Poems of Nicolás Guillén*. Amherst: University of Massachusetts Press, 1972.

Mullen, Edward J., ed. *Langston Hughes in the Hispanic World and Haiti*. Hamden, CT: Archon Books, 1977.

The Murder of Emmett Till. Dir. Stanley Nelson. PBS. Available at www.pbs.org/wgbh/amex/till.html.

New York Public Library. Sc Micro-F 1. 005, 268–1–2–3 Emmett Till (Press clippings).

Ojo-Ade, Femi. *Analytic Index of Présence Africaine: 1947–1972*. Washington, DC: Three Continents Press, 1977.

Sardinha, Dennis. *The Poetry of Nicolás Guillén*. London: New Beacon, 1976.

Suleri, Sara. Quoted in the introduction to *The Post-Colonial Studies Reader,* edited by Bill Ashcroft,
    Gareth Griffiths, and Helen Tiffin, 112. London: Routledge, 1995.

West, Cornel. *Democracy Matters.* New York: Penguin, 2004.

White, Clement A. *Decoding the Word: Nicolás Guillén as Maker and Debunker of Myth.* Miami: Edi-
    ciones Universal, 1993.

CHILDHOOD TRAUMA AND ITS REVERBERATIONS IN BEBE MOORE CAMPBELL'S *YOUR BLUES AIN'T LIKE MINE*

SUZANNE W. JONES

Novelist Bebe Moore Campbell was only five when Emmett Till was murdered on August 28, 1955. But in *Your Blues Ain't Like Mine* (1992) she seeks to answer the question that black teenagers in Mississippi, and indeed many people from all over the United States, asked after seeing the photograph of Till's mutilated and bloated body: "How could they do that to him? He's only a boy" (Dittmer, 58). Campbell embraces the view that Lillian Smith expressed in *Killers of the Dream* (1949): "The warped, distorted frame we have put around every Negro child from birth is around every white child also. Each is on a different side of the frame but each is pinioned there" (30–31). Campbell's decision to open her novel with the white woman's perspective and then move on to the black youth's consciousness signals her determination to name all the sources of pain and powerlessness that led to Till's murder. *Your Blues Ain't Like Mine* explores the consequences of being psychically abused during childhood, whether because of race or class or gender or color, and the possibilities for reconciliation between blacks and whites, between men and women, and across class lines. In a departure from the earlier literary chroniclers of Emmett Till's story, Campbell begins her novel with his murder but then writes hope into the aftermath. To accomplish this feat she widens her focus from Mississippi to Chicago and fast-forwards her narrative into the present.

In the 1991 dedication ceremony in which Chicago renamed sections of Seventy-first Avenue in honor of Emmett Till, Michael Eric Dyson explained the significance of the occasion: "By choosing to honor the memory of Emmett Till, we make a covenant with our past to own its pain as our responsibility and to forgive its failures only if the wisdom we derive from their doing is made a conscious part of our present pacts of racial peace" (267). In *Your Blues Ain't Like Mine,* Campbell similarly encourages her readers "to own" the pain of the past. Like other recent novelists who have interpreted the civil rights struggle, she takes as her task one that literary theorist Shoshana Felman describes in her analysis of Camus's *The Plague*: "to demolish the deceptive image of history as an *abstraction* (as an ideological and/or statistical, administrative picture in which death becomes invisible) by *bearing witness to the body*." Felman argues that "the specific task of the literary testimony is, in other words, to open up in that belated witness, which the reader now historically becomes, the imaginative capability of perceiving history—what is happening to others—*in one's own body*, with the power of sight (of insight) usually afforded only by one's own immediate physical involvement" (108). Campbell juxtaposes sharply contradictory sensory experiences in an attempt to shock readers into "immediate physical involvement." She also uses unexpected humiliation and violence to disrupt her plot, thereby hoping to re-create the shock of the senseless tragedies that occurred during the civil rights era and that echo in the American gun culture that thrives today.

In her attempt to allow readers to become "belated witnesses" to Emmett Till's murder, Campbell gives us access to the consciousness of her Till character, Armstrong Todd, on the night that a white man, Floyd Cox, murders him. As much as words allow, we feel the heat of that August night when the white men drive up to Armstrong's grandmother's house, we hear Armstrong's futile attempt to reason with the Cox brothers, and we experience at least some of the shock of his pain as they begin to kick him. We bear witness to his mental struggle as he strains to recall the self-effacing tactics his mother hastily taught him for dealing with southern white people, and we see the futility of his attempt to placate his attackers with what little money he has in his pockets. In *The Body in Pain*, Elaine Scarry points out that writers find it easier to describe psychological than physical pain, and she speculates about the reasons: "Contemporary philosophers have habituated us to the recognition that our interior states of consciousness are regularly accompanied by objects in the external world, that we do not simply 'have feelings' but have feelings *for* somebody or something, that love is love of *x*, fear is fear of *y*, ambivalence is ambivalence about *z* . . . This list and its implicit affirmation would, however, be suddenly interrupted when, moving through the human interior, one at last reached physical pain, for physical pain—unlike any other state of consciousness—has no referential content" (5). And yet in the several pages in which Campbell describes the "felt-characteristics" of Armstrong's physical pain that fateful night, she makes his body a "referent," thereby attempting to render Emmett Till's pain "knowable" to her readers.[1]

Campbell represents the kaleidoscopic last minutes of Armstrong's life by alternating descriptions of his body's realization that he is going to die (urine runs down his leg, his bowels release) with his imagination's desperate struggle to stay alive. Armstrong first imagines that he has not seen a gun, and later when he knows that he has, he hopes illogically that his father, who is in Chicago, will rescue him:

> Armstrong heard the click of the trigger, and he took a deep breath. He felt his bowels ripping through him, then a soft, warm mushiness in his pants. He heard an explosion; fire seared the inside of his chest. His head slammed into the dirt. Nearby, a tired dog began panting, its ragged breathing engulfing him. If only he could find the hound, he could maybe lean against its soft, warm fur, raise himself up a little. But he couldn't see anything. He pictured his father then, as the moans of pain dribbled from his lips: his father, tall and strong, coming toward him bathed in white light, his arms like steel bands, his hands stretched out for the boy to grab. As he heard the retreating footsteps in the air around him, he thought: *My daddy could whip all of you.*[2]

Campbell's verisimilitude here and elsewhere parallels Mamie Till Bradley's decision to leave the casket open at her son's funeral so that the world would be forced to confront the terrible reality of his mutilated body, bloated beyond recognition. Throughout the novel, Campbell's use of metaphors of physical pain to .convey searing psychological hurt follows Scarry's contention that often "a state of consciousness other than pain will, if deprived of its object, begin to approach the neighborhood of physical pain" (13). Whenever Armstrong's father, Wydell, is mentioned, Armstrong experiences the loss of his father's presence (his parents are separated) as if his body were in pain. When a black man he meets in Mississippi refers to Wydell as a "fool," Armstrong feels "as though someone was ripping a bandage off his bleeding sore" (12). When his grandmother criticizes Wydell as "trifling" and refers ironically to his drinking as "his job," Armstrong feels like he is "being punched in the stomach" (38–39). Later, Campbell similarly describes Wydell's despair when thinking about his own father's drunkenness and violence as a physical hurt: "he could feel the searing pain in his chest, as if his heart was on fire" (134). Such unexpected metaphors of bodily pain to describe psychological pain are surely Campbell's attempt to communicate the deep hurt of a father's absence to readers who have never experienced such a

loss. Near the end of the novel, when Wydell is listening to the blues, he feels
the "pain in the old man's voice": "There was grieving in his song, a mourning that was deep and profound. And when the old man was singing, it was as
though his hurt entered Wydell, because how else could he explain the blues
inside him, how else could he interpret his sudden tears" (361). In bearing witness to the body through her intensely metaphoric prose, Campbell attempts to
create a visceral experience for her readers.

When Armstrong looks into the face of his white murderer, he wonders,
"Where did all that hatred come from?" (43). This is the question that leads
Bebe Moore Campbell to imagine the childhoods of all those directly involved in
the racially motivated murder of an innocent teenage boy. To answer the question, she probes the psyches and allows readers to enter the consciousnesses of
Armstrong Todd, his murderer Floyd Cox, Floyd's wife Lily, and Jake McKenzie,
the dark-skinned black man who works in Floyd's pool hall, where Armstrong
and Lily encounter each other. Given the race, gender, class, and color hier-
archies involved, these four characters make up a volatile quartet. Campbell
suggests that insecurity, envy, and a desire for human agency motivate all four
people. She represents their actions and inactions as stemming from childhood
wounds that affect adult behavior. Because these wounds have not healed, they
have led to what cultural critic bell hooks terms "self-sabotage."[3] As she explores
psychological causes for behavior, Campbell also makes clear their link to social
issues and the dysfunction of a racially segregated society. At one time or another, each of these characters daydreams about leaving Mississippi.

But Campbell is also interested in current social problems: illiteracy, absent
fathers, the culture of welfare, unemployment, and drug and alcohol abuse. The
ways in which she changes some of the facts of the Till incident highlight these
concerns. Whereas Emmett Till's father was killed in World War II, Armstrong's
father is very much alive in the novel so that Campbell can explore the effect of
a living father's absence on his children. She gives Till a much younger brother
in order to examine the effects of gang culture on black families. Till's killer, Roy
Bryant, and his wife Carolyn had two sons, but Campbell gives Floyd and Lily
Cox a son and a daughter in order to use the feminist movement's lessons about
independence and female self-assertion to benefit Doreen Cox and eventually
to help Lily. Campbell makes Floyd and his accomplice full brothers, instead
of half-brothers, so that she can investigate the effect a parent has on two very
different children when he plays favorites and inculcates one narrow notion of

masculinity. Finally, while local black people in Money suspected that two black men, whom they termed "white folks' niggers," assisted in Emmett Till's abduction, Campbell complicates the possible motivation for such unlikely collusion and includes not only economic dependency on whites but also revenge for skin color bias within the black community.[4]

Using flashbacks to explain her characters' personalities and motivations, Campbell proposes that seemingly inexplicable human behavior can be understood and that apparently transparent actions are more complex than they seem. The behavior of Jake McKenzie, the black man who betrays Armstrong by tattling to the Cox men about Armstrong's brief encounter with Lily, seems especially paradoxical, but Campbell uses a flashback to Jake's childhood as insight. When Jake was growing up, lighter-skinned black children taunted him about his physical appearance, calling "Black Jake. Ugly as a snake!" (12). As a result, Jake takes an instant dislike to Armstrong Todd because he is light-skinned and handsome and because he lives in the very city where Jake has always dreamed of playing in jazz clubs. To punish Armstrong for being the person that he can never be, Jake makes disparaging remarks about Chicago, and when Armstrong responds by calling him "ugly," the word reverberates with the pain of Jake's childhood. Jake retaliates by telling Floyd that Armstrong has flirted with his wife. Thus, Jake ironically uses the racist white power structure, which he hates, against Armstrong, just as lighter-skinned black children used a white standard of beauty against him. Jake does not understand his envy of Armstrong and so considers their tense encounter Armstrong's fault rather than in any way his own. Uncomfortable with Armstrong's self-confidence and sophistication and angered by the familiar old retort, Jake denigrates the very qualities that he envies, saying Armstrong is "trying to be white" (78). When Jake hears of Armstrong's death, he represses his indirect role in the murder by mentally chastising Armstrong for disregarding the racist conventions that he himself detests, "Yella bastard shoulda kept his mouth shut" (80). By implicating Jake as an accessory to Armstrong's murder, Campbell suggests that racism's victims can become its unwitting perpetrators.

In a similarly complex way, Campbell examines Armstrong's motivations for speaking to a white woman in the Deep South, representing the action not simply as an impetuous boyish response to a dare but as a conscious refusal to let southern racial conventions define him. Campbell's Till figure is keenly aware of how subservient his country cousins are to white people, and he does not want to be seen in the same light, by either the black "*country fools*" (11) with whom he plays pool or the "poor-white-trash" (13) for whom they work: "He deliberately made his voice loud and condescending, so that everyone understood that he was a Chicago boy, born and bred, city slick and so cool that nobody better not mess with him" (11). Jake's disrespectful comment about Armstrong's father, whom Armstrong rarely sees, only increases Armstrong's determination to set himself apart from other black people so as not to be seen as a stereotypical fatherless black boy. To the uncomprehending black men in the pool hall, he shows off the French phrases he learned from his father, a World War II veteran: "*Voulez-vous danser avec moi ce soir? Vous êtes belle, mademoiselle*" (12). Nonsensical in this context, they simply suggest bravado. But when Armstrong unwittingly repeats the phrases in front of a white woman, they produce a different effect, although it is significant that Lily does not comprehend his French and so does not sense any provocation in his remarks. With their connotation of intimacy, however, these phrases suggest to readers just how daring Armstrong's subsequent eye contact and exchange of laughter with Lily is, transforming their chance encounter into an almost deliberate flirtation, which is exactly what Floyd Cox will accuse him of. That Campbell portrays the encounter as accidental only amplifies readers' shock at its outcome.

To establish the link between southern race and gender oppression, Campbell represents Lily, whose dreams have died in her stifling marriage, as pleased by Armstrong's attention. Lily unexpectedly experiences a powerful moment of sexual attractiveness and social daring because her encounter with Armstrong functions as a double defiance: first, of gender conventions (she has disobeyed her husband's order to stay in their truck) and, second, of southern racial conventions (she has had an encounter with a black man). While the stolen time exhilarates Lily, it threatens her husband's control over her body and focuses readers' attention on how inextricably southern white womanhood was linked to racial attitudes in the Jim Crow South. Immediately before Lily's encounter with Armstrong, Campbell depicts her as eager for sex with her husband who has been away on a job but repressed by Floyd's beliefs that only whores initiate intercourse. Campbell portrays Lily as a woman trapped—horrified by Floyd's plan to retaliate against Armstrong but economically dependent on him. This feeling of powerlessness inhibits Lily from acting on her better instincts and telling the truth about her encounter with Armstrong. Lily's failure to prevent his murder ends her budding relationship with Ida Long, a black woman she has encountered in the train station, a place that both women frequent in order to fantasize about escaping their circumscribed lives. Campbell suggests that the only way Lily can live with Floyd's emotional and physical brutality is to embrace a narrative of his heroism in protecting her from the proverbial "black male beast," even if he is actually a harmless teenage boy. So Lily consoles herself by thinking, "I've got a man who'll kill for me" (64, 150). As with Jake, Campbell uses Lily's childhood to explain her convoluted thinking about sex and sin and race. Lily is haunted by memories of an uncle who sexually abused her. Campbell flashes back to these awful memories whenever Lily doubts herself in the present, such as when she wonders whether her sexual desires for her husband are normal and whether the chance incident with Armstrong was her fault.

Finally, Campbell probes the psyche of Armstrong's murderer, once more following a trail of psychic pain back to childhood. She links Floyd's need to control his wife and his decision to kill Armstrong not only to southern society's sexist and racist ideology but also to a deep uncertainty about his own manhood, caused by a feeling of inferiority to his macho older brother and to a fear that his father loves John Earl more because his brother is more masculine than he is. Floyd's insecurities manifest themselves in violent behaviors toward those he avowedly loves when they disappoint him, like Lily and his son, and toward those his society has taught him to hate, like Armstrong. Floyd's father first questioned his son's manhood during his first hunting trip. Only nine and afraid of blood and guns, Floyd throws up when he sees the wounded "deer, still alive, bleeding and twitching, a terrible, hysterical lowing coming from its half-opened mouth." His father's callous gender-inflected response—"I didn't know I was taking a girl hunting" (121)—influences Floyd's choices for the rest of his life because he is forever trying to win his father's love by proving his own manhood. Floyd is always worried about his father's reactions and ever conscious of how his brother would act. As Campbell makes clear through Floyd's thoughts, an attempt to be appropriately masculine governs Floyd's reaction to Lily's encounter with Armstrong. The southern racial code his father has instilled in him requires that he confront Armstrong in order to affirm his masculinity. Only when Floyd has pulled the trigger that he could not pull at age nine does he win his father's qualified approval: "Well, you might can't fix everything that needs fixing, but damned if you can't make some things right." The reassurance that Floyd gains from finally "knowing that his father, at last, was satisfied with him" (43) is short-lived because his father blames him when all three Cox men are arrested for Armstrong's murder. Then the cycle of violence, in which an abused person becomes an abuser, begins all over again as Floyd discharges his emotional pain onto Lily, who absorbs his blows because of her own insecurities. For Campbell, the psychological wounds that Floyd experienced growing up combine with southern society's racism to provide the answer to Armstrong's question: "Where did all that hatred come from?"

There is a fifth significant player in Campbell's racial drama, although he is a passive onlooker. Her portrait of the closet liberal Clayton Pinochet answers a corollary question: Why didn't liberal white southerners do anything to stop the violence? After the not-guilty verdict that freed Emmett Till's murderers, a white minister from Atlanta, Joe Rabun, wrote to the *Atlanta Constitution*, expressing his shame and responsibility as a white man for Till's murder and the biased verdict that followed: "As long as we remain silent and inactive before the corruption of justice, all of us are criminal. When we see anyone deprived of his rights as an equal citizen in these United States, and make no objection, our own rights, lives and liberty are in jeopardy" (151–52). Clayton acts as such a "silent and inactive" witness to Armstrong's senseless murder because he does not do all that he could have done when Armstrong tells him he has gotten into "some trouble" with Floyd Cox. Rather than intercede, Clayton takes the easy way out, deciding to pay for Armstrong's college education to make amends for his cowardice: "He liked the grandness of the notion, and for a moment his high-minded intentions took hold of him and blotted out his nagging guilt. He didn't need to go to Floyd Cox; that wasn't his duty, he reminded himself" (25). Although after the murder, Clayton, a reporter, works behind the scenes to alert northern reporters, he has never told his neighbors what he really thinks about their prejudice or worked openly for racial justice or even contemplated marrying his long-time black mistress Marguerite. He is unhappy because he does not have the courage to defy his rich father or to face the disapproval of his neighbors. Campbell depicts Clayton as a complex product of his upbringing. He is in love with Marguerite, who reminds him of the black woman who raised him, but he is unable to give up his inheritance and the wealth to which he has become accustomed in order to marry her. As a result he loses her. The son of the richest white man in town, Clayton does have a social conscience, but the racial guilt money that he doles out behind the scenes is his father's, the product of cheap labor by poor blacks and poor whites.

Campbell's decision to intersperse scenes set in Chicago with those in Mississippi, especially in the second half of the novel, allows her to examine African

American migration from the Jim Crow South. Perhaps unexpectedly for some readers, Campbell draws a very clear line from old southern slave quarters to newer northern housing projects,[5] from sharecropping in the rural South at the beginning of the twentieth century to the disappearance of good factory jobs in the urban North at century's end, from early hopes of a promised land up North to contemporary despair in urban ghettos. The two settings remind readers that blacks who migrated North still had deep roots in the South (family ties, cooking, the blues, jazz), but they also suggest that, even today and well outside the South, African Americans are not out of the reach of what Campbell believes are the twin legacies of slavery and segregation: white racism and the potential for black "overidentification with being a victim," which can lead to feelings of powerlessness.[6] Campbell illustrates her point by giving Wydell and his cousin Lionel menial jobs in the same Chicago factory, which discriminates against black employees in the 1930s and 1940s. While Wydell becomes discouraged and turns to alcohol, Lionel saves his money, buys a small shoe repair business, expands to open a retail store, and sends his sons to college. In the first half of the novel, Campbell depicts many of her characters, white and black, as victims to one extent or another, but in the second half she pays special attention to those characters who rise above their unfortunate, painful childhoods. However, even as she champions constructive resistance to hardship, she does not downplay or obscure the effects of individual or institutional racism (or sexism or colorism or class elitism, for that matter).

After Floyd's trial, chapters alternate between the Todds in Chicago, struggling to make a life after Armstrong's death, and the Coxes in Mississippi, struggling to make a living in a town shell-shocked by the bad national publicity the family has brought down on their community. This juxtaposition between black and white families points up the irony of Campbell's title, *Your Blues Ain't Like Mine.* Muddy Waters and Robert Johnson are not Hank Williams and Patsy Cline, but Campbell links the pain that the lyrics of the blues and country music give voice to and the solace that the music provides—blues to poor blacks and country music to poor whites. Both the Todd and Cox families are dysfunctional, warped by childhood abuse and society's race, class, and gender biases. Both black and white fathers, Wydell and Floyd, attempt to escape family and employment problems through alcohol. Both black and white sons, W. T. and Floydjunior, are wounded by their fathers' lack of attention and by narrow notions of masculinity that are synonymous with domination. Both fall prey to drugs and violence. Both black and white women struggle with poverty and single parenthood as their husbands are increasingly absent, but it is the white woman, Lily, who goes on welfare, much to her daughter's dismay, and the black woman, Delotha, who works hard and opens her own beauty shop. By reversing racial stereotypes, Campbell underlines that some of the problems that demoralize the Coxes and the Todds—such as low wages and lack of education—are class related not simply race based, although she does not obfuscate the historical causes of the disproportionate link between race and class. By comparing these two working-class families, who because of white racism have not been able to see the similarities in their lives, Campbell prepares readers for the cross-racial labor coalition with which she concludes the novel.

The psychological realism that Campbell employs to probe the motivations of the characters linked by Armstrong's murder gives way to a more sweeping exploration of social change in Mississippi and Chicago over the three decades following Emmett Till's murder. Campbell needs those thirty years in order to arrive at her surprisingly happy ending, which leaves readers with hope that Mississippi (and the South) may rise above its notoriously racist past and that poor Mississippians, black and white, may someday come to understand that they share an economic struggle despite their racial differences. Wydell Todd and his son W. T. flee Chicago's violent, drug-infested streets for a bucolic sojourn in Mississippi, and Ida Long's son Sweetbabe and his family leave Chicago's cold weather and growing crime wave so that he can teach in his Mississippi hometown. Both returns are harbingers of the black migration back to the South which began in the 1970s and increased dramatically in the 1990s.

Clayton Pinochet, the closet liberal who has cowered behind his racist father's bank account, splits his inheritance with his biracial half-sister Ida, an act that foreshadows the late 1990s trend in fictional and nonfictional explorations of hidden black-white family connections as well as the debate about reparations for slavery. Indeed, the resolution of this subplot suggests that reparations may not be simply a handout for past social injustices but in some cases a rightful inheritance withheld—an inheritance, however, that Campbell clearly believes will not be shared without plenty of proof and provocation. Floyd and Lily Cox's daughter Doreen reaches across the color line during a labor dispute at the New Plantation Catfish Farm and Processing Plant where she works with Ida Long. Ida emerges as a spokesperson for black and white members of the working class. While incidents such as these can and do sometimes occur in the South, to conclude with all five surely paints a rosy picture of racial reconciliation in rural

Mississippi. In part because labor unions are rare in the South, the interracial alliance along working-class lines is an especially unusual occurrence, a fact that led one reviewer to conclude that "the ending tries to force an upbeat notion onto what is a bleak reality" (Katzenbach). In contrast to Campbell's novel, Anthony Walton's nonfiction portrait *Mississippi* (1996) depicts rural race relations as closer to polite but distant tolerance, and anthropologist Carol Stacks's study of African Americans returning to the rural Carolinas, *Call to Home* (1996), reveals more than a little white resistance to their new ideas and their increased presence in elected offices.

Campbell would more likely term her happy ending utopian rather than unrealistic, for the social changes she orchestrates in her novel do not come totally out of the blue, even though they may not exactly match current southern realities. Simply to chalk up her happy ending to the generic demands of popular fiction, as some reviewers did,[7] is to miss how the successes of her triumphant characters, also victims of a variety of social prejudices and pressures, drive home Campbell's strong personal belief in the possibility of rising above one's social circumstances. The contrast she sets up between Lionel and Wydell is one example; another is the contrast between Floyd Cox and his daughter. Doreen also grows up poor and prejudiced, but, unlike her father, she has encounters with African Americans at school and at work that broaden her perceptions of black people. While Campbell has Doreen acknowledge that she will probably never totally overcome the daily diet of racism on which she was raised, Campbell emphasizes through Doreen's exchange with her mother the economic reasons that nudge her toward a new way of thinking: "Mama, either I work with them or I get in the welfare line with them, and you know how I feel about that. I was raised around here, and even though I went to school with them, I always felt like they was different from white people, like I was better than they were. Hell, I was raised on that feeling, and I'll probably take it to my grave, but Mama, you know one thing: It's getting to where I just can't afford thinking like that no more. Them feelings just ain't practical when you work at the New Plantation" (377–78).

For Campbell's characters, white or black, to improve their lives, they must work hard in an adverse society as well as face the consequences of their own misperceptions and the actions or inactions that follow from them. Given the racist murder that provided the germ for her narrative, Campbell is especially interested in racial misperceptions and in strategies for overcoming them. In

Your Blues Ain't Like Mine, television and popular culture play no small role in reeducating working-class white women. Watching an acclaimed documentary on America's civil rights era, surely a reference to the 1980s PBS television series *Eyes on the Prize,* Doreen gains a different perspective on her father and mother's involvement in Armstrong Todd's murder. Even Lily admits aloud what she refused to say to anyone thirty years before: "He didn't deserve to die" (380). The ensuing years also teach Lily that Floyd did not kill Armstrong for her, the racist fantasy that she clung to when the murder occurred, a male master narrative that she finally abandons during a final confrontation with Floyd: "You ain't done nothing for me. Everything was for you. To make you feel good. Even that boy" (426). While Doreen grows up listening to black soul music on the radio (the Dells, Marvin Gaye, Diana Ross and the Supremes, Smokey Robinson and the Miracles, and the Temptations), television provides her mother with a new perspective on race. When Lily accidentally happens upon the *Oprah Winfrey Show,* she finds herself hooked because Oprah, like Lily, was molested by a relative when she was a child. As a testimony to Oprah's championing of women's self-help and to her appeal across the color line, Campbell has Lily watching Oprah when Floyd returns near the end of the novel. Although he expects to reunite with Lily, as he has done many times before, Lily for the first time is able to muster the will power to withstand his pleas. Oprah, with Doreen's encouragement, has given Lily the belief that she can assume responsibility for herself.

Cultural critic Benjamin DeMott argues that contemporary advertising and the popular media have promulgated a misleading and simplistic assumption that racism has to do "solely with the conditions of personal feeling" between blacks and whites—a shallow understanding of the problem that omits racism's "institutional, historical and political ramifications" (23). But despite popular culture's drawbacks, Campbell suggests that it can work to increase familiarity between the races, to dismantle some stereotypes, and to explore possibilities of interracial interaction. Unlike other popular novelists who write about race relations and focus on personal relationships, Campbell, whose mass-market paperbacks reach a large and varied audience, does not ignore the "institutional, historical and political ramifications" of racism. For example, in *Your Blues Ain't Like Mine,* when Stonewall Pinochet tries to enlist his son in his latest money-making venture, the New Plantation Catfish Farm and Processing Plant, Clayton refuses to become involved, privately mulling over concerns that Campbell clearly shares: "But he heard enough to know that the new industry his father was heralding offered nothing to the legions of poor whites and blacks who had become idle because of the mechanization of cotton farming. The profit margin of catfish farming would be maintained by the abundance of cheap labor in the area" (222). Clayton's more socially meaningful epiphany comes belatedly, after his father's death, when he realizes that no matter what his neighbors think he cannot in good conscience assume his father's old position among the town's white powerbrokers, the so-called "Honorable Men of Hopewell" (422). Thus, rather than continue to sympathize privately with black people and occasionally work behind the scenes, Clayton finally goes public with his liberal views and makes common cause with Ida Long in an attempt to change working conditions at the catfish processing plant. Readers last glimpse Clayton joining Ida and her co-workers on the picket line. Campbell does not sentimentalize Clayton's decision. She makes clear that his father's death has made Clayton's choice far easier and that Clayton's silence until his father's death has insured him an inheritance that leaves him financially secure. But his silence comes at a great personal cost, for in kowtowing to his father, Clayton, as a young man, gives up his romance with a poor white woman whom his father deemed inappropriate, and later Clayton loses the love of his long-term black mistress, Marguerite.

The lower-class white men, Floyd Cox and his son Floydjunior, are not as successful in altering their attitudes towards race and race relations as Doreen and Clayton because they never see beyond their own point of view. The Cox men equate black progress with stealing white jobs, and thus they label integration as the source of their own economic problems. They see themselves as victims of affirmative action and refuse to accept any responsibility for their own fate, a position Floyd regularly expounds on to Lily: "Now you got niggers with jobs, and white men can't find work. I ask you, is that right? In Birmingham I used to see niggers dressed in suits. Suits! Going to work. The women wearing high heels and dresses, going downtown to their jobs. That's what's done happened to us, Lily. I mean, why should the kids try hard in school when they know damn well that when they get out, everything that's worth having is going to them?" (308). Most insidiously, Floyd attempts to heal the bad relationship he has with Floydjunior by capitalizing on their mutual racism. After watching an interview on the nightly news about a black businessman who owns his own contracting company, Floydjunior yells, "Goddamn niggers have everything. There ain't nothing left for us." His father's reply—"They giving them everything. Affirmative action. And where's the affirmative action for white men?"

(338)—makes the Cox men, who are frequently at odds, realize that they do have one thing in common, hatred of black people.

This contemporary backlash against affirmative action parallels the 1950s backlash against the Supreme Court's *Brown v. the Board of Education* decision, which Campbell suggests led to the escalation of racial hatred and violence, such as the murder of Emmett Till. Campbell highlights how race and gender identities are intertwined with class because the Cox men are preoccupied with whether white people will view them as "white trash" if they work the same jobs as black men. In 1956 when Olive Arnold Adams published *Time Bomb: Mississippi Exposed and the Full Story of Emmett Till* under the sponsorship of the Mississippi Regional Council of Negro Leadership, she drew this character sketch of the lower-class southern white man: "he knows he is looked down on as 'white trash,' but he compensates for this by grinding his heel on the neck of the Negro. That way, he can be better than somebody, or at least feel better. Actually, he questions his superiority. He knows he does not command respect, so he demands it through acts of violence and terror" (216).

But in *Your Blues Ain't Like Mine,* misplaced blame does not occur on only one side of the color line. Delotha's attempt to bring Armstrong back to life by reuniting with Wydell in order to have another male child backfires when she begins to ignore her husband, to spoil her son W.T., and to blame his behavioral problems on the white teachers who try to intervene in order to stop his fighting. When a white policeman questions W.T. about a gang-related robbery, Delotha lies to provide him with an alibi. At first Delotha thinks she is protecting W.T. from white people, but eventually she begins to face up to a more complex truth. First, she acknowledges her responsibility in the family's breakdown—her mistake in trying to replace Armstrong with W.T.: "Had she pushed her daughters away from her and held her son too close?" (399). Although Delotha thinks she is being a good mother to W.T., her overindulgence, which she perceives as loving care, teaches "grandiosity rather than self-acceptance,"[8] and he takes to the streets first to avoid his parents' frequent fights and then to prove he is cool. Eventually, when Delotha finds a gun in W.T.'s room, she accepts the truth and concurs with Lionel's assessment of Chicago, "The streets is killing more black boys than the white folks ever could. We always had more than one enemy" (407).

Nor does Campbell let Wydell escape blame. While he proves himself an excellent father to his two daughters, he assumes that he does not know how to father sons because his own father was not a good role model. As a result, Wydell never establishes a good relationship with either Armstrong or W.T. but leaves the parenting of his sons to Delotha. Only when Wydell works through his own childhood trauma does he begin to understand his role in shaping W.T.'s fate. Wydell's intervention near the end of the novel literally saves W.T.'s life. Their trip to Mississippi, which removes W.T. from Chicago's perils, concludes the novel, functioning simultaneously as a lesson in family history and African American history. Significantly, the trip allows Wydell to introduce W.T. to the blues. Today's young black men prefer rap music to the blues, bell hooks argues, because they "do not want to hear an honest emotional expression of black male vulnerability": "They would rather hear rap music with its aggressive presentation of invulnerability. If the choice is between exposing the true authentic self and clinging to the false self, most males maintain their fantasy bonding rather than seek the real" (99). W.T.'s growing interest in the music that his father loves and used to sing suggests that he may finally be ready to express his own pain, rather than mask it with bravado.

By delving into the consciousnesses of all those involved in Emmett Till's murder and by extending her examination to those of the next generation as well, Campbell suggests that it is simplistic to read past racial incidents solely through the lens of race and problematic to see contemporary interracial interactions solely through the prism of past race relations. Embedded in *Your Blues Ain't Like Mine* is her strong belief that the act of verbally expressing pain—in this case both psychological and physical—is, as Scarry argues, "a necessary prelude to the collective task of diminishing pain" (9). Although Campbell suggests that watching Oprah on television may help Lily verbalize her pain, she is especially concerned with literacy and fashions several scenes in which learning to read paves the way to a better life, for children and adults. For example, Clayton Pinochet tutors Ida Long's son Sweetbabe so that he can go to college, and later he takes on other young black pupils. He even teaches Marguerite how to read with the result that she becomes a person with "her own opinions and demands" (315), eventually refusing to be a kept woman. With the importance of reading and education occurring as a leitmotif in the novel, Campbell shares a concern that hooks emphasizes in *We Real Cool* (2004), repeatedly showing that books can liberate the spirits of people demoralized by stereotypes, that books can teach people how to hope (38). In *The Body in Pain* Scarry argues that "the story of *expressing* physical pain eventually opens into the wider frame of *invention.*

The elemental 'as if' of the person in pain ('It feels as if . . . ,' 'It is as though . . .') will lead out into the array of counterfactual revisions entailed in making," in creating something new (22). Bebe Moore Campbell's *Your Blues Ain't Like Mine* simultaneously expresses America's complex racial pain, physical and psychological, and invents a cure for it. In functioning both as a way to express pain and a way to move beyond pain, Campbell's novel sings the blues for readers.

NOTES

1. Here I use Scarry's terms and theories in *The Body in Pain,* 13, to describe Campbell's technique and thus amplify and extend my own earlier analysis of Campbell's novel, which appeared in *Race Mixing: Southern Fiction since the Sixties,* 22–27, 217–19.

2. Campbell, *Your Blues Ain't Like Mine,* 42. Subsequent citations are indicated parenthetically in the text.

3. This is bell hooks's assessment of the consequences of psychological wounding in early childhood in *We Real Cool: Black Men and Masculinity,* 98.

4. To compare the fiction and the alleged facts, see Olive Arnold Adams, *Time Bomb: Mississippi Exposed and the Full Story of Emmett Till,* excerpted in Metress, *Lynching,* 217. In the Metress collection, see similar accounts by James L. Hicks and L. Alex Wilson. See also Whitfield, *A Death in the Delta.*

5. In *Mississippi,* 43, Anthony Walton points out this link on which I elaborate here.

6. Graeber, "It's about Childhood." Campbell's concern is one that bell hooks raises in her focus on black men in *We Real Cool:* "Excessive focus on the ways racism wounds black male spirits is often evoked to deflect attention away from all other sources of emotional pain. That deflection is disempowering because it sends the message that there is nothing black males can do to create positive change since they are 'powerless' to end white supremacy. Racism does damage black males, but so does sexism, so does class elitism with its hedonistic materialism, and so does abandonment and abuse in family relationships. All the sources of black male pain and powerlessness must be named if healing is to take place, if black males are to reclaim their agency" (100).

7. See the anonymous reviewer for *Kirkus Reviews* and Katzenbach, "Ricochets in Their Hearts." In Alison Light's discussion of feminist utopian fiction, "Fear of the Happy Ending," she argues that part of the "fear of the happy ending" has been a definition of radical politics that "conceives its job as one solely of critique" and rarely of desire fulfilled (92).

8. While hooks (*We Real Cool,* 94) sees the overindulgence as a product of patriarchal privileging of male children, Campbell seems to suggest that another cause may be the danger black men are exposed to, whether from white racism or black gang violence.

WORKS CITED

Adams, Olive Arnold. Excerpt from *Time Bomb: Mississippi Exposed and the Full Story of Emmett Till.* In Metress, 213–24.

Campbell, Bebe Moore. *Your Blues Ain't Like Mine.* 1992. New York: Ballantine, 1995.

DeMott, Benjamin. *The Trouble with Friendship: Why Americans Can't Think Straight about Race.* 1995. New Haven, CT: Yale University Press, 1998.

Dittmer, John. *Local People: The Struggle for Civil Rights in Mississippi.* Urbana: University of Illinois Press, 1995.

Dyson, Michael Eric. "Remembering Emmett Till." 1971. In Metress, 266–70.

Felman, Shoshana, and Dori Laub. *Testimony: Crises of Witnessing in Literature, Psychoanalysis, and History.* New York: Routledge, 1992.

Graeber, Laurel. "It's about Childhood." *New York Times Book Review,* 20 September 1992, 13.

hooks, bell. *We Real Cool: Black Men and Masculinity.* New York: Routledge, 2004.

Jones, Suzanne W. *Race Mixing: Southern Fiction since the Sixties.* Baltimore: Johns Hopkins University Press, 2004.

Katzenbach, John. "Ricochets in Their Hearts." *Washington Post,* 10 October 1992.

Light, Alison. "Fear of the Happy Ending: *The Color Purple,* Reading and Racism." In *Plotting Change: Contemporary Women's Fiction,* edited by Linda Anderson, 85–96. London: Edward Arnold, 1990.

Metress, Christopher. *The Lynching of Emmett Till: A Documentary Narrative.* Charlottesville: University of Virginia Press, 2002.

Rabun, Joe A. Letter to the editor of the *Atlanta Constitution,* 9 October 1955. In Metress, 151–52.

Review of *Your Blues Ain't Like Mine. Kirkus Reviews,* 15 June 1992, 733–34.

Scarry, Elaine. *The Body in Pain: The Making and Unmaking of the World.* New York: Oxford University Press, 1985.

Smith, Lillian. *Killers of the Dream.* 1949. New York: Norton, 1978.

Stack, Carol. *Call to Home: African Americans Reclaim the Rural South.* New York: Basic Books, 1996.

Walton, Anthony. *Mississippi: An American Journey.* New York: Alfred A. Knopf, 1996.

Whitfield, Stephen J. *A Death in the Delta: The Story of Emmett Till.* New York: Free Press, 1988.

GROTESQUE LAUGHTER, UNBURIED BODIES, AND HISTORY

Shape-Shifting in Lewis Nordan's Wolf Whistle

HARRIET POLLACK

You make a joke like that and you jes part of the problem.
—LEWIS NORDAN, *Wolf Whistle*, 102

Lewis Nordan's 1993 book *Wolf Whistle* is a fictionalization of fourteen-year-old Emmett Till's murder, written by a white writer who for thirty-eight years felt the story was not his to tell. His choices about emphasis, point of view, plot, and tone reveal the class and gender vulnerabilities that produced the insecure and destructive whiteness that feeds racial violence. Nordan, who grew up in Itta Bena, Mississippi, was one year older than Emmett Till at the time of the murder and speaks of having been haunted all his life by a newspaper description of the found body: "helpless feet and legs, upside down in the water, almost comic." In his essay "Growing Up White in the South," Nordan writes that Emmett Till's was "a death that marked not only a turning point in civil rights but, in a very personal way, in my own life as well" (3, 5).

> My racial identification with the murderers of Emmett Till still troubles me . . . I had never really thought there was something wrong with black and white schools, white and black water fountains, white and black bathrooms, blacks in the back of the bus, and grown people saying "Sir" to children . . . *Wolf Whistle* is in some ways an angry book. I still have a hard time talking about my upbringing in the South without an anger rising up in me. I feel angry sometimes that I was limited in these ways—although it's nobody else's fault . . . And the story I wanted to tell was what happened to the people in a community where murder was committed and they suddenly realized it might be their fault. This is the white story of the murder of Emmett Till. ("An Interview with the Author," 4–5)

Thirty-eight years after the event, Nordan finds a need and a voice to reapproach the incident. Unexpectedly, he writes a comic novel that is dead accurate, magically fantastic, seeking cultural transformation—a magic in its own right—and that is full of strategic shape-shifting.

The surprising choices Nordan makes, particularly mutations of the presumed events of history, are inventions that, if unpacked, may focus the central meanings of the past, even while they alter the story. In the postmodern twenty-first century, history is understood as a construct that can be told many ways for many purposes and is essentially so like fictional narrative (in its use of prefigured narrative conventions) that it is problematic to talk about "historical truth" versus "fiction." History is assumed to shift shape in language and to be in that sense unknowable. On the other hand, in the political twenty-first century, it is also understood that narrative is always political and that *how* history is told matters. In the genre of historical fiction and this novel in particular, history and fiction recurrently blur and unsettlingly shift shape.

In this novel, the disconcerting shape-shifting is strategic. The novel's tone shifts between comic and tragic, and damaged children and their unburied bodies shift one into the other.[1] In a parallel manner, shape-shifting between history and fiction is felt in the changed details of Bobo's shooting, in which, puzzlingly, he manages to shoot Solon first. It is felt in the altered characterizations of the historical players Roy and Carolyn Bryant and J. W. Milam, called in the novel Solon Gregg, Lady Sally Anne Montberclair, and her husband Lord Poindexter. The location of Money, Mississippi, is displaced into Arrow Catcher. And the meaning of the trial itself shifts shape when it partly transforms Alice Conroy and her attending fourth-grade class. So, my inquiry here concerns the conscious and unconscious transformations occurring in the writer's imagination.

What are the purposes of this shape-shifting? On one hand, I consider its usefulness in the analysis of whiteness and of racism, especially as it denies, challenges, and undercuts rigid boundaries—conceptual constructions that segregation fetishizes with ideas about purity and the danger of border crossing. Nordan's shifts erase borders rather than insisting on them as inviolable. On the other hand, I am also interested in the service shape-shifting performs in the expiation of the author's guilt and regret in national and personal history—dually triggered by the experience of the death of Emmett Till, national son, and by Nordan's own personal loss of two sons, one by suicide. Grief for these sons brings Nordan to connect and reconnect with the story of Emmett Till and his

Giuseppe Arcimboldo (1527–1593) *Wasser*, 1566.
Kunsthistorisches Museum, Vienna Austria © Erich Lessing. *Courtesy Art Resource, New York.*

double, Bobo, killed in Arrow Catcher, Mississippi. Nordan himself reports meeting and speaking to Mamie Till Bradley about their grief for lost sons.

Anyone who had not read Nordan's comic novel about the murder of Emmett Till could only be uneasy at hearing it described. Nordan's comic voice creates grotesque humor. The grotesque is a form that is about shape-shifting. It is easiest for me to reference the grotesque, and the genre's characteristic shifts, visually. Consider Giuseppe Arcimboldo's painting *Wasser* (Water), made in 1566 as part of his series of bizarre and fascinating paintings representing the elements and seasons. Seen close up, a mass of sea creatures can be recognized. And yet seen at a distance, the portrait resolves into a human face. The subject shifts shape in a glance, and the work is about perspective. The grotesque is a genre originating with paintings of fantastic creatures, combining human and animal elements, as in Lucas Cranach's 1523 *Der Papstesel* (The Pope), in which

The lynching of Rubin Stacey. *Courtesy Picture History.*

the Pope has the head of a cock, the belly of a woman, the feet of a donkey. The form, from its start, has been didactic, satiric, instructive—exposing deformity of the spirit. Contradictory visions shift shape—the comic is also tragic, the ludicrous is frightening, the droll is terrible, the customary is odd. This unsettling uncertainty harbors and promotes a potential provocation that urges an audience to uneasy thoughtfulness. The recent powerful installation and book *Without Sanctuary,* a collection of lynching memorabilia that is certainly not funny but plenty odd and overwhelmingly horrifying, today takes its power from the grotesque, as its images simultaneously fit both the categories of "ordinary" and terrifying: a young girl smiles into a camera before a notable landmark, but the landmark is a tortured black human body. The doubleness forces an audience to discomfort, awakening contemplation of our national racial history. Similarly, Nordan's grotesque humor shifts between the absurdity of and the prevailing horror of cultural circumstance and national trauma.

Speaking of his horrifying comedy, Nordan tells the story of having accepted an early criticism that his writing was too serious and without irony: "From that moment I became a comic writer, but I was always writing from the same place, that is, that deeply serious, melodramatic horror that's at the heart of my work . . . Something about me believes that comedy comes out of darkness and that all comedy is underpinned by loss. Often my revisions take that form. The first draft is just too serious and the second draft is comic . . . yet you never forget their seriousness either" (Maher interview, 118).

In Nordan's grotesque fibrillation between the too serious and the comic, laughter can attack the terrible. M. M. Bakhtin describes the grotesque as a genre through which immense "cosmic catastrophe . . . is . . . transformed into [comic] monsters" (336). In that transformation, there is the possibility of humanizing and undermining monsters by degrading them with subversive laughter. In *Wolf Whistle*, uncanny laughter attacks the assumed separateness of southern apartheid categories—particularly the not-at-all separate categories of prevailing and idiotic. Comic fibrillation challenges the notion of rigid category separation central to segregation—and undercuts apartheid's belief in and insistence on enforcing inviolable boundaries.

Yet even while celebrating grotesque laughter and authorizing the subversion of whiteness with it, Nordan builds the plot of *Wolf Whistle* to question and indict ambiguous laughter's less commendable uses, shifting the tones of the novel again. While provoking us to laugh out loud, in subversive assault, at what is not funny—white subjectivity and the sources of Solon's pathetic violence in his class, gender, and racial vulnerabilities—Nordan shifts and opens wide the question of what the Arrow Catcher community and, more problematically, we readers can laugh at too easily. Roy Dale enjoys jokes about Bobo's corpse, found in the river tied to a gin fan with barbed wire. The regrettable gag was that a black boy stole a gin fan—and was trying to swim across the lake with it. Laughter can be release or escape; it can expose and subvert. Laughter can transform. But laughter can also be the problem—it can signify willingness to callously turn horror into cartoon, to obscure behavior that should cause outrage. And Nordan shows us that laughter can be a testimony of membership in the clan of whiteness, reinforcing apartheid boundaries. The kids at Arrow Catcher High School laugh at their tall tale all day long, but in a central scene, Roy Dale tells the problem joke to Smokey Viner, a boy with a head so hard he enjoys butting it into walls—"blammo, the plaster . . . flying, smack" (*Wolf Whistle*, 203)—only to discover that he, Roy Dale has been the thick-headed one when Viner says:

"It ain't right . . . Y'all ought to be shamed of yourself, laughing about a boy got killed." The room was very quiet, no one was moving, or scarcely breathing. Some time passed like this. Then Roy Dale wondered why he hadn't known enough to say what crazy Smoky Viner said . . . Finally in a low voice, almost a whisper, some boy said, "Uh Smoky, it was a, you know, white lady. A colored boy and a white lady." This was gently said, a means of assuring that the record was straight.

Smoky Viner said, "It ain't right."

Somebody said, "We ain't said it was right, Smoky. We just kidding around."

Smoky Viner said. "I laughed too, I couldn't help it . . . Hope I live long enough to forgive myself for that laugh." (205–6)

As Rufus McKay, who speaks what he thinks, says after another joke, "You make a joke like that and you jes part of the problem . . . All y'all just as guilty as sin, as guilty as the gravedigger, as guilty as me" (102). And Nordan tells us this while, page after page, he is making us laugh our heads off uneasily and provokingly and guiltily at unreasonable and absurd class, gender, and race violence and vulnerability.

Edward Dupuy, in an interview with Nordan, connected humor to philosophy, citing Kierkegaard's having "said that humor was an intermediate stage between what he called the 'ethical' and 'religious' spheres of existence." In the same interview, Nordan talks about redemption in his fiction: "[There is] the charming boy that, at least fictionally, I seem to have been [identifying himself with Sugar Mecklin, a child who recurs in Nordan's novels], and then [there is] the unsavory adult I seem to have become, [identifying himself with all the alcoholic, self-absorbed fathers of his fiction,] and then a kind of redemption" (Dupuy interview, 103). Nordan's sense of pursing redemption in his fiction has to do with his "racial identification with . . . murderers," with his discovery through the Till case that he is "implicated." He's called *Wolf Whistle* "the white trash version of the Emmett Till murder . . . the story of the people who . . . didn't quite understand their own culpability in the situation" (84). He elaborated in a 2001 interview given to Thomas Bjerre:

That was a kind of modest put-down of the self. You know, "I'm just an old whitetrash boy." Maybe a little disingenuous, maybe a little jokey . . .

 [But] our voice was too silent during the fifties. We didn't say, "How dare you." Instead we just retreated and thought, "Oh my god, is this us who did this?" So we never really even talked about it at the dinner table, we were so horrified by it and so implicated in it, by our silences and by our casual use of racial epithets, and things like that. It was a turning point really. The truth is until I embraced who I actually am, certainly who I was, I had no way of writing that story effectively. So that's what I meant by the "white trash" version. (Bjerre interview, 374–75)

Brannon Costello in his reading of *Wolf Whistle*, "Poor White Trash, Great White Hope: Race, Class, and the (De)Construction of Whiteness," argues that Nordan undertakes the analysis of whiteness that Toni Morrison recommends for American fiction, showing that members of this social group called trash, because of "economic . . . and social marginalization, . . . cling fervently to their identities as white, but their classification as 'trash,' as the white Other, complicates that whiteness. Thus, [they] must constantly reassert . . . bonds with whiteness" (Costello, 210). He quotes Constance Penley on an insecure class that "must engage in the never-ending labor of . . . codifying . . . behavior so as to clearly signify a difference from blackness that will, in spite of everything, express some minuscule, if pathetic, . . . [assertion of] superiority" (Penley, 90). Historian Leon Litwack in "Hellhounds," his companion essay to *Without Sanctuary*, quotes the southern critic who observed that "men lynch most readily . . . when the black victim has 'offended that intangible something called *racial superiority*.'" Litwack's earlier history *Been in the Storm So Long: The Aftermath of Slavery* analyzes perceived offenses to "racial etiquette": "The freedman did not have to say anything in order to displease or raise suspicions in the whites; he only had to look a certain way . . . fail to exhibit the expected lowered head . . . [or] to yield enough by two or three inches in meeting on the sidewalk." Refusal to perform the mannerisms of "respect, humility, and cheerful obedience . . . were not so much discourtesies or intended provocations as positive assertions of [African Americans'] status as free men and women" (257–59). And so, the slightest, most subtle breaks from a strict code of racial etiquette were all that was needed to challenge distressed whiteness.

Nordan comments that he does not so much exaggerate or invent in his grotesque caricatures as elaborate on what is: "sometimes exaggeration is not exaggeration. Sometimes it's just looking very closely at what we usually look at very superficially . . . We say that somebody died and cover them with a sheet and call the undertaker. But if you linger at the moment of death, and you linger with what you see and hear and smell and touch, and develop a body of detail about this death, it becomes so large that it almost seems exaggerated. It seems larger than life just because it has been elaborated rather than exaggerated" (Maher interview, 119). And so, *Wolf Whistle*'s comedy looks closely and elaborately at the exposed position and insecurity of various allied classes of white males.

That emphasis on white male insecurity points to why Nordan transforms the historical Carolyn Bryant, a poor white store clerk, into the wealthiest woman in Arrow Catcher. The discourse of protecting the lady is, of course, deeply implicated in the story of American racial inequity and brutality. Sheltering the emblematic female—the lady embodying all the graces of the class system of the South—and protecting her (the woman and the class system) is a discourse used to justify, warrant, and excuse the restriction and brutalization of African American men. Lady Sally Anne Montberclair, however, is not a woman to invite or even allow protection. "Barelegged and rumored to be modern" (25), Sally Anne is an imposing woman, shockingly comfortable with herself—comfortable enough to enter Red's Good-looking Bar and Gro. and straightforwardly, before the drinking men, pay "hard cash for tampons, and on her face [wear] the look of a woman who meant to use them, as advertised" (32). Her female competency and class security nonplusses Red and every man present, who would all prefer to protectively euphemize her purchase—in order to shelter themselves (though in the name of chivalry and sheltering the Woman) from her unsettling threat to their notions of masculinity—the threat that she herself signifies. The men, represented by Red, are flustered, dazed, and unmanned by Sally Anne's dumbfounded refusal of their euphemisms and their protection; above all they feel unmanned by their own alarmed fear of and discomfort with the competent other-class female. Nordan's quick comic attention to the unutterable female fact of menstruation is all he needs to undermine the cultural construct of the lady, her fragile charms, and the allure of female delicacy. Simultaneously, and with the same quick comedy, he undercuts the insecure assertion of male control of the female body. Sally Anne is shameless when, prescriptively, she should be modest and shamed. The cultural vocabulary that in a single breath maintains apartheid boundaries by insisting on white female purity and black male danger is a coherent language, a single aggressive discourse unconfident about control of female and black. And so Sally Anne's fictional female provocation extends into Bobo's perceived but unwitting further challenge of Solon with "two huhs and a yeah" (38).

Bobo's voice in this scene, as in history's record, is hard to locate. On a "dee-double" dare (33), he says something to Lady Sally Ann, looking her "right square in . . . face." The text tells us, "He said what he said, Bobo did" (34). And then from that absence, we chart reactions. The blues singers stopped playing. Lady Montberclair noticed nothing. "Everybody else heard it, though . . . Runt heard it and wondered if he could teach his parrot to say hubba-hubba . . . Gilbert Mecklin heard it . . . Wolf whistle, real low." As in history's record of Till, Bobo's voice is absent, overwritten with cacophony, with reported interpretations. Then Solon said, "'What did you say?' speaking to the . . . child. He said this slow and deliberate and mean" (35–36).

If at one level Nordan's interest in redemption through fiction has to do with cultural and "racial identification with . . . murderers," there is another related and personal culpability that Nordan is tracking, connected to hard-drinking men behaving badly in Red's Bar and Gro. and in their family lives as well. Nordan writes about alcoholic men and their implied abuses of loved ones, particularly children, and perhaps also of the drinker's own unprotected inner child who is abandoned and further damaged by the destructive adult. Nordan is a writer with a career interest in articulating the culturally approved violation of children. Astonishingly and boldly open in interviews, he had said in his interview with Blake Maher: "Often when my wife is asked if my work is autobiographical, she says yes . . . It is emotional autobiography, that the loneliness I felt as a child is the loneliness that character Sugar Mecklin feels. There are factual similarities. The names of our fathers is the same, Gilbert; Sugar is a name that was applied to me sometimes by my parent. And my father, actually my stepfather—was a house painter as Sugar's father is" (Maher interview, 113). Later in the same interview, Nordan continues:

> People always have asked, "Are you Sugar?" But nobody's ever asked, "Are you Gilbert?" because Sugar speaks the words . . . But I feel very much a part of the life of Gilbert as well. My stepfather, on whom that character in some ways is based, was like anybody—sometimes loving and sometimes neglectful and sometimes urgently interested in me and sometimes indifferent to me . . . And so was I with my children . . . And sometimes when people say to me it must have been hard to have been the child of an alcoholic, identifying me directly with Sugar, they forget to say it must have been hard for you to be an alcoholic and know that your children suffered the same way Sugar did . . . So there is a great deal of love I have for Gilbert even beyond the love I have for Sugar . . . Where Gilbert's

life is not ruined and not wrecked, it is pretty far along the line of bad
choices and mistakes that he is going to have to live with, people that he's
hurt that he's going to have to acknowledge having hurt, and I feel very
deeply for him. (121–22)

Nordan's attention to the damage passed from father to son while enact-
ing culturally prescribed male behaviors is apparent in his earlier collection of
stories, *Music of the Swamp* (1991), in which Sugar and Sweet first discover in
Roebuck Lake the dead body that is only revealed as Emmett Till's in the later
novel *Wolf Whistle.*[2] Sugar comes home with the burden of the discovery, home
to his father, who, drunk, is listening to Bessie Smith records, his "wrist-cutting
music" (17). Gilbert's response to Sugar is "Hush, hush up, Sugar. Listen to this
song . . . Gilbert had not meant to say this. The last thing he meant to do was to
tell his boy to hush up. What he meant to say was that there was just so much
death in the Delta, it was everywhere, he didn't know how a child could stand all
of it . . . The music played and Bessie Smith sang on, and the Delta was bad, bad,
she was saying, and it was magic, it hypnotized you, you couldn't resist it even
if you tried, and now it was calling her back" (*Music*, 20–21). The night of the
Delta, bad, is something Gilbert feels in the blues. Barbara A. Baker has called
this Nordan's indictment of "geography"—a shorthand signifier for the power of
culture in this southern place synonymous with its problematic definitions and
divisions of gender, class, and race. Between Gilbert and Solon the intersection
is about guilt for behaviors not stopped in time. It is in this context of culturally
prescribed bad male behavior and children that I want to bring into focus the
two corresponding young bodies that Nordan's text looks at, Glenn Gregg's and
Bobo's, two bodies of damaged children and especially their gazing, reproaching
eyes.

   The act of looking is a coded image in the history of southern racial relationships and in the Till story in particular. In Nordan's text what Emmett Till said
is uncertain, but his gaze is not: whatever he said, he said it looking her "right
square" in the face (34). In the story of the interracial South, looking is written
as a tale of the averted eye. Emmett Till's mother focuses on the vocabulary of
the forbidden look when she describes "the talk" she gave her Chicago son before he went South in 1955.

   So, I had to talk to Bo about strange things in a strange, new place, things
   that lay in wait for him. He had to understand that he would not be in

Chicago and had to act differently. I wanted him to be aware of this at all times. That was so important. We went through the drill. Chicago and Mississippi were two very different places, and white people down South could be very mean to blacks, even to black kids. Don't start up any conversations with white people . . . Don't just say "yes" or "no" or "naw." Don't ever do that. If you're walking down the street and a white woman is walking toward you, step off the sidewalk, lower your head. Don't look her in the eye. Wait until she passes by, then get back on the sidewalk, keep going, don't look back. (Till-Mobley, 100–101)

The gaze not allowed, the code of the downcast eye, and the rule of don't-look-the-brute-in-the-eye: this code of not-looking was reversed during the civil rights movement when looking became an act of defiance, of national education, revelation, and accusation. In a master narrative of the 1960s, the black "boy" becomes a man by looking, and living to tell the tale. Deborah McDowell, discussing the photos of confrontations between police and civil rights workers, has shown how the conflict of protester and police is caught in a fixed gaze and a locked eye, and these photos convey as violent a tension as those reporting spilt blood. Photos of 1960s police beatings show what happens to those who have been, to use Ishmael Reed's title phrase, "reckless eyeballing." And the images of hosed, dog-bitten, and beaten bodies echo the bodies in lynching photos, revealing the oneness and indivisibility of two taboo acts: affronting vulnerable whiteness and looking, witnessing.

In this context I return to the maimed and mutilated children's bodies of Glenn and Bobo and to their open eyes. *Wolf Whistle* opens with our going to see, in the company of teacher Alice Conroy and her fourth-grade class, the body of Glenn, Solon's son. "Glenn poured gasoline, right on his daddy's bed; he was trying to burn up his daddy, when he burned up hisself instead" (17). Having caught fire while attacking his father with flame, the child Glenn is a living corpse when we are made to see him: "He [is] unrecognizable . . . even as a child . . . His eyes were wide open because the lids had been burned away. His teeth were white and prominent as a skeleton's, because he had no lips" (18).

We are brought to see this body, the result of daddy's behavior. We are led to see a child's unburied body just as we were when Mamie Till-Mobley—insisting on opening her son's casket for mass visitations and national viewing—brought us to see her murdered and mutilated son. Even if we avert *our* eyes, Glenn's eyelids still are burned off, leaving him a child witness to the culture that produced his anger and his victimization. This gaze makes me think of John Edgar Wideman's "The Killing of Black Boys," which tells of the day Till's face found him in *Jet* magazine: "Refusing to look, lacking the power to look . . . I sensed vaguely why a wrecked boy's face was displayed in the pages of a magazine. Guessed it would be dangerous not to look. Emmett Till had died instead of me and I needed to know how, why. Not returning his eyeless stare blinded me. In a faint, skittish fashion, I intuited all of this. Understood obscurely how the murdered boy's picture raised issues of responsibility, accountability" (reprinted in Metress, 279).

Glenn's lidless accusing stare shifts shape when we see another unburied boy, and we stay within Bobo's glare after he is dead, after Solon's "bullet had knocked from its socket [the eye] that hung now upon the child's moon-dark cheek in the insistent rain." From the witnessing gaze of that dead boy's eye, we see everything that we otherwise would not: "Solon was stealing a weight, a gin fan, and a length of barbed wire to tie the fan to Bobo's neck, to sink the body in the stream . . . Bobo could see all . . . with an appreciation of the dark and magical and evil world in which he had been killed" (176–78). He sees barbs of the twisted wire piercing his boyish Adams apple. And he sees the boys who find him, who see and read his body:

> And then he was in the water . . . Because he was magic now, Bobo . . . watched Sweet Austin find the body . . . Bobo entered Sugar's dream . . . The white boy woke up, he leaped from his bed and dressed hurriedly and ran down to the real-life pier on the lake bank and stood and scanned the waters with this innocent hope in his heart . . . Bobo called out from his death to Sugar, *I am the mermaid that you will love* . . . Most of all [Bobo] loved Sweet Austin, who found him . . . Bobo knew Sweet's mama would not come home on this night when Sweet needed her most, not until after the white boy was already deep in his horrible sleep. (181–83, 185–86)

She would wake him up and tell him: "'I'm home sweetening. I ain't drunk, ain't even smoked no cigarettes,' and then she would crawl in right alongside Sweet Austin on the steel bunk, and wake up with some kind of taste in her mouth like she been chewing tin foil . . . and no energy to apologize to her boy or anybody else, for all her regret" (186). To these damaged children, "Bobo sang, Don't look, don't look at me, preserve your innocence another moment longer" (186). But we all looked, a whole nation was made to look, and like Teacher Alice's fourth-grade class, those who were sheltered lost their innocence. When Mamie Till brought us to look at her determined ceremonial mourning, she altered the meaning of the lynched black body, changing it from a statement about white power somehow culturally accepted as "normal" enough to photograph and send on a picture postcard, to a statement about loving a lost child. In the photos Mamie Till arranged to have published, the image of the lynched body shifted its meaning as she modeled a gaze that was also an accusation.

This revelation of Bobo's body—this seeing what in 1955 Nordan feels "we" did not speak—is also, for Nordan, a displacement and a temporary concealment. Because the dead body he has brought us to see, as much as it is Emmett Till's, is also his own son's, reverberating with inconsolable loss. In his interview with Bjerre, Nordan comments: "As you know from reading *Boy With Loaded Gun* I had two sons who have died. One as an infant [from a congenital defect] and one as a twenty-year-old, from suicide" (370). In a 1998 interview with Sara Elliott, Nordan explains, "there are a lot of unburied bodies in my stories and it took me a while to figure out that that's what they are . . . Over and over I was finding evidence of unburied bodies and going and laying eyes on them. I didn't even know at the time that it was about my son's death" (45–46). In *Boy With A Loaded Gun,* published in 2000—his not-memoir in which he changed all the names and made up the conversations—Nordan leads us to the displaced body. We see it straight on when a car is found in the Arkansas wilderness with a son's decomposed body inside (*Boy,* 212). And the narrator asks, "Who is at fault in my son's death? Isn't someone to blame for this horror besides the boy himself? I am" (214). The lost son shifts shape with Emmett Till because the stories are parallel, because in both histories, adults who are responsibly facing irremediable horror, irreparable grief, and a mourning sense of "if only," must ask "Who is to blame?" and feel that "We are."

And so in *Wolf Whistle,* the bodies of damaged children, some dying, some recovering, shift one into the other, Glenn into Bobo into Sugar and Sweet, and then, most controversially of all, into Solon himself, the wounded son. Nordan changes history so that Bobo shoots and wounds Solon. Why? The damaged child attacks the problem and dies, but his death opens a wound.[3] Emmett Till died, yet his death attacked the culture of whiteness, wounding it. Glenn died as a result of attacking Solon along with the generations of adult behavior of which Solon is himself the product, as a child's suicide can be a way of assaulting adults. Students James Chaney, Andrew Goodman, and Michael Schwerner were other young people who died similarly attacking the behavior of adults. This is another master narrative in the civil rights movement history—the deaths of children exposing adult behavior. In an otherwise inexplicable transformation of the Till story, Solon is caught off guard when Bobo bolts from the car and shoots him; Solon, like an inattentive father ignoring the pain his child is expressing, is chatting about going fishing sometime in the future with the boy that he is about to kill. The conflation Nordan risks and makes here is between intended violence and the undirected behavior of an adult who is detached from a child's experience and vision. Bobo's death—like the others that elide with it, including those of the young civil rights workers who died in 1964— ultimately has a consequence on white fathers. They are—we were—and the nation was—shot while off-guard. After young Roy Dale and Sugar see Bobo's body and understand perhaps more than they should bear, their fathers, Cyrus and Gilbert, reform. The death of Emmett Till, which ultimately attacks and powerfully wounds whiteness, seems to shift shape and be one with Nordan's own inconsolable loss.[4]

The text conveys regretted white southern male culture creating horror for the children. It does so humorously, without pontification, and even with compassion for all those caught in this cultural inheritance. Nordan has commented on a failure of compassion in Flannery O'Connor's grotesque comedies, which he calls "so interested in the freakishness of her characters that she fails to see their humanity." Surprisingly, he says he finds it "discouraging to be compared to" her stylistically. His concern for the self-righteousness of judgments expressed in laughter is perhaps felt when Nordan risks shifting satire into a measure of compassion for "murderous, racist, homophobic" Solon Gregg (Dupuy interview, 100). Nordan brings Solon to his own moment of looking when he returns home to chastise his son Glenn for attacking him. Then he all at once sees his own effect on the child: "Oh Lord . . . he had no idea. Oh my Lord. He looked at his child's scars, the lidless eyes" (*Wolf Whistle*, 74). Solon sees the maimed child and is moved to the blues, to a moment Nordan describes as one "in which [Solon's] best self is trying to get out in the middle of all the horror that he's about to create" (Bjerre interview, 374). "From a corner of the room, Solon took up the tattered cheap-ass cardboard case that held his Sears and Roebuck guitar, the instrument that had first belonged to his rapist father, and then to himself" (*Wolf Whistle*, 74). What happens next could call up the title of James Baldwin's play written in response to the Emmett Till murder in 1964, *Blues for Mr. Charlie*. Mr. Charlie is, of course, the generic white man. As Mr. Charlie, Solon fingers the wound he has opened for others; silenced by what he all-at-once feels, he finds and plays the blues with his family:

> Solon held the guitar across his knees, secured around his neck by a heavy, old, sweat-stained leather strap, which Solon's father had used to beat Solon when he was a child. He sat in a straight back chair . . .
>
> Mrs. Gregg held a zinc washboard . . .
>
> Wanda, the beautiful daughter wearing daddy's shirt, held her strange instrument between her spread-out legs, where she sat, flat-footed, in her chair. It was a wash-tub from off the back porch, no different from the one that her mother leaned over on washdays . . .
>
> Wanda propped the free end of the broomstick against the raised rim on the bottom of the washtub. She could tauten or loosen the length of piano wire by raising or lowering the broom handle, and when she plucked the wire with her fingers, she made a deep and rich and metallic music of *thoom thoom thoom thoom,* to accompany her father's guitar.
>
> And so that is what they did now, the three of them, while the babies watched, this family together for the next to last time. They played "Bo Peep," the music of a black man named Blue John Jackson, who lived just a mile down the road . . .
>
> The Greggs played and sang in this way for an hour before they quit. It was the only verse they knew, maybe the only verse there was. (74–77)

Nordan risks inviting compassion here for Solon, the violated cultural son who has learned illogic, racism, class hatred, damaged sexuality, violence, aggression, meanness, and vulnerable insecurity. He risks compassion for the insanely unsound murderer, the horrifying comic monster, allowing him humanity and even the position of one more brutalized child—one who is too unaware to escape any of the damage done to him and who only knows how to inflict damage on others. In interviews, Nordan has commented on the risk of this shift: "As the book got ready to print, I thought, you know, this is possibly volatile.

This gives certain humanity to the evil villain, who murders a black child, and so on. I wondered whether that wouldn't seem like excusing him . . . or whatever" (Bjerre interview, 374). "Even Solon Gregg, the racist, homophobic murderer. I feel for him love and pity and compassion. One reason *Wolf Whistle* did not follow the boundaries of historical events was that I couldn't ever in my real heart love those people" (Eliott interview, 50). *Wolf Whistle*—which continuously and unsettlingly mines the blues' transformational promise of shifting grief into a shared song—allows Solon that connecting experience. Interestingly, in Solon's blues scene, Nordan is reinscribing a song based on "a different nursery rhyme: Li'l pig went to market. Wasn't to market, so he come truckin' back on down the line" (Bjerre interview, 374). In *Wolf Whistle*, the original's blue pig is displaced by Bo Peep's lost sheep while the other lyrics remain the same, an improvisation that extemporizes on the sacrificial lamb vocabulary that permeated civil rights–era discussion of Emmett Till's death. Does this imagery give the book's title another dimension, one that points to the distinction between the wolf and the lamb?

Nordan again rewrites history in the interest of telling it clearly when he changes Solon's relationship with Lord Poindexter Montberclair to diverge from the brother-in-law relationship of Roy Bryant and J. W. Milam. He instead emphasizes the class relationship of wealth to "trash"—of the wrought-iron fence around Montberclair's villa to the ripped screen doors of Balance Due. Montberclair exploits Solon's capacity for violent behavior, accepting Solon's assistance to bolster and protect his own vulnerable masculinity. He underwrites Solon's violence and yet abandons him to act "alone." This portrait is not about Bryant and Milam but about the murderers' relationship with the southern power system that came to the killers' aid during the iniquitous, grossly unjust travesty of a trial and then washed its hands of them. William Bradford Huie explains this relationship in "What Happened to the Emmett Till Killers?" when he follows up the story of Bryant and Milam after their acquittals. "Milam is confused. He feels whites still approve what he did. Why, then, should they be less co-operative then when they were patting him on the back, contributing money to him, and calling him a 'fine, red-blooded American?" (Huie, 63). "A responsible citizen of Tutwiler, in Tallahatchie County" spells out for Huie the management of the class relationship:

"Yeah, they came up here looking for land and a 'furnish,'" he said.

"But we figured we might as well be rid of them. They're a tough bunch. And you know there's just one thing wrong with encouraging one of those peckerwoods to kill a n———. He don't know when to stop—and the rascal may wind up killing you." (Huie, 65)

So Nordan in his portrait of Montberclair satirizes this relationship between white economic classes, their collaboration and partnership, and their antagonism and resentments.

Diverging from history in his creation of Solon and Montberclair, Nordan is still using shape-shifting to enable us to see a historical situation. I have said Nordan uses shape-shifting to reveal and undercut a culture constructed on rigid boundaries, one that fetishizes the purity of its conceptual boundaries and the danger of border crossing. Bobo's murder results from the insecure need to protect the everyday psychopathic cultural narrative of impervious, impermeable, cultural categories of gender, class, caste, and race. It is a murder designed to keep impregnable and impenetrable the otherwise entirely fictional boundaries of the apartheid South. The words for guarding against threat to these boundaries have sexual connotations; *impregnable* and *impenetrable* suit the southern narrative and cosmological mythology that highlights the ideological concepts of purity and danger, a purity emblematized in the symbolic construction of "white woman," protected from an again ideological black "danger."[5] This protection, of course, was above all about the idea of controlling the conceptual categories that organized the culture's idea of order. The suppression of felt threats to order were narratively and actually played out in the control of women and African Americans.

But in this novel, the murder, which is designed to protect these cultural categories, shifts shape to reveal the fictionality of those divisions. That is, in this "white trash version of the Emmett Till murder," as we shift our gaze from one page to the next, Bobo's black body changes place with bodies of damaged white children. This assault on cultural division is not made through trite generalization about how we are all victims in a racist culture. Instead, by means of the novel's shape-shifting habit, we see that behaviors meant to elevate and privilege the white male produce both the mutilation and death of the black child and of the white son. We witness the death of Glenn, then the risky portrait of Solon as victimizing father and as hopelessly damaged child, and finally the guilt of Gilbert and Cyrus, white fathers who realize the damage they perpetuate. Sins of the fathers visited on the children are recognized and witnessed by the women, by the children, by us, and are also acknowledged by Gilbert and Cyrus when they quit the drinking that Nordan guiltily identifies as one agent in the cultural script. The reform of these fathers is unexpected in the community. When Gilbert Mecklin stops drinking and becomes rare at Reds Bar and Gro., one of the drinkers remarks: "You mean he died, don't you? Seem like that would be a more likely explanation" (263). Nordan, not overreaching the idea of reform, balances these guilty/atoning/transforming fathers with those who don't change: the "new boys" who spend their time at Reds, lined up to hit each other over the head with ax handles. "Nobody might have died at all, no murderers might as well have got let off, as far as these boys were concerned." Cyrus thinks, "he didn't trust a man who was not changed by local horror" (261–62). Guilt is allowed to change into atonement, as horror again oddly shudders into comedy.

This shiver between guilt and atonement is also connected to the novel's bizarre narrative of arrow catching, a storyline with which Nordan further unpacks his idea of Arrow Catcher, Mississippi—the recurring invented location of his fiction, the cultural home place under investigation. The sport of arrow catching has something to do with expelling frustration, a violent expulsion that is dangerous if it hits another. Sometimes Roy Dale shoots a piercing rather than blunt arrow when he hurls out "something from inside himself, some abstraction requiring sudden and violent expulsion of the broken heart, hopeless dreams, a vastness of sorrow that outside of himself might be seen as beautiful and strange, but that inside of him was only poison and filth" (192–93). This dangerous and deadly blues arrow is what Solon shoots at Bobo, when he hurls onto a racially determined outside target his unmanageable frustrations—over how to be a father given that he is the son of a rapist father, emotions we know from his bizarre comic monologue in the Arrow hotel, where he counts his bullets while planning to surprise and shoot his family—the "least a daddy could do"—to treat their misery. The idea of arrow catching twitches spasmodically between two possible meanings. Is it that the target "catches it" in the sense of "is hurt by it"—or does the target catch the arrow in the sense of controlling and stopping violence? The image of Smoky Viner, who identifies the tragedy in Roy Dale's joke before anyone else, stopping Roy's arrow with his unexpectedly resistant head, fibrillates momentarily but literally with the destroyed body of Bobo. As the arrow whistles toward Smokey, we shift to Bobo, who has also "caught it."

The body of the Bobo-child dressed in a heavy garment of fish and turtles and violent death, reversed all its decay, and flesh became firm once more, eyes snapped back into sockets and became bright, bones unbroke themselves, feet became swift, laughter erupted like music, and bad manners and disrespect and a possessive disdain for a woman became mere child's play, a normal and decent testing of adolescent limits in a hopeful world.

[Then] the arrow hit Smoky Viner in the dead middle of his forehead. (208–9)

Bobo and Smokey are figures in another fibrillation, perhaps suggesting that Bobo/Till "caught it" in the two senses of being hit by racial violence but also catching it, as his death will eventually act to control it. Roy Dale, suddenly uncertain of whether the arrow he launched was blunt or barbed, abruptly empties his quiver and breaks the steel-tipped arrow over his knee, while repeating "I'm sorry, I'm sorry, I'm sorry" (210).

There is one last transformation of historical event to consider, and that is Alice's Conroy's fourth graders' presence at the murder trial. The actual trial courtroom also inappropriately had children in it—the sons of the murderers Bryant and Milam. News accounts such as James Gunter's in the *Memphis Commercial Appeal* (20 September 1955) describe the boys "scrubbed and neatly dressed in their Sunday best," sitting "quietly on their parents' laps for a few minutes" until they "grew restless . . . broke away and explored the courtroom . . . Relatives in the first row of the spectators area passed them drinking water from time to time and ran errands in efforts to keep the boys happy . . . Once, Bill Milam picked up a toy pistol and fired an imaginary shot at Roy Bryant Jr. Bill, the oldest child present, clambered over the rail and stamped down the aisle, making little boy noises. He ran his hand along the courtroom railing pickets, apparently deriving great satisfaction from the machine-gun clack-clack he produced" (quoted in Metress, 51). The idea of the inappropriate education that was provided for the children in the courtroom as well as children nationwide—who would receive the story of murder and the shocking photos of Till's body and news coverage of the trial—is part of the case's history.

But in Nordan's version, Teacher Alice brings her class to the trial, aggressively pursuing their education by taking them to see such sights as dying Glenn, the abused Mrs. Gregg, "the sewage plant where they rode in a motor launch on a sea of human waste, and the Prince of Darkness funeral home where they looked at a body" (224). In the courtroom "outing," not fully understanding the consequences of her behavior, Alice relies on the white privilege that entitles her to fill the first rows of the colored balcony, displacing "tons of black folks with just as much right as a bunch of lily white, thumb-sucking, hair-twisting, pants-peeing fourth graders to be watching the turning of the wheels of justice, such as they were in the sorriest state of the nation, but that was just too bad, too, because she wasn't giving up the seats she had fought so hard to get for her fourth graders, not a chance" (225). But from their position of white privilege in that black balcony, she looks down to see Uncle staring at a sea of whiteness, Uncle who like Moses Wright stands reasonably terrified and terrifyingly isolated, on the verge of doing what he had not done before, pointing his finger in a murdering white man's face and with eyes wide open pronouncing, "dar he," "there he is."[6] Suddenly aware of her contribution to his aloneness, Alice abruptly sees whiteness as an abomination: "White, white bird dooky, white, it was sickening, a pestilence!" (226). "All that white and miserable hatred, as ancient and impersonal as geology and fear. [Then] Alice hated the whiteness of her own skin, she ached in her heart for the white children . . . with her. The whiteness hit Uncle in the same way it hit Alice, like a deafening noise, as elemental as oceanic geography, glacial, straight in the face" (228). And suddenly, Alice called out, "we are here! We colored people are behind you!" (231). The fourth graders waved too: "we are waving our arms as our teacher waves hers, we are saying in loud voices that we are colored people when we know we are not, . . . denied our heritage for reasons unclear, we are suffering damage from this field trip that we may never recover from and we don't care because we love her and become visible to ourselves in her presence, and for reasons obscure we love you, too, old colored man, . . . we suffer your loss, we fear for your life, we don't know what is going on at all" (232).

We should not overstate, exaggerate, or romanticize what happens here. Alice, the teacher, brings her fourth grade class to some germ of a disconnect from racial identity. For a moment, all these young people color their identities—for a fleeting moment, although an important one. The moment is tied to the novel's end, in which Alice and Sally Anne meet after the trial at Swami Don's Elegant Junk, in the magic aisle. Amid fake flowers, tarot cards, magic wands, silk top hats containing white rabbits, escape trick manacles and handcuffs that do not hold, an empty tiger cage with heavy iron bars calling up the prison cell that contains no murderer, an astral flight coverlet, and a bag of John the Conqueroo—they discover a crystal ball for seeing the future. Its light shines with the quality of "hopeful planets" (290). And Nordan brings us all to ask, "do we believe in magic?"

This last scene is as ambiguous as all the transformations of the novel have been. In Swami Don's aisle of magic, a reader can wonder if the magic in Nordan's novel will be revealed as a mere illusion. While the novel draws to this close, Cyrus is trying to rename himself while others continue to call him Runt. Will reform hold? Will it matter? Measuring the loss that has brought Cyrus to want to change, he wistfully judges, "It's an evil world we live in." To which Coach replies, "I know, Cyrus. I know. We'll just have to make do" (276). Cyrus wants to "give back to Roy Dale some of what he took away," and Coach tells him "What's gone is gone forever" (274). Similarly, Mr. Archer tells Alice "These things happen, Alice . . . People die. Children die" (278). Here in this melancholy closing, loss and magic again shiver in the shape-shifting that is the hallmark of the novel. We witness once more, in Alice's memory, the vision of a dead child's body in a lake, caught in a raindrop. Certainly, we know the genuine reality of damage, waste, loneliness, loss, grief, racism, and evil. At the same time, the novel wants us to believe in magic and the possibility of cultural transformation. These are the shifting shapes at the novel's close—a melancholy recognition of inescapable realities shuddering with a longing for magical transformation. Is magic a metaphor for yearned-for transformations that only take shape with a sleight of hand, in spite of our desire to believe? Or can we trust its promise?

A clue to how to read Nordan's magic may come from its counterpoint with blues refrain. Just before coming across the ambiguous "magic stuff" at the junk shop, Sally Anne finds Robert Johnson's first guitar, if you believe as Swami Don does. Like the magic that we want to believe in, the blues is all about shape-shifting—to finger a wound and somehow sing it in music that transforms pain, loss, fear, and despair. The upbeat of a blues song fibrillates with its sorrow, and the loneliness of its grievance creates community with an audience that knows what brings the blues.[7] Like the blues, Nordan's magic admits the power of the lyrical imagination to uncover. The talking birds, the demon eye, the brightly colored African parrot that, by defecating, speaks for Bobo in the courtroom when Uncle's heroic accusing voice bounces off whiteness: throughout, this magic speaks. The unburied body that was never properly acknowledged at the time of the murder or in the aftermath of the subsequent trial—and that remained buried/unburied in Nordan's own consciousness and in that of white southern-ers, for that matter, speaks, sings, if only magically. Does that magic promise a transformation to follow loss? In the novel's very last lines, we still shudder with anxiety in the space between meanings. Looking into the crystal ball that is one of a kind while everything else in the magic aisle "seems stocked by the gross," Alice and Sally Anne "stood there, looking at it, into it. They could see nothing, nothing at all." The future is still unknown. These women—who know, judge, and yet are implicated in the guilty male Arrow Catcher culture—"continued to walk together through the store . . . They browsed; they spoke in low voices. They spoke, finally, from their hearts . . . Maybe, finally, they did weep together, and maybe held each other tight. Nobody but Bobo knows for sure what hap-pened next, but maybe, behind Alice and Sally Anne, the crystal ball in Swami Don's Elegant Junk shone with the bright blue light of empty loneliness and of faraway and friendly stars and all their hopeful planets and golden moons" (290). The novel's final lines do not know, but speculate on and hope for the magic that may shift shapes.

NOTES

1. The body of Glenn Gregg, the murderer's white son, shifts into that of Bobo, the murdered black child. And Bobo, dead, sings to the living but damaged boys, Sugar, Sweet, and Roy Dale—children who are the culture's products and victims.

2. Emmett Till's body was found in the Tallahatchie River by Robert Hodges, a seventeen-year-old white boy. Nordan often comments that he wondered for years about the discovery's effect on Hodges.

3. Fascinatingly and without other explanation, Nordan seems to forget or at least ignore that Solon wears this identifying and condemning wound in the courtroom; that is, during the trial the wound Bobo has placed does not yet show.

4. Myrlie Evers says of the unpredicted effect of Emmett Till's death: "It could have been just another Mississippi lynching. It wasn't. This one somehow struck a spark of indignation that ignited protests around the world. Kidnapped forcibly in the middle of the night, pistol-whipped, stripped naked, shot through the head with a .45 caliber Colt automatic, barb-wired to a seventy-four-pound cotton gin fan, and dumped into twenty feet of water in the Tallahatchie River, young Emmett Till became in death what he could never have been in life: a rallying cry and a cause" (Myrlie Evers, *For Us, The Living,* 1967; reprinted in Metress, 277).

5. See Patricia Yeager's *Dirt and Desire: Reconstructing Southern Women's Writing, 1930–1990* (Chicago: University of Chicago Press, 2000), 66, 274–77, for her discussion and application of Mary Douglass's *Purity and Danger,* one seminal anthropological work on the idea of culture and

the conceptual boundaries that cultures protect—that is, on the relationship between ideas of pollution and social order.

6. In "one of the most dramatic moments of the trial, the 64-year-old Rev. Moses Wright, Emmett Till's uncle, took the witness stand . . . He told of the two white men coming to his house—one with a gun in hand—and demanding 'the boy who made the big talk . . .'

With his thin body racked with emotion, but his face a deadly calm, the Rev. Mr. Wright arose, pointed a bony finger at a white man and declared: 'There he is'" (Hicks).

7. The lyrics of Robert Johnson's "Hellhound on My Trail"—performed in the novel but not in entirety—help drive the shudder between the novel's victims. I recommend looking at the lyrics, which I cannot here quote at length, for their relationship to the plot. It is Bobo who must "keep moving." But it is Glenn who "sprinkled hot foot powder all around [his] daddy's door." And Solon carries "a rambling mind, rider."

WORKS CITED

Allen, James, Hilton Als, John Lewis, Leon Litwack, and Congressman John Lewis, eds. *Without Sanctuary.* Sante Fe, NM: Twin Palms, 2000.

Baker, Barbara A. "Riffing on Memory and Playing Through the Break: Blues in Lewis Nordan's *Music of the Swamp* and *Wolf Whistle.*" *Southern Quarterly* 41, no. 3 (2003): 20–42.

Bakhtin, Mikhail Mikhailovich. *Rabelais and his World.* Bloomington: Indiana University Press, 1984.

Campbell, Bebe Moore. *Your Blues Ain't Like Mine.* NY: Ballantine; 1993.

Costello, Brannon. "Poor White Trash, Great White Hope: Race, Class, and the (De)Construction of Whiteness in Lewis Nordan's *Wolf Whistle.*" *Critique: Studies in Contemporary Fiction* 45, no. 2 (2004): 207–23.

Gunter, James. *Memphis Commercial Appeal,* 20 September 1955. Reprinted in Metress, 50–53.

Hicks, James. "Youth Puts Milam in Till Death Barn." *Washington Afro-American,* 24 September 1955. Reprinted in Metress, 87–88.

Huie, William Bradford. "Approved Killing in Mississippi." *Look,* 24 January 1956, 46–50.

———. "What's Happened to the Emmett Till Killers." *Look,* 22 January 1957, 63–65.

———. *Wolf Whistle.* New York: Signet, 1959.

Kenan, Randall. "Mississippi Goddam: Wolf Whistle by Lewis Nordan." *Nation,* 15 November 1993, 592–600.

Litwack, Leon. *Been in the Storm So Long: The Aftermath of Slavery.* New York: Knopf, 1979.

McDowell, Deborah. "Scripting the I/Eye: First Person Narrative and Civil Rights Photography." Paper delivered at the Unsettling Memories: Culture and Trauma in the Deep South conference, Jackson, MS, June 2004.

Metress, Christopher. *The Lynching of Emmett Till: A Documentary Narrative.* Charlottesville: University of Virginia Press, 2002.

Nordan, Lewis. "An Interview with Lewis Nordan." By Edward J. Dupuy. *Southern Quarterly* 43, no. 3 (2003): 95–108.

———. "Interview with Lewis Nordan." By Sara Elliott. In "Dead Bodies, Burned Letters, and Burial Grounds: Negotiating Place Through Storytelling in Contemporary South Fiction," PhD diss., Northern Illinois University, 1998.

———. "An Interview with Lewis Nordan." By Blake Maher. *Southern Quarterly* 34, no. 1 (1995): 113–23.

———. "Interview with Lewis Nordan, at his home in Pittsburgh, May 19, 2001." By Thomas Aervold Bjerre. *Mississippi Quarterly* 54, no. 3 (2001): 367–80.

———. "An Interview with the Author." In *Wolf Whistle,* 2d ed. Chapel Hill, NC: Algonquin, 1995.

———. *Boy with A Loaded Gun,* Chapel Hill, NC: Algonquin, 2000.

———. "Growing Up White in the South, An Essay." Chapel Hill, NC: Algonquin, 1993.

———. "The Making of a Book." *Oxford American,* March–April 1995, 74–88.

———. *Music of the Swamp.* Chapel Hill, NC: Algonquin, 1991.

———. *Wolf Whistle.* Chapel Hill, NC: Algonquin, 1993.

Penley, Constance. "Crackers and Whackers: The White Trashing of Porn." In *White Trash: Race and Class in America,* edited by Matthew Wray and Annalee Newitz, 89–112. London: Routledge, 1997.

Reed, Ishmael. *Reckless Eyeballing.* New York: St. Martin's, 1986.

Rubin, Anne Sarah. "Reflection on the Death of Emmett Till." *Southern Cultures* 2, no. 1 (1996): 45–66.

Till-Mobley, Mamie. *Death of Innocence: The Story of the Hate Crime That Changed America.* New York: Random House, 2003.

Wideman, John Edgar. "The Killing of Black Boys." *Essence,* November 1997. Reprinted in Metress, 278–88.

(DIS)EMBODYING THE DELTA BLUES

Wolf Whistle *and* Your Blues Ain't Like Mine

DONNIE MCMAHAND

As two novelized accounts of Emmett Till's murder, Bebe Moore Campbell's *Your Blues Ain't Like Mine* (1992) and Lewis Nordan's *Wolf Whistle* (1993) could not be more dissimilar. While *Your Blues* spans three decades, *Wolf Whistle* dramatizes the historical events of 1955 when Till, a black child from Chicago, ostensibly broke the cardinal rule of the South by soliciting a white woman, Mississippi shopkeeper Carolyn Bryant. Despite their differences in focus and style—Nordan's burlesque and Campbell's social criticism—both writers cull their characters from the complex psychological prism of the blues, promoting the social prevalence of blues music as a metaphor for what Barbara Baker, in discussing *Wolf Whistle*, terms "interracial consciousness" (20). Baker's phrase "interracial consciousness" vividly describes the tendency of the blues to transcend racial boundaries and to weave a bicultural mesh of shared experiences.

At the same time, Nordan and Campbell alike build into their representations of Till—as well as other black bodies—contradictory symbols of political compliance and social resistance. Centrally, I am intrigued by the novels' schismatic presentations of African American bodies as phenomenologically present and absent, there and not there, bodies vital and dying, abject and rebellious, whose textual representations combine images of a segregated and violent South with the cathartic and regenerative rhetoric of the blues. In the essay "Growing Up White in the South," Nordan emphatically declares, "In *Wolf Whistle*, Emmett, Bobo . . . is the fixed center . . . [the] *terra firma*" (vi). Terra firma, foundational, and "fixed," Emmett Till signifies for Nordan the very body of historical shift. Both Nordan and Campbell essentially meld the black body with the musical concept of a silent break, a rest measure, revealing instances in which the white separatist gaze, apart from acts of torture and killing, attains fulfillment through a continuous and pathological overlooking of the black presence.

Seeing as how "white only" justice (and consequently black absence) coincided historically with the production of blues music, the novels make their most subtle and profound use of the blues metaphor where two cultural systems—blues ethos and segregation—merge in the signifying figure of the black body. While *Wolf Whistle* suggests how 1950s black musicians ontologically and lyrically resisted the ongoing threat of white violence, *Your Blues* characterizes midcentury black migration through the complex blues trope of locomotion, racialized impediment, and freedom. Obviously, Nordan and Campbell are employing divergent strategies in their treatment of the blues. Drawing on the music's familiar theme of death defiance, Nordan, in the most visionary section of his novel, imparts a magical look at Till's murdered body, conferring on the child a prophetic consciousness that persists beyond the instance of his death. Campbell's more realistic storytelling synchronizes paradigmatic events and individual neuroses, the repression and sublimation that her characters experience—sitting at a train station or watching fieldworkers pick cotton—framed implicitly in relation to blues song. In both books, the blues surface and operate seminally as an interventionist text, or counternarrative, necessarily complicating the recorded history of the era as well as readers' perceptions of it now.

The act of the black body slipping into absence bestows an opportunity for empowerment and healing; it is a crisis moment, a challenge to the performer to transform bad into better. To be absented physically and subjectively in the making of popular American cultural consciousness and to invest that positionality of absence with vitality and purpose is, in many respects, cause to sing the blues. Both novelists, however, push their analogies beyond such tidy configurations of blues music and race. In a conversation printed after the text of her novel, Campbell comments, "I certainly feel that [all people's] blues are intertwined. Lily's blues of being a subjugated, molested white baby girl directly feed into Armstrong Todd's blues of being this murdered black boy." Clearly, Campbell objects to territorializing the blues and blues ethos to strict phylogenetic constructions of race and art. Meanwhile, in an interview in 2001, Nordan remarks, "The same year my book came out, *Your Blues Ain't Like Mine* [came out]. It was very hard for me to give myself permission to do [my book] until I realized that people like me . . . poor middle-class whites . . . we have a voice too. And our voice was too silent during the fifties" (quoted in Bjerre interview, 375). In the same interview, he notes, "When I wrote *Wolf Whistle,* I don't know I wrote a word of it first draft without blues playing" (375). Thus, as a *de-territorialized* text, *Wolf Whistle* not only reflects Nordan's immutable contact with the blues but also situates the music as a black and white cultural product, which impacted the (re)making of the biracial South. Concerning the scene in which child killer Solon Gregg sings the blues with his family, the author explains, "It's the only language he's got" (375). Nordan's statement here stresses the cross-infiltration of language and culture in his text and the humanity that blues music bestows even on the story's worst villain.

In *Seems Like Murder Here*, Adam Gussow contradicts the popular belief that traditional blues songs only evoke scenes of wanderlust, lost love, poverty, drunkenness, and lovers' quarrels. Theorizing that in addition to these themes racialized murder pervades many blues lyrics, Gussow further explains that the fear of white reprisal forced black singers to use veiled references to express their rage and lament. Like every other person of color living or traveling in the Jim Crow South, blues musicians existed in a panopticon of white surveillance, founded mainly on white fears of the black beast rapist. The covert killings that lasted long after the decline of public slayings reasserted the rule of white oppression, the rule that kept black bodies in their rightful place. Quiet as they were kept, these secret acts seemed as "unreal" and were as uncounted as the bodies that were destroyed.

Wolf Whistle and *Your Blues* demonstrate how Till's death, his disfigured corpse especially, countered this narrative of oppression and began the work of re-authoring the body politics of the South. To communicate this change, Nordan transfigures and redeems Bobo's flesh, setting it above the old lynch narrative and placing it, instead, in the recuperative framework of the blues. In a feat of magic, Nordan binds the image of the blues singer, strumming and singing into the jagged splinter of his life, with that of the slain boy's body singing out into the lush void of the Mississippi Delta. Bobo becomes with beatific grace the body of the blues. His song reaches far, eventually changing the landscape and the people who inhabit it.

This waterways singer represents the apotheosis of Nordan's undead blues artist. Before returning to this scene in the marsh, I wish to examine the other singers—The Rider, Rage Gage, and Blue John—who in their own way, rewrite the South, at least the part of the South they have been given. These men perform from a "joyful" reformation of their despair as nonentities, or ciphered spaces, or to borrow Houston Baker's phrase "from the (w)hole of blackness" (5). Their lyrics permeate Nordan's text, commenting on it like a Greek chorus or, more apropos, like a "signifying" audience who in turn propels the next phase of the story.

The blues artists make their debut in the novel, strumming their instruments and sitting on the porch of Red's Goodlookin' Bar and Gro. Their constant playing abruptly breaks off when "[Bobo] said what he said" to Lady Sally Ann Montberclair: "The blues singers had already stopped playing. They must have heard the children talking, must have suspected that the boy from Chicago didn't know no better" (*Wolf Whistle*, 34). Bobo's fatal indiscretion opens up a blues measure of chaos, with the singers on the porch and everyone in the room recognizing the shift. The silence marks the inability of art and language to absorb immediately the breaking of social boundaries. Stark and abysmal, the silence encloses the gap, or blank, of the black body. And, if nothing more, this breaking quiet portends the horror to come.

What the patrons and musicians understand is the imminence of white violence, how it lurks behind every corner, how it stalks the shadows, awaiting its next victim. These people also understand the code that governs when and where violence is unleashed, and they know that Bobo has just violated that code. Earlier in the scene, the blues singers give an encrypted foretelling of eruptive violence, using Robert Johnson's verses, "Hellhound on my trail, hellhound on my trail" (32). The song insinuates itself into the very narration of the text, moving outward from the men's thoughts: "the blues were falling down all around . . . like hail" (31), with an obvious pun on *hail* and *hell*. In the meantime, Johnson's song articulates the menace of the men's daily lives:

> I've got to keep movin' . . .
> And the days keep on worryin' me
> There's a hellhound on my trail.

The song and its performance also suggest an interior dialogue among the blues men, an exchange heard and *not heard* by Red and his customers. Invisibility here grants a shield, and the blues men take cover, permitting themselves and the music a disguised language of high intelligence that is indecipherable to its audience of oppressors.

A widespread trope in the rhetoric of the blues, the *hellhound* image connotes perilous pursuit and salvation. To elude hellfire—the lit torches of a lynching mob—the individual draws on the virtue of his wit and will to survive. But the encounter with death is elaborate and always impending. Again, the music anticipates and responds to the menace of racialized murder; one reality counterposes the other. Except, the blues, as Houston Baker asserts, smashes simple dualities (2–3), and in this light, the performer purposely locates the impetus for his music in the hazards of white fury. The blues performers do not hide from the white townspeople in Arrow Catcher; they do not physically remove themselves from white consciousness. On the contrary, they place themselves at its center, forcing a daily confrontation with their reality, spinning their blues lyric out of the potential risk inherent in the encounter. Regardless of the threat of violence and the absenting of bodies, the blues men take their positions in the store. What imperils also inspires, and vice versa.

Nowhere is this tie between violence and loneliness more pronounced than in these blues passages. Literalizing the disposition of the outsider in the stock symbol of the wandering artist, Blue John articulates the paradox of living an un-life. Blue John "sang about waking up in the morning and seeing the blues walking like a man. He sang, 'Come on, blues, take my hand'" (24). Typically on the go, the southern blues artist must stay two steps ahead of trouble, *hellhound* trouble. Blue John's words crystallize the concept of the absented blues persona, who defies death and fills the cipher of his life with music. The line "the blues walking like a man" serves as a metonym for the victims of racist villainy, as well as for the constant threat of violence, and functions as a mitigating force against the despair that white terror breeds. Blue John's song also affirms the need for personal attachment and companionship as the words depict John keeping company with a fellow artist, someone able to sympathize with his plight in life. Paying tribute to friendship and to the strategic use of invisibility, both the song and the scene it mirrors operate profoundly as coping devices.

Perhaps most remarkable about John's lyric is its use of myth making. Blue John mythologizes himself and his friends, a tactic that lends mystery to his own persona, safeguarding him—at least in his fantasy—from daily pitfalls. The myth that surrounds The Rider, a pink-skinned albino, depicted in the same scene, recapitulates the notion of death defiance: "Everybody was scared of The Rider. Everybody said The Rider had done been brung back from the dead by a hoodoo woman" (24–25). But again, as Nordan's anecdote about The Rider suggests, the denseness of blues aesthetics undercuts the facileness of duality. For even among his friends, The Rider is a person of isolation: "Wouldn't nobody talk to him. Everybody said The Rider had pink eyes like a grave rat" (24–25). He is an outsider among outsiders but always, nonetheless, at the core of his coterie.

If the scenes at the store and the barbershop present inverse sides of the segregated South, they also render, aesthetically and historically, an internal resolution. Contrary to any myth of death defiance, black bodies in real time "keep their place," careful not to disrupt the order of daily routine at Red's, where, for instance, Rufus McKay puts on the stereotype of "the old shoeshine boy . . . who slept all day and woke up singing songs from a former time" (95). But in the shared discourse of the barbershop, these men, most notably Rufus, bodily transform. No longer a passive shoeshine boy, no longer asleep, Rufus has literally shape-shifted into a new person, "tall and skinny and mean" (95). Also, the style of the men's singing changes, as the need for ambiguity has all but vanished at the barbershop. Protected by the night, the blues are transfigured alongside the men's bodies, appearing and sounding bolder, less disguised or hidden in plain sight, though no less artful.

Throughout the performance, the conversation continues, blurring the boundaries between art and unadorned speech, blending plain talk and blues tropes. Generating a "magic hour" effect, the musicians gain sweet release and a fullness of expression unattainable at Red's. But are these men as blameworthy of Bobo's murder as Solon and the other white men at the store? When Blue John tells a derogatory joke about the town's blacks, calling them "spear-chuckers," and The Rider laughs, Rufus fires back, "You make a joke like that and you jes part of the problem. All y'all just guilty as sin . . . guilty as me" (102). In reading this scene, Barbara Baker concludes, "Everyone in Arrow Catcher must share in the guilt of Bobo's tragedy" (37). What Baker overlooks is a more complex collective psyche in which the men's feelings of helplessness further exacerbate their sense of blame. Displacing his own responsibility, Blue John repeatedly provokes Rufus, asking, "What did you do . . . ?" adding, "Act like you's asleep and sing show tunes?" (99). But the provocations are self-implicating, further impelling the musicians to rehearse the scene at Red's, exhausting, at least temporarily, their pent-up anger and frustration in, as Houston Baker notes about the blues, "a veritable playful festival of meaning . . . a phylogenetic recapitulation—a nonlinear, freely associative, nonsequential meditation—of species experience" (5). Houston Baker's idea of blues performance as "the experiencing of experience" captures the men's struggle to make meaning of the morning at Red's, or at least to lend it an indestructible priority in the psyche, a painful subject to revisit, reexperience, possibly transmute into pleasure and solace. Finally, the men strum and sing with the presentiment that Bobo has indeed died even before Solon sets out to kill him. And their humor, Blue John's joke in particular, albeit crass and self-effacing, suggests, like their music, the need to laugh before crying—to evade, on the emotional level, open displays of vulnerability and defeat.

Away from the barbershop, Nordan powerfully probes the psychosocial dam-

age of black bodies systematically eclipsed by second-class citizenship. Patterned
in an identifiably white and alternately privileged and underclass point of view,
the novel, notwithstanding the barbershop scene, routinely portrays African
Americans as "disembodiments." These characterizations inscribe Nordan's
strategic use of the racist white gaze, permitting readers a visual and historical
insight into the killing mind, such as Solon Gregg's. Nordan, at the same time,
complicates the gaze, showing how white individuals, conditioned by racism,
could demonstrate kindness and compassion toward African Americans, while
still perceiving black bodies as specimens of negligible existence. When, for
instance, Runt Conroy walks to the Belgian Congo to warn Bobo's caretakers
of impending danger, he is certainly acting out of a beneficent impulse. Yet,
relying on his supremacist worldview he believes he can simply show up in the
streets and "holler up a nigger" (44). The people of the Congo decline his call
until finally "*a disembodiment answered him,* he reckoned that's what it was, old
woman's voice through the closed door of the house . . . *Runt spoke with ease to
disembodiments*" (45–46, emphasis added). Runt assumes the voice belongs to
an old woman, but because he cannot see the speaker, he cannot be altogether
sure. He simply observes the speaker as a "voice," a "disembodiment." Pointing out Runt's "ease" in speaking with absented persons (46), Nordan's narrator
confirms the conditioning of Runt's separatist (although not virulently racist)
outlook, his willingness not to see. In the meantime, the black speaker takes
advantage of the situation by telling Runt that the man he is looking for does not
exist ("Ain't no Uncle"), that Uncle is dead (46). She uses her invisibility strategically to absent another member of her community against the potential threat
of violence. Only after Runt explains the problem, that Uncle's nephew "had a
piece of white trash mad at him" (46), does the speaker relent, supplying reliable
information about where Uncle lives. And only after Runt promises not to hurt
anybody does an actual black person appear, whole and fleshed, from the dark
hull of the shack: "a girl about nine years old came out. Behind her, a long, skinny
black arm materialized from nothingness and poked out of the dark shack to try
to grab her back inside" (47). The child, Doe Rinda, dramatically "figured," and
perhaps the daughter or granddaughter of the disembodied voice, who is only
partially "materialized," rebelliously matches her face and body with her words,
defying the practice of avoidance and denial set in motion by the older voice.

Inevitably, the white construction of black invisibility forms a crucial nar-
ratological element in the capturing and killing of Bobo. During the scene of

his abduction, he *appears* in the text only once, when "Solon pulled Bobo out of the bed by his feet" (140). Nowhere else in the chapter (the sixth) do we *see* Bobo fleshed out on the page, even as Solon commands him to get dressed and walk down the steps of Uncle and Auntee's house into the waiting El Camino. Throughout the old couple's stalling tactics, what Solon calls "chit chat and foot dragging" (144), the narrator omits all description of Bobo's reaction to Solon or to his aunt and uncle. Even while he is forced to accompany Solon in the long car ride across the rain-soaked Delta, Bobo all but in a few passages *disappears* from the text. These erasures highlight Solon's racist tendency to see and not see black bodies, as his viewpoint takes over in these moments as the operative perspective of the novel. (The omissions also eerily re-evoke the instance of the blues artists riffing on Bobo's death as a foregone conclusion.) Solon's gaze has already absented him, has already marked him as deceased. As the tragedy looms closer and closer, Bobo's textual death prefigures his actual one.

Only in death does Bobo's textual presence expand, encompassing the thriving rhetoric of blues resurrection. Nordan collapses into the moment of Bobo's dying what I read as an enchanted blues performance and an empathetic landscape that listens and responds. Prior to this moment, the narrative amasses images of a primordial underwater consciousness, "transformations, angels and devils, worlds invisible to Bobo before death" (175). These magical depictions remake the murderous history of the Delta, while at the same time suggesting a blues ethos and aesthetic. The rain-soaked land rehearses daily events, reworking, the way a blues artist does, the ordinary and the tragic into ornate cadence: "The music of the spillway water in the swamp sounded like soft, faraway plucking on the strings of the guitars of the blues singers on Red's front porch" (166). Significantly adding to this link of earth and bluesman is the image of the black corpse consigned repeatedly over time to the Mississippi waterways. When Alice tells Runt about her vision of a drowned child, he responds, matter of fact, "These Delta rivers are full of niggers, honey" (88). Evidenced in Alice's vision and in Runt's remark, the swamp does not obliterate but recycles, constantly penetrating the collective psyche of the living with reminders of the slaughtered. In this light, Bobo literally and magically fleshes out the implied blues subject of the traumatized black body.

Nordan's fantastical image of Bobo's corpse captures the racial antithesis of the Jim Crow South, as encapsulated by the scenes at Red's store and Rage's shop. Bobo's spillway performance reiterates the audacity of his verbal stunt

inside the store while aggrandizing the blues men's transfigurations at the barbershop. In a limbo state of semiconsciousness, with a blown-out "demon eye"
and chanting mermaid voice, Bobo synthesizes those qualities that make up the
individual musicians of the novel. For one, his submersion in the lake imparts
special insight into the reality of absented bodies: "The gin fan was . . . the
weight *to hide Bobo's body*" (emphasis added, 178). But, of course, he does not
stay hidden: he uses his dead space creatively. Same as The Rider, "brung back
from the dead by a Hoodoo woman" (24–25), Bobo in the spillway becomes a
reoriginated life force, shrouded in mystery and defiant of the finality of death.

"Blues song," Gussow notes, "was [a] way of reconstituting the pleasure of
racialized torture . . . redistributing it away from a sadistic white lynch mob and
toward the 'suffering' black blues subject and his community" (29). Nordan's
magic essentially compresses the amount of time that usually separated Negro-
phobic violence and black musical complaint. Bobo's song, therefore, transcends
the rigors of temporal space, an indication of the extent to which the child's
death embodies, much like the blues artists, the psychic and physical trauma
that informs black life in the 1950s. Gussow observes, "The blues singer in one
characteristic guise proposes him—or herself as an abject, isolated, tortured but
articulate sufferer, the voice of a black body's aching parts refusing to be scattered and silenced" (29).

Citing several recently published memoirs of blues singers, Gussow locates
the blues' paradoxical recognition of the "utter dissolution" (28) of the tortured,
dismembered body and the body's figurative rebirth and subversive continu-
ance in the life and lyrics of the singing artist. One such account, that of Texas
singer Mance Lipscomb, recalls the 1906 lynching of a black man in Navasota,
Texas: "Man didn have a face! Body near about like mush . . . And I'm still here,
playin on this old gittah" (quoted in Gussow, 28). Lipscomb's statement of defiance focuses the relationship between a distressed black populace and its chosen
recourse of musical invention. Although metaphorical, Bobo's transformation
similarly transcodes the fatalism of the spillway as well as the wound of racist
violence with his very being, or nonbeing. Bobo moves the implicit meaning of
the swamp away from silence and death to vocalized resistance.

This textual representation of Bobo's nonbeing has long troubled readers
and critics of the novel who deliberately ask: Where is the historical Emmett,
his consciousness prior to his demise, or any depiction of his character as a
black teenage boy? If, in fact, Nordan's creative design contains any limitations,

they are perhaps most pronounced in the murder scene, where without the racist gaze (Solon soon departs the waterway), Bobo might be expected to come alive as more fully human, his thoughts touched less by mythic charm and more by realism. The scene at Rage's shop, where Nordan effectively negotiates his way into a sustained, interior representation of the black subject, evinces the writer's ability to render dimensional black characters. The author's claim in "Growing Up White in the South" (iii–iv) that Bobo (Emmett) occupies the firm moral ground, around which the novel's fanciful, unearthly action revolves, rings true. Less convincing is Nordan's suggestion in the essay that Bobo remains untouched by the strange, the unearthly. To be fair, in a book where buzzards engage anthropomorphically in humanlike dialogue and a parrot sounds off like a cash register, a murdered child singing in the spillway appears more mundane—by comparison only. Nevertheless, Bobo's death song hardly reads as realistic; rather, it reflects Nordan's sentimental regard for Till as terra firma, as his most precious and sacred link to the historical events. Either way, Nordan's reluctance to interrogate in *Wolf Whistle* the boy's feelings and thoughts leaves the child a holy object, a centerpiece lacking in the nuances of personal experience.

In place of the child's interiority is a rendering that stylizes the significance of Till's highly publicized corpse as an iconic epiphany of racial injustice. Here then, if nowhere else, *Wolf Whistle*'s magic best mirrors its historical source. Sounding the battle cry for the civil rights movement, the unsightly image of the child's corpse would immensely affect U.S. history and social policy, an impact well documented by historical narratives as well as accounts of those who experienced firsthand various aspects of the social revolution. Seizing the authority and command of this watershed event, Bobo's body sings out to Sugar Mecklin and Sweet Austin, the two boys who discover his corpse, "*I am the mermaid, I am the lake angel, I am the darkness you have been looking for all your sad lives*" (184). Then, suddenly, transposed into a Gospel aesthetic, "with a choir on the far side of the lake" (183), Bobo's song harmonizes all the "voices" of the anonymous or half-forgotten lynched, converting covert murder into public spectacle. A reconstructed corporal identity, Bobo undermines the authority that spectacle killings once held for white society: "In death, Bobo was patient . . . Soon enough they would see the weight, the wire, the bullet holes, the magic eye" (185).

As Grace Hale explains in *Making Whiteness*, often in the white imagination the lynched black body subsumed the meaning of the savage crime enacted on it while many white Americans clung to pristine characterizations of themselves as inherently civilized and virtuous. Hale reminds readers how the propagandist "image of the 'black beast rapist' . . . remained[,] . . . and by the late 1930s representations of lynchings worked almost as well as lynchings themselves" (226–27). But without accusations of rape or assault, without even the delusional script of justice, the spectacle of Till's corpse would reverse the effect of clandestine killings and only verify the barbarism of a small southern town. The enchanted song that Nordan bestows upon his memory of Emmett Till, who, incidentally, did not fall into the hands of buyers and dealers trafficking in lynched body parts, anticipates the possibility of a new social order. Terra firma, Bobo invites Sugar and Sweet to see his ravaged carcass, trusting prophetically that the sight will begin the work of dismantling the paradigm of rampant racist fury.

Your Blues Ain't Like Mine similarly explores the crumbling of white supremacy after a cataclysmic contact across the color line, namely, the lynching of Armstrong Todd. Like Nordan, Campbell refers to a childhood haunted by the Emmett Till case, telling interviewer Jane Campbell in 1999, "I was five when he died . . . I'd hear my dad talking about him. . . He was not an historical figure. He was not like Harriet Tubman or Sojourner Truth or Fredrick Douglas. He was my age just about" (958). The novelist further explains how Till became "a reference point" (958) for her family in a society on the brink of convulsive change. To re-create an atmosphere of historical shifts, Campbell weaves throughout her narrative the aesthetics, aura, and subject matter of the Delta blues. In that blues artists typically, as Graeme Boone asserts, "distill the theme of self-determination . . . in a context of social adversity" (85), Campbell's novel contextualizes personal struggle and psychological torment within rather transparent instances of social crisis.

The novel is largely a forum of cross-experiences, a crossroads dynamic of yours versus mine, which Campbell exploits at various levels of identity, including but not limited to black and white masculinity and white womanhood. The narrative also examines the depths to which racial and economic oppression impact virtually every sexual relationship in the segregated South, from Marguerite and Clayton, to the Todds, to Ida Long's parents, and especially Lily and Floyd, the interpolation of race and sex in each case instancing yet another preferred subject of the blues. Moreover, the novel invokes vis-à-vis its very structure the historical migration of blues music from Mississippi and Memphis to Chicago. By cross-sectioning her story, moving it repeatedly from the South to the North, between white and black, male and female perspectives, Campbell duplicates the multidirectional vocalism of a call-and-response blues performance.

Reinforcing this twin concept of mobility and change, of lives in transit and transition, is the novel's provocative use of railroads, one of the blues' best-trafficked tropes. Particularly telling is how the text combines distinct concepts of locomotion and the absented black body to evoke the motive force of budding social revolution. In anticipation of Delotha's plan to transport her son's remains to Chicago for a publicized burial, Stonewall Pinochet proposes a counteroffensive during a meeting of the Honorable Men of Hopewell, Campbell's reproduction of the real-life Citizens' Councils of Mississippi: "We can't let that body outa Hopewell. No telling what all might happen if she gets to Chicago with it. She might have a notion to call the newspapers up there; she might call the damn NAACP . . . That body's got to stay right here" (*Your Blues,* 91). Betraying an inherent sense of self-correctness, Pinochet locates in Armstrong's murder hard evidence of white southern atrocity.

Roughing up the heroic surface of a mother's intrepid train ride out of Mississippi, Campbell charts the psychic toll Delotha continually pays in dealing with her loss years after her dead son's exposure in the media. For her, Armstrong's body lives on, invading her thoughts and nightmares. Unable or unwilling to channel her anguish into a more recuperative expression, as Blue John, The Rider, and Rage Gage are able to do, Delotha descends into a pit of posttraumatic insensibility, turning to dead-end schemes of revenge against the Coxes and her estranged husband Wydell for his negligence as a father. Traveling as far as Memphis, Delotha eventually gives up her homicidal venture and returns to Chicago. While Campbell celebrates the idea of movement here, she suggests through Delotha's breakdown that, as a signifier of social disturbance, mobility alone does not always yield positive change. The novel's tableau of the impoverished, miserable lives of black exiles from the South keenly illustrates this reality. Just as Delotha's crisis in Memphis signifies her inclusion in this predicament of the disillusioned black northerner, her ultimate immobility also echoes the thwarting of other Southbound women whose lives hang in transit/transition. Lily has long set her sights on a romanticized Memphis, but by novel's end she has given up her hopes of traveling there. Determined to spare her son the death that befalls Armstrong, Ida endures many setbacks to her plans to escape the South; ultimately, she settles into a life in Hopewell, Mississippi, where she redirects her desire for travel and change into a burgeoning political activism.

Delotha's activist transportation of her son out of Mississippi only brings her temporary satisfaction; the simple truth is Delotha cannot accept her son's death. When her plans of revenge fall through, she embarks on a seemingly fruitful plot of reconciling with her husband, starting a business, and having more children. But upon giving birth to her fourth child, a second son, Delotha finds, "He was so much like her first boy. 'Armstrong,' she said softly . . . 'No white person will ever hurt you'" (220). Delotha has suspended her acceptance of Armstrong's death in an irrational hope to reconstruct him bodily. In her mind, Armstrong's death simply signifies an untimely (and temporary) absence, inverse to the absenting that predetermined his lynching in the South. Her happiness rests in the illusion that she has conceived and birthed a second Armstrong to replace and redeem the death of the first, to fill up the void left inside her body and mind. Inclined by grief to favor her new son, W.T., over her daughters, she immediately demonstrates her bias, hoarding the child from Wydell (whom she still secretly resents), breastfeeding her baby boy when she gave the girls Similac. Delotha's preoccupation with W.T. worsens through the years, as her sharper judgment gives way to an obsession with sheltering and protecting his body from the dangers of the world. Spoiled, undisciplined, and discontented, W.T. turns to the streets in search of a surrogate family. Ironically, as Suzanne Jones points out, Delotha's failure to heed police warnings and the advice of W.T.'s white teachers further places her son in fatal danger, not necessarily from whites but from other delinquent black boys (27).

Like Delotha, Wydell does not foresee the emergence of gangs and black-on-black crime, nor does he predict the havoc they soon wreak on black families. His judgments arise from the former paradigm of white violence; he, like his wife, has stalled, his life put in limbo by his inability to transport himself mentally from the ravages of his southern past. Unlike Delotha, he is far more apprehensive at the birth of their second son: "Another boy, he thought. They kill the boys, the men. Hang them by their necks and then torch their lifeless bodies. Throw them on the chain-gang for nine hundred years" (*Your Blues*, 222). Clearly, Wydell's trepidation harks back to his youth, one full of fear and imprinted by a world antagonistic to his survival. As a result, he has a limited, mostly negative concept of black manhood, specifically black fatherhood. In the South he has left behind, black fathers are generally powerless to protect their children and themselves. Scripted almost entirely by their bodies into inferior, subordinate roles, these black men, as field and factory laborers, caretakers, and attendants, form twin trajectories of physical and economic subjugation.

But their victim status tells half the story, for some black men, Wydell's father included, would mimic their white masters, borrowing their violent customs, particularly the practice of whippings. After Armstrong's killing, Wydell recalls "how when he was a boy, *his father would walk out of Pinochet's fields with the expression of a whipped dog* . . . He would stand in front of the big man, naked and shivering, and his father would walk toward him, holding the whip high in his hands, saying, 'Didn't I tell you? Didn't I tell you?' Didn't I tell you to put lime in the outhouse; to weed the garden, to put paper in your shoes and not go barefoot in the rain? To not throw in your daddy's face everything you learned at that fool schoolhouse, 'cause it ain't gon' do you no good no way'" (emphasis added, 155). Bolstering his father's defeatist outlook, the beatings mangle Wydell's general perception of himself as a black man. On one hand, Armstrong's phantom body proves vital in the re-membering of his parents' marital life together. His torture and murder, however, continue to cast a shadow over their lives, compelling Delotha's fixation to reproduce a dead child while aggravating Wydell's uncertainty about his ability to raise boys. Without the benefit of a *generative* backward glance, the couple's reunion, even their commercial success, yields a superficial riff on the deafening pause and chaos of their first son's death. Wydell takes up drinking again, while Delotha willfully denies W.T.'s gang and drug-related activity.

Realizing at last the hollowness of their lives, Wydell takes W.T. on a retreat to Mississippi. His attempt to wrest his son and himself from a sequence of self-destructive behavior reverses Wydell's usual response to crisis. Traveling back to his place of origin, he begins the task of experiencing the experience, of confronting the center of his psychic terrors. Only by breaking their hold can he become a more capable father. Integral to Wydell's definition of roots is a love of the blues. He tells W.T., "We picked that cotton until our fingers bled. And sometimes when it got bad—and boy, it could get real bad—we'd be in them fields just a-singing, you know. 'Cause them songs, them songs could get you right" (332). For Wydell, geography and song figure as highly intimate representations of the other. The music disperses feelings of racial cohesion through an otherwise tattered network of labor, the base of Pinochet's agrarian empire. As impulsive and tactical as a musical riff, the journeying back to the land of original blues production signifies not so much perfect resolution as it does a viable, new beginning. As Wydell craves a drink, W.T. reaches out to comfort him, asking, "Dad, what did you useta sing?" (332).

Contradicting this rehabilitative association of body and song, of travel and new beginnings, is Campbell's portrait of pool hall manager Jake McKenzie. In both the South and North, Jake disrupts the novel's twofold design of blues ethos and black mobility. A casualty of internal racism, Jake has heard the same taunt since childhood: "Black Jake. Ugly as a snake" (64). Embittered, he informs on Armstrong and later relocates to Chicago to sing blues in a bar that caters to a predominantly white clientele. In the city, Jake embeds under his skin his sycophantic costume, performing blackness and waggish sexuality as one and the same for an audience of white college types and yuppies: "The more the people hooted, the harder he twirled his hips, too lean for his pants. He turned around, unbuckled his belt, and his pants began slipping and sliding down, revealing his scrawny, naked behind, until there was no music, just yelling and screaming as the old blind man stumbled around the stage, twitching and shaking his ass" (317). Patronizing the crowd's prejudices, Jake's song and dance resemble Rufus McKay's ingratiating routine at Red's store in *Wolf Whistle*, except Campbell's bar scene stages an added element of wild, derisive spectacle, eerily reminiscent of a public lynching. Jake is still a joke, but now by his own doing and according to the misbegotten logic that he controls the laughter. In truth, he is a wasted figure, "who looked as if he didn't weigh more than 120 pounds" (317). Although Jake takes control, he distorts the freedom spirit of the music he sings, renegotiating its purpose through the degrading manners of minstrelsy. Where Nordan's singers protest lynching, Jake reaffirms its cultural intentions; by deliteralizing the act of murder, he in essence lynches himself.

No less complicated is Lily Cox's relationship with the blues, which she can only appreciate through the barrier of her prejudice. Jake has absorbed the white gaze to the point of transforming himself into the embodiment of its projection. Lily, on the other hand, possesses the gaze, but like Jake, her use of it comes at the expense of her own intuition and self-awareness. Through Lily's view, for instance, black fieldworkers and blues singers appear merely as persons of mystique, unknown and unknowable. Her perspective underscores Campbell's larger narrative of the black body as atmosphere, remembrance, and desire, these significances variously determined for characters divided by race. Interspersed throughout the novel are scenes that bind absented (almost phantasmal) black bodies with the southern landscape. Campbell frames her narrative with images of a singing earth (images which, incidentally, chime with Nordan's depiction of a musical swamp), but by the book's end, with Wydell and W.T. looking out on a flooded plain formerly a cotton field, the land is only ghostly populated via memory and imagination. The singing bodies, a chorus of fieldworkers, shown so vividly in the novel's first scene, have literally vanished by the last. As the novel opens, Lily wakes, taking pleasure in the black song performance of the Pinochet fieldworkers: "Colored people's singing made her feel so good" (9).

The field singers might as well be physically absent in the novel's first scene; however devoted Lily finds herself to the "colored people's singing," she retains the advantage of detachment. The singing happens at a distance, lessening the likelihood of physical contact, which, in Lily's mind, avers her social privilege. Lily's dependence on distance, symbolic and literal, persists throughout her life, especially during periods of personal crisis. As a child, during an incident of molestation, she learns to displace her feelings, to distract herself from her pain by focusing on the field songs. Years later, sitting on her back porch with her daughter Doreen, Lily confesses, "I wish I could shut my eyes and see them fields full of singing niggers. It's beautiful when they make background music for your life" (233). Without the romance of the singing field, Lily's life at middle age has lost its air of superiority. Looking back and idealizing her youth, she elides the scarring memory of her uncle molesting her while she watched fieldworkers just as easily as she overlooks now the reality of the workers' exploited labor. To act and feel otherwise in either case would divide her from her husband and all the other white men in her life. As a result, the black body surfaces in her thoughts strictly as a "singing nigger," as innocuous entertainment. Only "the voices" of these disembodied persons "seemed to be inside her" (9).

Indeed, Lily's attraction to the sensuality of the singing, the sexual connotation of its sound and rhythm, "loud and searing, almost violent" (10), stresses the divided nature of her consciousness. Safe from her husband's fumbling touch, Lily's separate existence that she lives vicariously through the art of the "Other" draws vibrancy from the very taboo of its imagination. No black man has actually intruded upon the private space of her marital bed, the classic threat of unconscionable transgression. And yet, Lily's attraction to the singing has developed into a sublimated desire that essentially transports African American bodies across the field into her bedroom.

Lily's sublimation of carnal desire into "colored people's singing" holds devastating implications on the race and power dynamics of the Mississippi Delta. Specifically, Lily's unconscious longing informs her sex life with Floyd, which consistently proves disappointing for her: "he had to push hard to enter, because she was like a desert inside" (47). Floyd's insensitivity perpetuates a pattern established by Lily's molestation. Confronted by his own insecurities, Floyd struggles with his father's imperious model of masculinity, steeped, as it were, in the cause of white supremacy. The pool hall incident merely elevates Floyd's nervousness to critical proportions; his homicidal actions continue the already long chronicle of white male fear and sexual angst: "What made terror slam into Armstrong like a lash across his back was the fear he saw in Floyd's eyes" (37). Armstrong, at this crucial moment, figures as the incarnation of projected hate, his flesh bearing the brunt of white patriarchy, epitomized by the Coxes, but also by the Pinochets and even Wydell's father, who, as I have suggested, interpolates the white standard of dominance and violence into his own code of masculinity. The image of the lash breaking over Armstrong's back reverberates with Wydell's memories of his father beating him, drawing upon the theme of economic control and threatened virility in both black and white men.

Herself the victim of Floyd's brutality, Lily briefly turns her back on white male supremacy during a short-lived, biracial friendship with Ida Long. What really fascinates Lily about Ida is her boldness and sexual independence: "She don't have no husband telling her what to do" (32). The women bond, if only for a moment, over their dream of escaping the stifling atmosphere of Hopewell, Mississippi. Campbell literalizes the sympathetic attachment of the two women with the town's train junction, what Houston Baker calls the "way-station of the blues" (7). In *Railroad: Trains and Train People in American Culture,* theorist James Alan McPherson captures the multiple historical meanings of the train station, which during the nineteenth century thrived semiotically and tropically in the imagination of the black working class. The blues, born in the cash crop fields of the South, would expand, as McPherson explains, via the promise of freedom, democracy, and mobility that became synonymous with the very sound of steam blowing whistles and churning wheels (6–9). Ida and Lily likewise draw hope from the sign of the crossroads, the opposing tracks, and the station itself, as all these markers signify impelling force and escape. Even their relationship bears a crossroads design as over the years the women move toward each other, then away, then toward each other again through Doreen's budding friendship with Ida.

Like Delotha and Wydell, Lily represses her honest feelings about Armstrong's lynching. Not until the morning of Floyd's imprisonment does she finally begin to uncouple herself from her husband's worldview. This same morning, Floydjunior blames his parents as the source of their family's misery; his outburst forces Lily to confront "for the first time that the death of Armstrong Todd was not behind her. She felt his memory growing inside her like a new life" (*Your Blues*, 200). Only now does Lily begin to experience Armstrong's death, allowing it to enter her body, granting it due space in her consciousness. With the memory of Armstrong comes the hard realization of her complicity in his murder and in her husband's acquittal. Lily's repression points up Delotha's. Although experiencing the tragedy from different angles, both women suffer greatly from repressing the pain of their blues. As suggested by the crisscross trace of the narrative design, only until Delotha and Lily recognize and embrace their troubled and connecting history, pushing through the tacit racial barrier of "yours and mine," seeing how their blues bind them at the more immediate level of experience, can they gainfully move forward. However, these women never fully reach this point. Withholding closure but implying its possibility in the arc of Lily's growing remorse, Campbell emphasizes the urgent necessity of healing (interracially and within the South) by evoking the poignancy of its incompleteness.

Part penance, part attrition, Lily's memory of the singing bodies, soon vacated by time and the black migration north, morphs into a lyric "seep[ing] into the land like spilled blood" (9). It is Armstrong's blood that Lily considers; it is his blood that reverberates in the absence of the colored peoples' song and singing, "in the dry wind whispering through the grass" (328). Her frustration grows at not remembering the words or melody, her memory of the music diminished and replaced by the void of Armstrong's death. The murdered body and the song entwine, spiraling over Lily like a "vanishing echo . . . just another shadow on her soul" (9).

Campbell's fusion here of blues song and the absented black body parallels Nordan's depiction of Bobo in the spillway. Like Armstrong's, Bobo's empowerment happens posthumously, and in both instances, the black body accomplishes in death what it cannot do in life: it rewrites the political culture of the South. That these two novels of such contrasting imagination are, nevertheless, able to capture faithfully the historical significance of Emmett Till's murder, not so much by restaging the actual event but by invoking the impact of artistic response on cultural memory, speaks powerfully to the convergence of cultural reform and blues performance. Where Campbell's rail scenes give witness to the blues spirit of freedom and motion, Nordan's work stresses the ministrations of the Mississippi landscape in its molding of a collective musical mindset, the senseless destruction of black bodies reiterated in lyrics and raindrops.

Your Blues and *Wolf Whistle* also concur in their depictions of the ruinous racist gaze, which Campbell uses to map out the black body as a taboo subject, indicating how for Lily the black body, when absented from view, develops into a double helix of sexual menace and attraction. Nordan, meanwhile, pushes the gaze toward its most violent occupations, toward its capacity to negate, to disembody, to stabilize scorn and admiration in equal quantity, as when Solon tells his accomplice Poindexter Montberclair, "Muddy Waters might be a nigger, but he spoke the truth" (127). Here in the El Camino where Solon and Poindexter are making their way to Uncle, Auntee, and Bobo and where Solon has tuned the radio to WOKJ, "the all colored station in Jackson" (127), blues music suffuses the men's thoughts. That the music reveals a black presence flourishing even in the crosshairs of white terror only enriches the gritty rhythm and rhetoric of southern consciousness in the 1950s. In the momentous killing of Emmett "Bobo" Till, black and white culture collided at the crossroads, *the* blues emblem of a bustling and fluid paradigm. The fictions intricately document the buildup and fallout of this collision, suggesting the fullness and power of the blues as an iconic art and as intervening historical record that, at the time of Till's death, bestowed an illuminating focus on the interracial turmoil occurring in the Delta and throughout the country.

WORKS CITED

Baker, Barbara A. "Riffing on Memory and Playing Through the Break: Blues in Lewis Nordan's *Music of the Swamp* and *Wolf Whistle*." *Southern Quarterly* 41, no. 3 (2003): 20–42.

Baker, Houston A., Jr. *Blues, Ideology, and Afro American Literature: A Vernacular Theory*. Chicago: University of Chicago Press, 1984.

Boone, Graeme M. "Blues." In *The Oxford Companion to African American Literature*, edited by William L. Andrews, Frances Smith Foster, and Trudier Harris, 84–87. Oxford: Oxford University Press, 1997.

Campbell, Bebe Moore. *Your Blues Ain't Like Mine*. New York: Ballantine, 1992.

Campbell, Jane. "An Interview with Bebe Moore Campbell." *Callaloo* 22, no. 4 (1999): 954–72.

Gussow, Adam. *Seems Like Murder Here: Southern Violence and the Blues Tradition*. Chicago: University of Chicago Press, 2002.

Hale, Grace Elizabeth. *Making Whiteness: The Culture of Segregation in the South, 1890–1940*. 1998. New York: Vintage, 1999.

Johnson, Robert. "Hellhound on My Trail." *The Complete Recordings*. Sony/Columbia, 1990.

Jones, Suzanne. *Race Mixing: Southern Fiction since the Sixties.* Baltimore: John Hopkins University Press, 2004.

McPherson, James Alan. *Railroad: Trains and Train People in American Culture.* Random House: New York, 1976.

Nordan, Lewis. "Growing Up White in the South." In *Wolf Whistle.* 1993. 1st ed., 2d printing. Chapel Hill: Algonquin, 2003.

———. "Interview with Lewis Nordan at His Home in Pittsburgh, May 19, 2001." By Thomas Aervold Bjerre. *Mississippi Quarterly* 54, no. 3 (2001): 678–91.

———. *Wolf Whistle.* 1993. Chapel Hill, NC: Algonquin, 1995.

LITERARY REPRESENTATIONS OF THE LYNCHING OF EMMETT TILL

An Annotated Bibliography

CHRISTOPHER METRESS

The following bibliography lists more than 140 literary works (novels, stories, poems, plays, songs, musical scores, and movie and television scripts) that are based upon—or make significant reference to—the Emmett Till lynching. Annotations are provided for works that were not discussed in the preceding essays, and, where possible, original publication information is given for each entry. This bibliography is designed to aid those who are interested in learning more about the full extent of Emmett Till's place in literary memory and imagination. The bibliography is also available at http://faculty.samford.edu/~cpmetress/till -bibliography.html. Having this resource on-line enables others to contribute updated information and entries, thus assuring that the bibliography remains current and representative.

Alloy. "Emmett Till." Engine Records. 1993. Songwriter unlisted.
>Hard rock song with two lines: "If I were black: / hanging from a tree."

Alston, Nelson G. "Little Emmett." In *A Time for Glory and Hate: The American Civil Rights Movement*, 15. Denver: Alpha Books N Press, 1993.
>Short poem that asks a series of retrospective questions about the murder, everything from "Where were you when they killed that boy?" to "How did you feel when that all white jury / found those murders / Not guilty?" Accuses the country of indifference, complacency, and hypocrisy.

Anderson, Devery. Untitled poem. Available at http://emmetttillmurder.com (accessed 1 September 2006).
>In this poem by one of the leading historians of the case, Till is remembered as an "only child, a mother's son" who "moved a sleeping land." Now, in death, Till is "one of heaven's angels" who "move[s] us once again."

Ascher, Rhoda Gaye. "Remembrance (for Emmett Till, murdered Aug. 31, 1955)." *Freedomways* 9, no. 2 (1969): 138.

> Poem reflecting on how, even though the "night cries are gone now" from the Tallahatchie River, "delta lips are [still] red" with racism: "Take a rotting log from the circling river, / Wear it, piercing your heart, in remembrance."

Baldwin, James. *Blues for Mister Charlie*. New York: Dial, 1964.

Barr, David, and Mamie Till-Mobley. *The Face of Emmett Till*. In *New Plays from Chicago*, edited by Russ Tutterow and Ann Filmer, 309–65. Chicago: Chicago Dramatists Press, 2005. Original title: *The State of Mississippi vs. Emmett Till*. Directed by Douglas-Alan Mann. Pegasus Players. Premiere at Truman College Theatre, Aurora, Illinois, 9 September 1999.

> The play opens with Mamie Till-Mobley preparing to deliver a speech at the dedication of the Civil Rights Memorial in Montgomery, Alabama (5 November 1989). From here, the play moves back and forth across time as it recounts Till's kidnapping, his subsequent lynching, the return of his corpse to Chicago, and the trial of his murderers. Relying heavily on documentary sources and Mamie Till-Mobley's memory of the events, the play occasionally works with a split stage—for instance, as Moses Wright gives his court testimony about Till's kidnapping, that kidnapping is reenacted elsewhere on stage. In addition to the play's most powerful scene, in which Till-Mobley remembers opening the casket at the train station, other scenes of note include a re-creation of Till's beating and a series of scenes depicting Till-Mobley's conflicts with Roy Wilkins and the NAACP over the role that organization would play in seeking justice for Emmett's murder. In the closing scene, Till-Mobley's plea to remember the civil rights martyrs who "paid the ultimate price . . . for the freedoms we enjoy" is followed by a full-cast rendition of "Woke Up This Morning with My Mind on Freedom."

Barry, Quan. "Emmett Till's Open Casket as *La Pietá*." *Green Mountains Review* 17, no. 1 (Spring/Summer 2004): 112. Reprinted in *Controvertibles*, 44. Pittsburgh: University of Pittsburgh Press, 2004.

> Poem that reflects on the death of Mamie Till-Mobley. After recalling the "litany of injuries" marking Till's corpse, the poem concludes, "When Mary holds the dead Christ in her arms / she has seen everything / but the Resurrection."

Beecher, John. "The Better Sort of People." In *To Live and Die in Dixie*, 42–43. Birmingham: Red Mountain Editions, 1965.

> Condemnation of southern racism by a left-wing southern poet. The racist persona claims that "Our Negroes here are satisfied" until they head up North and "come back with notions." Although the persona concludes that such Negroes "somehow get spoiled / and need the fear of God / thrown into them again," he is against what "ignorant rednecks do." It was "unnecessary / to beat that little Negro boy to death."

Sure, "he was uppity," but a "good horsewhipping should have been enough." The "better sort of people" in Mississippi "love our Negroes" and "the violence you hear so much about" comes from the "poor white trash."

Bilbrew, A. C. "The Death of Emmett Till—Part 1 and Part 2." Dootone Records 382. Performed by the Ramparts. Published by Dootsie Williams Incorporated, B.M.I. 1955. Lyrics published in *California Eagle,* 29 December 1955.

Song retelling what happened to Till, whose "name will be a legend we all know." When Till agrees that Carolyn Bryant is good looking, saying "Wheee! You're right," that "remark cost him his life." The two white men at trial "grinned and smoked and chewed / As the fearful witnesses all did testify." In the end, however, it was to no avail, and we "won't see little Emmett any more."

Black, Daniel. *The Sacred Place.* New York: St. Martin's, 2007.

This novel reimagines the events leading up to and immediately following the kidnapping and lynching of Emmett Till. When fourteen-year-old Clement, visiting from Chicago, goes into a grocery store in Money, Mississippi, to buy a root beer, he puts his nickel on the counter. When the white woman working the register demands that he pick it up and put it in her hand, Clement laughs at her and walks away, telling her that "Slavery's been over." A few days later, four white men show up at Jeremiah Johnson's house, demanding to see the boy from Chicago. When they try to force entry, however, Jeremiah and his son Enoch kill three of the men and vow to take up arms against any local whites who try to seek retaliation. After Clement is eventually kidnapped and killed, the remainder of the novel deals with how Jeremiah and Enoch organize the black community into a "liberation movement" willing to use violence to overturn the social order. In the novel's penultimate scene, an armed black community confronts local whites, and when a white man fires on one of the black men, the armed community fires back, killing a young white boy and the sheriff, and affirming Jeremiah's threat that "For every Black funeral, it's gon to be a white one."

Brooks, Gwendolyn. "A Bronzeville Mother Loiters in Mississippi. Meanwhile a Mississippi Mother Burns Bacon." In *The Bean Eaters,* 333–39. Harper: New York, 1960.

———. "The Last Quatrain of the Ballad of Emmett Till." In *The Bean Eaters,* 340. Harper: New York, 1960.

Brown, Frank London. "In the Shadow of a Dying Soldier." *Southwest Review* 44, no. 4 (Autumn 1959): 292–306.

Story about a black Chicago reporter assigned to the Till trial. Having to face Deep South segregation for the first time, the reporter comes to understand both the depths of racial hatred felt by whites and the modest but growing resistance being expressed among blacks. When a local racist marks him as an outside agitator, the reporter must flee Mississippi before the trial is over. Although incredulous when he learns of the verdict, the reporter is in the end comforted somewhat by the lingering image of local blacks "standing on the lawn day after day in the white sun—in the shadow of the Confederate soldier—unafraid, dead set on showing Mrs. Bradley we're behind her."

Browne, L. Anthony. "Yours' [sic] to You." *Baltimore Afro-American*, 7 January 1956.

Poem addressed to Mississippi, pointing out the hypocrisy of those in the state who praise America but deny rights to the likes of Emmett Till. This poem by a Newark, New Jersey resident, expresses lingering outrage over "that horrible night," warns Till's killers that one day they "will hang [their] heads in shame," and questions how we can still call this country "the land of the free."

Burrell, Brian. "Emmett Till." Premiere at Theatre-Theatre, Hollywood, California, December 1994.

Play reviewed in the *Los Angeles Times*, 16 December 1994. This unpublished play is characterized as a "brutal tragic comedy" about the marital breakup of a black sitcom writer and his white wife.

Campbell, Bebe Moore. *Your Blues Ain't Like Mine*. New York: Putnam, 1992.

Cassells, Cyrus. "Strange Fruit." *Callaloo* 18 (Spring-Summer 1983): 5–6.

An older narrator recalls being "frightened by Billie's song" into "Learning a grief / That is a racial." He then remembers how with Till's lynching "the strange fruit was given / A face, a body like my own—." Now, years later, he sees a "boy's body / Swinging from a tree" and wonders if one day "fear" will die, "That one word, if we could grasp it, / Which might stop a child from becoming strange fruit."

Césaire, Amié. "Message sur l'état de l'union." *Présence Africaine*, n.s., 6 (February/March 1956): 119–20. Revised heavily as "Sur l'Etat de l'Union." In *Ferrements: Poèmes*, 76–78. Paris: Éditions du Seuil, 1960.

Coleman, George M. "Some Negro Mother." *Atlanta Daily World*, 13 September 1955.

Inspired by Till's lynching, this four-stanza poem meditates on the fears that southern black women feel after giving birth. The poem's mother wonders if she should "Teach [her son] of the Stars and Stripes / And a nation's glowing spark, / Or of the Klan and the blinded vet / To whom the world is dark?"

Coleman, Wanda. "Emmett Till." *Callaloo* 27 (Spring 1986): 295–99.

Beginning with "river jordan run red," this five-section poem uses the image of a river to recount how Till's lynching "quickly courses thru / the front page news" and reveals a fragmented national psyche. Till's whistle, "a smooth long all-american hallelujah" that stirs up a "whole tributary of intolerance," calls into question the promise of America. Interspersing lists of rivers (*"the colorado the columbia the connecticut the cumberland"*) with indictments of American exceptionalism ("oh say Emmett Till can you see Emmett Till"), the poem also explores the redemptive power of Till's lynching: the opening image of "river jordan run red" is echoed in the concluding lines *"on that third day / he rose /* and was carried forth to that promised land."

Collins, Durward, Jr. "Temperate Belt: Reflections on the Mother of Emmett Till." In *Beyond the Blues: New Poems by American Negroes,* edited by Rosey E. Pool, 68–69. Kent, England: Hand and Flower Press, 1962.

Employing a series of surreal images drawn from the circus, the poet reflects on Mamie Till as a "Sidewalk barker in yellow silk" who "shook that tiny skull until / pity bled from our eyes." Poem ends in melancholy as we see her "charming fewer / and fewer" and glimpse her "once or twice, lying in the tracks / of the tilt-a-whirl, full of quarters / among the weeds that sprung from [her son's] grave."

Collins, J. C. Letter to the Editor. *California Eagle,* 13 October 1955.

Letter cast in the voice of Emmett Till as he begs God to avenge his death. Asking God to let his "tortured and mutilated face and [his] agonizing scream . . . haunt [his murderers] continuously both day and night," Till hopes for a similar torment for all those who clapped "their hands with glee as they beheld my murderers escape the just penalty." Requesting that God put a curse on the Sumner courthouse—"that house of mockery"—so that all who enter it do so with grave "misgivings lest some evil befall them," Till urges that God move quickly and "stay not thy hand, lest those who have done this deed further pollute this land."

Cooper, Mary Carson. "A Tribute to Emmett Till." *Cleveland Call and Post,* 22 October 1955.

Short poem by a reader from Akron closes with the lines, "It's time all Negroes did fight back / With their own lynching team!"

Cornish, Sam. "Calls Me From the Thunder." In *1935: A Memoir,* 138. Boston: Ploughshares, 1990.

Prose poem characterizing Till as "more child than man" who died for "attempting to climb the pedestal where his white woman stood."

———. "The Cross." In *1935: A Memoir,* 167–68. Boston: Ploughshares, 1990.

Reflecting on all the black "men and women weighed with anchor and anvil, battered beyond recognition" in the Mississippi, this prose poem seeks to debunk the 1950s mythos surrounding the "Eisenhower years of barbecue and cocktail hours."

———. "Emmett Till (August 1955)." In *Folks Like Me,* 92–93. Cambridge, MA: Zoland, 1993.

Told from the perspective of a young black man who has always lived up north (whose identity is, at first and only momentarily, conflated with Till's), this poem expresses anger against southern Negroes "sitting / in backs of buses / bags of food / in their laps / bladders tight / in silence sweating."

————. "The Floating Line." In *1935: A Memoir,* 141. Boston: Ploughshares, 1990.

Short prose poem that attributes the beginning of a bus boycott in Memphis to "the people who walk, Emmett Till in their memory."

————. "The Good Men." In *1935: A Memoir,* 140. Boston: Ploughshares, 1990.

Poem about the "lessons that are never taught in / school," in particular how Bryant and Milam (the "good men") pistol-whipped Emmett Till. Juxtaposes this unspoken history with the stories of other good men (Frederick Douglass, Nat Turner) whose lives also go untold.

————. "The Heart That Breaks." In *1935: A Memoir,* 140. Boston: Ploughshares, 1990.

Poem condemning President Eisenhower for not wishing "to legislate the heart." Points out that "it is the heart that ties the fan to the / body / of Emmett Till."

————. "In Memoriam." In *1935: A Memoir,* 137. Boston: Ploughshares, 1990.

Brief prose poem that remembers Till as a "snappy fellow in good clothes" who "if he lived long enough would have gone to fat in his late twenties from beer, liquor, soul food and lack of exercise."

————. "Langston Variations 1955." In *Cross a Parted Sea,* 67. Cambridge, MA: Zoland, 1996.

Brief poem that fuses the language of Langston Hughes with recollections of Emmett Till's photo in *Jet* magazine.

————. "Life Was Poor." In *Cross a Parted Sea,* 101. Cambridge, MA: Zoland, 1996.

Told from the perspective of a black domestic, this poem contrasts the lives of white people in Money, Mississippi—who "sing / the praises / of the lord and keep / his world and word"—with the lives of blacks, who live in forced segregation.

————. "My Lord What a Mourning." In *Cross a Parted Sea,* 103. Cambridge, MA: Zoland, 1996.

Poem in which the persona recalls viewing the corpse of Emmett Till.

————. "One Hundred Million Black Voices." In *Cross a Parted Sea,* 97. Cambridge, MA: Zoland, 1996.

Poem proclaiming, among other things, that "in America everywhere / on death row / we are / Emmett Till Medgar / Evers / the Strange Fruit / that Billie sings."

————. "A River the World Knows." In *Cross a Parted Sea,* 102. Cambridge, MA: Zoland, 1996.

Poem in which Moses Wright recalls the moment he saw Till's ring and "knew that [it] was my nephew / pulled from the river like so / many others."

———. "The South Is My Home." *Obsidian III* 1, no. 2 (Spring–Summer 2000): 67–68.

Till is twice mentioned in this litany of ennobling and disgraceful reasons for why the poet considers the South central to his sense of identity.

———. "The South Was Waiting in Baltimore." In *1935: A Memoir*, 168–70. Boston: Ploughshares, 1990.

Till's photo in *Jet* magazine surfaces in this poem about racism in Baltimore.

———. "Tough in the Streets Dead in Mississippi." In *1935: A Memoir*, 139. Boston: Ploughshares, 1990.

Prose poem depicting Till as "made tough on the streets of Chicago" and not understanding "dark children of Southern blacks" whose "words are so measured they melt in the mouth."

Crowe, Chris. *Mississippi Trial, 1955*. New York: Phyllis Fogelman Books, 2002.

Young adult novel (grades 6–8) that tells the story of Hiram Hilburn, a white boy who has grown up with his grandparents in Mississippi but whose civil-rights minded father moves him away to Arizona so that he will not adopt the racist ways of his home state. The summer Hiram turns sixteen, he is allowed to visit his aging grandfather. Here, he renews some of his childhood acquaintances and meets Emmett Till (whom he saves from drowning). When Till later turns up dead, Hiram suspects that his boyhood friend R.C., now a racist bully, has helped Milam and Bryant commit the murder. Hiram is served with a subpoena to testify in court, but Hiram's racist grandfather will not allow him to attend the trial, especially if Hiram testifies against white men in favor of a "colored boy who didn't know his place." Against pressure, he decides to testify, but in the end he is not called to do so. When Hiram sees the courtroom celebration following the not-guilty verdict, he feels sick and wants "to get out . . . of Mississippi, and back home where things and people weren't so crazy." After the trial, Hiram learns that his grandfather helped to kidnap Till. When Hiram returns to Arizona, he keeps this secret but now understands why his father had to break with Mississippi and the past.

Dasher, Joseph R. Unpublished song about Emmett Till (title unknown). File 1, box 20. Papers of the NAACP. Library of Congress.

In late 1955 (November?), Dasher attended an NAACP rally in Baltimore. In a letter to Glouster Currant of the NAACP, received 1 February 1956, Dasher says that, "at the rally I presented a group of young fellows who are known as the 'Honeyboys,' to sing a song that I had written as a campaign song in memory of the late Emmit [sic] Till." Dasher notes that he is enclosing a copy of the song, but the song was not found in the files.

Davidson, Richard. "A Cause for Justice." *Daily Worker*, 11 October 1955.

This free-verse poem alternates between depictions of "Mr. and Mrs. XX"—a white Mississippi couple who attends the Till trial—and "the echo of a boy's voice" that emerges from Till's grave in Chicago. As Mr. and Mrs. XX go on with their lives after the trial—wondering to themselves "what was all the shouting about"—the voice from Till's grave "grows louder." Whereas the white couple finds it easy to forget, Davidson proclaims that Till's "death becomes part of our living flesh. / His killing a waking cry of our conscience."

————. *Mississippi*. Premiere at Pantomime Art Theatre [Second Avenue], New York City, 20 January 1956. File 1, box 20. Papers of the NAACP. Library of Congress.

According to a playbill, this "new play based on the Emmett Till Case" was directed by the author and had a scheduled run of three performances. The cast list, containing such characters as "Will Price" and "Judith Mason," suggests that the play obliquely refers to the Till case. No known transcript exists.

————. "Requiem for a Fourteen-Year-Old." *Daily Worker*, 12 September 1955.

This earliest-known poem about the case recounts Till's funeral, where "Ten thousand heard the service which gave him / To the cool earth." The memories among those ten thousand vary: some remember Till as "a nice kid with his cap slung back on his head; others remember how he was "sweet / on a girl lived down the block." The poem ends with an ironic turn, depicting how Till's buddies leave the funeral "Whistling a low moaning blues," while later that night in Washington "someone remarked / about the need for a strong colonial policy."

Davis, Ossie, and Ruby Dee. *What Can You Say to Mississippi?* 1956. Original performance date unknown.

In their memoir *With Ossie and Ruby: A Life Together*, Davis and Dee recall writing and performing a play about Till's murder (staged for Local 1199 in New York City as part of the union's 1956 Negro History Week celebration). Sidney Poitier also starred. All attempts to recover a script of the play have failed.

Davis, Stephanie (a.k.a. "Ainka"). "For You Emmett Till." 1996. Available at www .timbooktu.com/ainka/ainka.htm (accessed 1 March 2005).

Claiming Till as "My bright eyed son," the poet wonders what Till "would have grown to be." The answer is "Black and strong . . . / Proud like me . . ."

Dente, Wade. *A Good Place to Raise a Boy*. Premiere at Hotel Theresa, New York City, 1956. File 1, box 20. Papers of the NAACP. Library of Congress.

The contents of this play are unknown, and the only evidence that it existed is a flyer found in the NAACP papers. According to the flyer, "the whole story was never told in the newspapers," and "Unless this story is told, the valiant efforts of the few Negroes and Poor [sic] whites struggling in the South will be useless."

Dickerson, George. "On the Murder of a Black Boy." 1979. In *Selected Poems: 1959–1999*, 136. New York: Rattapallax Press, 2000.

Poem recited during an autobiographical one-man show entitled *A Few Useless Mementos For Sale* (originally produced in 1979 as *Fragments from a Broken Window* at the American Renaissance Theatre, New York). Near the end of the drama, the main character, a world-weary writer in his late fifties who is holding a rummage sale in his apartment, recalls how, during the 1950s and 1960s, "the world was outdoing me in its madness." In particular, he recalls the assassinations of JFK, Martin Luther King, Bobby Kennedy, and the "memory of Emmett Till." He then recites his poem, in which he condemns the "mouths white with agreement" that "turn so quickly to evening tea."

Diop, David. "A Un Enfant Noir" (To a black child). In *Coups de Pilon*, 24–25. Paris: Présence Africaine, 1973.

Although unmentioned in this work by French West African poet Diop, Till is clearly the boy depicted as killed for gazing "on a mouth on breasts on a body of a white woman." The American South is described as a "country where one places one hand on the Bible / But where the Bible is not opened."

DJ Nasty Knock. "Emmett Till." *Sex*. Street Records. SS-31008-2. Released 27 February 1996.

Song dedicated to Till, "Who should never be forgot," who serves as "A reminder to the racists who make this world rot." DJ's retelling relies heavily on Huie's *Look* narrative; Till, who "went down to Mississippi all strong and lean," is cast as a defiant hero, a role model for current black youth. Claiming that Till boasted "I'm better than you" to his murderers, DJ pleads that today's black man must "remember those words and hold your head high."

Dumas, Henry. "The Crossing." *Negro Digest* 14 (November 1965): 80–86.

This initiation story involves two young black boys who, upon crossing a bridge in rural Louisiana, begin to discuss the Till murder. When one threatens to scare the other's little sister and throw her into the river, the other boy recounts his version of the lynching. This version is filled with widely inaccurate exaggerations (including dozens of robed Klansman and a three-day stoning), suggesting that Till's story has become a larger-than-life example of the racial hatred all black children must learn about as they cross from adolescence into maturity.

Dylan, Bob. "The Death of Emmett Till" [a.k.a. "The Ballad of Emmett Till"]. First performed 26 January 1962. Recorded 2 July 1962. Lyrics in *Writings and Drawings*, 19. New York, Knopf, 1973.

Recounting the details of the lynching and the trial, the song is notable for its activism and its errors. Dylan not only claims that Milam and Bryant confessed to the crime before the trial started, but he also asserts that "on the jury there were men who helped the brothers commit this awful crime." The song ends with a call to action, for if "we gave all we could give / We could make this great land of ours a greater place to live."

Emanuel, James A. "Emmett Till." 1963. Original place of publication unknown. Reprinted in *The Treehouse and Other Poems*, 9. Detroit: Broadside Press, 1968.

A haunting lyric that opens with "a whistling / Through the water" and imagines Till as one who "swims forever, / Deep in treasures, / Necklaced in / A coral toy."

———. "Where Will Their Names Go Down?" In *The Treehouse and Other Poems*, 9. Detroit: Broadside Press, 1968.

Crying out for "Our bloodied boys / Sunk link by link" into the "Tallahatchie, the Mississippi, and the Pearl," this poem affirms the memory of those who have been martyred: "From swollen prayers we rise to fiercely shake a chain of days / That blurry hang across that dying scrawl."

Falsey, John. "I'll Fly Away: Then and Now." Public Broadcasting System. Directed by Ian Sanders, 11 October 1993.

The thirty-ninth and final episode of the acclaimed network series moves back and forth between the early 1960s and the early 1980s. Lilly Harper, now a grandmother, is trying to educate her indifferent grandson about his heritage (in particular the racial injustices of the past). To do so, she tells the story of Elden Simms, a black youth from Detroit who was lynched in her Georgia hometown for being "uppity" to a white woman. Lilly's father is the only one who can identify the two white men who killed Elden and, in a scene reminiscent of Moses Wright, he does so at the trial. Fearing for their lives, Lilly and her daughter have to flee the Bedford family household. The episode ends with the grandson now understanding the sacrifices that were made by the civil rights generation.

Fields, Beryl. "One Way Out." *New York Amsterdam News*, 19 November 1955.

Short poem by a reader from the Bronx who encourages subscribers to write to their congressman. "Remember the pen is mighty as the sun," she exhorts, "So write and fight and make it plain / That the Emmett Tills have not died in vain."

Fields, Julia. "Mississippi Green, or, Something Is Unfinished Here, Emmett Till." In *Slow Coins*, 65. Washington, DC: Three Continents, 1981.

Surveying a desolate Mississippi landscape (where one "almost expect[s] / To see a black man's hand" rise out of the "idle" swamp), this poem's narrator wonders "why Emmett's mother / Would ever even bring / Him for a visit."

Flanagan, Thomas Jefferson. "The Wolf-Whistler: He Was in the Heart of the Mississippi South." *Atlanta Daily World*, 27 September 1955.

Poem by a regular contributor to the *Daily World*. Focusing on the whistle—prompted by the "boundless joy" Till must have felt to be so "Far from the State Street slum" of Chicago—the poem concludes with Till's soul lingering "at the beautiful gate [of Heaven] / Where one can wolf-whistle to God."

Francis, Vievee. "Emmett, I Said Wait." *Callaloo* 26, no. 3 (2003): 630–34.

Poem from the perspective of Carolyn Bryant as she recalls many years later what happened on that fateful day. With sleep haunted by images of Till, she recalls how she was offended by his "nasty sound" but "did not say / take him to the river." Staring at her from "the magazine / years old," "the crack in [Till's] face / is a question mark," and in her dreams she both eroticizes the young boy (smiling "into his slender throat") and tries to comfort him with soothing hushes.

Gilliam, Mary. "Little Boy from Chicago." *Baltimore Afro-American,* 26 November 1955.

Poem expressing horror over the killing but also an abiding faith that God "knows who and where his murderers are / And in His own way and His own time, / They will be brought before the Judgment bar."

Giovanni, Nikki. "All Eyez On U (for 2Pac Shakur 1971–1996)." In *Love Poems*, 62–64. New York: Morrow and Company, 1997.

Poem written after the murder of 2Pac Shakur. According to Giovanni, "this generation mourns 2Pac as my generation mourned Till as we / all mourn Malcolm." Shakur's memory "will not go away," just as "Emmett Till did not go away."

———. "Bring on the Bombs: A Historical Interview." In *Quilting the Black-Eyed Pea*, 65–72. New York: William Morrow, 2002.

An interview poem recounting the story of Daisy Bates, who recalls how Till's murder "rang a resounding bell" and "put some iron in our backbone."

———. "A Civil Rights Journey." In *Blues: For All the Changes*, 56–58. New York: William Morrow, 1999.

Prose poem opens with Giovanni's memory of Till's murder, which she calls the "defining event of my generation." Unable to "make sense" of what happened, Giovanni asks questions that mark the beginning of her "civil rights journey."

———. "For Tupac Shakur (1971–1996)." In *Love Poems*, 61. New York: Morrow and Co., 1997.

Prose poem about how Shakur's "spirit will flower and who like Emmett Till and Malcolm X will be remembered by his people for the great man who could have been."

———. "Hands: For Mother's Day." In *To Those Who Ride the Night Winds*, 16–18. New York: William Morrow, 1983.

Reflecting on how "hands must be very important" to women's lives (and how "wives and mothers are not so radically different"), Giovanni remembers: "I saw a photograph once of the mother of Emmett Till . . . a slight, brown woman with pill-box hat . . . white gloves . . . eyes dark beyond pain . . . incomprehensively looking at a world that never intended her son to be a man."

———. "Here's to Gwen." In *Quilting the Black-Eyed Pea,* 30–31. New York: William Morrow, 2002.

In this prose poem tribute to Gwendolyn Brooks, Giovanni calls "Bronzeville Mother" the "most brilliant work on the murder of Emmett Till."

———. "Lorraine Hansberry: An Emotional View." In *To Those Who Ride the Night Winds,* 13–15. New York: William Morrow, 1983.

In this tribute to Hansberry, Giovanni ruminates on the fate of black Americans since 1619, issuing a list of things she wishes would have been different. Among them, she writes: "I wish we had been enslaved . . . at the same rate we were being set . . . free . . . It would be . . . an entirely different story . . . I wish the battleships . . . had sailed down the Mississippi River . . . when Emmett Till was lynched . . . at the same speed they sped to Cuba . . . during the missile crisis."

———. "Rosa Parks." In *Quilting the Black-Eyed Pea,* 8–9. New York: William Morrow, 2002.

Prose poem in tribute to Rosa Parks and to the Pullman Porters "who organized when people said they couldn't." Among other things, it imagines the porters who "welcomed a fourteen-year-old boy onto their train in 1955" and who later "got Emmett's body on the northbound train" back to Chicago.

———. "Visible Ink." In *Blues: For All the Changes,* 15–16. New York: William Morrow, 1999.

In this poem, Giovanni includes Mamie Till Bradley among those "greatest heroes [who] probably have no idea . . . how heroic they are."

"Goodbye to Dixie, Chicago Here We Come." Unpublished poem. Referred to in *Jackson Clarion-Ledger,* 8 November 1955.

Sent to columnist Tom Ethridge by a resident of Bright Bank Plantation, Midnight, Mississippi, this poem was supposedly written by an "exasperated Chicagoan" (Ethridge's words). According to Ethridge, some sample lines read: "Tell all the folks to board the bus . . . the Mayor's done give this town to us. He'd sell his very soul for votes . . . man, it's fun to sow wild oats! Romp all over a white man's place . . . guarded by cops while you spit in his face!"

Graham, Donald G. (Dante). "April 5th." *Understanding Black Poetry: Black Speech and Black Music as Poetic References,* 320–21. Edited by Stephen Henderson. New York: William Morrow, 1973.

In the wake of King's assassination, the narrator tries to remember King's words but can only recall "three little / girls malcolm X medgar evers / emmett till and the soft / touch I had die last night." Proclaiming "non-violence is dead," the poem concludes with "Lord strike their ass / for they know what / they do."

Guillén, Nicolás. "Elegias a Emmett Till." *Propósitos* [Buenos Aires], 21 August 1956, 3. Reprinted as "Elegy for Emmett Till," in *Man-Making Words: Selected Poems of Nicolás Guillén,* translated, annotated, and with an introduction by Robert Márquez and David Arthur Murray, 87–91. Amherst: University of Massachusetts Press, 1972.

Holland, Endesha Ida Mae. "From the Mississippi Delta." Unpublished, 1988.

    Emmett Till is mentioned in the opening lines of this short play adapted from Holland's memoir of the same name. A performance of the play is noted in the *New Yorker* (5 September 1988), and Cleanora Hudson-Weems mentions it in *Emmett Till: The Sacrificial Lamb of the Civil Rights Movement* (Troy, MI: Bedford, 1994).

Huff, William H. "The Emmett Till Case." *Baltimore Afro-American,* 21 January 1956.

    Short poem written by Mamie Till Bradley's legal counsel in an attempt to explain why he withdrew his support from her NAACP-sponsored speaking tour.

———. "Let's Have that Anti-Lynching Bill." *Pittsburgh Courier,* 15 October 1955.

    Short didactic poem urging readers to think of "a youngster's body floating / Where his own race is kept from voting" and "combat" the filibuster against the antilynching bill before Congress.

Hughes, Langston. "I Feel Mississippi's Fist in My Own Face, Simple Says." *Chicago Defender,* 15 October 1955.

    Story about how Simple feels in the wake of the Till lynching. Berating his fellow blacks for staying down South in the first place, Simple begins to express his anger about how blacks should respond to the lynching. When he suggests that blacks ought to "get themselves an arsenal," the narrator accuses him of "advocating race war." Responding that "there's no race peace there," Simple grows angrier and angrier as he begins to relive the lynching. Finally, he exclaims, "I do not want to talk about it anymore, so do not ask me what I would do if I was there, nor how I would protect myself because I might be forced to show you, so do not ask me."

———. "Mississippi—1955." *Daily Worker,* 26 September 1955. Earliest version, "Emmett Till, Mississippi, and Congressional Investigations," is in an unpublished draft dated 16 September 1955 in Hughes, 317, James Weldon Johnson Papers, Beinecke Rare Book and Manuscript Library, Yale University. Another draft dated 23 September 1955 is in file C, 13, box 18, Papers of the NAACP, Library of Congress.

———. "The Money, Mississippi Blues." In *The Lynching of Emmett Till: A Documentary Narrative,* edited by Christopher Metress, 296–98. Charlottesville: University of Virginia Press, 2002.

Blues song with lyrics by Hughes and music by Jobe Huntley. Attached to a 4 October 1955 letter to Henry Lee Moon (file C, 13, box 18, Papers of the NAACP, Library of Congress), the song was submitted to the NAACP for use in fundraising campaigns. It incorporates some of the language of "Mississippi—1955" and works off variations of the line "I don't want to go to Money, Mississippi." Characterizes Till as a "little old boy" who was "beaten because he was so bold" and wonders why Mississippi would do this to the child of a man who "died for democracy."

Huie, William Bradford. "Wolf Whistle." Unproduced screenplay. 21 May 1960. Folder 350. William Bradford Huie Papers. Ohio State University.

Huie's screenplay relies heavily upon his 1956 *Look* magazine account. While visiting his black kinfolks in Mississippi, Chicago-born Bobo Wilson brags about his white girlfriend, whose picture he carries in his wallet. Highly sexualized in Huie's screenplay, Bobo (who is seventeen in this script) is dared to enter a local store and ask a white woman, Clara Matlock, for a date. Because "the picture has trapped him," he "*must* enter the store." Innocently holding her hand "for a beat," Bobo tries to save face, but Clara is alarmed and grabs a pistol. Soon, according to Clara's husband Ray, "every nigger in the Delta is talking about it," and so he and his brother Big Matt Matlock must do something. The screenplay then cuts to the trial, much of which is seen through the eyes of Thomas Darnell, a famous magazine writer from Alabama who also serves as the movie's narrator. (In his trial scenes, it should be noted, Huie often diverts from the historical record.) The screenplay ends with a post-trial flashback. Darnell has secured a confession from Big Matt Matlock, who now narrates how Till was kidnapped and murdered. Echoing Huie's *Look* account, Big Matt tells how the two men beat the boy mercilessly while he defiantly asserts that "I'm as good as you are. . . . . An' you know som'pin. I got a white girl." After we witness Till being shot in the head, the screenplay ends with a close-up of the "questioning face" of Darnell, who muses, "the question which caused Big Matt to murder Bobo . . . still tortures many white men. What should a white man *do* when a Negro youth reaches for the hand of a white girl?"

———. "Wolf Whistle." Unproduced screenplay. Revised 29 June 1960. Folder 352. William Bradford Huie Papers. Ohio State University.

Some scenes are rearranged and/or deleted, but the most significant changes involve the way the murder is recast and how the screenplay ends. Instead of being saved until the final scenes, Till's murder is placed early, in its appropriate chronological sequence. This version ends with the not-guilty verdict. Immediately afterward, in full view of others in the courthouse lobby, Darnell asks the two men if they murdered Till, and they proudly confess that they did. Instead of ending with Darnell's musing on "what should a white man *do* when a Negro youth reaches for the hand of white girl," the screenplay now ends with the image of Big Matt having to plow his own field and ostracized by the white community for publicly confessing to the crime.

Ice Cube. "Cave Bitch." *Lethal Injection.* Priority Records. P2–53876. 1993.

> Song warning a "white bitch" who wants a "Mandingo" to "ease back." Unattracted to her "Stringy hair—no derrier—frontin' and fakin' with your silicone pair," he warns black men against this "cave bitch" who is "looking for dark meat" because "sooner or later, the bitch'll yell rape." And "Soon as daddy found out you a jigaboo / He'll kill you like he did Emmitt [*sic*] Till."

Jackson, Mary Coleman. "The Ballad of Emmett Till." 10 October 1995. File C, 13. Box 18. Papers of the NAACP. Library of Congress.

> A Los Angeles native, Jackson submitted this poem to Roy Wilkins and the NAACP "to use as they see fit (or throw away)." For most of the eleven stanzas, Jackson recounts the kidnapping and murder from the perspective of Milam and Bryant, who plead that "We let the Till boy go free." In the end, however, Jackson warns, "woe to the men and the women of Money," and "Woe to their children for they'll reap the fruit / That grew when men murdered a boy."

Jackson, Reuben. "Thinking of Emmett Till." In *Fingering the Keys,* 27. Cabin John, MD: Gut Punch Press, 1990.

> Black narrator of this brief poem asks a white waitress for sugar and is met "with / bloodthirsty / smile." No direct mention of Till but for the title.

Johnson, Bryan. "Emmit [*sic*] Till." *Denver Quarterly* 34, no. 2 (Summer 1999): 57.

> Surrealist poem refers directly to Till only in the title. By indirection, the poem uses Till as a metaphor for the redemptive powers of suffering as it tells the story of an unnamed Mississippi woman who is dreaming of transcendence in her world of mundane poverty.

King, Rev. Joseph. "Death in Dixie." *American Negro* 1, no. 2 (October 1955): 17.

> This poem points out the hypocrisy of American freedom in the wake of Till's lynching, for despite the claims of our democracy, "Death is our law! Murder our order of justice." It concludes with a call for "Justice against the beast men! / Black men, human men wrestle down the terror beast deep / down in Mississippi."

Kramer, Aaron. With music by Clyde R. Appleton. "Blues for Emmett Till." *National Guardian,* 7 November 1955. Reprinted in *Sing Out* 6, no. 1 (Winter 1956): 3.

Comparing Till to a bird whose "feathers were all brown," the singer bemoans that in Mississippi such a bird "Better not chirp when Mrs. Bryant's around." "Slow down when you pass a courthouse, and laugh about that word— / Laugh about 'Justice,' friend, and cry for the young brown bird."

Loeb, Chas. H. "Refugees." *Cleveland Call and Post,* 8 October 1955.

This poem, submitted as an "editorial in rhyme" by a *Call and Post* columnist, reflects ironically on the Cold War policy of having "a fund for displaced Poles / . . . [and] every poor assorted coot / Who wants to try the way of life / We call democracy," while blacks are denied similar protections. "Who cries out when little kids / are lynched—and lynchers freed?" Loeb asks. "Should foreigners get all the breaks / While our own citizens catch hell?"

Lorde, Audre. "Afterimages." *Cream City Review* 17, no. 2 (Fall 1981): 119–23.

Mair, Ernest. Untitled Poem. *Baltimore Afro-American,* magazine section, 15 October 1955.

Opens by wondering how southerners, "made in [God's] image," could "become / lower [than] the venomed rattler that crawls." Ends by calling for a "Hercules" to wash America's "garments clean of Southern slime."

Malone, Russell. "Flowers for Emmett Till." *Russell Malone.* Columbia CK 52825. New York: 1992.

Jazz instrumental. No lyrics.

Maly, Christopher. "This Unsafe Star: The Story of Emmett Till." Original music by Matthew Boring and Christiana Wismer. Premiere at Lincoln High School, Lincoln, Nebraska, 12 October 2006.

Accompanied by three muses (and by brief appearances from such figures as Langston Hughes, James Baldwin, and Arthur Ashe), an elder Mamie Till-Mobley narrates her son's story. Beginning with Christmas 1954 and concluding with the aftermath of the trial, the play draws its title from Amiri Baraka's 1966 poem "Jitterbugs," which condemns white racism for making "this star unsafe, and this age, primitive." Against the bleakness of Baraka's poem, however, Maly's play offers hope. In the closing lines, Bryant and Milam's *Look* magazine confession is followed by the appearance of Rosa Parks, who claims, "When I was on that bus, I thought of Emmett the entire time." According to one of the muses, the story of Mamie and her son "is about the power one woman and one child can have over this star unsafe." This hopeful vision is confirmed when, at the very end, Emmett and his mother come together on stage for the first time and a "young Mamie" recites a few lines from Countee Cullen's "These are no wind-blown rumors," a sonnet affirming the power of love to endure even in the face of death.

Matthews, Ralph. "Thinking Out Loud [Aftermath of the Till Case]." *Cleveland Call and Post*, 19 November 1955.

In this brief "fiction," published in an editor's column, Bruno Hauptman returns from hell to meet with Bryant and Milam after their acquittal on kidnapping charges. Hauptman wants to know how two "ignorant country bumpkins" escaped punishment when he had "to pay with [his] life." Hauptman's problem, the locals tell him, is that his crime didn't exploit race and keep "niggers from getting too biggity." Hauptman responds, "Now I understand . . . The boys in Hades will be glad to hear this and they'll tell you so themselves when you come down. We'll be waiting for you." Upon saying this, he vanishes.

McAllister, Brewster. Lost poem. 1955.

In an October 15 column in the *Chicago Defender* ("White Reader Admires Negro's Fight Against Bigotry, Bias and Hatred"), Albert Barnett discusses a letter he received from McAllister and notes, "The poem sent in by Mr. McAllister will be printed in this column next week." It was not.

McBrown, Gertrude P. "Brotherhood Paradox (Mississippi Way)." *Baltimore Afro-American*, 3 December 1955.

Brief poem noting the paradox between a "proud nation" that "boast[s] / Of democracy, justice and brotherhood" and "the gasping death groans / Of a black boy hanging from a tree."

McDaniel, Eugene, and Jonathan Muhammad. *The Guardian.* Produced by Je'Caryous Johnson. Premiere at Cullen Performance Hall, University of Houston, Houston, Texas, 20 January 2000.

According to the play's author and producer, "*The Guardian* begs the question of where was Emmett Till's guardian angel during his time of need" and "examines why divine powers allowed such a tragic event to occur." An earlier version of the play was known as "Heaven's Child: The Legacy of Emmett Till." All attempts to secure a script of either version have failed.

Merriam, Eve. "Money, Mississippi." *Montgomery, Alabama, Money, Mississippi, and Other Places.* New York: Cameron Associates, No Date [1956].

Poem condemning "Dirty Money town," "Bloody Money town," "Rotten Money town," "Evil Money town" for its sanctioning of Till's murder. Ends with a call to "Bring home the body of Emmett Till / From that terrible Money town. / Bring home the body of Justice / With her blood-stained shining crown."

Miller, Jeanne. "Can I Write of Flowers?" *Essence,* 1 December 2001.

Beginning "Must I write / of Emmett Till / problems plaguing / Black Folks / Still," the poet asks to be freed of history. Confessing that "Emmett Till sleeps / in my bed / haunts me with his swollen / head," she begs to write of "flowers please / ducklings / swans and / honeybees." Someone else must express the "violent rage / that I can't capture / on my page."

Millet, Martha. "Emmett Louis Till (1941–1955)." *Baltimore Afro-American*, 22 October 1955.

Poem that imagines "a river of righteous men" taking vengeance for Till's murder by seeking to "topple" the "altar" of white supremacy.

———. "Mississippi." *Masses and Mainstream* 8, no. 10 (October 1955): 42–48.

Radical poet Millet retells the bloody and racist history of the Mississippi River so that "The blood cries out / speaking truth to your lies / Mississippi." This retelling is interspersed with images of the Till case, from the cries of young Emmett ("*Why have you done this to me?*") to the strength of his mother ("the blood of your child / rose up in you for their damnation"). Poem ends by asking Mississippi what it will do, where will it hide, when "the avenger comes among you"?

Morrison, Toni. "Dreaming Emmett." Premiere at Marketplace Theatre, Albany, New York, 4 January 1986.

If print or recorded versions of the play exist, they are not being made available to the public, and thus these details about the drama are drawn from a handful of newspaper accounts and reviews. According to Margaret Croydon, "Toni Morrison Tries Her Hand at Playwriting," (*New York Times*, 29 December, 1985), "the characters and the action shift back and forth in time and place, and there is a play within a play. The nonlinear story involves an anonymous black boy who was murdered. In a dream state he suffers the pain of remembering his death 30 years before. Seeking revenge and a place in history, he summons up the perpetrators of his murder, as well as his family and friends, all to be characters in the dream. But his ghosts refuse to be controlled by his imagination; all see the past in their own way, as the boy doggedly searches for a meaning to his death—and thereby his life. At one point he is challenged by a member of the audience, a black woman who rejects his dream and provokes a confrontation on sexual issues." According to Harlow Robinson, "Dreams of a Prophetic Past: Novelist Tony Morrison Tries Her Hand at Playwriting," (*American Theatre*, January 1986, 17–19), all of Emmett's ghosts—unlike Emmett—have aged thirty years and are "marked by their experiences of the last three decades." The black woman who challenges him is a "sassy" woman in her early twenties named Tamara, and her confrontation "exposes Emmett as both less and more than he pretends to be." Requests to secure a script from the playwright have been denied, and the play's producers—the Albany Capital Repertory Theatre—confirm that, after the 1986 production, Morrison collected all records of the play and refuses to release them.

———. *Song of Solomon*, 79–83. New York: Penguin, 1977.

Early in this novel, a group of black men in a barbershop overhear radio reports about a "boy [who] had whistled at some white woman, refused to deny he had slept with others, and was a Northerner visiting the South. His name was Till." Some men are silent; others condemn Till for his brashness; still others defend him for being a man. All agree, however, that Till's murderers will never be convicted, and the scene ends with the men beginning to "trade tales of atrocities, first stories they had heard, then those they'd witnessed, and finally the things that had happened to themselves." Eventually, this "litany of personal humiliations, outrage, and anger turned sicklike back to themselves as humor."

Nelson, Marilyn. *A Wreath For Emmett Till.* Illustrated by Philippe Lardy. Boston: Houghton Mifflin, 2005.

A heroic crown of sonnets (fifteen interlinked sonnets, with the last sonnet comprised of the first lines of the preceding fourteen) accompanied by illustrations. Marketed as "juvenile poetry" but rich in meaning, these poems explore how, "like a haunted tree / set off from other trees in the wildwood / by one bare bough," Till's presence informs America's racial memory. For Nelson, "Emmett Till's name still catches in my throat," and she confesses her desire to put him in a "parallel universe" where he would "live through a happy childhood." But knowing that she cannot free him from the "obscene theft" of his life, she explores ways to gather honest flowers for a wreath that will not let us forget that theft, for such "Forgetting would call for consciencelessness." Instead, "we must bear witness to atrocity" and remember Till as he was "dragged along, blood spattering" upon "white petals as he, abandoning all hope, gasped his agonizing last breath." If we forget this, we risk "unforgettable shame."

Nichols, John. "Don't Be Forlorn." 1959. Manuscript made available by the author.

Unpublished first novel by the author of *The Milagro Beanfield War,* written while he was a sophomore at Hamilton College. In a 2001 memoir, Nichols confessed, "The plot of *Don't Be Forlorn* is seriously warped by the weight of catastrophically maudlin writing. Mawkish stereotypes and an absolute lack of subtlety abound on both sides of the race question; my writing is outlandishly melodramatic . . . But my story does indicate a desire for social justice." Despite Nichols's misgivings, the novel manages to convey an important message about the need for compassionate identification with those who suffer injustice, especially in the conversion of Carter Fitzgerald, the white lawyer who seeks to convict the men who have murdered young Laury Emmons, a well-educated northern black boy who has been too bold in his talk with a local white girl.

Nielsen, Aldon. "A Good Place to Raise a Boy." *Talisman* (Spring 1994): 94–95.

This poem of fragments connects Till's lynching to the Birmingham church bombing, reflecting on racism as the "complexion of the end of the century."

Nordan, Lewis. *Wolf Whistle.* Chapel Hill: Algonquin Books, 1993.

Ochs, Phil, and Bob Gibson. "Too Many Martyrs." Originally "The Ballad of Medgar Evers." *All the News That's Fit to Sing.* Wea-Elecktra. 1965.

This song begins with the image of a man who sees Emmett Till, his "friend," "a hanging" because "color was his crime." The "blood upon his [Till's] jacket left a brand upon his mind." In the next stanza we learn that this branded man is Medgar Evers, and "he walked his road alone / Like Emmett Till and thousands more whose names we'll never know."

Packer, Vin. *Dark Don't Catch Me.* Greenwich, CT: Gold Medal Books, 1956.

Pappas, Nikos. "Emmet [sic] Till." 1958. In *To My Collaborators: The Greek Poets,* 154–55. River Vale, NJ: Cosmos Publishing, 1999.

In this poem by an award-winning Greek writer known for his outrage against social injustice, the narrator addresses Till directly and bemoans the shallowness of an age marked by "the assured careers of the young who drive / hot rods crammed with corruption." While "Toughs with silk shirts / and high-school diplomas encircle us / beat up their mothers / smoke hashish and gulp gin," the narrator and Till "write verses, / our thirst still unquenched by the cataracts of silence."

Parks, Mary. "For Emmett Till." *Daily Worker,* 13 October 1955.

Poem describing a one-sided classroom lecture about American history. Praising "Plymouth Rock / The Pilgrims, the Mayflower," the teacher neglects to mention "Those who came on the slavers' ships," and when the teacher professes that "all men are created equal" the poet asks "But what of the slaves? What was the sequel?" Wondering "How many boys in Chicago" have learned of Garrison, Turner, Vesey, Tubman, and John Brown, the poet urges us to remember "this boy with a shattered head / Who died in a muddy river bed."

Pitcher, Oliver. "Salute." In *Beyond the Blues: New Poems by American Negroes,* edited by Rosey E. Pool, 68–69. Kent, England: Hand and Flower Press, 1962.

Poem "saluting" Milam and Bryant and "all self-anointed / men / who dole out freedoms to other / men." Poet decries "all things / Worthy of my confusion."

Platt, Donald. "Amazing Grace Beauty Salon." *Southern Review* 38, no. 1 (Winter 2002): 57–62.

A male narrator enters a beauty salon and overhears two women—one black, one white—joke and "small talk" about their men. When the white one jokes about her man looking "like he's black" because he dresses in "bright colors," the narrator hears the "history squeezed into the silence" that follows. The image of Till "carrying / on his back the seventy-five-pound cotton-gin fan, lashed / with barbed wire / to his neck, across the ruts of the night field / to the Tallahatchie River" rises up between the women, and Till's story becomes like a river whose "floodwaters overflow the casual / conversation" of us all.

Plumpp, Sterling. "Unremembered." In *Ornate With Smoke,* 29–32. Chicago: Third World Press, 1997.

    Narrator of this brief poem recalls how his father gave him a piece of rope his own father found near "the pass from Money where Emmett / Till was killed." The rope then begins to tell "moaning narratives" of the "black boys and / black men" who have met death at the hands of lynchers.

Ragland, J. Farley. "Methods in Mississippi." *Richmond Afro-American,* 24 September 1955.

    Although "the lad had done no wrong," "prejudice was strong," and "Ghoulish hate went wild / To lynch a helpless child!" On the eve of the trial, the poet waits "to see what fate / A crime like this shall rate."

Razaf, Andy. "Timely Question." *Washington Afro American,* 12 November 1955.

    Brief, ironic poem by the famed lyricist begins with the question, "Is your town a good place to / Raise a boy?" (referring to the slogan of Sumner, Mississippi). No mention of Till, but by allusion the poem mocks "true democracy" in Mississippi.

Reed, Ishmael. *Reckless Eyeballing.* New York: St. Martin's, 1986.

    In this satirical send-up of 1980s feminism, Reed has his protagonist, the black playwright Ian Ball, write a play called *Reckless Eyeballing,* which is about how a southern white woman demands that the corpse of a black boy be dug up from its grave and put on trial again. The boy, Ham Hill, is clearly a stand-in for Emmett Till, and although Ball has written the play to appease his feminist critics, the play gets recast and much goes awry. In Reed's complexly plotted novel, the Ham Hill story serves to implicate white and black feminists (in particular Susan Brownmiller and Alice Walker) for perpetuating self-interested caricatures of violent and sexualized black men.

Richardson, W. James. *The Ghost of Emmett Till.* Bloomington, IN: Authorhouse, 2005.

    Freelance journalist Jamal Peterson travels to Mississippi to cover the Till trial. Deeply moved by the heroism of local blacks and angered by the intractable racism of southern whites, he returns to Detroit determined that "Emmett's death be a lighting rod for justice and a ramrod against oppression and injustice everywhere." Soon after the trail, strange events begin to occur in the Delta as Emmett's ghost begins to mete out its own justice (for instance, one by one, the jurors suffer misfortunes). As Jamal grows more involved with the civil rights movement (covering the Montgomery bus boycott and other events), he almost loses his own life. Through all his tribulations, however, Jamal is strengthened by his memory of Till's sacrifice. When he returns to Mississippi in 1975 for a statue dedication in honor of the slain boy, he learns that blacks throughout the Delta have drawn a similar strength from Till's memory.

Ristau, Harlan. "Elegy on the Death of Emmett Till." *Free Lance* 4 (1957): 5.

A poem of mourning in which the narrator wonders if "this boy died / only a symbol of gigantic wrongs unredressed." Urging remembrance and a rejection of violence, the poem closes with pity for "those diseased in mind / those sick in private darkness."

Robinson, Bruce. *Marching to Freedomland.* Premiere at Mitchell-Robinson Youth Theatre, Germantown, Pennsylvania, May 1998.

Reviews note that this play tells the story of the civil rights movement through the eyes of children, with particular emphasis on Emmett Till and the Birmingham church bombing. Script unavailable.

Roper, William. "Poem for Emmett Till: A Freedom Song." Written for Erika Duke-Kirkpatrick. Composed May 2000. First performance unknown.

According to the notes, this violoncello solo "is an abstraction of those events in the life of Emmett Till." The work is divided into eight episodes, ranging from "Emmett in the womb" and "Emmett's birth" to "Emmett's ascension" and "The cry of our mothers." Wanting the musician to "communicate what you feel about this moment in history," Roper warns that "If you feel nothing, it might be more wise to not play the piece."

Seese, June Akers. "Emmett Till and the Men Who Killed Him." In *James Mason and the Walk-in Closet,* 75–78. Normal, IL: Dalkey Archive Press, 1994.

Story dealing with a white woman's memory of her racist uncle, a northerner "unmatched in his hate." As she grows older and thinks of what happened to Till, who "whistled at a white woman standing on the hot sidewalk and before the sun went down . . . [and] was buried in concrete," she understands that her uncle "could have done it if he had been in Mississippi with the mob," could have been one of "those men who went home and ate their suppers in the heat with wet concrete on their pants, bragging, in my uncle's voice."

Serling, Rod. "Noon on Doomsday." Unproduced teleplay. Undated [November–December 1955?]. Box 71. Ts. Rod Serling Papers. U.S. Manuscript Collection, 43 AN. University of Wisconsin, Madison.

Set in Demerest, Georgia, this unproduced teleplay explores the aftermath of the murder of a nineteen-year-old black man, Henry Clemson, by a twenty-year-old white man, John Kattell. At first, the local police hope to cover things up, but when the Atlanta papers pick up the story, local law enforcement charges Kattell with murder. Led by the town lawyer, Demarest rallies around Kattell, an unlikable bully. Soon, secrets about the town's dark past begin to emerge, in particular the lynching thirty years earlier of a black man who allegedly raped a white woman. After Kattell is acquitted, he confesses to his crime, and, after being mocked by his lawyer's father, he stabs him with the same knife he used to kill Clemson. When Kattell tries to escape through the stunned crowd, the sheriff warns him to stop but is forced to shoot him down. This teleplay was rejected by the sponsors of the U.S. Steel Hour, and Serling was forced to revise it heavily so that all references to race and the South were omitted.

———. *Noon on Doomsday.* Teleplay. *United States Steel Hour.* Broadcast 25 April 1956. Box 71. Rod Serling Papers. U.S. Manuscript Collection, 43 AN. University of Wisconsin, Madison. Reprinted in *Television Plays for Writers: Eight Television Plays with Comment and Analysis by the Authors,* edited by A. S. Burack. Boston: The Writer, 1957.

In this revised version (the result of at least four rewritings, one of which included the unwelcome addition of a wolf-whistle to the alleged crime), Serling's story is no longer set in the South; instead, the murder happens in a small New England village. As the story opens, the town is awaiting the jury verdict in the case of John Kattell, an angry white man in his early twenties who has murdered Moses Chinik, a seventy-seven-year-old arthritic Jewish grocer, after a scuffle in Chinik's store. Kattell is clearly guilty, but the national press coverage of the trial is making the town defensive in the face of outside agitation. When the jury acquits Kattell, his lawyer has an angry confrontation in the town square with his own father, who accuses his son of acquiescing to prejudice and defending a guilty bigot. Kattell overhears this accusation and attacks the father, but then a northern Jewish newspaper man accuses Kattell of preying on the defenseless and challenges him to a fight. Kattell senses that the town is turning on him and, knife in hand, falls to his knees and begs for forgiveness. Serling's final direction captures the teleplay's explicit moral: "The camera starts a slow dolly away from Kattell until he remains a tiny dot in the middle of a loneliness. What we are looking at is John Kattell's desert, the one he's going to live in for the rest of his life."

———. *A Town Has Turned to Dust.* Broadcast 17 June 1958. *Playhouse 90.* Rod Serling Archives: *Playhouse 90* Television Scripts. Ithaca College.

Final version of Serling's heavily revised "Untitled Original Draft" of 19 June 1957. Set in the 1870s Southwest, this story is about a Mexican American teenager named Pancho Rivera who is awaiting trial on charges that he robbed the store of a white man, Jerry Paul. Paul leads a mob that strings up the young boy from the town flagpole. This lynching recalls a similar one in which the town sheriff participated. This past lynching, however, has none of the black-white racial overtones of Serling's original draft, and no one in town can quite remember why the man was lynched (rather than saying he was lynched for whistling at a white woman). The story ends with the sheriff killing Jerry Paul.

———. "Untitled Original Teleplay." Draft. 19 June 1957. Ts. Rod Serling Archives: *Playhouse 90* Television Scripts. Ithaca College.

The story of the trial and acquittal of Jerry Paul, a twenty-three-year-old white

merchant accused of killing a Mexican American teenager who was allegedly trying to rob Paul's store. The story is set in a contemporary Southwest town, where
most people know that the teenager and Paul's wife were attracted to each other.
A reporter covering the trial learns that another lynching took place in town many
years ago, this one involving a "colored man" who "whistled at a girl or something
like that." In a fate similar to John Kattell's in *Noon on Doomsday,* Jerry Paul watches
as the town turns on him in the wake of his acquittal. In a final public confrontation,
Paul strikes a man dead in a bar fight and, fleeing, is shot in the back by the sheriff.
Commissioned by *Playhouse 90* in 1957, the teleplay was rejected by sponsors. Later,
with revisions, it was produced as *A Town Has Turned to Dust.*

Skelton, T. R. Untitled poem [submitted as a letter to the editor]. *Pittsburgh
Courier,* 8 October 1955.

This poem asks how Mississippi will "wash the boy's blood" from its hands after
acquitting Till's murderers.

Smith, R. T. "Dar He." *Ploughshares* 31, no. 1 (Spring 2005): 134–37.

Older white poet recalling how "I was not yet eight / when the news hit and can
remember my parents at dinner / . . . / shaking their heads in passing and saying it
was a shame / but the boy should have been smarter." Needing "a revelation to lift
me from the misery of remembering," the poet claims he has long been haunted by
Moses Wright's court testimony "like a scene /from some reverse *To Kill a Mockingbird.*" The poem ends, however, with the poet wondering if all this remembering is
"an exercise in sham shame" or something true and genuine.

Sneed, Pamela. "Eyes on the Prize." In *Imagine Being More Afraid of Freedom Than
Slavery.* New York: Henry Holt, 1998.

Black narrator of this poem traces her anger to Till's face "bloated, beaten, /
burning in my mind / every time I climb the stairs / to my house." Addressing a white
friend, she tells how she hears "white laughter gurgling / from courtrooms / when
they say you're free / to kill niggers whenever you like," noting that the difference
between black and white is that "You are free."

Spicer, Kevin. "The Baby in Emmett Till's Eyes." Highways Performance Space.
Santa Monica, California. 1994.

Content of this performance piece unknown, except that it dealt with violence
toward black men. See www.lacitybeat.com/article.php?id=2537&IssueNum=116 and
www.dogonvillage.com/african_american_news/Articles/00000252.html (accessed
1 August 2006).

———. "The Murder of Emmett Till: 50 Years Later." Premiere at Highways
Performance Space, Santa Monica, California, 26 August 2005.

A group of performance pieces by Spicer and other local multimedia artists. For best details, see www.dogonvillage.com/african_american_news/Articles/00000252 .html (accessed 1 August 2006).

Stephens, Georgia. Untitled Poem. 3 October 1955. Submitted as an addendum to a letter to the NAACP. File C, 14. Box 18. Papers of the NAACP. Library of Congress.

> Long, handwritten poem sent to the NAACP for use in fundraising purposes.

Stevens, Ernest Wakefield. "Blood on Mississippi." *Cleveland Call and Post*, 15 October. 1955.

> Poem castigating Mississippi for a killing that will reflect poorly upon American efforts to promote democracy: "Bow your head low, Mississippi, / For the damage you have done / To the efforts of our country / In its fight for everyone."

Strong, Alfred. "For Emmett Till." *Baltimore Afro-American*, 10 December 1955.

> Poem hoping that good will come from Till's murder, for "Somewhere there shines / The morning that will see such horrors gone, / When men with hearts of beasts will be unknown."

Tarpley, Natasha. "Slow Dance." *Callaloo* 15, no. 4 (Fall 1992): 928.

> Recollection of a slow dance that took place during the "summer they dragged / Emmet [sic] Till's almost body out of the Tallahatchie." The two dancers are left "holding each other up, / finding our rhythm in those blues."

Thompson, Julius E. "Till." *Blues Said: Walk On.* 1977. Galveston, TX: Energy Earth Communications, 1977. Reprinted in *Black Southern Voices: An Anthology of Fiction, Poetry, Drama, Nonfiction, and Critical Essays,* edited by John Oliver Killens and Jerry W. Ward Jr., 288–89. New York: Meridian, 1992.

> Poet wonders if his readers are able to imagine "a black son, walking / down a mississippi highway headed / home" and to "feel the four hundred years." "Can you awake to see / yourself / dead like he died?" the poet asks. "Can you, can you, / can you save one black son / who god didn't save?"

Untitled play. Performed at the Jewish Cultural Club, 924 E. 123rd Street, Cleveland Ohio, 8 October 1955.

> In a letter to the editor of the *Cleveland Call and Post* (15 October 1955), Jerry Gordon, chairman of the Ohio Labor Youth League, mentions the performance of this play. No known transcript exists.

Vargas, Fish. "The L.I.F.E. Foundation of Emmett Till." 2004. Available at www .louderarts.com/poets/fish (accessed 1 August 2006).

> Poem published on the louderARTS Project webpage by a middle-school creative writing teacher who tells his young students about the lynching. When Vargas urges them to see Emmett Till "as every facet of prejudice you face," the students respond

by seeing all the Emmett Tills in their own lives: their friends who have been shot, beaten, and mistreated. When one student responds, *"Emmett Till could have been / Martin Luther King,"* the poet is "met by a face stretched with sadness / eyes lost."

Walker, Alice. "Advancing Luna—and Ida B. Wells." In *You Can't Keep a Good Woman Down*, 85–102. San Diego: Harcourt, Brace, Jovanovich, 1971.

> Story about the development and disintegration of a close friendship between the narrator—a nameless black woman from Georgia—and Luna, a rich white girl from the North. The two meet in the summer of 1965 during a voter registration drive in Georgia, and a year later they share an apartment in New York City. It is here that Luna confides to the narrator that she was raped by a black civil rights worker the previous summer, and while the narrator believes her, she reflects on the historical privileges that give Luna, a white woman, the power to destroy, on her word alone, the life of a black man. These reflections lead her to think of, among other things, the lynching of Till, and force the narrator to question conflations of race and gender.

Walton, Anthony. "The Lovesong of Emmett Till." In *Mississippi: An American Journey*. Knopf: New York, 1996.

> Poem wondering about the identity of the young Chicago white girl whose picture Till allegedly had in his wallet. "More than likely she was Irish / or Italian, a sweet child who knew him / only as a shy clown," and Till that day in Mississippi was "just showing / off, showing the rustics / how it was done." But Till "paid the price of / not innocence but affection," affection for a girl "who must by now be an older / woman in Chicago, a woman / who will never know."

Ward, Jerry W., Jr. "Don't Be Fourteen (In Mississippi)." 1982. In *Black Southern Voices: An Anthology of Fiction, Poetry, Drama, Nonfiction, and Critical Essays*, edited by John Oliver Killens and Jerry W. Ward Jr., 296–97. New York: Meridian, 1992.

> Poem comparing Till's lynching to the sentencing of Robert Earl May Jr., a fourteen-year-old black boy convicted of a crime. With the haunting refrain "Don't be fourteen / black and male in Mississippi," this poem characterizes Till as a "guilt-offering to blue-eyed susans."

Warren, Nagueyalti. "Till's Death Did Us Part." In *Lodestar and Other Night Lights: Poems*, 11. Lewiston, NY: Edwin Mellen Press, 1992.

> This loss-of-innocence poem recalls how the days of "grandiose memories," when children could "run wild / And free in the woods," ended in the summer of 1955, "When fear paralyzed" and left children "with no space to run."

Weeks, Ricardo. "Song for Emmett Till's Mother." *Washington Afro-American*, 8 October 1955; *Pittsburgh Courier*, 8 October 1955.

Poem from Mamie Till Bradley's perspective as she laments her son's death and hears God commanding her not to weep but to "find a way."

———. "Too Tight." *Washington Afro-American,* 29 October 1955.

Poem that wonders whether Too Tight Collins truly did witness Till's murder. If so, the poet pleads, Too Tight "should speak / And not stand by / Shaking in the shadow / Of Truth."

West, Kanye. "Through the Wire." *College Dropout.* Roc-a-Fella. B0001AP12G. 2004.

Written two weeks after West was in a near-fatal car accident in October 2002 and had his jaw broken in three places and his mouth wired shut. West sings about a public appearance and asks, "just imagine how my girl feel / On the plane scared as hell that her guy look like Emmett Till."

Wideman, John Edgar. *Two Cities.* New York: Houghton Mifflin, 1998.

Several times in this novel, fifty-year-old Robert Jones remembers "the photograph of a black boy's face that turned me to stone." In particular, he recalls seeing the *Jet* magazine photo in 1955 and trying to "read the story squinting, eyes narrowed to avoid Till's crumbled face."

Wiley, Mike. "Dar He: The Lynching of Emmett Till." Directed by Serena Ebhardt. Multimedia Design by Ben Davis. Premiere at Virginia State University, Petersburg, Virginia, 26 February 2006.

This innovative, ninety-five-minute, one-man, multimedia stage show weaves together some of the most important source material about the case with imaginative re-creations of key events. Wiley plays a dozen-plus characters, from William Bradford Huie, Moses Wright, and Mamie Till to Wheeler Parker, Carolyn Bryant, and Willie Reed, as he tells the story from different perspectives and time periods. All the while, the story is played out against a background of shifting media images. The result is a moving and sophisticated drama that raises important questions about historical memory and the power and obligations of retelling.

Wright, Richard. *The Long Dream.* New York: Harper, 1958.

Although Wright's final novel doesn't directly mention Till, many critics have noted the presence of Till's lynching in the fate of Chris Sims, best friend to the novel's protagonist Fish Belly. After Chris is discovered in a hotel room with a white woman, a white mob lynches him. At his father's mortuary, Fishbelly takes a long hard look at Chris's brutalized corpse, in particular his "bloated head and torso." Throughout the novel, Fishbelly is haunted by Chris's face—with its "mouth, lined with stumps of broken teeth . . . an irregular, black cavity bordered by shredded tissue that had once been lips."

A Statement on the FBI Report

On February 27, 2007, a grand jury in LeFlore County, Mississippi, declined to issue an indictment against Carolyn Bryant-Donham for her alleged role in the lynching of Emmett Till. The indictment for manslaughter was brought by District Attorney Joyce Chiles, who based her charges on a three-year FBI investigation that yielded more than 8,000 pages of evidence. A month after this grand jury decision, the FBI released its report to the public, and it is currently available at http://foia.fbi.gov/till/till.pdf.

The FBI's 464-page report is not a literary representation of the case, but it does contain significant material for those interested in how the Emmett Till narrative continues to circulate in the contemporary memory and imagination. Although the text is highly redacted and is thus difficult at times to decipher (for privacy protection, the names of all living persons are covered over), the report includes two sections—"Timeline" and "Sequence of Events"—that offer new ways of conceiving what happened between the evening that Till was kidnapped and the morning when his body was discovered. Moreover, the report also contains a section on "Admissions." This section begins with a summary of one of the ur-narratives of the Till case—Huie's "Shocking Story of Approved Killing in Mississippi"—and then presents new evidence intended to challenge that narrative. Of particular interest are revelations that J. W. Milam told several people about his role in the murder and that Roy Bryant was audiotaped making a confession to a confidential source in 1985. Moreover, Leslie Milam twice acknowledged his role in the crime, once as a deathbed confession. Finally, the report also includes a retyped trial transcript. For years, this transcript was feared lost, and its inclusion in the FBI report recovers for scholars an important primary document.

CONTRIBUTORS

KATHALEEN AMENDE is Assistant Professor of American Literature at Alabama State University. This is her first published essay. She is currently revising her dissertation on sexuality and religion in the works of southern authors Rosemary Daniell, Sheri Lee Reynolds, and Lee Smith.

LAURA DAWKINS is Associate Professor of American Literature and the Director of Graduate Studies in English at Murray State University. Her articles on American literature and culture have appeared in *LIT: Literature Interpretation Theory, 49th Parallel,* and in two collections, *The American Child: A Cultural Studies Reader,* edited by Caroline Levander and Carol Singley (Rutgers University Press, 2003) and *Prose and Cons: Essays on Prison Literature in the United States,* edited by D. Quentin Miller (McFarland, 2005). She is currently working on a book, "Speaking for the Silenced: Racial Violence and the African American Literary Imagination," which examines literary responses to historical incidents of racial violence in the United States.

SUZANNE W. JONES is Professor of English and Women, Gender, and Sexuality Studies at the University of Richmond. Her articles on southern fiction have appeared in a variety of journals and collections. She is the author of *Race Mixing: Southern Fiction since the Sixties* (Johns Hopkins University Press, 2004) and the editor of three collections of essays, *Poverty and Progress in the U.S. South since 1920* (with Mark Newman, VU University Press, 2006), *South to a New Place: Region, Literature, Culture* (with Sharon Monteith, Louisiana State University Press, 2002), and *Writing the Woman Artist: Essays on Poetics, Politics, and Portraiture* (University of Pennsylvania Press, 1991), and two collections of stories, *Crossing the Color Line: Readings in Black and White* (University of South Carolina Press, 2000) and *Growing Up in the South: An Anthology of Modern Southern Literature* (New American Library, 1991; Signet Classic, 2003). Her current project is a study of the reappearance of the mixed-race figure in contemporary American literature.

SYLVIE KANDÉ teaches African Studies at SUNY Old Westbury and Caribbean History at the New School. Her work deals mostly with the new urban identities resulting from slave trade and subsequent migrations between Africa and the West. Her first book, *Terres, urbanisme et architecture 'creoles' en Sierra Leone, 18ème-19ème siècles* (L'Harmattan, 1998), is a study of the repatriation of black people to Sierra Leone and the resulting Creole culture that developed in Freetown. She is the editor of the proceedings of an NYU colloquium she organized in 1997 on mixed racial identity in the Francophone context, published by l'Harmattan under the title *Discours sur le métissage, identités métisses. En quête d'Ariel* (1999). Her third book, *Lagon, lagunes* (Gallimard, 2000), is a long piece of poetic prose, with an afterword by Edouard Glissant. She has published numerous essays on African, African American, and Caribbean literature and cinema in scholarly books and journals such as *Research in African Literatures, Quarterly Black Book Review, Sulfur,* and the *Cambridge History of African and Caribbean Literatures.*

VIVIAN M. MAY, Assistant Professor of Women's Studies at Syracuse University, recently published *Anna Julia Cooper, Visionary Black Feminist: A Critical Introduction* (Routledge, 2007). Her articles on African American literature, feminist theory, and interdisciplinarity have appeared in such journals as *Callaloo, Hypatia, Prose Studies, NWSA Journal, Women's Studies Quarterly,* and *Studies in the Literary Imagination.* Her essays have appeared in several collections, including *New Essays on James Baldwin's "Go Tell It On the Mountain,"* edited by Trudier Harris (Cambridge University Press, 1996), and *Women's Studies for the Future,* edited by Elizabeth Lapovsky Kennedy and Agatha Beins (Rutgers University Press, 2005). She has also co-edited an issue of *Womanist Theory and Research.*

DONNIE MCMAHAND, a graduate student in English at Tulane University, is also currently a lecturer at the University of North Carolina at Chapel Hill. In his dissertation, he traces the shifting significances of the African American body in literature from and following the civil rights era. His essay "(Dis)embodying the Delta Blues" looks forward to this larger project. He thanks his mother Gloria and dissertation director Rebecca Mark for their encouragement.

CHRISTOPHER METRESS is Professor of English at Samford University in Birmingham, Alabama. His essays on southern literature and history have appeared in such journals as *South Atlantic Quarterly*, the *Southern Review*, *Studies in the Novel*, and *Mississippi Quarterly*. He is the editor of *The Lynching of Emmett Till: A Documentary Narrative* (University of Virginia Press, 2002), and he is currently at work on a study of white southern writers and the civil rights movement.

SHARON MONTEITH is Professor of American Studies in the School of American Studies at the University of Nottingham in the UK. She writes on contemporary British fiction and on film history as well as the American South. She is the author of *Advancing Sisterhood? Interracial Friendships in Contemporary Southern Fiction* (University of Georgia Press, 2000) and co-editor (with Suzanne Jones) of *South to a New Place: Region, Literature, Culture* (Louisiana State University Press, 2002) and (with Peter Ling) *Gender and the Civil Rights Movement* (Garland, 1999; Rutgers University Press, 2004). She co-authored *Film Histories* (Edinburgh University Press, 2007) and has contributed essays on southern fiction or film to a variety of collections, including *The Blackwell Companion to the American South*, edited by Richard Gray; *Memory and Popular Film*, edited by Paul Grainge; and *The African American Freedom Struggle*, edited by Brian Ward. In 2001–2002 she was a Rockefeller Humanities Fellow (Race and Gender in the Mississippi Delta) at the University of Memphis. She is currently finishing a book on American culture in the 1960s and writing another called "The Civil Rights Movement in the Melodramatic Imagination."

BRIAN NORMAN, Assistant Professor of English at Idaho State University, teaches twentieth-century American, African American, and multi-ethnic U.S. literature. He is the author of *Addressing Division: The American Protest Essay and National Belonging* (SUNY Press, 2007). He has a longstanding interest in James Baldwin and other literary figures who also serve as political advocates, especially for American social movements such as civil rights. He is co-editing with Piper Kendrix Williams a special issue of *African American Review* on "Representing Segregation," which will appear early in 2008. His current research concerns contemporary literary representations of Jim Crow, and recent articles of his appear, or are forthcoming, in *African American Review*, *MELUS*, *Canadian Review of American Studies*, *Women's Studies*, and *differences*.

HARRIET POLLACK, Associate Professor of English at Bucknell University, is the co-editor with Suzanne Marrs of *Eudora Welty and Politics: Did The Writer*

Crusade? (Louisiana State University Press, 2001) and the editor of *Having Our Way: Women Rewriting Tradition in Twentieth-Century America* (Bucknell University Press, 1995). She has published in the areas of southern fiction, history, politics, race, and gender in such journals as *Mississippi Quarterly, Southern Literary Journal,* and *South Central Review,* and her work has been reprinted in such volumes as Harold Bloom's Biocritiques series (*Eudora Welty,* Chelsea House, 2004), and *The Critical Response to Eudora Welty,* edited by Laurie Champion (Greenwood, 1994). She received the SCMLA Kirby Prize and is a past president of the Eudora Welty Society. Her recent work is about what is encoded on the body in southern fiction and in American racial discourse. Her next book is tentatively titled "The Body of the Other Woman in the Fiction and Photography of Eudora Welty."

MYISHA PRIEST, a recent recipient of UCLA's President's Post-Doctoral Fellowship, received her PhD in English in 2003 from University of California, Berkeley, and holds an MA in Africana Studies from Cornell University. Her dissertation "Memories of the Flesh" (2003) is a study of African American literature. She is currently completing a book on African American children's literature.

INDEX

Aanerud, Rebecca, 105

Abbot, Shirley, 141n2

Ace in the Hole (Wilder), 38

Adams, Oliver Arnold, 174

—*Time Bomb,* 174

"Afterimages" (Lorde), 10, 12

Alcoff, Linda Martín, 106

Algeria, 147–48, 155

Ali, Muhammad, 16–18, 27

All God's Chillun Got Wings (O'Neill), 90

Amende, Kathaleen, 11, 128–42

"American" (McKay), 155

Anzaldúa, Gloria, 103

Arcimboldo, Giuseppe, 180

—*Wasser,* 180

Atlanta Daily World, 23

Baby Doll, 34

Bahktin, M. M., 182

Baker, Barbara, 187, 202, 207

Baker, Houston, 205–6, 207

Baker, Josephine, 147

Baldwin, James, 9, 21, 75–97, 192; declining fame of, 84; on integration, 77; meeting of with Robert Kennedy, 75; and "Negro" as white invention, 87; on nonviolence, 78–79

—*Blues for Mister Charlie,* 9, 21–22, 75, 78–97, 192

—*Devil Finds Work, The,* 94

—*Evidence of Things Not Seen, The,* 75

—*Fire Next Time, The,* 77, 78–79, 87–88

—"Letter from a Region in My Mind," 75

—"Words of a Native Son," 79

Balfour, Lawrie, 83

Ballad of the Sad Café, The (McCullers), 47

"Ballot or the Bullet, The" (Malcolm X), 78

Bandung Conference, 155

Baraka, Amiri, 94–95

Barry, Quan, 24

—"Emmett Till's Open Casket as *La Pietà,*" 24

Bartley, Numan V., 32

Been in the Storm So Long (Litwack), 184

"Behold Thy Son" (Driskell), 24

Bell, Inge Powell, 141

Benjamin, Walter, 40

Birmingham church bombing, 119, 130

Birth of a Nation (Griffith), 41

Bjerre, Thomas, 183, 190, 191, 192, 203

Black Arts movement, 94

black body, the, 53–72 passim

Black Boy (Wright), 132

"Black Christ, The" (Cullen), 20

black Diaspora, 12

Black Monday (Brady), 39

Black Muslims, 92

Black Nationalism, 86, 88, 94

Black Power, 81, 87, 88, 92

Block, Sam, 141

Blues for Mister Charlie (Baldwin), 9, 21–22, 75, 78–97, 192

blues music, 13, 70, 155, 156; Gussow on, 204, 210; in *Wolf Whistle,* 187, 191, 192, 193, 198, 199, 202–11; in *Your Blues Ain't Like Mine,* 175, 176, 212–19

Body in Pain, The (Scarry), 162, 175–76

Boone, Graeme, 212

Boucher, Anthony, 37

Boy With Loaded Gun (Nordan), 190

Bradley, Mamie Till. *See* Till-Mobley, Mamie

Brady, Tom P., 39
—*Black Monday*, 39
Breland, J. J., 39, 40
Brooks, Gwendolyn, 9, 10, 18–19, 98–111; praise
    of for Audre Lorde, 126n3; reasons of for
    writing Till poems, 113
—"Bronzeville Mother Loiters in Mississippi,
    A," 10, 18–19, 21, 28, 39, 98, 100–109,
    112–17, 125
—"Last Quatrain of the Ballad of Emmett Till,"
    10, 98, 102–4, 109
Brooks, Peter, 33
Brownmiller, Susan, 41
Brown v. Board of Education, 31, 36, 47, 48, 49n1,
    147, 174
Brown v. Board of Education II, 31
Brunstein, Robert, 91
Bryant, Carolyn, 2, 3, 5, 45, 202; court testimony
    of, 5, 58, 108; depiction of by Brownmiller,
    41; depiction of by Huie, 39, 43; depiction
    of in fiction, 45, 164, 166–67, 169–73, 175,
    179, 185, 216–18; depiction of in poetry, 10,
    18–19, 39, 98, 99–109, 112–27; as remem-
    bered by Eldridge Cleaver, 17
Bryant, Jerry H., 41
Bryant, Roy, 2, 6, 7, 33, 146, 151, 193, 196; con-
    fession of to Huie, 35, 36; depiction of in
    drama, 80; depiction of in fiction, 45, 47,
    48, 162, 167–73, 217–18; depiction of in po-
    etry, 100, 102, 104–8, 113–17, 150–53
Byrd, James, 1

Caldwell, Erskine, 37, 43
—*God's Little Acre*, 37
California Eagle, 7, 23
Call to Home (Stacks), 171
Campbell, Bebe Moore, 12, 13, 14, 161–76, 202–
    4, 212–19; on the blues, 203; on remember-
    ing Till's murder, 212
—*Your Blues Ain't Like Mine*, 12, 13, 14, 21, 161–
    76, 202–4, 212–19
Campbell, Jane, 212
Camus, Albert, 162

—*The Plague*, 162
Carter, Hodding, 6
Castro, Fidel, 144
Cawelti, John G., 33, 45
Césaire, Aimé, 11–12, 143–57
—*Ferrements*, 12
—*Notebook of a Return to My Native Land*, 151
—"On the State of the Union," 12, 144, 149–51
Chaney, James, 35, 75, 191
Chatham, Gerald, 4, 5, 6, 57
Chicago Defender, 6, 7, 22, 25, 61, 63, 99, 103
Citizens' Councils, 32, 49n1, 135, 212
civil rights movement, 4, 9, 11, 156, 188, 191,
    211; and Anne Moody, 128–42; and James
    Baldwin, 72, 75–78, 86, 89, 92
Cleaver, Eldridge, 17, 86, 130
—*Soul on Ice*, 17, 86
Cleveland Call and Post, 7, 24
Cobb, James C., 42
Cobb, Martha, 143, 155–56
Coleman, Wanda, 8, 154
—"Emmett Till," 24
Collins, Patricia Hill, 118
Coming of Age in Mississippi (Moody), 11, 17,
    128–42
Communism (Communist Party), 144, 146, 148,
    155, 157n4
Cone, James, 67–68
Congress of Racial Equality (CORE), 128, 141
Cook, Pam, 48
Coombs, Orde, 94
Costello, Brannon, 184
Council of Federated Organizations (COFO),
    129
Cranach, Lucas, 180
—*Der Papstesel*, 180
Crime and Punishment (Dostoevsky), 90
Crisis, 33, 53, 55, 146
Cullen, Countee, 20, 155
—"The Black Christ," 20

Daily Worker, 6
Damas, Léon Gontran, 146

Dark Don't Catch Me (Packer), 8, 34, 37, 44–48
Davies, Carol Boyce, 103
Davis, Angela, 41, 155
Davis, Kenneth C., 37
Davis, Richard Harding, 38
Dawkins, Laura, 10–11, 112–27
Death in the Delta, A (Whitfield), 42
DeCarava, Roy, 9, 66–72
Delta Democrat-Times, 6, 59
DeMott, Benjamin, 172
Der Papstesel (Cranach), 180
Derrida, Jacques, 144
Devil Finds Work, The (Baldwin), 94
Dittmer, John, 141
Douglass, Frederick, 139
Douglass, Kirk, 38
Dreaming Emmett (Morrison), 42
Driskell, David, 24
—"Behold Thy Son," 24
Driver, Tom F., 91
DuBois, W. E. B., 33, 80, 146, 155
Dupuy, Edward, 183
Dyson, Michael Eric, 8, 26, 161

"Elegy for Emmett Till" (Guillén), 11, 147, 149–55
Elliot, Sara, 190, 192
Ellison, Ralph, 53, 54, 69
—"Twentieth-Century Fiction and the Black Mask of Humanity," 53, 54
"Emmett Till" (Coleman), 24
Emmett Till narrative, the, 7–14
"Emmett Till's Open Casket as *La Pietà*" (Barry), 24
Esquire, 1
Estes-Hicks, Onita, 128
Evers, Medgar, 4
Evers, Myrlie, 129, 199n4
Evidence of Things Not Seen, The (Baldwin), 75
Eyerman, Ron, 17, 19, 20
Eyes on the Prize, 172

Fabre, Geneviève, 112

Faulkner, William, 31; press statement of on Till lynching, 154
—*Intruder in the Dust*, 38
—*Light in August*, 38
—"Mississippi," 34–35
—"On Fear," 31, 32
—*Sanctuary*, 33
Felman, Shoshana, 162
Feracho, Leslie, 156
Fire Next Time, The (Baldwin), 77, 78–79, 87–88
Fontaine, William, 146
Fraser, Cary, 147

Gabbin, Joanne V., 113
Gable, Clark, 38
Gannett, Lewis, 66–67
Gates, Henry Louis, Jr., 94
Girl on the Bestseller List, The (Packer), 37
Glover, Clifford, 119
God's Little Acre (Caldwell), 37
Goodman, Andrew, 35, 75, 191
Gourevitch, Philip, 157
Green, Ernest, 62
Green Mile (King), 41
"Growing Up White in the South" (Nordan), 27–28, 178, 202, 211
Guillén, Nicolás, 11–12, 143–57
—*Elegias*, 11
—"Elegy for Emmett Till," 11, 144
—*Movitos de Son*, 144
—"Road to Harlem," 154
—*Songoro Cosongo*, 144
Gunter, James, 196
Gussow, Adam, 204, 210
—*Seems Like Murder Here*, 204
Gutman, Herbert, 118–19

Halberstam, David, 4
Hale, Grace, 211–12
Harlem, 9, 66–72, 77, 85
Harris, Trudier, 98, 101
Hartman, Saidiya, 66, 69

Hearst, William Randolph, 38

Heath, W. L., 34

—*Ill Wind,* 34

—*Violent Saturday,* 34

Heilman, Robert, 35

Herbers, John, 4

Hernton, Calvin, 90

Hewes, Harry, 80

Hicks, Granville, 80

Hicks, James, 4

Highsmith, Patricia, 37

hooks, bell, 131, 164, 175, 176n6

—*We Real Cool: Black Men and Masculinity,* 175, 176n6

Howard, Dr. T. R. M., 4

Howe, Irving, 92

Hudson-Weems, Cleanora, 24

Hughes, Gertrude Reif, 114

Hughes, Langston, 56–72, 154; columns of on the Till case, 61–62; influence of on Guillén, 144, 155, 157n2

—"Mississippi—1955," 9, 56, 62, 63–65

—*Sweet Flypaper of Life, The,* 9, 56, 65, 66–72

Huie, William Bradford: as a hero-journalist, 38–39; motion picture contract of, 36; and new journalism, 49n8; review of by French press, 149; suing of by Mamie Till-Mobley, 50n13; and use of melodrama, 8, 35–48

—*Klansman, The,* 35

—*Revolt of Mamie Stover, The,* 35

—"Shocking Story of Approved Killing in Mississippi," 3, 7, 8, 36, 47, 108, 146, 157n5

—*Three Lives for Mississippi,* 35

—"What Happened to the Emmett Till Killers?" 36, 193–94

—*Wolf Whistle,* 8, 40

—"Wolf Whistle," 34, 35, 36, 38, 39, 41, 42, 47

Hurley, Ruby, 4

"I Have a Dream" (King), 78

Ill Wind (Heath), 34

Intruder in the Dust (Faulkner), 38

It Happened One Night, 38

Ivy, James W., 146

Jackson State University, 141

Janiewski, Dolores, 133

Johnson, James Weldon, 155

Johnson, Robert, 200n7, 205

Johnson, Sam, 6

Jones, Curtis, 41

Jones, Suzanne, 12, 161–77, 214

Kandé, Sylvie, 11–12, 143–61

Katzenbach, John, 171

Keating, Analouise, 99

Keller, Joseph, 92

Kellum, J. W., 32–33

Kempton, Murray, 4, 5

Kennedy, Robert F., 75–76

Killers of the Dream (Smith), 34

"Killing of Black Boys, The" (Wideman), 41, 189

King, Martin Luther, Jr., 35, 77, 83, 94, 130, 156

—"I Have a Dream," 78

Klansman, The (Huie), 35

Kubayanda, Josaphat, 156

Ku Klux Klan, 32, 34, 148

Ladner, Dorie, 141

Ladner, Joyce, 141

Lang, Charles, 62

"Last Quatrain of the Ballad of Emmett Till" (Brooks), 10, 98, 102–4, 109

Laub, Dori, 104

Lee, Marvin E., 24

Leeming, David, 75

Le Monde, 146, 147, 149

"Letter from a Region in My Mind" (Baldwin), 75

L'Humanité, 146, 149

Life, 24, 36

Light in August (Faulkner), 38

Lipscomb, Mance, 210

Litwack, Leon, 184

—*Been in the Storm So Long*, 184
Long Dream, The (Wright), 49n4
Look, 3, 7, 34, 36, 146, 149
Lorde, Audre, 10–11, 107–8; on black mother-
  hood, 118; and building coalitions between
  women, 124–25; praise of by Gwendolyn
  Brooks, 126n3
—"Afterimages," 10, 12, 113, 117–25
—"New York City 1970," 119
—"Now that I am Forever with Child," 117–18
—"Power," 119
—*Sister Outsider*, 118, 124–25
—"Woman, A / Dirge for Wasted Children," 119
"Lynching, The" (McKay), 20

Maher, Blake, 184–85, 186
Making Whiteness (Hale), 211, 212
Malcolm X, 77, 78, 83
—"Ballot or the Bullet, The," 78
Marrow of Tradition, The (Chestnutt), 38
May, Vivian M., 8–9, 98–111
McCarthy, Joseph, 61
McCullers, Carson, 47
—*Ballad of the Sad Café, The*, 47
McDowell, Deborah, 186
McKay, Claude, 20, 155
—"America," 155
—"Lynching, The," 20
McKay, Nellie, 132
McMahand, Donnie, 13–14, 202–20
McPherson, James Alan, 218
Meeker, Marijane. *See* Packer, Vin
Memphis Commercial Appeal, 196
Mencken, H. L., 34
Merle, Robert, 148
"Message on the State of the Union" (Césaire).
  See "On the State of the Union" (Césaire)
Metress, Christopher, 1–15, 16–30, 56, 63, 76,
  95n3, 130
Middle Passage, 119
Milam, J. W., 3, 5, 7, 33, 138, 146, 196; confes-
  sion of to Huie, 35, 36, 38, 40, 42, 43, 44;

as compared to a gendarme auxiliaire, 148;
  as depicted in fiction, 45, 46, 48, 179, 180,
  185–95, 202, 208–10; as depicted in poetry,
  149–53; on Emmett Till's last words, 150
militancy, 75–92 passim
Mills, Charles, 98, 100, 105
"Mississippi" (Faulkner), 34
Mississippi (Walton), 171
"Mississippi—1955" (Hughes), 9, 56, 61, 62–65
Mississippi Regional Council of Negro Leader-
  ship, 174
Mississippi State Sovereignty Commission, 32
Molina, Papusa, 98
Mollet, Guy, 155
Monteith, Sharon, 8, 31–52
Moody, Anne, 11, 17; on discovering white
  privilege, 134; disillusionment of with non-
  violence, 130; and rejection of violence,
  139–40
—*Coming of Age in Mississippi*, 11, 17, 128–42
Moore, Amzie, 4, 49n2
Morrison, Toni, 42, 184
—*Dreaming Emmett*, 42
Mortimer, Lee, 38
Movitos de Son (Guillén), 144
Murder of Emmett Till (Nelson), 3
Murrow, Edward R., 38
Music of the Swamp (Nordan), 187
Myrdal, Gunnar, 34

National Association for the Advancement of
  Colored People (NAACP), 11, 32, 59, 136,
  139, 146, 147, 213
National Organization of Decent Literature, 33
Native Son (Wright), 81, 83
Negrismo, 12, 143, 149, 152
Négritude, 12, 143, 146, 149, 151, 152, 157
Negro American Literature Forum, 92
"Negro Madonna, The" (Salamunich), 24
Nelson, Stanley, 3
Newquist, Roy, 113
New Republic, 91

"New York City 1970" (Lorde), 199

New York Times, 37, 91

nonviolence, 3, 45, 75–92 passim, 129–31

Nora, Pierre, 10, 112

Nordan, Lewis, 8, 13, 14, 27–29, 178–99, 202–11; anxiety of for expressing sympathy with murderers, 193; and autobiographical nature of work, 186–87; on being a comic writer, 180; on the blues, 203; and death of his sons, 190; on Flannery O'Connor, 191; racial identification of with Till's murderers, 178; reason of for writing *Wolf Whistle*, 27–28; on speaking with Mamie Till, 180; on unburied bodies in his fiction, 190; and use of exaggeration, 184–85; on whiteness, 184

—*Boy With Loaded Gun*, 190

—"Growing Up White in the South," 27–28, 178, 202, 211

—*Music of the Swamp*, 187

—*Wolf Whistle*, 13, 14, 27–29, 178–99, 202–11, 216, 219

Norman, Brian, 7, 9, 75–97

Notebook of a Return to My Native Land (Césaire), 151

"Now That I am Forever with Child" (Lorde), 117–18

O'Connor, Flannery, 31, 48, 191

Olsen, Tillie, 130

O'Meally, Robert, 112

One Hour (Smith), 42

O'Neill, Eugene, 90

—*All God's Chillun Got Wings*, 90

"On Fear" (Faulkner), 31, 32

"On the State of the Union" (Césaire), 12, 144, 149–55

Oprah Winfrey Show, 172

Ottley, Roi, 98

Packer, Vin, 8, 34; and use of melodrama, 35–48

—*Dark Don't Catch Me*, 8, 34, 37, 44–48

—*Girl on the Bestseller List, The*, 37

—*Spring Fire*, 37

—*3 Day Terror*, 37

Parker, Wheeler, 2, 3

Patterson, Orlando, 55, 119

Payne, Ethel, 99, 103

Penley, Constance, 184

Peyton Place (Metalious), 44

Phenix City Story, 34

Pierre, Henri, 147

Pittsburgh Courier, 23

"Poem for Emmett Till" (Roper), 24

Pollack, Harriet, 1–15, 178–201

Porteous, Clark, 4

Port Huron Statement, 83–84

"Power" (Lorde), 119

Présence Africaine (Paris), 12, 149

Priest, Myisha, 9, 53–74

Puzo, Mario, 93–94

Raines, Howell, 41

Rampersad, Arnold, 66

reckless eyeballing, 186

Reed, Ishmael, 95n3, 188

Reed, Willie, 3, 5

Regarding the Pain of Others (Sontag), 121

Revolt of Mamie Stover, The (Huie), 35

Rich, Adrienne, 87

Rishoi, Christy, 129, 138

"Road to Harlem" (Guillén), 154

Rob Roy (Scott), 31

Roper, William, 24

—"A Poem for Emmett Till," 24

Rose Tattoo, 34

Ruark, Robert, 38

Salamunich, Yucca, 24

—"Negro Madonna, The," 24

Sanctuary (Faulkner), 33

Saturday Review, 80

Scarry, Elaine, 162, 163, 175–76

—*Body in Pain, The*, 162, 175–76

Schwerner, Michael, 35, 75, 191

Scott, Walter, 31

—*Rob Roy,* 31

Seems Like Murder Here (Gussow), 204

Senghor, Léopold Sédar, 146, 155

"Shocking Story of Approved Killing in Mississippi, The" (Huie), 3, 7, 8, 36, 47, 108, 146, 157n5

Sister Outsider (Lorde), 118, 124–25

Skelton, T. R., 23

Smith, George, 3

Smith, Lillian, 34, 39, 44

—*Killers of the Dream,* 34, 161

—*One Hour,* 42

—*Strange Fruit,* 34, 38

Smith, Robert, 4

Smith, Valerie, 99, 102

Sollors, Werner, 112

Songoro Cosongo (Guillén), 144

Sontag, Susan, 121

—*Regarding the Pain of Others,* 121

Soul on Ice (Cleaver), 17, 86

Southern Review, 132

Spelman, Elizabeth V., 20, 102, 106

Spender, Stephen, 92, 93

Spring Fire (Packer), 37

Stacks, Carol, 171

—*Call to Home,* 171

Stein, Gertrude, 128

Stein, Sol, 94

Strange Fruit (Smith), 34, 38

Strider, Harold C., 5, 6, 57, 58

Student Nonviolent Coordinating Committee (SNCC), 94, 128, 141

Suleri, Sara, 143

Sumner, Mississippi, 4, 6, 31, 40, 58, 60, 148; and town slogan, 59

Sumner, W. G., 42

Swango, Curtis, 4

Sweet Flypaper of Life (Hughes and DeCarava), 9, 56, 65, 66–72

Tallahatchie River, 3, 5, 6, 24, 57, 147, 151

Taubman, Howard, 91

Teacher's Pet, 38

Terkel, Studs, 24, 26

Thomas, Kendall, 94

3 Day Terror (Packer), 37

Three Lives for Mississippi (Huie), 35

Till, Emmett: as Aristotelian tragedy, 150–51; and being dared to enter the Bryant grocery, 150, 185; as biblical narrative, 152; connection of to James Byrd lynching, 1; as depicted by Huie, 40, 43–44, 108; father of, 164; funeral of, 4, 33, 61, 156; as impetus to the civil rights movement, 89, 126n2, 129, 141, 156, 199n4, 211; *Jet* photograph of, 4, 33; likening of to Christ, 19–29; on possessing pictures of white girls, 43; stutter of, 73n2, 110n7; and summary of lynching and trial, 2–7; and the wolf-whistle, 2–3, 23, 41, 59, 108, 112, 136, 138, 150, 186

Till-Mobley, Mamie, 2–5, 8, 57, 156, 180; advice of to her son, 2, 187–88; and changing the meaning of the black body, 9, 56–57, 65, 71–72, 190; decision of to display her son's corpse, 33, 56, 60–61, 65, 67–72, 109, 156, 163, 188–89, 190; as depicted by Huie, 50n12; as depicted in fiction, 169, 174–75, 180, 213–15; as depicted in French press, 148; as depicted in poetry, 98, 100–109, 113–16; lawsuit of against Huie, 50n13; likening of to a Madonna, 24; and rebuttal of Huie, 158n9; on son's likeness to Christ, 22–26; story of as told to Ethel Payne, 99–100, 103

Time, 35, 84

Time Bomb (Adams), 174

To Kill a Mockingbird (Lee), 38

Tom Dent Collection, 141

Toomer, Jean, 155

Topeka Plaindealer, 5

Tougaloo College, 140

trauma, 12, 18, 20, 22, 26, 64, 110n5, 175–76, 209, 210, 213; cultural trauma, 8, 14, 17, 19

Tropiques, 155

Tulane University, 141

Turner, Darwin, 91

Tuskegee Institute, 62

Violent Saturday (Heath), 34
Violet, Indigo, 99

Wakefield, Dan, 4
Walton, Anthony, 171
—*Mississippi,* 171
Washington, Jesse, 33
Wasser (Arcimboldo), 180
Watkins, Melvin, 88, 90–91
Weixlmann, Joe, 89–90
Wells, Ida B., 55
We Real Cool: Black Men and Masculinity (hooks), 175, 176n6
"We Shall Overcome," 129–30
West, Cornel, 156
"What Happened to the Emmett Till Killers" (Huie), 36, 193–94
Whitaker, Hugh Stephen, 42
White, Clement, 155
White, Hugh, 4
whiteness, 8, 87, 101, 131–32, 134, 211–12; in Nordan's *Wolf Whistle,* 178, 179, 182–84, 188, 197, 198
Whitfield, Stephen J., 42, 50n15
Whitten, John, 6, 58
Wideman, John Edgar, 41, 189

—"Killing of Black Boys, The," 41, 189
Wilder, Billy, 38
—*Ace in the Hole,* 38
Williams, Tennessee, 43
Winfrey, Oprah, 172, 175
Without Sanctuary (Allen), 181, 184
Wolf Whistle (Huie), 8, 40
"Wolf Whistle" (Huie), 34, 35, 36, 38, 39, 41, 42, 47
Wolf Whistle (Nordan), 13, 14, 27–29, 178–99, 202–11, 216, 219
"Woman, A / Dirge for Wasted Children" (Lorde), 119
Woodward, C. Vann, 42
Woolworth sit-ins, 128
"Words of a Native Son" (Baldwin), 79
Wright, Moses, 2, 3, 5, 43, 151, 197; as depicted in French press, 148; on identifying Milam and Bryant in court, 5, 39, 146, 200n6
Wright, Richard, 49n4, 92, 132, 141, 155
—*Black Boy,* 132
—*Long Dream, The,* 49n4
—*Native Son,* 81, 83
Wright, Simeon, 3
Wursmer, André, 148

Your Blues Ain't Like Mine (Campbell), 12, 13, 14, 21, 161–76